RED CLOUD AT DAWN

RED CLOUD AT DAWN

TRUMAN, STALIN, AND THE END OF THE ATOMIC MONOPOLY

MICHAEL D. GORDIN

FARRAR, STRAUS AND GIROUX | NEW YORK

Farrar, Straus and Giroux
18 West 18th Street, New York 10011

Distributed in Canada by D&M Publishers, Inc.
Printed in the United States of America
First edition, 2009

Library of Congress Cataloging-in-Publication Data
Gordin, Michael D.
    Red cloud at dawn : Truman, Stalin, and the end of the atomic monopoly /
Michael D. Gordin.— 1st ed.
       p.   cm.
    Includes bibliographical references and index.
    ISBN-13: 978-0-374-25682-1 (hardcover : alk. paper)
    ISBN-10: 0-374-25682-9 (hardcover : alk. paper)
    1. Nuclear weapons—History—20th century.   2. Arms race—History—
20th century.   3. World politics—1945–1955.   4. Truman, Harry S., 1884–1972.
5. Stalin, Joseph, 1879–1953.   6. United States—Foreign relations—Soviet Union.
7. Soviet Union—Foreign relations—United States.   8. United States—Foreign
relations—1945–1953.   9. Soviet Union—Foreign relations—1945–1991.   I. Title.

U264.G67 2009
355.02'17094709044—dc22

                                                                        2009001424

Designed by Debbie Glasserman

www.fsgbooks.com

10   9   8   7   6   5   4   3   2   1

For Loren R. Graham,
mentor and friend

Tyger! Tyger! burning bright
In the forests of the night,
What immortal hand or eye
Could frame thy fearful symmetry?

In what distant deeps or skies
Burnt the fire of thine eyes?
On what wings dare he aspire?
What the hand dare sieze the fire?

And what shoulder, & what art,
Could twist the sinews of thy heart?
And when thy heart began to beat,
What dread hand? & what dread feet?

What the hammer? what the chain?
In what furnace was thy brain?
What the anvil? what dread grasp
Dare its deadly terrors clasp?

When the stars threw down their spears,
And water'd heaven with their tears,
Did he smile his work to see?
Did he who made the Lamb make thee?

Tyger! Tyger! burning bright
In the forests of the night,
What immortal hand or eye,
Dare frame thy fearful symmetry?

—WILLIAM BLAKE, "THE TYGER"

CONTENTS

ABBREVIATIONS

AAF	Army Air Forces (after 1947, USAF)
ADA	Atomic Development Authority
AEC	Atomic Energy Commission
AFMSW-1	Air Force Deputy Chief of Staff for Materiel, Special Weapons Group, Section 1
AFOAT-1	Air Force Deputy Chief of Staff for Operations, Atomic Energy Office, Section 1 (administrators of long-range detection)
CIG	Central Intelligence Group
cpm	counts per minute
FAS	Federation of American Scientists
GAC	General Advisory Committee of the AEC
GRU	Chief Intelligence Directorate (Soviet military intelligence)
JCAE	Joint Committee on Atomic Energy, United States Congress
JCS	Joint Chiefs of Staff
LTBT	Limited Test Ban Treaty
MAD	Mutually Assured Destruction
NKGB	People's Commissariat of State Security (Soviet foreign intelligence)
NKVD	People's Commissariat of Internal Affairs (Soviet secret police)
NRL	Naval Research Laboratory
NSC	National Security Council
ORE	Office of Reports and Estimates; also Office of Research and Evaluation
OSS	Office of Strategic Services

PGU	First Chief Directorate (*Pervoe glavnoe upravlenie*)
PPS	Policy Planning Staff, Department of State
RDB	Joint Research and Development Board
SAC	Strategic Air Command
UNAEC	United Nations Atomic Energy Commission
USAF	United States Air Force

RED CLOUD AT DAWN

INTRODUCTION
WHAT HAPPENED AT POTSDAM

And mutual fear brings peace,
Till the selfish loves increase:
Then Cruelty knits a snare,
And spreads his baits with care.
WILLIAM BLAKE, "THE HUMAN ABSTRACT"

It was not supposed to happen this way. Somebody had to tell him, and soon, before anything was final. He was going to be suspicious. He might ask questions, questions that could not or should not be answered. And what should he be told, anyway? The important thing was to make him think he knew everything, without actually letting him know anything important. Time was running out.

The path to Cecilienhof Palace runs through a picturesque garden alongside the lakes of Potsdam. Calling it a palace might be a tad grandiose. It was built as the residence of Crown Prince Wilhelm just before World War I, and it looks like nothing so much as a bloated Tudor country home somewhere in East Anglia. It would be a lovely place for a casual meeting among friends, except this was no casual meeting, and there were no friends here.

In July 1945, this picturesque garden happened to be located in the Soviet sector of occupation a few miles to the southwest of the smoldering rubble that had been the capital of Adolf Hitler's Third Reich. Here, in the suburbs of Berlin, American President Harry S. Truman arrived with his diplomatic and military entourage for a meeting, code-named Terminal, with the heads of state of the United Kingdom and the Soviet Union. Only five months had passed since their previous meeting at Yalta, yet the cast of characters had changed almost as completely as the setting. Winston Churchill had been defeated in the elections earlier that month by Labour Party leader Clement Attlee, and the Tory came along more as an honored guest and adviser than as one of the Big Three. Franklin Delano Roosevelt had died on April 12 and was succeeded by Truman, former Missouri senator and onetime haberdashery salesman who, like Attlee, did not have the benefit of knowing what had happened, exactly, at Yalta. Only Joseph Stalin stood as a fixed point of this final postwar meeting. He was once again the host.

The Big Three had a great deal to discuss at Potsdam, but the issues clustered around one major and one minor axis: negotiating the postwar settlement in Europe and orchestrating the entry of the Soviet Union into the Anglo-American war with Japan. (Stalin had abrogated his neutrality pact with Japan in April but had not yet initiated hostilities in Asia.) Most of the discussions—often heated—concerned the former set of questions: What to do with Poland? Were there to be reparations, and if so, how much? How was an occupied Germany to be governed? An occupied Austria? All of these issues were contentious, and the faint fissures that would crack into the chasms of the cold war began to snake across the surface of the wartime alliance.[1]

The minor axis was touchier, because Truman and his new secretary of state, James F. Byrnes, were not positive they needed Soviet entry to conclude the war against Japan. If it could be avoided, they certainly did not *want* it; dealing with the Soviets in Europe was bad enough. Military advisers to Truman still called for Soviet entry, and the sooner the better: Pinning down Japanese land forces in China and Manchuria would be difficult without the Red Army, and every bit of force was welcome. But Truman and Byrnes at times thought they could do without the Soviets, for they had something else, something new, something that might permanently give the West an edge over the Communists—not to mention over Emperor Hirohito.[2]

On July 16, a day before Terminal began, scientists working for the Manhattan Project had detonated the world's first atomic explosion in the desert outside Alamogordo, New Mexico: Operation Trinity. Atop a hundred-foot-tall tower, pieces of plutonium (a heavy metal generated from enriched uranium in atomic reactors—themselves new inventions), carefully machined and sculpted into segments of a sphere, were imploded into a dense core, which then began to fission. The heavy nuclei in the centers of the plutonium atoms split apart, releasing enormous amounts of energy. This physical process was discovered only in December 1938; plutonium was first secretly synthesized as recently as the winter of 1940–1941, and now the Americans held a deliverable weapon. The test had gone perfectly, and the Fat Man bomb, and a simpler uranium 235 gun model, code-named Little Boy, were being shipped off to the Pacific to be detonated over specially selected Japanese cities. Perhaps the Soviets were not needed after all.

But still, Stalin needed to be told. Officially, he was an ally, although neither party trusted the other, and technically he was *not yet* an ally in the Pacific war. Many of the American attendees harbored a growing feeling that Roosevelt's wartime alliance with Stalin either had been a mistake or was about to become one. Perhaps this was one area where the tendency to get too cozy with the Soviets could be checked. The Manhattan Project, begun as an Anglo-American collaboration, had deliberately and explicitly excluded the Soviet Union from the beginning.[3] As far as Truman and Byrnes knew, Stalin remained completely ignorant of their determined efforts to weaponize uranium and plutonium—but he would certainly know once the first city was destroyed in early August, and he would know he had been left in the dark on purpose. Byrnes's initial impulse was to leave him there.

Secretary of War Henry L. Stimson disagreed. Stimson was an aged and dedicated Roosevelt appointee and onetime secretary of state under Republican President Herbert Hoover. (Stimson remained an adamant Republican under the two Democratic presidents he served.) Byrnes, not wanting the interference, made a point of not inviting him to the Potsdam meeting, but Stimson came anyway, mostly to advise Truman about S-1 (his code name for the Manhattan Project). The time for stalling Stalin was over. The minutes of the recent meeting of the Anglo-American Combined Policy Committee on July 4, 1945, record that the secretary of war was already convinced that Potsdam was the place to lift the veil for the Soviets, at least a little:

> If nothing was said at this meeting about the T.A. [tube alloys = atomic] weapon, its subsequent early use might have a serious effect on the relations of frankness between the three great allies. [Stimson] had therefore advised the President to watch the atmosphere at the [Potsdam] meeting. If mutual frankness on other questions was found to be real and satisfactory, then the President might say that work was being done on the development of atomic fission for war purposes; that good progress had been made; and that an attempt to use a weapon would be made shortly, though it was not certain that it would succeed.[4]

The Interim Committee—a group of civilian and military officials lightly peppered with scientists that Stimson had convened to discuss the wartime and postwar implications of the atomic bomb— had earlier "unanimously *agreed* that there would be considerable advantage, if suitable opportunity arose, in having the President advise the Russians that we were working on this weapon with every prospect of success and that we expected to use it against Japan."[5]

At first, Truman was hostile to the idea of informing Stalin, and

Winston Churchill was equally resistant. But the news of Trinity changed everything—for them and for Byrnes. Stimson recorded in his diary that Churchill "now not only was not worried about giving the Russians information of the matter but was rather inclined to use it as an argument in our favor in the negotiations." He continued: "The sentiment . . . was unanimous in thinking that it was advisable to tell the Russians at least that we were working on that subject and intended to use it if and when it was successfully finished."[6]

On July 24 around 7:30 p.m., after a hard day of negotiations on European issues, Truman sauntered over to Stalin during a pause in the discussions, leaving his interpreter behind, and exchanged a few words. We will never know exactly what he said, or exactly what Stalin answered. The exchange would have enormous repercussions, but Truman, Stalin, and the latter's interpreter, V. N. Pavlov, have left no immediate transcript of what happened. Truman's interpreter, Charles "Chip" Bohlen, stayed back as his boss made his move:

> Explaining that he wanted to be as informal and casual as possible, Truman said during a break in the proceedings that he would stroll over to Stalin and nonchalantly inform him. He instructed me not to accompany him, as I ordinarily did, because he did not want to indicate that there was anything particularly momentous about the development. So it was Pavlov, the Russian interpreter, who translated Truman's words to Stalin. I did not hear the conversation, although Truman and Byrnes both reported that I was there . . . Across the room, I watched Stalin's face carefully as the President broke the news. So offhand was Stalin's response that there was some question in my mind whether the President's message had got through. I should have known better than to underrate the dictator.[7]

Bohlen was not the only one who thought there might have been a miscommunication. Everyone in the know—Bohlen, Stimson, Byrnes, Churchill—watched the conversation carefully, although not *too* carefully, for they did not want to tip off Stalin that the exchange was important. As Byrnes recalled in his 1947 memoirs:

> He [Truman] said he had told Stalin that, after long experimentation, we had developed a new bomb far more destructive than any other known bomb, and that we planned to use it very soon unless Japan surrendered. Stalin's only reply was to say that he was glad to hear of the bomb and he hoped we would use it. I was surprised at Stalin's lack of interest. I concluded that he had not grasped the importance of the discovery. I thought that the following day he would ask for more information about it. He did not. Later I concluded that, because the Russians kept secret their developments in military weapons, they thought it improper to ask about ours.[8]

By 1958, in his second set of memoirs, he had slightly revised his view:

> I did not believe Stalin grasped the full import of the President's statement, and thought that on the next day there would be some inquiry about this "new and powerful weapon," but I was mistaken. I thought then and even now believe that Stalin did not appreciate the importance of the information that had been given him; but there are others who believe that in the light of later information about the Soviets' intelligence service in this country, he was already aware of the New Mexico test, and that this accounted for his apparent indifference.[9]

The Soviet dictator did not leave his own account of the exchange, but some in his delegation did. It is hard to take Soviet Foreign Minister V. M. Molotov's memoirs as completely reliable, for he recalled something that no one else in the room managed to observe—his own presence at the conversation—yet it seems certain that Stalin informed him about it immediately after. Here is Molotov's account: "Truman took Stalin and me aside with a secretive look and told us they had a special weapon that had never existed before, a very extraordinary weapon . . . It's hard to say what he himself thought, but it seemed to me he wanted to shock us. Stalin reacted very calmly, so Truman thought he didn't understand. Truman didn't say 'an atomic bomb,' but we got the point at once."[10] There are three important features about this Soviet version: Truman never specifically mentioned the nuclear character of the weapon; the Soviets knew what was actually behind his words, although they did not reveal it; and Stalin and his entourage saw this as a veiled threat. Marshal Georgii Zhukov, the commander of the Red Army and thus a crucial figure at Potsdam, believed that Truman had gone up to Stalin "obviously with the goal of political blackmail," but noted that Stalin "didn't give away any of his feelings, acting as if he found nothing important in H. Truman's words."[11]

Which leaves us with the important question: What *did* Stalin think? What, in fact, did he really know about the atomic bomb before Truman's comment? Truman was certain that he knew nothing. As he stated in an interview in 1959: "When [*New York Times* journalist William Laurence] says that Stalin knew, he did not. He knew nothing whatever about it until it happened . . . He knew no more about it than the man in the moon."[12] Yet, as is now abundantly clear in evidence from the Soviet archives, Truman misjudged his opponent. Stalin knew quite a lot. On August 7, the day after the destruction of Hiroshima by the Little Boy uranium bomb, Molotov (now back in Moscow) met with U.S. Ambassador Averell Harriman. He told the American: "You Americans can keep a secret when you want to."[13] Harriman observed "something like a smirk" on Molotov's face, and later noted that "the way he put it convinced me that it was no secret at all . . . The only element of surprise, I suppose, was the fact that the Alamogordo test had been successful. But Stalin, unfortunately, must have known that we were very close to the point of staging our first test explosion."[14]

Harriman's intuition was correct. Zhukov noted that Stalin took Molotov aside that evening of Truman's casual conversation and said, "We need to discuss with Kurchatov the acceleration of our work."[15] Igor Kurchatov was the scientific director of the Soviet atomic bomb project. Stalin not only knew about the bomb, he was building his own; Truman had not only failed to forestall Soviet proliferation, it appears he had accelerated it.

We now know that Stalin had authorized a Soviet atomic project much earlier, although it was still far from achieving a working nuclear device. Years away, in fact. Vladimir Merkulov—a commissar of the NKGB, the foreign intelligence branch of the People's Commissariat of Internal Affairs (NKVD) and thus under the direct command of Lavrentii Beria, Stalin's secret police chief and also overall director of the Soviet atomic project—reported immediately after the Yalta conference: "No time-frame of any certainty is available for the production of the first bomb, since research or design work has not been completed. It is suggested that the production of such a bomb will require one year at least and five years at most."[16] Meanwhile, Stalin had to act calm. It would not do to show the Americans that he was concerned about the atomic bomb or about the fact that the Americans were the sole possessors of this new weapon. In an often-quoted September 17, 1946, interview with *Sunday Times* correspondent Alexander Werth, Stalin dismissed the notion of atomic blackmail:

> I do not consider the atomic bomb as serious a force as certain political actors are inclined to consider it. Atomic bombs are designed to frighten the weak of nerves, but they cannot decide the fate of a war, since there is a completely insufficient number of atomic bombs for this. Of course, monopolistic possession of the secret of the atomic bomb creates a threat, but against that there exist, at least, two remedies: a) monopolistic possession of the atomic bomb cannot continue for a long time; b) the use of the atomic bomb will be banned.[17]

This playing down of the bomb became the standard strategy of Soviet diplomacy during the American atomic monopoly, and we can see its origins in that very exchange between Truman and Stalin at Cecilienhof Palace. Stalin remained poker-faced, indicating that nothing terribly new had happened, nothing to get upset about. This was an eminently sensible approach to handling an East-West confrontation that looked as though it was going to get worse.[18] (Privately, Stalin may have felt more strongly. His daughter Svetlana reported that her father turned silent on hearing the news of Hiroshima, sullenly withdrawing to his chambers, at which point he became ill.[19])

The day after Truman's conversation with Stalin, on July 25, the initiation of atomic bombing was authorized, and on the 26th the United States and United Kingdom—but without the Soviet Union, which was not yet a belligerent in the Pacific war—issued the so-called Potsdam Proclamation, which threatened Japan with "prompt and utter destruction" if it did not unconditionally surrender immediately. Here Truman also did not explicitly mention the atomic bomb. Only on August 6, 1945, would the world understand what he had meant.[20]

Truman was by that date in the middle of the Atlantic on the USS *Augusta*. He had left Germany immediately after the conclusion of the conference on August 1—"I don't want to have to answer any questions from Stalin," he told an aide.[21] And he would never have to. In a press conference on May 27, 1948, he informed America that "I have never had any communication from Mr. Stalin since Potsdam."[22] Yet this should not lead us to believe that the conversation had been meaningless. The awkwardness of the way Truman first broached the topic of nuclear weapons between the two superpowers gave Stalin an excellent pretext to change his policy of cooperation with the West, and in the meantime inclined Truman to dig in his heels about any further revelations on the atomic front. J. Robert Oppenheimer, the scientific director of the atomic-bomb-designing laboratory of Los Alamos, thought that the failure to be absolutely clear and open had already soured any potential for cooperation with the Soviets regarding the international control of nuclear weapons, and somewhat melodramatically told Secretary of Commerce Henry Wallace that "the mishandling of the situation at Potsdam has prepared the way for the eventual slaughter of tens of millions or perhaps hundreds of millions of innocent people."[23] We now know that the global nuclear holocaust did not happen, but Oppenheimer's worries that secrecy would breed animosity and then overt aggression seemed real enough at the time. The most important implication of Potsdam, however, may have been in what Truman did not say: the words "atomic bomb." Given that Stalin already knew about the Manhattan Project and American plans to use it against Japan, the roundabout and vague way Truman went about "informing" the Soviet Union of his plans spoke volumes. As the historian Tsuyoshi Hasegawa perceptively put it: "To Stalin, the most important revelation was that Truman was withholding information about the atomic bomb."[24] By trying to be oblique, Truman turned out to be too clever by half. It was not supposed to happen this way.

The main character in this book is not a person or an organization but an event: a nuclear explosion. The world's first atomic bomb was detonated by the Americans on July 16, 1945, in the Trinity test in Alamogordo, New Mexico. The second bomb destroyed the city of Hiroshima and the third the city of Nagasaki in the final days of World War II. The fourth and fifth nuclear explosions took place on the Bikini Islands in mid-1946 as part of the U.S. military's Operation Crossroads. The sixth, seventh, and eighth explosions were part of Operation Sandstone at the Pacific island of Eniwetok and marked the first significant postwar innovations in nuclear weapons design. The ninth explosion, on August 29, 1949, was the first non-American detonation, in the deserts of Kazakhstan at a test site called Semipalatinsk-21. This ninth explosion, which Soviet scientists dubbed "First Lightning" and the

Americans called "Joe-1" (in ironic homage to Stalin), is our star character.

The first Soviet test was not simply a technical experiment that confirmed the ability of the Soviet Union to build nuclear bombs; it was equally an international event that marked the beginning of an arms race that would ultimately lead to nuclear proliferation beyond the two superpowers. From the moment the Manhattan Project successfully produced the first nuclear weapon—even earlier, in fact—Americans were fraught with anxiety over the possibility that these explosives would spread over the world. It would be bad enough if a "friendly" nation, such as Britain or France, weakened American dominance by developing a nuclear capacity of its own; it would be far worse if these weapons fell into the hands of a potentially threatening enemy. In the context of the incipient cold war, it required little imagination to see the Soviet Union as that future antagonist. But how would the Americans be able to *know* that the Soviet Union in fact had acquired the bomb? For that matter, how were the Soviets themselves to know that they "had" it?

From very early on, arms-control proposals, espionage, and scientific devices were marshaled in an effort at first to forestall, then detect, and finally react to a Soviet nuclear test. Above all, it was important not to be caught off guard by the test when it happened. Surprise, as the historian Walter Laqueur has noted, is the very thing intelligence is supposed to prevent: "A major mistake leads to surprise and thus an intelligence failure; the main function of an intelligence service, therefore, is to shield those it serves against surprise."[25] Throughout my story, I will focus on the Soviet test and *knowledge* about the test—what was required to conduct one, what was required to detect one—as a crystallization of problems of intelligence in general, and nuclear intelligence in particular.

We might be tempted to think about the story of the ninth nuclear explosion as either about the Soviet Union (how did it manage to produce an explosion?) *or* about the United States (how did it learn about the Soviet bomb, and how did it react?). It is a story about both and neither. The Soviet test happened against a background in which the United States already possessed an atomic bomb and had used it, and so neither the motivation nor the process of Soviet proliferation can be understood without fore-grounding the Americans. Likewise, in the period from 1945 to 1949—the atomic monopoly, a unique period in which only one power possessed nuclear weapons—every American atomic decision was fundamentally built around the potentiality of a Soviet bomb. So although this book is most concerned with events in the United States, those events were always internationally inflected and reactive, usually to actions by the Soviet regime; the substantial narrative devoted to Soviet actions likewise resonates with how the Americans and Europeans interpreted them. This book is a history of the atomic monopoly, and thus an American story, but it also is a story of how that monopoly collapsed—which makes it an international one.[26]

Both the national and international dimensions can be seen clearly in that awkward conversation between Truman and Stalin on July 24, 1945, in a palace on the outskirts of Berlin. The Potsdam exchange—for all its uncertainties, omissions, and misdirections—tells us a great deal about the intersection of geopolitics, intelligence, and the atomic bomb, the triumvirate that dominates this story. Seen from the perspective of the end of the cold war, we have an understandable tendency to emphasize two countries: the United States and the Soviet Union. And, indeed, these were the dominant players (represented by Truman and Stalin) in the Potsdam exchange. But others were involved at the dawn of the nuclear arms race, and they are often forgotten in hindsight. Great Britain was part of the discussion about revealing something (however little) about the atomic bomb to the Soviets, and the entire exchange took place in a Germany devastated by war. In the account that follows, the British, the Germans, and the legacy of World War II are never far from our view. The arms race was born into a world that was fast becoming split into two opposing camps, but that world was not merely bipolar. Every discussion of the

American atomic bomb always reflected fears of a Soviet bomb, the failure of the wartime German nuclear project, and British aspirations for their own.

The world of atomic weapons is shot through with espionage, secrecy, intrigue, misinformation, deception, and supposition; it is, in short, a story of intelligence, that is, the dedicated gathering and interpretation of raw information about international matters. In any situation in which you have two or more parties (individuals, groups, nations) that are both trying to learn something about their opponent(s) and at the same time prevent the other(s) from learning anything useful, paradoxes of concealment and revelation abound. What one side (for example, the United States) chooses to reveal to its opposite number is subjected to a series of questions: Was this an honest revelation? What was left out? Why tell specifically *this* piece of information? Why tell us *now*? How can one be sure it is reliable, especially since one cannot simply repeat "observations" as is often the case with a scientific experiment? How should one react to the news without revealing too much about one's own position? These problems inhere in every piece of intelligence data but were dramatically intensified if the information came through illicit channels.[27] Say, written in invisible ink made of milk on the margins of a newspaper in a code based on Walt Whitman's *Leaves of Grass* (which actually did happen).

When Truman told Stalin of an unusually powerful explosive that was soon to be released on Japan, he both revealed something (the existence of a bomb) and concealed something (its atomic character). Yet even more was revealed to Stalin, despite Truman's intentions: The concealment itself was an interesting piece of data. Stalin, in turn, concealed the extent of his knowledge, and could do so only through a posture of blissful ignorance: Go ahead and use that bomb, see if I care. Now Truman and Byrnes had to interpret *that*, and Stalin had to interpret their reaction, and . . . The dialectical dance continued. Once one side started down this line of reasoning, mirroring the behavior of the opposite party became an intensely destructive self-fulfilling prophecy; one simply came to expect the worst possible behavior from the opposition, which would respond in kind. Over and over again, we will see this back-and-forth dynamic of atomic intelligence, a repeated exchange that shaped the character of the cold war arms race in numerous fundamental respects.

I refract the Soviet story through the American one, and vice versa, chiefly because atomic weapons have always been enmeshed in an adversarial context, replete with the smoke of deception and the mirrors of inference. The Manhattan Project was initiated out of fear that Hitler's Germany would develop a nuclear bomb first, and the hope was that an Allied atomic bomb could serve as a deterrent against that weapon's use. Thus, what eventually came to be known as Mutually Assured Destruction (MAD), one of the dominant nuclear strategies of the cold war, was imagined as the normal state of affairs before anyone had even come close to building an operational weapon, let alone considered using it. The commanding general of the U.S. Army Air Forces in World War II, Henry "Hap" Arnold, described this oddly symmetric feature of nuclear weapons clearly in 1946: "The anticipated cheapness of destruction with atomic explosives, coupled with the fact that their use with air-power weapons such as rockets prevents adequate defense, means that in the future the aggressor who destroys his enemy's cities may expect his own destroyed in turn." This sounds decidedly gloomy, but Arnold anticipated that this would paradoxically increase security: "Neither side may care to fire the first atomic shot and thus bring destruction to its own cities and population as well as to the enemy's."[28] This statement was made three years before the Soviet Union detonated the first non-American bomb, at a time when there was no credible aggressive threat, atomic or otherwise, to the American heartland. Throughout the following chapters, therefore, we must focus not just on what both sides were doing in parallel, but also on what each side thought the other side was doing, and how each imagined the other would react—and so on down the chain.

This resonates with one particular difficulty in how Truman and

Stalin interacted with each other—the problem of knowing what the other knows about what you know—but this was only one problematic feature of intelligence revealed in the story of the atomic monopoly and its breakdown, and perhaps the least significant one at that. Three other dominant problems about the uncertainty of information, and the obstacles such uncertainty posed for the historical actors, were even more salient.[29] The first problem concerned how one could obtain any information at all from a remote entity, something very difficult to gain access to (the inside of the Soviet nuclear complex, underground uranium deposits), and then come to an evaluation of how reliable that information was. Once you had some information, however limited, a new problem arose with respect to making predictions based on a series of unknown variables: How far along were the Soviets in making their atomic bomb? Could the Soviets purify enough uranium for a stockpile of weapons? Could scientists leapfrog over the atomic bomb to build a hydrogen bomb? Once one had a set of predictions in hand (five years to a Soviet bomb; uranium would be hard to obtain; the hydrogen bomb was likely feasible), then one had the problem of how to make use of this uncertain knowledge, of basing policy decisions in the real world on a foundation that one knew to be of only questionable reliability or certainty. These questions and uncertainties are endemic to the work of nuclear intelligence, and it is no surprise to find them again and again in debates over the nuclear status of any particular country, whether that country is China, Israel, India, Pakistan, North Korea, Iraq, or Iran.

Each chapter in this book follows a different aspect of the problems of intelligence: How much can you reveal to another party without giving away all the information needed to make a bomb? How much can you infer from limited data and how do you predict the future based on it? How do you evaluate the reliability of information that comes from dubious sources (like jittery scientist-spies)? How do you turn incomplete and uncertain data into something useful (like a nuclear bomb)? How do you gather scientific data from a remote entity and establish its veracity? How do you make that information relevant to political actors? How do you react in a world where each reaction generates counterreactions, and a misstep could lead to disaster? Truman, Stalin, and their advisers were continually forced to confront these issues from Potsdam forward.

There are many ways one could solve these problems, and American and Soviet politicians, intelligence officers, scientists, and bureaucrats adopted a variety of strategies across this important period. In broad terms, we observe two different styles of intelligence work adopted by the Soviet Union on the one hand, and the Western powers (primarily the Americans, but also the British) on the other. The Soviets obtained most of their information on foreign programs through human informants, either intelligence agents who gathered publicly available information and sent it back to Moscow, or clandestine spies who worked deep within the Manhattan Project or the postwar atomic-energy establishment. The Americans, on the other hand, had exactly *zero* human informants in the Soviet Union, relying instead on technical means of intelligence acquisition (tapping phones, intercepting cables, cryptography, airborne radiation sampling). Throughout this book, we will see both the human and the technical modes of intelligence gathering (HUMINT and TECHINT in today's jargon) deployed as means to solve these serious problems of uncertainty. Both mechanisms had advantages and drawbacks, and those features set the constraints for many of the predictions and the policies built upon that information by each side.

Why is this a story about information at all? At root, a nuclear weapon is an apparatus designed to assemble a specific metal (either uranium or plutonium produced from irradiated uranium) into an explosive device. Surely, then, the story of the atomic monopoly and its disintegration should be not just a story of information but also of materials and technology. Indeed, early arms-control efforts stressed the central importance of controlling materials to slow or stop the spread of nuclear weapons. Those efforts foundered quickly, however, and with their demise, the materials-centric way of thinking about the problems posed by nuclear weapons faded as well. Today, the emphasis on materials has started to reemerge, but this has been a recent resurgence.[30] When materials dropped from the minds of policy makers (mostly, but not exclusively, Americans), what remained was the situation at Potsdam: circling around the problem of uncertain, insecure, transient intelligence data.

This is not the way atomic history is often told. The emphasis tends to be on the devices themselves rather than on the knowledge about those devices; usually, the story is not reflected in international reactions and counterreactions, but kept within the confines of one country. Such an approach makes the development of a nuclear device a story of technological progress and breakthrough, culminating in a success—typically in the form of a mushroom cloud. This is a picture composed of individual stages and driven from the very inception by its final goal: a working bomb. Thus, we find many histories of the Soviet bomb, the Chinese bomb, the Israeli bomb, the French bomb, and so on.[31] There are some serious problems with thinking about the development of nuclear weapons in this way.

First, despite the tendency of historians to focus on atomic bomb development within specific national contexts, no state has ever developed a nuclear device on its own. For the Manhattan Project, the Americans engaged in extensive cooperation with the British and Canadians and employed a full cohort of German émigré physicists. The British used American information, Canadian and South African uranium, and its own complement of German émigrés (previously on loan to the Americans). The Indians derived a great deal from the British; the Israelis from the French; the Chinese from the Soviet Union.[32] The only nation that attempted to develop an atomic bomb "in house" was Nazi Germany, and it famously failed in the endeavor. The monolithic "national" nuclear histories thus miss out on one of the central features of these weapons: They are immensely complicated devices built from many resources, domestic and international. Primary among the resources crossing borders was information. By emphasizing what people knew and how they knew it (and how reliable they assumed that knowledge to be), this book brings to the forefront some of the actual uncertainties of the problems of building a bomb, and it does so in the terms of the historical figures themselves. In the national framework, each design decision and each political calculation was focused on producing a working device; in the informational perspective, these calculations are much more contingent, much more revisable, and more clearly resemble political decision making as we see it today.

Historians' relative minimizing of the international contributions in the supposedly "national" technology of the nuclear bomb would be remarkable in itself, but there is the additional assumption that projects the "American" (also silently British, German, Danish, Italian, Canadian) experience during the Manhattan Project as normative, the standard against which all other programs are measured. In intelligence parlance, this fallacy of reasoning is called "mirror imagining." The American development of nuclear weapons in World War II repeatedly stands as the yardstick of atomic progress, the metric against which all other proliferations are defined. True, the Manhattan Project was successful (it produced a working explosive device), yet that does not imply that it should be taken as representative, as constituting the necessary path along which all other atomic programs would travel. There is some reason to doubt how informative a model the American experience is. No one has ever managed to make a bomb as rapidly as the three and a half years it took the U.S. Army to move from initial research to test. The first atomic program was the fastest.[33] It was also built in the context of wartime mobilization, a characteristic no other program shared, and it was built by the wealthiest country on the planet.

It is important not to get trapped into this standard model of the American program, for it flattens out a great deal of what was distinctive about both the American project and all the subsequent ones. Each effort certainly followed paths that were in some way similar—they all sought to release the energy produced by the fission of uranium or plutonium nuclei—but they all undertook their programs for radically different reasons, and differed from the Manhattan model in important ways. Differed, not deviated. The Soviet program was not simply a Soviet Manhattan Project; it was its own beast and should be understood on its own terms, even if those terms prove not to be wholly contained within the confines of the Soviet Union itself and involve in part American data and German scientists.[34] (The Soviet effort was also certainly not a *Russian* Manhattan Project. Throughout this book, I use the word "Soviet" to refer to the project and its scientists, as many of them were not Russian, but rather Ukrainian, or Georgian, or German.) Through a 1995 edict by Russian President Boris N. Yeltsin, we have access to a spate of declassified documents about the workings of the Soviet atomic program, including its extensive use of espionage garnered from the American and British projects.[35] Without these documents, employed extensively here for the first time in a study that folds the Soviet Union and the United States together, any look into the Soviet program would suffer the same problems of uncertain information that bedeviled Truman's advisers in the late 1940s.

The first full narrative of an atomic bomb project was Henry DeWolf Smyth's *Atomic Energy for Military Purposes*, the official history of the Manhattan Project, released on August 12, 1945, before the surrender of the Japanese government and the end of World War II. Interest in these weapons, in their various guises, has not subsided since then. This book draws heavily on the sixty-odd years of research that have gone into telling this history, and in addition to offering new information on neglected aspects of this period, it provides an account of the dawning of the cold war complementary to the standard pictures one can pull off the shelf. It differs, often significantly, from other accounts not only by focusing on "what happened" at specific moments in history but also by asking "who knew about it, and how?" at each of those junctures. The facts were real enough, but politicians, military officials, and scientists did not react to the facts—they reacted to the facts insofar as they knew and understood them. This approach injects a degree of uncertainty and tension into the crucial decisions of these years, a mood manifest in almost every document produced by these individuals on both sides of the Iron Curtain.

For example, the fulcrum of the cold war is often taken to be 1948, the year of the Czechoslovakian coup, the Berlin blockade, the peak of the *Zhdanovshchina* cultural purge in the Soviet Union, and Truman's reelection. That was indeed a year of great importance, but in my story of geopolitics, intelligence, and the atomic bomb, the crucial year for the cold war was 1949. Three dates that year were pivotal to the launching of the arms race. On August 29, the Soviet Union detonated their test bomb—and then did nothing. There was no official or unofficial announcement, no change in external behavior. In the silence, Soviet scientists simply continued production of more devices. The Americans had no idea that anything had happened at first. Then, on September 3, the long-range detection system, which the Americans had thrown together as a stopgap that April, was activated for the 112th time with an elevated radiation warning. This proved not to be a false alarm. Within two weeks, the data from the detection system had been interpreted to be proof that a Soviet explosion had happened. On September 23, President Harry Truman announced publicly that there had been an "atomic explosion" in the USSR.

The atomic monopoly was over. Now there were two powers that could build atomic weapons, and the arms race was afoot. This seemingly obvious connection between a Soviet nuclear capability and a bilateral arms race was not straightforward in 1949. Many observers thought that the Soviet detonation might be a trigger that would reinvigorate negotiations for viable international arms control, or that the Americans would respond to the Soviet test with moderation. As it turned out, the explosion led not to more negotiations and disarmament but rather to the terrifying stockpiling of nuclear weapons. When the Korean War broke out in June 1950, dreams of peace vanished.

The result is the world we live in now: nuclear armed and at risk of becoming more so every day. This book offers an account of how that happened, how the world moved from the tension at Potsdam and the nuclear destruction of two Japanese cities to a planet that had two nuclear powers—and then many more. The story of the development and testing of the first Soviet atomic bomb was not just an episode in the cold war between the superpowers, it was also the first proliferation, the first detonation of a nuclear device by a power not part of the initial wartime coalition to develop atomic weapons. First Lightning initiated shockwaves that continue to reverberate through the nonproliferation policies that have carried over into our post–cold war present. The dust from that explosion has yet to settle.

ONE
ATOMIC MONOPOLY

> Those who restrain desire, do so because theirs is weak
> enough to be restrained; and the restrainer or reason usurps
> its place & governs the unwilling.
>   And being restrain'd, it by degrees becomes passive,
> till it is only the shadow of desire.
> WILLIAM BLAKE, "THE MARRIAGE OF HEAVEN AND HELL"

What did the world really know about nuclear weapons on August 15, 1945, the day the Japanese government surrendered and World War II was declared over? Not much. Everyone knew that the Americans had developed a new "atomic bomb," and that they had used it, twice, on Japanese cities. The residents of Hiroshima and Nagasaki knew most directly the horrific destruction of fission bombs, but they had very little access, until the end of American occupation and censorship, to knowledge about how the bomb worked and its implications.[1] The citizens of the world knew essentially three facts about the bomb: that a strange metal called uranium could power a massive weapon, that the Americans were the only ones to have done so, and that the Americans would not hesitate to use these weapons. These were the new facts; the new theories about what to do with them would take some time to emerge.

For while the world had changed after the war, it had not changed completely. Many of the problems that had beset the industrialized nations in the 1930s—labor unrest, economic disruption, Stalinism—remained all too evident, only to be supplemented by dramatic new crises. Some of these, such as the wartime carnage and destruction that transformed demographic, economic, and agricultural patterns radically across Europe and East Asia, were to be expected. Others seemed to pose new dilemmas, ones that few had considered before the end of the war simply because most were ignorant of what lay on the horizon. The atomic bomb posed a series of such new dilemmas, ones most people (including most Americans) professed themselves unprepared to meet.

Nuclear weapons became facts at precisely the moment that global geopolitics was beginning to freeze into an East-West standoff: a confrontation between the Soviet Union and its allies on the one hand, and the United States and its coalition on the other. The transition from a wartime alliance that was never extremely close between Franklin Roosevelt and Stalin to a brittle and hostile state of extreme tension in the postwar years happened rapidly but not instantly. The recriminations and accusations about who "started" the destruction of East-West cooperation began even before the deterioration of relations had fully set in. Atomic weapons and the cold war not only were born at the same time, but each also deeply shaped the development of the other. America demobilized from its wartime footing remarkably quickly. By December 31, 1945, almost 1,670,000 men and women had been released from the U.S. armed forces ahead of schedule, and it soon became apparent that Soviet ground forces dwarfed any possible American counterpart. While American military budgets were constrained under the tight bookkeeping of the Truman administration, Soviet military expenditures increased by perhaps 30 percent between 1948 and 1949, and American intelligence estimated that the Soviets could mobilize 470 divisions and 12 million men within six months, not to mention their 2.5 million–man standing army.[2] Conventionally speaking, the West was outmatched.

Various influential parties in the United States were convinced that the bipolar postwar settlement in Europe was only the prelude to an armed confrontation, and since the Americans could not hope to deter any potential Soviet aggression with manpower, the atomic bomb was quickly seized upon as a panacea. General Lauris Norstad, high-level planner for the Army Air Forces, had already in mid-September factored the atomic bomb into his calculations to balance Soviet forces, requesting from General Leslie Groves at the Manhattan Project a stockpile of 123 atomic bombs as a minimum with an optimum of 466 (taking into account only large-yield strategic bombs, like the ones used in Japan, and not supplementary, as yet nonexistent, tactical nuclear weapons). Although Norstad counted on such stockpiles, the American president did not accelerate nuclear production. When Norstad was writing, for example, there was exactly one nuclear bomb in existence. General Carl Spaatz correctly noted the problem America faced if it was to rely on nuclear deterrence: "The bomb is enormously expensive and definitely limited in availability."[3]

Spaatz was correct: The bomb was expensive. The only military option more expensive, however, would have been to maintain a high level of conventional forces. Choices about forestalling the Soviet Union, about defending Western Europe, about restructuring Japan, about building nuclear weapons, about demobilizing the American army were in large part economic decisions. The United States was in a favorable position to make such choices, being the only major belligerent to suffer no wartime destruction in its heartland. At the end of the war, America possessed two-thirds of the world's gold reserves and three-quarters of its invested capital; it contained more than half the world's manufacturing capacity, and produced more than one-third of the world's goods. It also dominated shipping and export markets. In 1945, the gross national product of the United States was three times Soviet Russia's and

five times Great Britain's.[4] At war's end, America believed it faced
a national security problem in Stalin's Soviet Union, but it also had
the economic and—with the fortuitous advent of the atomic
bomb—the military means to counter it.

Perhaps unsurprisingly, their solution for the military problem
was framed in economic terms: monopoly. Specifically, an atomic
monopoly. The terminology of monopoly was omnipresent, even
though this was not, strictly speaking, a monopoly because there
was no closed market, no opportunity (or desire) to trade in
nuclear weapons. But the language was suggestive. Although the
world at large may have known little about atomic weapons, the
scientific, military, and political elite in Washington knew a great
deal. They knew, for example, how to make a bomb, knew that
they had the production process ready to make more (albeit not as
many as one might think, and not as rapidly)—but they also knew
that the Soviet Union was starting to work on nuclear weapons,
and that, unless action was taken, it would likely succeed. The
Americans also believed in this postwar world that there was
something historically unique in being the sole possessors of this
weapon, as the Yale University political scientist Arnold Wolfers
observed in 1946: "Until that day [the monopoly's end] comes, and
if only for a passing moment of history, this country occupies a
unique position among the nations—one, in fact, that has no parallel in history . . . There may never have been a time when all
other great powers were so dependent upon the attitude of one
major country."[5] This chapter is about that attitude.

The atomic monopoly—the control of this new weapon by the
United States alone—contributed heavily to the emphasis on
nuclear weapons for deterring the Soviet Union, and also to the
sense of American exceptionalism that fueled the ideological fires
of the cold war. The very notion of a monopoly implies control, and
that control meant staving off any proliferation of nuclear weapons
for as long as possible, ideally forever. Thinking about the monopoly in terms of what would later be called a "nonproliferation
regime" forces us to think about not just a monopoly of hardware,

of bombs, but also in terms of a monopoly of knowledge and information. The attempt to control atomic knowledge led to a series of efforts to prevent a nuclear arms race, and those efforts would all eventually fail. How and why they did proves not only interesting but crucial for understanding the emergence of a nuclear cold war arms race.

We now know that the Soviet Union proliferated in 1949, and that early nuclear arms control was a staggering failure. But we should also heed the Princeton physicist Eugene Wigner's observation that those in the monopoly did not necessarily expect it would take this course: "Today it is puzzling that so many able people could have seriously hoped that the atomic bomb would bring world peace. But it is important to recall that we did."[6] Part of the reason the Americans were cautiously optimistic about preventing an atomic arms race lay in the fact that during World War II tight American controls on information had played a role in preventing the nuclear proliferation of Nazi Germany, in the sense that the Germans remained unaware of the existence and extent of the Manhattan Project and thus did not prioritize their own work on nuclear weapons. The wartime framework thus set the first expectations of how to keep a lid on the atomic genie.

The first advocates of tight control of nuclear information even before the war started were, like Wigner, not military men but nuclear physicists. Shortly after the discovery of the fission of the uranium nucleus in December 1938, scientists around the world noted the possibility that the tremendous energy released by the process could be harnessed in an explosive. Since the discovery of fission took place in Berlin, physicists in Britain and America (especially refugees from Hitler's Germany) understandably expressed concern that the Nazis might begin work on such a weapon. No American scientist wanted to inadvertently help them.

The solution was not to stop research but to stop publishing that research. Here we see a pattern that would continue throughout the atomic monopoly: not to change the practices of science in the laboratory but instead to change the flow of knowledge. The easiest way was to self-censor, no longer submit or publish articles on fission. Gregory Breit of the Uranium Committee in the United States managed to coordinate a cessation of publication through the National Academy of Sciences and a few other contacts. The British were also able to stanch the leakage of scientific information fairly easily by contacting the editors of the six main scientific journals concerned with physics and convincing them to submit any articles on uranium fission for vetting to the Directorate of Tube Alloys (the British organization in charge of its atomic project, suitably concealed behind a meaningless code name).[7] Once the scientific press was under control, the popular press was less worrisome. If the Germans wanted to learn about the properties of uranium, they were going to have to work it out themselves.

Among the Western Allies, only the French refused to play along with self-censorship; while Soviet magazines continued popular discussions of the physics and implications of uranium fission well into 1943—long after complete silence on these matters had settled over all the other belligerents. Soviet openness can be attributed both to lack of coordination between the organs of military and civilian censorship in the Soviet Union, and to the limited interest in weaponizing uranium.[8]

That low level of interest was to change rather dramatically during the war, and it changed, ironically, more than anything else because of Anglo-American self-censorship. The point of the physicists' censorship was twofold: primarily not to provide valuable information to German scientists, but also to downplay the importance of fission by not talking about it, the silence drawing attention away from the furious pace of investigation in the Manhattan Project. This led to some unintended consequences. Georgii N. Flerov, one of a small prewar group of Soviet nuclear physicists, submitted an article to the American *Journal of Physics* on the spontaneous fission of uranium—an interesting phenomenon but one with no applications for atomic weapons.[9] The American physicists, after some deliberation, decided to print the article, believing that not printing it would tip off the Soviets to their budding nuclear program.

Flerov anticipated at least some scientific reaction to his piece, but there was nothing. Not only did no one respond, no one responded to any of the *earlier* articles on fission. And it was not as though the American nuclear scientists had moved on to different, nonnuclear topics; they simply were not publishing any research at all. This silence was troubling, and Flerov wrote to S. V. Kaftanov, the scientific consultant to the State Defense Committee, in November 1941 to alert the Soviet government to his fears:

> Well, the fundamental point is that in all foreign journals there is a complete absence of any kind of work on this question. This silence is not the result of the absence of work; they are not even printing articles that appear as the logical development of earlier printed work. There are no promised articles. In a word, the stamp of silence has been laid on this question, and this is the best sign of what kind of burning work is going on right now abroad.[10]

Where there is no smoke, there might be fire. When Kaftanov did not move fast enough to satisfy Flerov, he wrote directly to Stalin, urging him to begin an atomic-weapons program (although he cautiously estimated the chances of success at 10–20 percent).[11]

Flerov's inferences demonstrate an important feature of classification regimes: When a censor blacks out lines in a document, he or she alerts others—and not always just the intended foe, which in this case was Nazi Germany, not Soviet Russia—that his or her country is trying to hide something and often tells them a good deal about the nature of what is supposed to remain hidden. For example, in early 1945, Leslie Groves persuaded the U.S. Army Air Forces to bomb the Auer Company's metallurgical facilities in Germany. Rather than forestall Soviet specialists from acquiring the relevant technology, the choice of this specific facility because of certain equipment it contained for uranium purification allowed Stalin's scientists to deduce which equipment that was.[12]

General Groves's strict conception of security thus often proved counterproductive. After the end of the European war, the Soviet Union celebrated the 220th anniversary of the founding of its Academy of Sciences and invited leading scientists from around the world to attend. The guest list happened to include some scientists working on the Manhattan Project. After visas had already been granted and attendance confirmed, Groves yanked a number of physicists with no explanation. Nobel laureate Irving Langmuir, one of the Americans who did attend (he performed no atomic work during the war), testified succinctly to Congress about the implications: "I believe that these attempts to maintain secrecy resulted in giving to the Russians the very information which the Army most wished to keep from them. Any sensible Russian scientist knowing of these facts would have believed that we were developing an atomic bomb and were keeping it secret from the Russians."[13]

The Americans, British, and Canadians wanted to keep both Germany and the Soviet Union out of the nuclear race, and they were to be kept out by information denial. The Quebec Agreement between Franklin D. Roosevelt and Winston Churchill of August 1943 created a subsidiary secret alliance within the Big Three alliance of the United States, the United Kingdom, and the Soviet Union. Churchill and Roosevelt concluded: "We will not either of us communicate any information about Tube Alloys [i.e., atomic weapons] to third parties except by mutual consent."[14] The only third party in serious question was the Soviet Union, which was thus excluded—only with respect to atomic information—from other extant wartime weapons-sharing agreements. The postwar exclusion of the Soviet Union from the atomic alliance followed as a matter of course.

Retiring Secretary of War Henry Stimson acutely felt the impending problems posed by atomic energy and initiated the first serious attempt within the Truman administration to address them. The so-called Stimson Plan had a very short life—proposed in mid-September 1945, it was dead by the end of the month—yet it exposed two features that permeated American thought about nuclear arms control for decades: the centrality of the atomic monopoly for American thinking about relations with the Soviet Union, and the postulate that all negotiations should be transacted in the currency of knowledge.

Stimson's "plan" was more of a suggestion than a full-fledged proposal, but the absence of other serious alternatives elevated the secretary's concerned musing into the first battleground of the arms-control wars. The visit to Potsdam had deeply troubled the venerable Republican, who had served as secretary of state in Herbert Hoover's administration what must have seemed a lifetime ago. Potsdam revealed not just the destruction modern war could bring (even excluding nuclear weapons); it also exposed Stimson to the extent and severity of Stalin's secret-police regime, which hosted and monitored the Allied visitors. It seemed to him that such a government should not be allowed to have an atomic bomb, and yet how to prevent it? As he wrote to Truman on September 11, time was running out, to the tune of "a minimum of say four years or a maximum of twenty years." This led Stimson to an uncomfortable proposal: "Accordingly, unless the Soviets are voluntarily invited into the partnership upon a basis of cooperation and trust, we are going to maintain the Anglo-Saxon bloc over against the Soviet in the possession of this weapon. Such a condition will almost certainly stimulate feverish activity on the part of the Soviet toward the development of this bomb in what will in effect be a secret armament race of a rather desperate character." The United States, backed by Great Britain, should skirt around the fledgling United Nations and make the Soviets an open-ended offer to exchange information on nuclear matters. One could not know the benefits that might accrue, and the risks seemed low. Not only was the atomic bomb a stick to threaten the Soviet Union with, but sharing information in exchange for important political and economic concessions could also be America's most valuable carrot. "I consider the problem of our satisfactory relations with Russia," Stimson concluded, "as not merely connected with but as virtually dominated by the problem of the atomic bomb."[15]

The plan was vague—talk to the Russians about talking to them about the bomb—but it did suggest a set of principles: exchange information for security in the form of promises not to proliferate and a moderate inspection regime. Harry Truman, out of respect for this revered public servant, presided over the longest cabinet meeting of both his administrations on September 21, 1945, to discuss the risks and advantages of Stimson's proposal. "The discussion," recalled acting Secretary of State Dean Acheson, "was unworthy of the subject."[16] Secretary of the Navy James V. Forrestal recorded an extended account of the meeting in his diary, colored with his own stance against any concessions to the Soviet Union, atomic or otherwise—Truman's only military policy adviser to feel this way.[17] Forrestal noted of a cabinet lunch a few days earlier: "He [Truman] said his present disposition was to disclose the principles of atomic energy to the Russians and others of the United Nations but not the method of making the bomb. He said he proposed to have full discussion. I said I was forced to say now that I was violently opposed to any disclosure and I thought the country would be."[18] The "discussion" eventually changed few minds and instead consisted of the articulation of previously formulated positions on the viability of atomic sharing.

Truman's cabinet split into essentially three camps: the Forrestal wing, which opposed any sharing with the Soviet Union on principle; the Stimson faction, which supported some overtures along Stimson's lines in an effort to forestall an inevitable arms race; and Secretary of Commerce Henry A. Wallace, on his own. Wallace, as Roosevelt's vice president in his third term (and thus during most of the war), was one of the few cabinet members who had been briefed on the Manhattan Project before Hiroshima informed the rest of the American government (and the world). He felt that this experience and his technical training (in agricultural science) granted him a privileged position. Forrestal, perpetually irritated by Wallace, characterized the latter's stance as "completely, everlastingly and wholeheartedly in favor of giving it to the Russians."[19] Wallace, in his diary, understandably painted his position as more nuanced: "It was impossible to bottle the thing up no matter how much we tried; if we took the attitude of being dogs in the manger with regard to scientific information that we would develop for ourselves a scientific Maginot Line type of mind, thinking we were secure because of our past attainments, while at the same time certain other nations were going beyond us."[20] Nuanced or not, his difference of opinion with Forrestal would rebound disastrously for his reputation. News of the discussion was leaked to the press—almost certainly by Forrestal—and the Stimson Plan was unfairly attributed to Wallace. Given that Wallace publicly advocated, both then and in his later 1948 presidential campaign on the Progressive Party ticket, strengthening relations with the Soviet Union through concessions, as well as consistently liberal social policies, his support automatically gave the Stimson Plan a more pro-Soviet appearance than an association with Stimson would have.[21] (Stimson would himself recant his ideas privately and publicly by the end of 1946.[22])

With the cabinet split in three, the meeting was of course inconclusive, although Truman was not conducting a vote: He wanted to hear views; he would make the decision to share or not on his own.[23] To the extent there was any consensus, it hinged on estimates of how long the monopoly would last. Forrestal characterized the opinion of former head of the War Manpower Commission, Paul McNutt, in these terms: "Agreed with the principle of keeping your powder dry but said in this case it looked to him as if we couldn't keep our powder dry because of [Vannevar] Bush's statement that our atomic power knowledge must necessarily eventually be equaled by the Russians."[24] For Secretary of War (and Stimson's successor) Robert Patterson, support hinged directly on the assumption that the Soviets "could, without any aid or assistance from us, produce atomic bombs within a period of from four to twenty years. In other words, we can take it as fairly certain that our present control of atomic bombs to the exclusion of Russia will not extend beyond twenty years at the outside."[25] As Vannevar Bush, the wartime director of science policy (including jump-starting the atomic bomb project) and the architect of the postwar National Science Foundation, pointed out: "From one standpoint it is important to make the move at once. If Russia becomes fully embarked on an extensive program, it will be hard to deflect her effort. Moreover we wish her to choose the path of international understanding, and first impressions are important. From this standpoint we lost something when we could not make the move until the bomb actually exploded. Now no unnecessary time should be lost."[26] The Americans had to act fast, for they had both the monopoly (sole possession of the bomb) and the knowledge; to preserve the former, perhaps they should weaken their hold on the latter.

Truman certainly paid attention, but he did not agree with any of the three sides: do nothing, do Stimson, do everything. He felt he had to do something, and he took a middle-of-the-road approach that adopted some of the weakest features of the Stimson Plan without capturing its likeliest benefits. It is impossible to make sense of the so-called Agreed Declaration of November 1945 without a clear view of the jumbled mess that was America's foreign policy apparatus at the end of the war.

Franklin Roosevelt had loved foreign policy, and loved running it himself, which accorded with an anemic State Department and an ineffectual secretary of state (the last of the series was Edward Stettinius). Neither passion was a terrible liability either in a climate of 1930s isolationism or during the war, when the War Department naturally eclipsed its diplomatic sibling. But FDR's successor, Harry S. Truman, neither liked nor had a gift for foreign policy (his only foreign experience before the presidency being a tour in World War I). Truman, more than any recent president, needed an efficient State Department.[27] He did not have it—but he would get it.

No thanks to his first secretary of state (after furloughing Stettinius), James F. Byrnes. Byrnes was a lion of the Senate, a clever Southern logroller, and the man who felt Truman's nomination in 1944 had robbed him of the vice presidency (and hence the presidency). Truman trusted Byrnes, and Byrnes trusted himself, so the latter ran an idiosyncratic and somewhat independent foreign policy until Truman called him to heel and replaced him with George C. Marshall in 1947.[28] Marshall would in turn be replaced by Dean Acheson in 1949. The State Department in the years of Marshall, the heroic army chief of staff who directed American forces in World War II, and Acheson, a white-shoe lawyer with a long history of public service, grew dramatically: By January 1949, there were five times as many employees in its new building in Foggy Bottom as there had been in the old establishment; the department had a little over six hundred employees in the 1920s, one thousand on the eve of the war, and six thousand by 1948.[29] But Truman's early staff was bare-bones, Byrnes was perpetually wandering the globe alternately appeasing and antagonizing the Soviet Union, and Truman was frustrated at being kept in the dark.

Byrnes was in a sense the least of Truman's problems. The president may have been out of his depth with the intricacies of both atomic energy and Soviet diplomacy—and, to his credit, he knew it—but he was also a former senator with tremendous respect for the balance of power between the executive and legislative branches. Truman, by inclination, wanted to keep Congress in the loop. After the midterm elections of 1946, he had to.

The first postwar year and the process of economic reconversion had not been kind to the juggernaut American economy, and Truman shouldered a lot of the blame. Almost none of the news was good. Americans were hit with an unprecedented housing shortage, leaving Chicago alone with 100,000 homeless veterans (not to speak of the others). Most wartime price controls were removed in June 1946, which generated runaway inflation as consumers competed for scarce products. The Consumer Price Index rose from 129.6 to 153.3 (using a baseline of 1935 = 100), and the wholesale price index was even worse.[30] The upshot of all this was a battering for the Democratic Party in the congressional elections of 1946; the 80th Congress brought a Republican majority to both houses, as the long, cold winter of opposition dating from 1932 came to an end.[31] Truman was an unpopular president faced with a deteriorating economy, a hostile foreign adversary, and an even more hostile Congress. To deal with either of the first two, he needed to compromise with the third.

Necessity, buttressed by Truman's Congress-friendly outlook, gave birth to his bipartisan foreign policy—a pattern of cooperation on foreign affairs, especially with respect to the Soviet Union, that lasted until the end of the cold war and represents one of Truman's most enduring achievements. The point man in Congress for a cooperative, anticommunist, anti-isolationist foreign policy was Senator Arthur Vandenberg of Michigan, elected in 1928 and the only Republican from a large industrial state to be reelected in 1934 (he ranked second in seniority in 1946). Vandenberg had started out as an isolationist, but the rise of fascism in Europe persuaded him that a commitment to engage with world affairs (especially European affairs) was necessary to avoid worse destruction in the future. Vandenberg thus balanced the more doctrinaire GOP factions led by presidential hopeful Robert Taft ("Mr. Republican").[32] Any policy that involved Truman offering to share atomic secrets with the Soviet Union had to be sold to Vandenberg, and Vandenberg had to sell it to Taft. These dynamics highly constrained the available moves.

Stimson's plan was not among them; it would reveal too much sensitive information without requiring enough concrete concessions from the Soviets. The Republicans in Congress would eat the president alive. Instead, Truman offered a compromise: the Agreed Declaration of November 15, 1945. The declaration stemmed from two sources: first, British Prime Minister Clement Attlee's request, in a letter to Truman of September 25, for further Anglo-American atomic discussions; and Truman's own address to Congress requesting speedy enactment of atomic-energy legislation.

Truman was explicit about the temporariness of the monopoly: "Scientific opinion appears to be practically unanimous that the essential theoretical knowledge upon which the discovery is based is already widely known. There is also substantial agreement that foreign research can come abreast of our present theoretical knowledge in time."[33] Yet he and Byrnes (and Attlee, for that matter) all believed that the duration of the monopoly would be long, provided the Americans kept their information to themselves.

And preserving unfettered control of the bomb was, despite appearances, the goal of the Agreed Declaration. Truman announced, on behalf of the three nations involved in the Manhattan Project (the United States, Britain, and Canada), that discussions on sharing atomic information—and ceding control of atomic-energy regulation to an international authority—would be put before the United Nations for discussion.[34] Truman thus appeased those groups that wanted some firm action, while deferring the action for later and the discussion to others. Truman also contravened the central point of Stimson's plan, the important feature that the deal be offered to the Soviets directly as a bilateral exchange (supported by Britain). Stimson felt the Soviet Union would have no respect for the United Nations and would perceive the proposal as a stall tactic. Truman managed to conjure the worst of both worlds: He invoked the UN and he spoke for the three atomic powers in a move that could only look like ganging up on Stalin.[35]

In light of Truman's particular constraints, it is hard to imagine what else he could have done. Given his disinclination for foreign policy, the nuances of inducing Stalin to behave were not to his taste. He had to deal with a split cabinet, and one that had already shown a dispiriting capacity to leak to the press. And he was able to smell the coming right turn in Congress on the winds of the polls. Any international control on custody, production, or use of the atomic bomb was not popular. A public survey of August 22, 1945—before the Stimson Plan was discussed or even truly conceived—found that 73 percent of respondents opposed ceding control to the UN Security Council. (In contrast, in Britain, which was not the monopolist, a poll of January 12, 1946, showed 74 percent approving of such control.) And the very idea of UN control only fell in popularity: In April 1946, 61 percent of Americans wanted to continue producing bombs, and by November that had risen to 72 percent.[36] Truman understood the numbers; the United States would continue making bombs, he told Americans in late November 1945, for "experimental purposes."[37]

As of the fall of 1945, one proposal to preserve the atomic monopoly by sharing limited information had collapsed, and the alternative to replace it merely deferred the option. International efforts were not abandoned (the Agreed Declaration was still U.S. policy), but the Americans had not yet settled on the form their international proposals to the Soviet Union would take. Meanwhile, Congress was working out domestic control—preservation of the government's monopoly of atomic energy within the United States—at exactly the same moment. One might think in America in August 1945 that the logical party in the government to control atomic weapons (and atomic energy more generally) should be the body that created it: the U.S. military, specifically the army, whose Corps of Engineers directed the Manhattan Project. This was not the path Congress chose. For even before the end of the war, the "scientists' movement," largely organized by the Federation of Atomic Scientists (soon to become the Federation of American Scientists: FAS), lobbied Congress extensively and effectively against the proposed May-Johnson bill, which would perpetuate military administration, and in favor of some form of civilian control. By 1946, they had achieved their goal.[38]

That goal was realized by the Atomic Energy Act of 1946, otherwise known as the McMahon Act, after the self-appointed "Atomic Senator," Democrat Brien McMahon of Connecticut. As opposed to May-Johnson, which would have created a single cabinet-level position and reverted many of the day-to-day decisions about the exploitation of atomic energy to the control of military officials, the McMahon Act promoted a slew of subsidiary organizations, a complex interweaving of committees upon committees, and a murky division between civilian and military control (although rhetorically it sided definitively with the former). The act created a five-member Atomic Energy Commission (AEC), all ostensibly equal but with a chairman who served as primus inter pares, advised by a nine-member scientist-staffed General Advisory Committee (GAC), and overseen by an eighteen-member, statutorily bipartisan Joint Committee on Atomic Energy (JCAE), one of the most powerful joint committees in congressional history.[39] The McMahon Act instantly created three problems: leadership, custody, and information.

The leadership problem was particularly acute, because such a five-member governance structure for an executive agency was unprecedented. Its leader would have to be respected, flexible, and industrious, for he would have to clear a hostile congressional confirmation process, deal daily with a broad spectrum of political opinions (Truman insisted on appointing political opponents to the AEC to foster a bipartisan climate), and create an institutional culture from scratch. Truman's selection was inspired: former director of the Tennessee Valley Authority David E. Lilienthal. Among the public, the light-haired, smiling Lilienthal was one of the most widely respected public servants, having tirelessly devoted himself to the electrification and modernization of the Appalachian countryside, but he was also an old New Dealer, an inveterate liberal, and a Harvard Law–educated intellectual. He rubbed a lot of people in Washington (including Truman in his former Senate guise) the wrong way, but he was an experienced administrator with new, technology-based organizations, he knew something about atomic energy (as we shall see shortly), and his nomination helped shore up Truman's support among the left wing of his party.[40] And so Lilienthal, after a tense confirmation fight, became chairman of the AEC.

Lilienthal kept a detailed diary, replete with extensive and thoughtful reflections, and thus we have an inside (albeit partial) view of the formation of the AEC. At first, Lilienthal was optimistic about the possibilities for cooperation among his four peers, especially conservative Republican Lewis L. Strauss (pronounced "Straws"), a self-made lawyer and financier who represented a sincere attempt by Truman not to let atomic energy fall to partisan bickering.[41] The relationship between Lilienthal and Strauss deteriorated as the latter became increasingly concerned about potentially lax security in atomic policy. Within a year, Lilienthal considered AEC chairman "probably the world's worst job," and by early 1949: "L[ewis Strauss]'s attitude is one that makes me increasingly unhappy. My respect for him has suffered a considerable blow, not because of his *views*, as such, but the air of circumlocution."[42] By that September, on the eve of the news of the first Soviet test, Strauss had almost driven Lilienthal to resign: "Lewis has made it almost impossible to enjoy the Commission as a family, as we did when we started out, something I worked hard to develop."[43] Coupled with repeated harassment by Republican senators and the JCAE during the 80th Congress, Lilienthal stooped under the weight of his new task. He served as AEC chairman for almost the entire monopoly, although the events within it so harried him that he resigned in early 1950. Yet his views and his leadership, for all their faults, shaped almost every feature of that period.

This is perhaps nowhere clearer than in the issue of custody over nuclear weapons. According to the terms of the Atomic Energy Act of 1946, the AEC had a domestic monopoly over atomic-energy concerns. That is, it controlled the production and disposition of uranium fuel, and thus it determined how much fuel was available to build nuclear weapons, what form those would take, and where they would be distributed. For the first time in American history, a military weapon lay outside the control of the military. As a last-minute intervention in drafting the law, Arthur Vandenberg inserted an amendment that created a Military Liaison Committee to coordinate between the AEC and the armed forces, but its ambit was undefined.

Forrestal, in his dual status as secretary of the navy (and, after

1947, of defense) and as Strauss's friend, repeatedly lobbied Truman to resolve the confusion over who actually was in charge of the weapon—ideally, for Forrestal, resolving it in favor of the military. Custody of the physical weapons was a microcosm of the problem of being a monopolist, mirroring domestically the problems posed by granting control of any aspect of atomic energy to the United Nations. Forrestal insisted that in order to be prepared to use nuclear weapons—which he saw as a real possibility given the contemporary situation in Europe—the military needed to gain "familiarity" with them. How could one plan to use nuclear weapons if one did not know in advance how many one had, how many could be produced and how quickly, and what their physical features (both their size and their blast yield) would be? Yet the Atomic Energy Act was clear that the AEC had complete jurisdiction over the nuclear material. (Even nuclear command remained vague until September 1948, when Truman asserted control over authorization for the use of nuclear weapons.)[44] A murky compromise was worked out in principle, whereby the AEC still controlled the fuel in the weapons, but the military controlled the physical bombs, and the civilian president controlled the decision to use this category of weapon. In practice the problem was resolved by granting ever more authority to the Military Liaison Committee (and thus the Department of Defense), subverting the original intent of the law. The result of the custody debate, therefore, was much like all other American moves in the atomic arena: centralize and monopolize control, even while making sincere efforts to divide responsibility.

The third problem with the McMahon Act was Section IX, which made it illegal for any American (including any member of government, and thus also the president) to share any information about anything nuclear with any foreign power, the most sweeping assertion of governmental secrecy yet in American history.[45] It sent a very clear signal to the British—the initiators of the American atomic effort—that they would not obtain technical assistance or information from the Yankees very easily or very soon. The British remembered their contribution to the Manhattan Project (most visibly represented in the twenty scientists sent to Los Alamos, but actually present at every stage of the wartime effort), and Attlee and his citizens were furious at the McMahon Act's passage.[46] Specifically, the act revoked the clauses of the secret Quebec Agreement of 1943 which permitted sharing of nuclear information among Britain, America, and Canada. Congress had not been informed about the highly classified Quebec Agreement, and in any case had written the law in such a way as to revoke the standing executive agreement.

The British, however, wanted nuclear knowledge, and the only place they could get it was America. The British were building a nuclear bomb, and they required more information than they had obtained at Los Alamos and other sites in the Manhattan Project. Why was the United Kingdom proliferating? A good question, yet one difficult to answer because the decision to acquire an "independent nuclear deterrent" was taken for granted to such an extent that the active reasoning was rarely spelled out. The first discussion of a British atomic bomb came from the chief of the air staff in August 1946 (building on the deliberations of Gen 75, an inner ring of senior ministers who intensely debated atomic-energy matters), but only on May 12, 1948, almost two years later, was the issue broached openly in the House of Commons, to little discussion.[47] To the extent that there was a concrete rationale—beyond a vague yearning for "great power" status in the wake of decolonization and the dawning of the cold war—it was structured by anxiety about the Americans. As Foreign Minister Ernest Bevin put it in January 1947, "We could not afford to acquiesce in an American monopoly of this new development."[48] (This was uncommonly close to Soviet reasoning, as it happens.)

Unlike the Soviet Union, the British could force the United States to listen to them. Because of the structure of the Combined Development Trust (the wartime and postwar uranium monopoly discussed in the following chapter), the British controlled half of the "Allied" uranium supply and thus could potentially heavily restrict the number of atomic bombs the Americans could build. Forrestal in particular worried about how to get this raw material out of British hands; they were sitting on a resource they could not use but would not share it with those who could.[49] Forrestal was too gloomy: The British were happy to share; they just would not share for free. They wanted technical information to assist in the construction of nuclear reactors, isotope separation facilities, and perhaps weapons themselves, and they would pay for it in metal. There were two problems here: It was illegal to tell the British anything under the strict terms of the McMahon Act, and it also might not be wise. Forrestal noted in his diary, in response to the arguments of Vannevar Bush and Lilienthal, that "the kind of information which the British might ask for might conceivably now be given without any injury or loss of security," that "we could not ignore the fact that there was a substantial bloc in the Labour Party in England and some people in the Cabinet, headed by [Stafford] Cripps, who were full out for complete collaboration with Russia and that we therefore had to take the risk that whatever we gave them by way of information might ultimately get to Russia."[50] Communists could not be trusted, and Labour seemed pretty pink to him.

Compromise was essential, however, because the bombs could not be made if the British did not play along, and the Americans could not afford to wait. The need for uranium became particularly acute in 1947, as Truman later related in his memoirs, with the deteriorating state of Soviet-American relations, the stalling of atomic arms control, and the frantic recognition by the Americans of the puny size of their supposedly mighty atomic stockpile.[51] (The optimal size for an atomic stockpile is, of course, a relative assessment based on how many bombs one thinks one needs. To speak more precisely, Truman's expectations for the number of bombs necessary for an effective nuclear war–fighting strategy had risen, and thus the extant bombs appeared to him to be too few.) George F. Kennan, the architect of America's containment posture in the cold war and the leading interpreter of Soviet intentions for the Truman administration, was pulled off his other assignments as director of the State Department's Policy Planning Staff and assigned to this issue.[52] In 1947, Kennan and his interlocutors came to an aptly named solution: the Modus Vivendi. The British now had to give up a great share of the uranium, which they would not have used anyway, and they got some limited cooperation within the terms of the McMahon Act (primarily information about reactor design and isotope separation). The Americans, in turn, accepted the British nuclear program and acquiesced to the latter's plans to maintain bombs and facilities in the British Isles.[53] The Modus was due for renegotiation in two years. As fate would have it, the Soviets detonated their first device just before that date and disrupted everything.

No one should have been terribly surprised at either the Soviet explosion or the British program, since by 1949 atomic arms control had demonstrably failed to all but the most Pollyanna-like observers. But when the Atomic Energy Act was passed, this outcome was by no means obvious. In fact, indications were good that the Agreed Declaration would actually bear some fruit: Both the British and the Soviets might compromise with the Americans into some form of international control. Truman and Byrnes were willing to cede some authority over atomic matters to a future United Nations Atomic Energy Commission (UNAEC), but—as befitting the keepers of the atomic monopoly—they did not want to lose any more control than necessary. The administration wanted to have a detailed atomic-control proposal ready for discussion by the time UNAEC deliberations were slated to begin in summer 1946, and Dean Acheson put together a committee to work out an agenda. During their deliberations, the members were clear that there were two possible monopolies over the bomb: one over raw materials, and one over information. The committee's report recognized that, unlike the raw materials that went into a bomb, information was a volatile substance, not to be constrained for long: "The knowledge possessed by the United States, and to a lesser degree by the United Kingdom and Canada, concerning the atomic bomb is only a temporary monopoly, a wasting asset which, if it is to be exploited to gain some form of international control, must be brought to bear promptly."[54]

Thus was born the Acheson-Lilienthal Report "to study the subject of controls and safeguards respecting atomic energy necessary to protect this country," named after both its State Department patron and the committee's nominal chair, David E. Lilienthal, more than a year before his confirmation as chair of the AEC.[55] (The legislation creating the commission, the McMahon Act, had not even passed yet.) Aside from Stimson's general suggestions and Truman's vague deferral, this was the first concrete and sustained attempt to think about nuclear arms control as a fundamentally *new* problem, not one that could be analogized (as Stimson had) to efforts to regulate submarine warfare or chemical weapons. As such, the group needed exceptionally gifted individuals from the multiple constituencies affected by atomic energy, which Acheson and Lilienthal interpreted as essentially scientific, governmental, and industrial. They drafted Chester I. Barnard (president of New Jersey Bell), Allen Thomas (vice president and technical director of Monsanto Chemical Company), Harry A. Winne (vice president in charge of engineering policy at General Electric), and J. Robert Oppenheimer. Noticeably and deliberately absent was any military representation.

After weeks of intense discussions, during which Oppenheimer tutored all present on the basic physics of a nuclear bomb, the final report was written during four all-day sessions at the Dumbarton Oaks mansion in Washington, D.C. Although the report was written in an impersonal tone without attributing particular insights to specific individuals, the final proposal bore strong similarities to arms-control ideas Oppenheimer had expressed in the fall of 1945. "All the participants would, I think," Dean Acheson recalled later, "agree that the most stimulating and creative mind among us was Robert Oppenheimer's."[56] Considering the proposal that would soon bear his name, Lilienthal was ecstatic: "We have developed a really original, distinctive, and I think completely sound idea as the theme of our recommendation on the atomic bomb."[57]

The Acheson-Lilienthal Report was a direct and unabashed defense of monopoly as *the* strategy for atomic arms control. Stated bluntly, the report advocated relinquishing the American atomic monopoly to a new monopolist, an Atomic Development Authority (ADA), which would literally own all nuclear material on the planet and produce atomic energy for the sake of all nations while being itself sovereign and, in some respects, above even the United Nations. Once international control was established, and the ADA held its monopoly, it would also own all the atomic bombs the United States already possessed (or was then manufacturing), and the UN would be entirely in charge of decisions about their use. The point of the proposal was to exploit atomic energy for peaceful purposes *and* to eliminate nuclear arms as potential aggressive weapons, at the same time preventing any future powers from developing the technology to proliferate on their own. At the dawn of the nuclear age, Oppenheimer—troubled by the destruction of Hiroshima and Nagasaki—helped steer the Acheson-Lilienthal Committee to advocate a form of nuclear disarmament for the United States.

The first point the committee needed to establish in its report was that the American monopoly was temporary: "Today the United States has a monopoly in atomic weapons . . . It has been recognized that this monopoly could not be permanent. There have been valid differences of opinion on the time which it would take other nations to come abreast of our present position, or to surpass it; but it is generally admitted that during the next five to twenty years the situation will have changed profoundly."[58] So, since time was of the essence, a new structure needed to be erected to replace the American monopoly with a more permanent one. Scientists around the world would work for the ADA and produce nuclear devices, and thus would be loyal not to their respective nations but to the planet as a whole. That is, they would be supranational in allegiance, conducting their atomic research for the benefit of the world and not an individual sovereign state (the latter having already given up some of its sovereignty to the ADA in the first place). The mechanism for this to work was the second major argument of the report: The only effective control of atomic weapons must center on monopolizing the raw materials of fission—uranium (and thorium) ores. If the ADA controlled this material, then there was no way any nation could proliferate. This required a shift from thinking about information to thinking about materials.[59] The point was not just to control atomic energy but also to set up an inspection regime under the ADA so that, while it could not prevent a determined proliferator, it could at least provide a year's warning. At which point the UN Security Council might authorize the threat or the use of nuclear weapons to prevent other nations from acquiring their own atomic arsenal.

Perhaps inadvisably, the Acheson-Lilienthal Report was leaked to the press and published without Truman or Byrnes ever having made a clear decision about whether this proposal was in fact going to become the official policy of the United States. Never mind that it was highly unlikely that a treaty containing an ADA— and particularly the *monopolization* by an *international* authority of *private* mining resources—would ever clear the Senate, Acheson and Lilienthal wanted the report distributed both to force Truman's hand and to alert the public that atomic arms control was going to require some new thinking. As Acheson testified to the JCAE during Lilienthal's confirmation hearings, "This plan is an attempt to show that international control is possible, provided that other nations are willing to make the necessary sacrifices to put it into effect."[60] As such, the report was an existence proof, evidence both that atomic arms control was possible and that it was going to be difficult.

Acheson eventually had his way, although perhaps not as he had envisioned, and he would eventually come to regret it. Acheson-Lilienthal did become the proposal of the U.S. government before the United Nations, after a fashion. The only way members of the UNAEC would learn the details of the Acheson-Lilienthal Report was by reading it themselves, for the official proposal put before them was an altered—some might say distorted, or gutted, or bowdlerized—version, modified by the seventy-six-year-old financier and adviser to Democratic presidents since Woodrow Wilson, Bernard M. Baruch.

To read Truman's account in his memoirs, the appointment of Baruch was sensible and uncontroversial—gastric ulcers, chronic napping, and bad hearing aside: "Bernard M. Baruch seemed to me to be the logical man, and for several reasons. Not the least important of these was that Baruch enjoyed considerable esteem in the Senate. His association with the administration's plan for the control of atomic energy might help remove some of the opposition to the McMahon bill in Congress."[61] It was not trivial to talk Baruch into accepting the task. Not, as one might suppose, because he was exhausted after extensive public service dating back to his organization of the American economy during World War I, but because he wanted to be in charge, and he felt that the publication of the Acheson-Lilienthal Report had marginalized him, turned him into a simple messenger boy. Secretary of State Byrnes had to engage in significant flattery to persuade Baruch to take the post at all.[62]

But attitudes to the appointment in the scientific and diplomatic communities—the two groups most invested in the radical approach of the report—ranged from underwhelmed to outraged. Scientists, especially those represented by the FAS, an organization composed largely of Manhattan Project veterans, thought the aging Southerner too ignorant of the technical issues to shepherd the proposal through and absolve them of their responsibility for the weapon they had created. The diplomats sensed that Baruch had lost any finesse or charm he might have once had as he slid into his dotage. But he was certainly a reasonable choice to assuage the fears of senators who would have to ratify any arms-control treaty and were already panicky about the leakage of atomic "secrets" to Communist hands. (The first of several atomic spy rings was publicly blown in February 1946, at the very moment the Acheson-Lilienthal Report was being written.) Baruch supposedly had a strong reputation for reliability with the Washington establishment, although Acheson, never one to mince words, later noted, "My own experience led me to believe that his reputation was without foundation in fact and entirely self-propagated."[63] Lilienthal, no less invested than Acheson in the appointment of the emissary to the UN, was blunter: "When I read this news last night, I was quite sick. We need a man who is young, vigorous, not vain, and whom the Russians would feel isn't out simply to put them in a hole, not really caring about international cooperation. Baruch has none of these qualifications."[64] Even the patrician and well-mannered Vannevar Bush told Baruch, as the latter recalled in his memoirs, "point-blank that, in his opinion, I was the most unqualified man in the country for the task."[65] Baruch harangued Lilienthal and Acheson to give him a quick rundown on all this atomic business, an impossible task given the technical complexity of the subject, even had the two of them been willing. Oppenheimer was so incensed that he refused to cooperate with Baruch.

This denial of the most qualified advice meant that Baruch more or less had to feel his own way, and he surrounded himself with his usual cadre of advisers, publicity men, and sycophants to prepare the American position for the first UNAEC meeting in June. (Truman and Byrnes had more pressing cold war worries and apparently did not try to strong-arm any cooperation.) Baruch was undaunted and not above brandishing the bomb, as he noted to Lilienthal: "America can get what she wants if she insists on it. After all, we've got it and they haven't and won't have for a long time to come; I don't know how long, but it will be some time."[66] Given the short time frame and lack of expertise, there was no question that the Acheson-Lilienthal Report would serve as the basis of Baruch's eponymous plan, focusing on the international monopolization of uranium. But in the interest of operationalizing it—and of putting his own "personal stamp" on it—Baruch made three major changes to the proposal. Those changes reflect an important feature of the Baruch Plan: It was a domestic compromise, not an international one, designed to appease American political instincts.[67] This domestic, inward focus of the plan—seen even in Truman's retrospective justification of the appointment as facilitating the McMahon Act's passage, not international arms control—generated Baruch's three modifications, each of which created its own sticking point.

The first change was to impose sanctions on violators: "swift and condign punishment," in Baruch's terms. As he put it in his opening speech to the UN on June 14, 1946 (a speech he also arranged to be printed and extensively broadcast through his personal public-relations staff), "If I read the signs aright, the peoples want a program not composed merely of pious thoughts but of enforceable sanctions—an international law with teeth in it." This imposed an international inspection regime and brought with it the clear implication that the Security Council (at the very least) would be obligated to punish violators, either through sanctions or military action. The second change would eventually raise the most comment: "There must be no veto to protect those who violate their solemn agreements not to develop or use atomic energy for destructive purposes."[68] The third change bore the marks of American capitalist reasoning: The international authority would indeed own all of the uranium in the world, but only once it was mined out of the ground; while still encased in the earth, it would remain private property, thus enabling a free-market trade in uranium-rich land up to the point the ore was extracted.

Each of these changes sparked enough criticism that the central principle enunciated in the Acheson-Lilienthal Report—that the royal road to atomic control was through control of raw materials—was seldom questioned. The entire debate focused on procedure.[69] Even if we accept that the Soviet Union would never have agreed to *any* restraints on its ability to proliferate, the procedural debates provided much room for stalling and eventually discredited the central assumption of emphasizing raw materials in nonproliferation regimes—with unfortunate consequences lasting to the present.

The insistence on maintaining private ownership of uranium still in the ground instantly tipped off critics to the central theme of the Baruch Plan: monopoly. As one of many left-wing commentators noted, "On an international scale, the cartel represents the same intermixture of government and monopoly. In the sphere of diplomacy the most direct expression of the cartel's program for control of the world's atomic resources is the Baruch scheme for international control of atomic energy."[70] That is, one outcome (intentional or not) of the Baruch Plan would be to limit control of uranium and nuclear weapons technology to a few select individuals sanctioned by international law. Given the geographical distribution of nuclear expertise in the mid-1940s, it was obvious that the staff of the ADA would be primarily American. Over time, the scientific contingent of the ADA would become more international—assuming that one trusted the ADA to be autonomous of American interests, which the Soviets did not. In the meantime, the Americans could still have the world's nuclear knowledge and matériel under their control. Soviet ambassador to the United Nations, Andrei Gromyko, was blunt in his memoirs about this feature of the Baruch Plan: "America had established a monopoly on the manufacture of nuclear weapons and wanted to retain that monopoly."[71] This interpretation of the Baruch Plan became the official Soviet line from the very first days after its proposal, expressed by Soviet Foreign Minister V. M. Molotov as "a control so shaped as, on the surface, to appear international, while in reality it is designed to secure a veiled monopoly for the United States in this field."[72]

Simply cold war propaganda? Perhaps. But then why did the United States insist on continuing to produce nuclear weapons while the Baruch Plan was under discussion at the United Nations? The plain text of the Baruch Plan, as well as its later elaboration by American officials, rejected a moratorium on the production of nuclear weapons for the American stockpile: First the plan needed to be approved, then the ADA would be set up and begin inspections, and only *then* would the United States destroy its bombs. In the meantime, the stockpile would grow.

On a practical level, as Baruch's staff recognized, the "U.S. has gone so far in its demobilization of the Army and Navy that if we were to stop making bombs we would be almost defenseless and would certainly have only a modicum of military power with which to stand up to the U.S.S.R."[73] But the insistence on continued production of bombs was more than realpolitik; it also reflected, to American minds, the deep asymmetry between the world and the United States in the nuclear arena, and thus the generosity of the Baruch Plan. America was the only power with this weapon, and instead of holding on to it, it was volunteering to give it up! If the president wanted to retain bombs for a few years until he felt secure, that was his prerogative. The alternative was simply for the United States to arm itself to the teeth. "Certainly," wrote Baruch adviser John Hancock, "we couldn't equalize [the atomic situation] unless we gave up all the information, destroyed all our plants, killed the scientists, destroyed the know-how of production and the plants in which such know-how could be applied."[74] The asymmetry was part of the status quo, and the Soviets would have to deal with it.

Not surprisingly, Soviet diplomats disagreed. Five days after Baruch's speech, Gromyko (who, like all other members of the commission except for Baruch, was also their nation's chief representative to the UN) issued his response:

As one of the primary measures for the fulfillment of the resolution of the General Assembly of 24 January 1946, the Soviet delegation proposes that consideration be given to the question of concluding an international convention prohibiting the production and employment of weapons based on the use of atomic energy for the purpose of mass destruction. The object of such a convention should be the prohibition of the production and employment of atomic weapons, the destruction of existing stocks of atomic weapons and the condemnation of all activities undertaken in violation of this convention.[75]

In essence, the Soviets inverted the structure of the Baruch Plan: *First*, every nation must renounce the use of nuclear weapons and destroy their nuclear facilities; only then would there be symmetry among all countries and an inspection regime could be erected. Whereas Baruch proposed using the atomic monopoly held by the United States as the framework for international arms control, Gromyko wanted to annihilate the monopoly altogether and place the atomic issue on a par with other, nonmonopolistic, problems. The U.S. State Department correctly assessed this premise of the Gromyko proposal: "Obviously, his position seems to be that atomic energy poses no new problem, as far as the United Nations is concerned, and that the Security Council should handle this problem in the same way that it is empowered to handle other problems relating to the maintenance of international peace and security, to breaches of the peace, and to acts of aggression."[76] Given the assumption, by then widespread in the United States, that atomic weapons presented a revolutionary transformation of the rules of warfare and of statecraft, it was hard not to see the Soviet proposal as Henry Wallace did, "as a counterproposal for the record . . . It is almost impossible to take it seriously"; or, as American ambassador to the Soviet Union Walter Bedell Smith noted, "Viewed from this Embassy, Gromyko's atomic control proposal is thoroughly disingenuous proposition which tends to (1) seize for USSR moral leadership on atomic question and (2) obscure the basic issue, which is inspection."[77]

There is no question that obscuring the terms of the debate by emphasizing the moral problems of atomic warfare was one of the tactics Gromyko deployed, and deployed effectively. The second was his emphasis on matters of procedure. Here Baruch's second amendment to the Acheson-Lilienthal Report—the suspension of the veto—played a key role. Each of the five permanent members of the UN Security Council (the United States, the Soviet Union, the United Kingdom, France, and China, which at this time meant Chiang Kai-shek's Nationalist government) wielded a veto over any proposed enforcement action that would entail intervention by the UN member states under the council's direction. Baruch did not suggest eliminating the veto altogether, only suspending it on questions of atomic energy, based on the reasonable guess that one of the Security Council members (the Soviet Union, of course) might in fact be found in violation by the ADA and thus would be in a position of moral hazard: subverting the norms of international law out of self-interest.

The Soviets stood very firmly behind the retention of the veto for *all* Security Council business, the securing of this right having been essential to induce them to join the San Francisco Charter that established the United Nations. According to Molotov, the veto represented unanimity of major-power action, which was substantially more relevant to important issues like arms control than the simple majority rule Baruch proposed.[78] As one of Baruch's assistants, D. F. Fleming, reported to his boss when Soviet recalcitrance became clear: "Their conception of the U.N. is one in which the few big powers will make the main decisions by agreement—preceded by much hard bargaining. They may be very perverse and wrong in this attitude, but for years to come they will not do business on any other basis."[79] In fact, by October 1946, the Soviet Union had already used its Security Council veto eleven times, and by the following August had added seven more—far more invocations than any other permanent member—prompting pundits to worry that the veto might kill the UN as an effective institution.[80] Whether pragmatic, self-interested, or principled, the veto provided a handy excuse for the Soviets to stall on the Baruch Plan; Chester Barnard, one of the original members of the Acheson-Lilienthal Committee, called it "an irrelevant blind alley in which the Russian bear could do a lot of dancing if he wished."[81] And dance he did.

Gromyko's alternative to the Baruch Plan was extensively debated within the UNAEC but was definitively rejected on April 5, 1948, by a nine-to-two vote—the minority being the Soviet Union and Poland (already a satellite). It was dismissed in a joint statement penned by the Canadians, Chinese, British, and French:

> The Soviet Union proposals are not an acceptable basis for the international control of atomic energy. The UNAEC cannot endorse any scheme which would not prevent the diversion of atomic material, which provides no effective means for the detection of clandestine activities and which has no provision for prompt and effective enforcement action. The Soviet Union Government has not only proposed a scheme that is fundamentally inadequate for the control of atomic energy, but at the same time has made the overriding stipulation that they will not agree to establish even such a feeble scheme of control until all atomic weapons have been prohibited and destroyed. It is completely unrealistic to expect any nation to renounce atomic weapons without any assurance that all nations will be prevented from producing them.[82]

Since the Soviet Union was the most likely nation next to develop an atomic bomb, it was the single most crucial party the Americans had to convince—and they failed. So why did the Soviet Union insist on global nuclear disarmament rather than on constructive negotiation? Frederick Osborn, Baruch's successor as chief atomic negotiator, found himself "forced to the conclusion that the Soviet delegates were more interested in propaganda than in negotiations, and that their propaganda was directed almost entirely to the emotions of the people on their side, rather than to the intelligence of their audience."[83] As usual, the columnist Walter Lippmann offered a commonsense answer: "We have to conclude that as a matter of fact the Soviet government expects us to continue to have the monopoly of the atomic bomb, that it does not believe we can use it effectively, and will, therefore, make no concessions to us. For the net result of Mr. Gromyko's argument is that we continue to have the bomb."[84] Perhaps the monopoly did not scare the Soviet Union after all.

It certainly did not scare them enough to endorse the Baruch Plan when their own proposal was rejected. It was not at all clear, given the different premises of both proposals, starting from a notion of asymmetry (Baruch) or symmetry (Gromyko), whether the two could ever be reconciled by compromise.[85] By September 1946, Baruch could confidently write to Truman that there was no way unanimity—the sine qua non of any realistic effort to prevent Soviet proliferation—would emerge.[86] Noteworthy here was only the lateness of Baruch's realization; Lippmann had figured this out within ten days of Baruch's first speech: "I am very much afraid that Mr. Baruch's presentation of the American proposals has prejudiced them so deeply that it will be difficult to make any kind of reasonably quick progress to an understanding."[87] Baruch resigned his post as negotiator to the UNAEC in January 1947, to be replaced by America's representative at the UN, Vermont Republican Warren Austin, who was by then in his seventies.[88] Austin and his team of negotiators, while more persistent than Baruch's flighty cohort, made little progress.

No great surprise. By mid-1947, even J. Robert Oppenheimer, one of the fiercest advocates for some variant of atomic arms control, had lost his faith: "It seems to me that to continue negotiations under these conditions is an act of bad faith, and that in time this bad faith will catch up with us."[89] In what was to become a pattern for Oppenheimer, a lack of attention to politics had doomed his ideas (chiefly an emphasis on raw materials). As Osborn reported on a conversation with Oppenheimer in his diary: "He thinks that the substitute of the Russian plan—however strengthened and improved—for the majority plan would be impossible, dangerous and unacceptable in the present state of the world. He feels that the weakness of the Acheson-Lilienthal Report is that it did not sufficient[ly] define the state of the world necessary for any effective plan of control."[90] That was in February

1948. By summer, it had become hopeless. The distinguished Chicago sociologist Edward Shils lamented the new status quo: "At present the situation is so unpromising as far as atomic energy control as such is concerned that even if the Soviets were to accept the majority plan, the American people and their leaders might indeed be too distrustful of the Soviets to accept their scheme which they themselves had proposed."[91] In June, the majority (supporters of a modified Baruch Plan) and the Soviet Union had hardened their stances to a deadlock, and in the fall of 1948 the UNAEC referred the issue to the General Assembly. It would bounce around for another year, only to die quietly in November 1949 after Soviet proliferation rendered the issue moot.[92] Two days after the Security Council abandoned the problem in 1948, the Soviet Union shut the roads into their sector of occupied Germany. The Berlin blockade had begun.

The story of atomic arms control, uninspiring failure though it was, contained the seeds of much that followed. The Soviet-American arms race—particularly the nuclear component of that race—did not happen against a neutral background; it happened against *this* background, and thus in the failure of the Baruch Plan and the Soviet counterproposal we can detect several of the assumptions that would guide both parties' behavior over the course of the monopoly.

The Soviets pursued two solutions to the American monopoly. The first, and obviously highly classified, approach was to break the monopoly and develop a Soviet nuclear bomb. The other alternative, the public one, justified the so-called Peace Offensive, whereby the Soviet Union cast itself as the advocate of arms control and disarmament as opposed to a capitalist West that refused to relinquish its atomic arsenal. Beginning in 1946, Andrei Zhdanov, Stalin's second in command, orchestrated a public-relations campaign with a dual function: to embarrass the United States so they would not use their atomic advantage, and to assure their own client states that the absence of a Soviet deterrent was not a liability.[93] It affirmed the correctness of the historical struggle against Western imperialism.

This was the public stance of the Soviet Union, but what about its private stance? Given the topography of power, that meant the personal views of Joseph Stalin about nuclear weapons. Unfortunately, we know very little about what Stalin thought about the bomb. He spoke far less often in public than the average Western leader in the postwar years; during the war he had delivered a number of lengthy speeches, but from 1945 to his death he delivered only one extended public speech (aside from his intervention in ideological debates about linguistics), and granted only about four short interviews annually.[94] Stalin's account of military doctrine—the official Soviet interpretation—minimized the importance of nuclear weapons or any other kind of technological innovation. For Stalin, military strategy was built around the five "permanently operating factors": the stability of the rear, the morale of the army, quantity and quality of divisions, state of (conventional) armament of the army, and the organizational ability of the command. The only "transitory" factor was surprise. There was no place for "revolutions" in warfare caused by very large bombs powered by some obscure physical process in uranium—and thus the Peace Offensive made perfect sense.[95]

While the East called for peace, the West contemplated war. The central presumption behind all of the arms-control proposals, from Henry Stimson's on, was that the American monopoly was temporary. When the Soviet Union eventually obtained the atomic bomb, its utility in offsetting Soviet conventional superiority in Europe would be greatly vitiated. Why not take advantage of the transient technological edge and initiate a preventive war against the Soviet Union? The Berlin blockade was interpreted by American hard-liners as presaging a Soviet invasion of Western Europe and thus made the issue much more acute within the corridors of power (although publicly government officials distanced themselves from outright calls for preventive war). The hawks never got very far, mostly because the military never expressed confidence that it had enough troops, planes, or (crucially) bombs actually to "knock out" the Soviet Union.[96] Truman could never be certain of the outcome.

All he could be sure of is that Soviet-American relations—never cozy, not even at Potsdam, which was beginning to look like a Golden Age—had deteriorated severely. In 1948 confrontation seemed unavoidable. On March 1, Communists in Czechoslovakia engineered a coup that shocked the Western world. The looming Italian elections a month later raised the possibility that Communists might triumph at the ballot box, and the United States mobilized a series of tactics (more or less unsavory) to ensure that the left would lose. When the Soviets blockaded Berlin on June 24, the cold war threatened to turn hot. Truman arranged for an airlift, jointly with the British, to supply the starving western sectors of the city, thereby preserving it from integration with the East and—as a by-product—helping secure his surprise victory in the American presidential elections that November. The airlift forestalled criticisms of containment by his Republican opponent, Governor Thomas Dewey of New York, and Truman was able to astonish the pundits with a narrow upset. Democrats in Congress benefited too: The 81st Congress had a 54–42 and 263–171 Democratic majority in the Senate and House of Representatives.[97] Domestic politics were back under control, Europe was locked in a bipolar split, and Truman was firmly in charge.

In charge of what, exactly? The wartime Manhattan Project scientists and administrators had correctly recognized the problems the atomic bomb would pose for the postwar order: The Americans would be dominant, but that dominance would be transitory; the Soviets would be defensive, and that defensiveness would breed divisiveness. Nothing had changed in the first three postwar years, studded as they were by the failure of proposal after proposal to restrain an atomic arms race. And yet, strange as it might now seem, the situation in 1945 did not appear to be necessarily headed in this direction; agreement and cooperation between the

Americans and the Soviets did not seem utterly impossible. British Ambassador to the Soviet Union Archibald Clark Kerr perceptively captured the mood on the ground in Moscow in December 1945:

Then plump came the Atomic Bomb. At a blow the balance which had now seemed set and steady was rudely shaken. Russia was balked by the west when everything seemed to be within her grasp. The three hundred divisions were shorn of much of their value. About all this the Kremlin was silent but such was the common talk of the people. But their disappointment was tempered by the belief inspired by such echoes of foreign press as were allowed to reach them that their Western comrades in arms would surely share the bomb with them. That some such expectation as this was shared by the Kremlin became evident in due course. But as time went on and no move came from the West, disappointment turned into irritation and, when the bomb seemed to them to become an instrument of policy, into spleen. It was clear that the West did not trust them. This seemed to justify and it quickened all their old suspicions. It was a humiliation also and the thought of this stirred up memories of the past. We may assume that all these emotions were fully shared by the Kremlin.[98]

There seemed no alternative to the straightforward conclusion: Absent meaningful arms control, the Soviet Union would soon develop an atomic bomb. The only question was, How soon?

TWO

HOW MUCH TIME DO WE HAVE?

> The hours of folly are measur'd by the clock; but of
> wisdom, no clock can measure.
>
> WILLIAM BLAKE, "THE MARRIAGE OF HEAVEN AND HELL"

Polls from 1945 onward consistently reflected the widespread view that the Soviets would be the next nuclear power.[1] "Only two people out of a hundred," the Social Science Research Council observed, "think other countries will be unable to make the bomb."[2] And, in January 1946, it seemed that the inevitable had happened. To considerable newspaper fanfare, Dr. Raphael E. G. Armattoe, the director of the Loneshire Research Center for anthropology and human biology in Londonderry, Northern Ireland, announced that he had learned from secret sources that the Soviets had produced an atomic bomb the size of a tennis ball. The story was deemed so important that President Truman himself issued a flat refutation of Armattoe's claim at a press conference.[3] The Central Intelligence Agency concurred: "There are no indications that the Soviets have an operational atomic bomb."[4]

That did not stop further reports of Soviet proliferation—or of something even worse. Apparently bored by accounts of an object so humdrum as an atomic bomb, journalists produced sensationalist stories that the Soviets had developed an extremely lethal cosmic-ray bomb, or even a "death ray"—the latter backed by no less an authority than German Nobel laureate in physics Werner Heisenberg in March 1949.[5] Most of these reports came from right-wing European newspapers and may have been motivated in part by a desire to stiffen American resolve for the defense of Europe.[6]

Taking down Armattoe's allegations was one thing, but Truman was obviously too busy to deal with all of these reports, and refutations began to issue from lower and lower down the administrative totem pole. Even though American intelligence was pretty sure that these reports were fictions or disinformation, how sure could they really be? Some, such as the American naval attaché to the Soviet Union, in dismissing reports of a Soviet nuclear test in Chita in 1946, felt it safest to hedge his bets: "While we are inclined to view with considerable skepticism specific atomic rumors which have come to our attention, we do not feel it would be safe to assume in general that USSR has not yet developed atomic bomb. Until there is pretty conclusive evidence one way or another, it would seem to be sound to proceed on assumption that USSR may have produced and tested or will soon produce and test atomic bombs."[7] This position had been dominant among cautious civil servants even before the end of World War II. A position paper from April 1945 reveals both the fear of eventual Soviet proliferation and American ignorance of their progress: "While information concerning Russian activity in this field is incomplete, there is reason to believe that Russian scientists are at work in the general field of nuclear energy."[8] But the Soviets did not have the bomb yet—of that the Americans were confident. Even Joseph Stalin, the last person one would expect to minimize Soviet strength, announced in an October 1946 interview that he had no nuclear weapon.[9]

After Armattoe had been put to rest, other Soviet reports seemed to refute Stalin's sanguine assertions. On November 6, 1947, on the thirtieth anniversary of the Bolshevik Revolution, Soviet Foreign Minister Viacheslav Molotov hinted at Soviet success. In the midst of a rousing celebratory speech, he cryptically added, "As we know, a sort of new religion has become widespread among expansionist circles in the U.S.A.: having no faith in their own internal forces, they put their faith in the secret of the atomic bomb, although this secret has long ceased to be a secret."[10] Two weeks earlier, Andrei Zhdanov, Stalin's second in command, had announced in Warsaw that while the Americans had a monopoly on nuclear weapons, that monopoly was "temporary." Andrei Vyshinsky, who would replace Molotov as foreign minister in 1949, concurred with Molotov that the Soviets "possibly" had the bomb, and then later affirmed that the monopoly was an "illusion."[11] Could it be that the Soviet Union had in fact developed an atomic bomb—and so early, in 1947?

Absolutely not, the Americans concluded. The rejection was so definitive that one might think that some obscure penetration agent or defector had alerted the Truman administration to the spuriousness of Molotov's claims. There was no such thing. Officials merely paid close attention to the foreign minister's wording: "this secret has long ceased to be a secret." If Molotov meant to say he had a bomb, he surely would have said so; instead, he declared that the secret did not exist. The claim that there was no "secret" to the atomic bomb was one that physicists in the United States had been making for a long time—that the biggest secret was that the bomb was feasible, and Hiroshima had given that one away—and, according to Ambassador Walter Bedell Smith, Molotov was merely echoing this sentiment. He had meant, Smith opined, "that Soviet scientists had reached a laboratory solution, and that the next step would be some sort of test, which might well come in the near future."[12]

But when? Already, as the mushroom clouds were dispersing over Japan, a wide array of Americans with diverse assumptions and information pondered a simple question: When would the Soviet Union have the bomb? In other words, to preview a mantra that saturated American airwaves during civil defense drills in the 1950s: How much time do we have? This question was literally everywhere in the postwar United States; it was, if anything, the central question of the atomic monopoly: When would it end? Widely touted predictions ranged from two years, to twenty years, to never.[13]

How was such a staggering range of numerical values possible? Obtaining any knowledge about the Soviet nuclear effort was extremely difficult. At one level, the problem was one of intelligence gathering. Americans had very little information (and even less *reliable* information) about what was happening beyond what Winston Churchill had already in 1946 dubbed the Iron Curtain. But it would be a mistake to assume that the problem was simply one of faulty input; the very circuitry of decision making was problematic, and problematic at every stage.

Any estimate of how long it would take for the Soviet Union to "have the atomic bomb" relied on a series of (usually unstated) assumptions that radically affected what number any reasonable estimator churned out—even omitting the very significant political and personal biases that also shaped interpretations of highly uncertain data. Those posing estimates in the late 1940s, whether it was their job to do so or not, had to explicitly or implicitly answer a series of questions:

How hard is it to build an atomic bomb? The Americans had just produced such a bomb, but that did not mean they could easily answer this question. First, very few Americans had a complete sense of the Manhattan Project, and so they might be inclined to overestimate or underestimate the difficulties the project had faced. And even if someone did know all the features of the American effort, he or she would still have to answer a Goldilocks-style question about whether the American experience was fast, slow, or just right. There were, after all, only two historical analogues for the presumed "Soviet atomic effort": the Manhattan Project, which yielded a working nuclear bomb in roughly three and a half years; and the Nazi project, which yielded a bomb in . . . never.[14] The Soviet Union would probably fall somewhere between those two. The émigré Dutch physicist Samuel Goudsmit, who led the advance team into Europe that produced the first look into the failed German program, raised a cautionary note in 1947: "We made a safe error by overestimating the Germans. Let us avoid overestimating ourselves."[15] But were the Americans truly overestimating the difficulty of building an atomic bomb when they gave a large number for their estimate of Soviet proliferation? It was (and still is) difficult to say.

How smart are the Soviets? Aside from a very select set of nuclear physicists, no American had a very good sense of the know-how and ingenuity of Soviet scientists or the competence of Soviet engineers. Ingrained biases and some wartime experience led many (especially among the military) to believe that the answer to the question was "not very." For scientists, especially physicists, their own array of private information gleaned from personal meetings (dating mostly from the 1930s, a time of extensive international interactions among nuclear physicists) and following the specialist literature led to precisely the opposite conclusion. In either case, since an atomic bomb required a developed scientific and technological base, a certain minimum level of talent was required to produce one at all, and increased speed needed brighter talent.

When did the Soviets begin? Suppose you concluded, from industrial and scientific fundamentals, that it would take the Soviets eight years to build an atomic device. When did they start? Eight years from *when*? As the British nuclear physicist P.M.S. Blackett pointed out as late as 1956, "There does not seem to be available in the West any reliable published information as to when the Soviet atomic energy programme really started."[16] There was little to do but guess.

How much espionage has leaked? The Soviet Union had an advantage over the Americans: They knew that an atomic bomb was feasible, that it would in fact explode. As postwar director of Los Alamos Norris Bradbury later reflected, "They, surely, had one major start. They knew it *could* be done, which we did *not* know. The great thing that Alamogordo said, and that Hiroshima and Nagasaki said, was that a nuclear explosion was possible."[17] But, as many elite Americans knew already in 1945 (Secretary of the Navy James Forrestal had worried about it in his diary), and everyone knew in February 1946, some important information about the American atomic bomb had been passed to Soviet hands through spies.[18] *Which* information? And how much of it? Was it outdated or incidental data, or did it reveal the most crucial parts of the project?

How hard are they trying? It was difficult enough to execute a large and complicated task in secret; it was even more complicated to do so in an economy utterly devastated by the war, as the Soviet economy was. Was Stalin devoting all of his resources to building a bomb, or was it one priority among many? Was the fact that very little information on the Soviet effort was leaking out of the Soviet Union a sign that they were not working very intensively, or just that they were working in tremendous secrecy? How did one interpret the absence of evidence? Was it, in this instance, evidence of absence?

The debates surrounding all of these questions hinged on a fundamental problem of secrecy in atomic matters. Anyone making an estimate had to rely on his or her own sources of information to produce answers, but various individuals—even equally highly placed public servants—had very different security clearances and different access to public, secret, personal, or scientific information. Their estimates hinged on what they knew and how they knew it, but they were literally prohibited by law from explaining to anyone else *why* they believed their estimate, which sources they were using. In the midst of this confusion born of secrecy, a solution eventually emerged: a convergence of estimates to five to ten years. This "consensus" concealed another problem of information: five years from when?

Presumably, if anyone knew how hard it was to build an atomic bomb, it was Major General Leslie R. Groves, the wartime head of the Manhattan Project. While J. Robert Oppenheimer is more famous today as the "father of the atomic bomb," he was actually the scientific director only of Los Alamos, the bomb-designing facility. The portly, mustachioed Groves was the superior of not only Oppenheimer but also the directors of the plutonium-production and uranium-separation plants, the mining concerns, reactor design facilities, and so on. And Groves used his authority to offer a numerical value of how long it would take the Soviets to build a bomb. In fact, he answered it multiple times. His various estimates shared one feature: a high number. The atomic bomb was hard to make, and the Soviets were not up to the task of doing it quickly.

Even within the span of three months in 1945, Groves gave three different government audiences three different numbers, each suitably hedged. Addressing the War Department in September, he opted for a ten-year estimate: "With regard to Russia, [Groves] estimated it would take her three years to develop the scientific knowledge (assuming efficient administration and access to German scientists) and five years by major effort to solve the industrial problems, or seven to ten years under a program of normal peacetime emphasis."[19] But when the House of Representatives called him as an expert witness in October, he shrouded his answer in vagueness. He did not mention the Soviet Union, and he did not give a precise time scale: "I believe that for another country to do this work, if it had the power of the greatest countries left in the world, but had no particular ideas, that it would take them from 5 to 20 years, and the difference in time would depend entirely on how 'all-out' they made their efforts and how much they threw security to the winds."[20]

By November, testifying before the Senate, he had drilled down to a firmer number: twenty years. This was the number he would invoke time and again in newspaper interviews, lectures, and correspondence. Even here, however, he was careful to state some of the assumptions behind his estimate: "If they did it in complete secrecy, probably within from 15 to 20 years—more likely the latter. If they did it without secrecy and with a great deal of help from the United States and from England and Switzerland—and I say Switzerland because she is a manufacturer of precision machinery—it could be done in 5 to 7 years, probably seven."[21] All of these estimates from 1945 were linked (by Groves and conservative allies in Congress) to the Truman administration's efforts at atomic arms control. If one wanted an atomic monopoly of long duration—and who didn't?—then it was important to isolate the Soviet Union from foreign help, especially American help.

Groves came to his estimate based on several factors, some of which he disclosed to the public, others of which he kept secret. When speaking openly to the press, he emphasized the technical difficulty of the construction of nuclear weapons, especially the required precision engineering. Even if some would dispute Groves's cavalier dismissal of Soviet physicists, the consensus affirmed his slighting of Soviet *engineers*. Groves polled the industrial directors of aspects of the Manhattan Project to collect their estimates of proliferation risks around the world. He telephoned G. M. Read of DuPont—which designed and built the plutonium-production facility in Hanford, Washington—on May 21, 1945 (months before the end of the war), to ascertain how long it would take other nations to replicate Hanford. At first Read claimed that "even if they had all the plans I don't think they would live long enough to build one of these things," basing his assessment on poor engineering. He later retreated from his blanket dismissal but still gave a long estimate: "But would say on W [Hanford] it would be 4 to 5 years on the Russians, 2 to 3 on the Englishmen and damn near eternity on the French."[22]

This emphasis on the prowess of American engineering—and

supposed Soviet incompetence—bolstered the normative status of the American experience with the Manhattan Project. In his September 1945 rejection of the Stimson Plan for sharing atomic information with the Soviet Union, Treasury Secretary John Snyder was perhaps the first to sound an American exceptionalist note:

> It is not a question of cold science, or the application of certain mathematical laws. We know that in the production of the atomic bomb there was a certain element of American mathematical and mechanical genius which has given us the automotive industry, the great development of the telephone industry, and countless other inventive processes which are not always developed in every land, and which seem to be peculiarly the result of long years of mechanization of industry within the United States.[23]

Kremlinologists agreed. In Forrestal's diary entry of September 24, 1948, he paraphrased the views of Ambassador Walter Bedell Smith along very similar lines: "The Russians cannot possibly have the industrial competence to produce the atomic bomb now and it will be 5 or even 10 years before they could count on manufacture of it in quantity. They may well now have the 'notebook' know-how, but not the industrial complex to translate that abstract knowledge into concrete weapons."[24]

This view became popular among pundits and was expressed in the most widely distributed popular article on estimates, appearing in *Look* magazine in 1948. An engineer who had worked on the Hanford plutonium-production plant and a specialist on the Soviet economy together came to the conclusion that precisely because "in productive capacity, the key atomic industries in Russia average 22 years behind these industries in the United States," and therefore "the Russians might make their first mushroom cloud in 1954, nine years from their start and six years from now."[25] (This article was translated into Russian as a brochure in 1948 and would later form a touchstone for Soviet bragging rights.)[26]

In public, Groves stressed the engineering gap; in private, among a very small circle of individuals with the requisite security clearance, he enunciated stronger reasons behind his high number. As Groves would later admit to an interviewer, "I was thinking of the industrial effort and also the supply of ore, particularly the latter."[27] Or, as Groves put it at the 1954 security clearance hearings for Oppenheimer: "Our reliance on what the Russians could or could not do was based on primarily the supplies of material which I felt would be available to them, that is raw material."[28] The supply of uranium, then, was crucial for Groves's estimate. The fundamental premise behind both the Acheson-Lilienthal and Baruch plans for international control of atomic energy, after all, had been the vital importance of supplies of uranium ore for weapons development. Yet neither plan was implemented, and presumably there was an ongoing international search for uranium ore. How, then, could Baruch's assistant Fred Searls come to the conclusion that "it may well be ten years before they [the Soviets] can become possessed of an adequate supply" of uranium?[29] What did Searls—and his source, General Groves—know that others did not?

Groves had managed, before the end of the war, to virtually monopolize the world's known uranium under the so-called Murray Hill Area Project of the Manhattan Engineering District (in keeping with the intermittent vogue of assigning code names linked to the geography of New York City). The atomic monopoly was buttressed by a real monopoly on raw materials.[30] Before World War II and the scramble by various powers to develop nuclear weapons, uranium was not a widely sought-after commodity, its primary uses being in ceramics and paint coloring. Overnight, after the destruction of Hiroshima, it became one of the most important, and most frightening, resources on the planet. As of 1945, there were only a few known mines that produced high-grade uranium, and none was richer than the 65 percent uranium oxide produced by the Shinkolobwe mine in the Belgian Congo. In May 1939, the British had managed to persuade Edgar Sengier, the managing director of Union Minière de Haut Katanga, to sell all current and future production of the Congo mines to the British, to keep it out of the hands of the Germans.[31]

As with so many aspects of the development of nuclear weapons, the British at first shared control of the uranium monopoly—managed by the newly established Combined Development Trust—but then lost their dominance to the Americans, and particularly to Groves. (The British and the Canadians maintained equal shares in the trust, however, long after they lost control of the weapons made from the ore, and this served as their only leverage with the Americans to wheedle out classified atomic information.) Groves negotiated (secret) contracts with the Belgian Congo, with Brazil, and with the rich uranium mines near Great Bear Lake in Canada, leaving only the high-grade Joachimsthal mines in Nazi-occupied Czechoslovakia and those in the hands of neutral (and recalcitrant) Sweden out of his control.

During the war, the Manhattan Project was powered by this monopolized uranium. The Combined Development Trust had cornered about six thousand tons of uranium oxide ore during the war, thirty-seven hundred (two-thirds) of which came from the Belgian Congo and eleven hundred tons (roughly one-sixth) from the Canadian mines. The remaining eight hundred or so tons were gathered from American ores (tailings of the vanadium-mining industry). The Brazilian ore was precautionary. In December 1945, Groves informed the Combined Development Trust that it controlled 97 percent of the world's known uranium output. The monopoly was not total—the blasted Swedes!—but it was impressive; the Soviets could not catch up: "Russian resources of raw materials are far inferior to those of the Trust group of nations and in all probability these could not be made available unless costs of production are completely disregarded."[32]

The power of the trust remained, of course, a closely guarded secret. If the world's suppliers knew that the consortium was attempting to corner the world's uranium market, that would have sent prices skyrocketing, as well as alerted the Soviets to the vital importance of concentrating most of their efforts to assembling uranium.[33] Groves could state his twenty-year estimate with high confidence, but he could not say *why* he felt so confident: He had the uranium, Stalin did not.

This secrecy provision presumed that the Soviets did not know about the global scarcity of free uranium, and it would not be a good idea to let them in on the news. The flaw in this was that Stalin was in fact entirely aware of the U.S. monopoly on the Congo uranium and had for some time set his sights on German and Czechoslovakian ores.[34] The Soviets knew, but the Americans did not know they knew—a distinction that made all the difference in the world. The Americans even worried that the Soviets were faking their poverty in uranium, deliberately hinting in public that they had access to only low-grade ore to lull the Americans into complacency. According to one of the intelligence operatives of the U.S. Atomic Energy Commission, "It is also possible that they deliberately tried to plant the impression that the Soviet Union is weak in uranium resources."[35] Even Groves, for all his vaunted confidence in the Trust, knew that the monopoly was not total and in 1949 emphasized the dire state of American ignorance: "We do not know how much raw material Russia has been able to assemble. We do not know how many tons of ore she is getting, or its richness, or how much uranium she is getting out of the ore. We do not know the losses in her other processes in getting the uranium into the form for use in an atomic furnace."[36] Were the Soviets actually uranium-poor?

Definitely. NKVD chief and director of the Soviet atomic program Lavrentii Beria was informed already in January 1945: "From the poor quality of uranium ores (from 0.1 percent to 0.3 percent uranium oxide in the ore) the obtaining of metallic uranium presents great difficulty, and if we do not find richer sites of uranium, we will need a number of years in order to obtain just the quantity of metallic uranium which is necessary for the conducting of scientific and experimental work on the resolution of the task of creating a uranium bomb and a uranium pile."[37] How Beria and his minions solved this problem is a question for the next chapter, but suffice it to say that publicly available sources in the West by 1949 reported substantial uranium deposits even within Soviet borders (although presumed to be of poor quality), not to mention the satellite states of Soviet-occupied Germany and Czechoslovakia. The Soviet Union in fact held about 40 percent of the world's known uranium reserves, as we now know.[38] But Groves (and Beria) knew none of this during the monopoly.

The main reason to take Groves's egregiously mistaken estimate seriously is that everyone else did, whether they were in on the Murray Hill Area secret or not. In fact, Groves's predictions carried more weight with the public than anyone else's, precisely because he was the individual expected to have the largest amount of secret information upon which to base an estimate.[39] Few challenged him directly, although those who did—typically scientist veterans from the Manhattan Project—lamented his influence. Harrison Brown, chairman of the Atomic Scientists of Chicago, one of the groups lobbying for civilian control of atomic energy, charged that "men like Gen. Groves . . . who say publicly that it's going to take Russia 15 years are deluding the public."[40] For his part, Groves did not believe that the estimates of the scientists were worth very much. "The truth is," he said in July 1949, less than two months before the Soviets in fact did detonate their first nuclear device, "that scientists are not in the best position to make sound estimates. The real problems faced in such a development are those of management and engineering, rather than the purely scientific ones."[41] The scientists, in order to make themselves heard, had to claim that they had access to their own private information upon which they could stake a public estimate.

Even a single individual with a very definite set of assumptions, like General Groves, found it difficult to come to a single answer to the question: How long until the Soviet Union has the atomic bomb? The amorphous group often referred to as "the scientists" found it even harder. Despite persistent myths about the uniform support of scientists for the Acheson-Lilienthal Report, the scientific community included diverse individuals with heterogeneous views. Given the sensitivity of the proliferation estimates to initial assumptions, there is no single number that encapsulates the scientists' views. The simple fact that most scientists offered no prediction at all indicates that there was no party line. As a generalization, however, one can say that individuals with scientific training in nuclear physics tended to offer estimates that averaged lower than those offered by industrialists, engineers, or military personnel.

Scientists on the Manhattan Project began to formulate predictions before the war had ended. Those at the Metallurgical Laboratory in Chicago issued the Franck Report in the summer of 1945, which advocated warning the Japanese before using the atomic bombs in combat, but also offered perhaps the first written scientific estimate of the probable date of Soviet proliferation. As an aside, the authors noted that "the experience of Russian scientists in nuclear research is entirely sufficient to enable them to retrace our steps within a few years, even if we would make all attempts to conceal them . . . Thus, we cannot hope to avoid a nuclear armament race, either by keeping secret from the competing nations the basic scientific facts of nuclear power, or by cornering the raw materials required for such a race."[42] A group of Los Alamos scientists, who may or may not have seen the Franck Report, passed a letter immediately after the war to the American leadership through Oppenheimer that echoed the prediction of "a few years": "It is therefore highly probable that with sufficient effort other countries, who may in fact be well underway at this moment, could develop an atomic bomb within a few years."[43] In October 1945, atomic gadfly Leo Szilard, Groves's bête noire, testified to Congress that it might be six years.[44] These were hedged estimates, but they were certainly lower than Groves's.

We should perhaps not be surprised that the most explicit exploration of the question came from the pens of two scientists with direct experience of the American project: Frederick Seitz and

Hans Bethe, the latter the wartime head of the theory group at Los Alamos. In 1946 they published an article titled "How Close Is the Danger?" which carefully weighed the necessary ingredients for constructing an atomic bomb and put a numerical value to the estimate. In simple, clear prose, Bethe and Seitz outlined what it would take for Russia, France, China, Argentina (or a South American coalition), Sweden, or Switzerland to make atomic weapons (they excluded Great Britain on the grounds that it had been a direct participant in the wartime project). One had to assess the nations' incentives, scientific talent, technological ability, starting point, and (of course) access to uranium. Bethe and Seitz were not yet aware of the Murray Hill Area Project, but they were fairly sanguine about Soviet prospects: "Considering the ubiquitous nature of uranium it is hard to believe that a nation with the surface area of Russia, for example, could find difficulty in locating deposits of sufficient size to go into large-scale production ultimately." They were also aware of a generalized tendency to assume that the Soviets were going to copy the American pathway. They recognized the flaws of this assumption:

> For one thing, we have adopted all along the somewhat provincial viewpoint that the nation engaging in the work will be less effective than we have been, and this viewpoint may be entirely unjustified. Also, it should be kept in mind that work in one or another nation may already be much farther along than external facts would indicate. Finally, it must never be forgotten that men of genius in other countries may devise methods which are much superior to our own and which would greatly reduce the time involved; our previous estimates have been based on the assumption that a foreign nation would simply copy our own pattern of attack.[45]

Their conclusion: five years. That is, five years from 1946, more or less, which meant around 1951.

The five-year estimate proved remarkably popular among scientists. Arthur Holly Compton, who had directed the Metallurgical Laboratory at the University of Chicago and who was as well informed as anyone about both Soviet scientists and the uranium monopoly, told a reporter in 1948 that he felt it would be at least four years—that is, 1952—before the Soviets obtained a bomb, but that "I won't be surprised if they don't get it before 1970."[46] Less cocky, but no less dismissive of the potential threat, was J. Robert Oppenheimer, who asserted in a letter that same year: "With all recognition of the need for caution in such predictions, I tend to believe that for a long time to come the Soviet Union will not have achieved this objective, nor even the more minor, but also dangerous possibility of conducting radiological warfare." Confronted with this letter at his security clearance hearings in 1954, five years after the first Soviet nuclear test, Oppenheimer hung his head: "This was a bad guess."[47] Even more privy to state secrets, Vannevar Bush, the director of science administration during the war and the postwar force behind the founding of the National Science Foundation, surely had as much access as Groves to the highest levels of information (such as the existence and function of the Combined Development Trust), but was at first not as optimistic as the general about the prospects for a Red bomb. At the cabinet meeting on September 21, 1945, to discuss the Stimson proposal, Forrestal paraphrased Bush as predicting that "the Russians can get to about the place we are now in five years *provided they devote a very large part of their scientific and industrial effort to it.*"[48] James Bryant Conant, the president of Harvard University and Bush's exact peer in wartime science administration, was somewhat looser but held to an estimate of five to fifteen years, which he later rationalized as "vague enough to be almost certainly correct."[49]

The Joint Chiefs of Staff (JCS), the coordinators of military planning, perhaps unsurprisingly drifted toward the "consensus" of five to ten years.[50] The same could not be said of the various branches of the slowly unifying American military. For example, the postwar navy experienced tremendous anxiety that the advent of atomic warfare would render a seaborne military service obsolete. The longer the Soviet Union remained a conventional power, the longer the navy could argue for a greater share of the unified appropriations pool, since the navy would be essential to keep the sea-lanes open to supply Western ground troops in Europe. If the Soviet Union proliferated sooner rather than later, then the air force was in a stronger position. Air force estimates reasoned directly from Manhattan Project progress tables, echoing the scientists' normative assumptions and guessing at a Soviet start date of 1942. Assuming that the Soviets would be at least as efficient as the Americans, they predicted a Soviet test in the latter part of 1949—which turned out to be correct.[51] The fact that the air force was right means no more than that they guessed well, for they had access to no more information than anyone else and they filtered it through their own interests. Nonetheless, after the Soviet test, the prediction of 1949 generated substantial prestige for air force intelligence, which continued to argue for dire predictions of Soviet progress, culminating in the spurious "bomber gap" of the 1950s.

Yet the drift toward five years spanned the ideological and professional spectrum, even among the most stalwart cold warriors. At first, these latter, for all the anticommunist rhetoric of the late 1940s about robotic Russians and their mindless lack of creativity, tended to predict a shorter duration for the monopoly, reasoning from Communist duplicity, espionage, and the striking speed of industrialization exhibited by the Stalinist five-year plans. Senior Republican Senator Arthur Vandenberg—the backbone of Truman's bipartisan foreign policy—on December 10, 1945, wrote: "We agree that Russia can work out this atom science in perhaps two years."[52] But even Vandenberg was not immune to the subliminal pressure of the five-year estimate; less than six months later he had revised his view in line with conservative journalists like Drew Pearson: "Our 'secret' in respect to atomic bombs probably will not be a 'secret' for more than five years."[53] Even President Truman agreed with this assessment. He told his first secretary of state, Edward Stettinius, that "we had perhaps from four to ten years," but it seems clear that he relied heavily on Groves's assessments of a long monopoly and leaned toward the latter number.[54]

The uniformity of this single time estimate tends to mask the heterogeneity of opinions because even though the number was the same, the reasoning of the estimators diverged, often dramatically. The convergence on a five-year estimate was only one effect of uncertainty; a more disturbing one was that the estimate was so ubiquitous that it floated unmoored across the years. That is, people who said five years in 1945 would say the same in 1947 and in 1949. Five years slowly came to mean "five years from now," not "five years from when they started" or "five years from my first prediction." Herman Kahn, the enormously influential nuclear theorist of the 1950s and 1960s—so much so that he was one of the templates for Dr. Strangelove in Stanley Kubrick's movie— retrospectively diagnosed the effect in 1960: "The reason why those who predicted five years were surprised [by Soviet proliferation in 1949] was because there is a very human tendency to forget the passage of time and think of five years as being always five years after the moving present rather than as five years from a fixed date . . . Once a number like five years is repeated often enough, it gets to be sacred."[55] From 1945 to the middle of 1949, both within the government and in newspapers and magazines, the common estimates varied between five and ten years—*every* year, regardless of whether the same individual had claimed five years in 1945 and it was now 1948.[56] This tune became so ubiquitous as to blend into the background, and people began to ignore it.

They could ignore it because so little new information filtered through to change anyone's presumptions. The naked truth was that the American intelligence infrastructure was in disarray during the atomic monopoly—so much so that it is a stretch even to speak of an "infrastructure." The first standing foreign intelligence organization that the United States ever had (aside from the Federal Bureau of Investigation, which, despite perpetual director

J. Edgar Hoover's fondest wishes, was constrained to counterintelligence functions) was the wartime Office of Strategic Services (OSS), heavily sculpted by the venerable British intelligence agencies and mightily mistrusted by many politicians in Washington, who harbored a traditional suspicion of intelligence organizations in general and were offended by the Ivy League elitism of its agents. One of those politicians was Harry Truman. On September 20, 1945, just before convening his cabinet to discuss the Stimson Plan, Truman signed Executive Order 9621, abolishing the OSS, transferring the intelligence-gathering components to the army where they became the Strategic Services Unit, and moving all the research and assessment to the Department of State.[57] William "Wild Bill" Donovan's stable of spies was no more. (To be fair to Truman, the OSS was so riddled by Soviet agents by the end of the war that it was unlikely it would have served very effectively against its new presumptive target.)[58] The United States now had no standing intelligence apparatus to deal with peacetime concerns, just like before the war.

Such a lacuna could not remain unfilled. General Carl Spaatz, among other military officials, in October 1945 filed a report insisting that "the requirement for a world wide intelligence service has been emphasized . . . It is necessary that we have detailed knowledge of all scientific, political, economic and military developments and trends in all nations of the world."[59] Each of the individual services in the armed forces had its own intelligence divisions (G-2 for the army, N-2 for the navy, A-2 for the air force), but they were poorly coordinated, unable to formulate coherent pictures for the president to evaluate. Truman refused to bring back the OSS and opted instead to build a new agency from the ground up.

The reconstruction began with the appointment of a director of Central Intelligence and the creation of the Central Intelligence Group (CIG) in 1946, the latter of which was transformed in 1947 into the Central Intelligence Agency. Despite its name, for years the CIA was hardly the unified, coherent organization it was intended to be. The first DCI, Truman's Missouri friend Admiral

Sidney Souers, had hired seventy-one people at CIG and put the organization on a reasonable footing, but his successor, Air Force General Hoyt Vandenberg (nephew of Arthur), realized that this barely scratched the surface of the problem and requested an expansion to three thousand employees the following year. He also obtained an extra $10 million from Truman's usually frugal administration, almost doubling the CIG budget. With the Office of Reports and Estimates (ORE) and the Bureau of National Estimates, both established in 1946, Souers and then Vandenberg were supposed to unravel the secrets of the Soviet Union, the famously closed society that almost never leaked.[60]

The CIA was understaffed, underfunded, and a long way from its goal of synthesizing and correlating American intelligence. Each of the various military intelligence organizations remained, generating its own information, supplemented by intelligence outfits at the FBI and other government offices.[61] The National Security Agency, in charge of electronic and signals intelligence, did not exist during the monopoly (it was established in November 1952). There was no Science and Technology Directorate at the CIA until August 1963 (although there was an office of Scientific Intelligence as early as 1948), and no National Photographic Interpretation Center until 1953. Much of the infrastructure now used to gather intelligence of any kind—let alone highly sensitive atomic intelligence—simply did not exist.

Ordinarily, these difficulties could have been overcome or at least ameliorated with human intelligence—American agents on the ground in the Soviet Union. But the Workers' Paradise was "denied territory" in intelligence parlance: there were *zero* American ground agents in the Soviet Union. In 1949 the CIA began a five-year program to recruit and train former Soviet citizens to be air-dropped back on Soviet territory to serve as informants. Almost all of them were arrested immediately and unceremoniously shot. Those few who produced information were not trusted by the Americans, who feared that they had been "turned" and were now double agents transmitting disinformation.[62]

No spies, no leaks, no information. None of this absolved the CIA and other intelligence organizations from providing estimates of the expected termination of the atomic monopoly. The ORE admitted that its methods involved some creative induction:

> An estimate of capabilities ten years hence obviously cannot be based on evidence, but only on a projection from known facts in the light of past experience and reasonable conjecture. The estimates herein are derived from the current estimate of existing Soviet scientific and industrial capabilities, taking into account the past performance of Soviet and of Soviet-controlled German scientists and technicians, our own past experience, and estimates of our own capabilities for future development and production.[63]

Senator Bourke Hickenlooper, a hawk on all matters of nuclear security, was substantially less charitable and stormed into soon-to-be-named Secretary of Defense James Forrestal's office in a rage about the status of nuclear intelligence, as the latter reported in his diary of July 8, 1947:

> He is under the impression that intelligence activities of the CIG are not effective, that the organization is flimsy and handicapped by the impression of an impermanent status, due, a good deal, to the rapid turnover in the position of top director. The collection of external intelligence is lagging, with particular reference to any information on activities of other countries in the field of atomic energy. There is no knowledge, for example, of what progress Russia has made either in the field of actual assembly of the bomb or of the availability to them of the necessary materials.[64]

For Hickenlooper, this was just one more instance of poor management of atomic matters. He was routinely displeased, dismayed, even disgusted.

Especially with AEC chairman David Lilienthal. (Hickenlooper spent the summer of 1949 conducting hearings into Lilienthal's alleged "incredible mismanagement" of the AEC, a personal vendetta against the liberal New Dealer that proved to be groundless.) But on the matter of atomic intelligence, they were in complete accord. The situation was simply dreadful, Lilienthal felt:

> The thing that rather chills one's blood is to observe what is nothing less than the lack of integrity in the way the intelligence agencies deal with the meager stuff they have. It is chiefly a matter of reasoning from our own American experience, guessing from that how much longer it will take Russia using our methods and based upon our own problems of achieving weapons. But when this is put into a report, the reader, e.g., Congressional committee, is given the impression, and deliberately, that behind the estimates lies specific knowledge, knowledge so important and delicate that its nature and sources cannot be disclosed or hinted at.[65]

Or, as Lilienthal would put it more pithily a year later, "In my opinion our sources of information about Russian progress are so poor as to be actually merely arbitrary assumptions."[66]

There seemed to be no solution except to bypass the CIA entirely and set up a parallel structure for atomic intelligence, thereby compounding the problem the CIA was ostensibly created to solve. Every DCI knew that something was wrong and a stopgap solution was needed. Sidney Souers reviewed the situation and placed the AEC's director of security and intelligence, Rear Admiral John Gingrich, on the Intelligence Advisory Board (and later on the Joint Intelligence Committee, which was also intended to coordinate information from various sources). Gingrich's staff, however, was minuscule: W. C. Truheart, Paul Fine, and W. A. Shurcliff. And even with Gingrich folded into the loop, the CIA remained too possessive of its contacts to trust him with the information that he needed and that only he was competent to assess.

Samuel Goudsmit was called in to evaluate the situation by the AEC's General Advisory Committee, and was pessimistic: "The summary reports show that at present almost no authentic data about Russian developments are available. Estimates of probable dates for Russian accomplishments are unreliable because they are based too much upon comparison with and analogous to our own project."[67] The very problem the scientists had of mapping potential foreign progress onto a Manhattan Project timeline was replicated within the intelligence community.

The situation was undoubtedly bad, but it was not completely hopeless. Despite the absolute prohibition on exchange of nuclear information with foreign powers decreed by the McMahon Act in 1946, a fair degree of cooperation over nuclear intelligence persisted between the Americans and the British.[68] In the absence of penetration agents or defectors, the chief sources of American information were analyses of budgets and gathering whatever data could be had from postwar Germany. It proved extremely hard to figure out how much the Soviets were spending on atomic research by the first method. In the 1947 budget, there was a line for "scientific research" valued at 6.5 billion rubles, three times the prewar figure. But was that *everything* that was spent, or were more funds under other line items? And why should one believe Stalin's official budget anyway?[69] The information from Germany was slightly more reliable, although not very useful. Operation Wringer (begun in June 1949) interrogated Germans repatriated from the Soviet Union, and much accurate information about the Soviet program was developed from these sources—although this was possible only *after* 1955, when the major German atomic scientists were deported. The information was invaluable as a historical source, but the Soviets made sure that no one was released until any data he or she had was rendered inoperative by a "cooling off" period of isolation.[70] Strategically, the Americans (and the British) knew basically nothing.

Yet intelligence officials still made estimates. They had to; it was their job. Given the inadequate sources of information, we should not be surprised that the first CIG estimate of July 23, 1946, was vague and uninspiring: "The Soviets will make a maximum effort to develop as quickly as possible such special weapons as guided missiles and the atomic bomb." For *this* one needs an intelligence infrastructure? The report also noted an ambient fear that "the Soviets may already have an atomic bomb of sorts, or at least the capability to produce a large atomic explosion," before dismissing it as unlikely.[71]

The estimates continued to pour forth regularly from the CIA— predictions of Soviet proliferation being as important as the situation in Berlin, or the advance of the Communists in China—but it had as little to go on as anybody else. Less, in fact, since it is not clear that the CIA was fully aware of the Combined Development Trust. A year before the Soviets actually proliferated, in September 1948, the CIA devolved, as almost everyone else had, to a five-year estimate: "The earliest date by which the Russians may have exploded their first bomb is mid-1950; the probable date by which they will have exploded their first test bomb is mid-1953."[72] Notice how this splits the difference of "five years": 1950 was five years from the first nuclear explosions of 1945, and 1953 was five years from the present. Either way you sliced it, the relevant number was five.

It is in the nature of foreign policy that officials (elected and otherwise) have to make assessments about the world situation when they have only partial, corrupted, or nonexistent evidence. With hindsight, we can see how mistaken these estimates of Soviet proliferation were, but it is important to highlight that many of them were rational given the limited data available, combined with the American experience on the atomic project and scattered suppositions about what the autarkic Soviet Union was like. These estimates tell us far less about the Soviet Union than about the scope of American anxiety during the monopoly period.

But what did those numbers mean? It is very hard to say, because most of these numbers, and thus the estimates, were not predicated. That is, only very rarely did anyone say what the estimates were estimates *of*, other than "having the bomb." But what did it mean to say the Soviets would "have a bomb" in five years? Did one mean five years until the Soviets uncovered the basic information of how to make an atomic bomb? Five years until a working reactor? Until the establishment of the production process for nuclear fuel? Until the first Soviet atomic test? Until a sizable stockpile? Until the assembly of a delivery system capable of striking the American heartland? Most estimators were vague about what they meant, and so it was possible, in good conscience, to keep reiterating "five years," because the five years may have referred to something different each time.[73]

Yet the estimates mattered as historical facts in the late 1940s. The numbers—large or small—concretely affected American decision making and thus structured the contours of nuclear policy in ways that leave traces down to the present. The most obvious way the estimates shaped Americans' expectations was in setting the groundwork for the tremendous shock they felt when the Soviets did proliferate in 1949. But they also affected two concrete policy areas: preemption and declassification.

The first immediate effect of a lengthy estimate was to discourage a preemptive strike against the Soviet Union. This was, for most Americans, the most crucial value these predictions had. As the journalist William Laurence succinctly summarized, "The shorter we believe the time to be the more likely we are to be overcome by fear, leading inevitably to a state of mind in which 'hit-'em-fustest-with-the-mostest' would appear to be the only possible choice. On the other hand, the more time we have, or think we have, for considered judgment, the greater the chance reason may prevail."[74] Yet the Americans did not know how long it would take. As David Lilienthal noted in a speech in April 1946, this anxiety was the worst aspect of being the atomic monopolist:

But sooner or later other nations will be able to produce atomic bombs—that seems to be an inescapable fact. Whether other nations will be able to make bombs in five years, or ten years, or whether it will take fifteen years or more, no one can be sure. And as things now stand, we won't know what progress other nations have made as the months and years go by. We will wish like hell we knew, and we'll worry about it—but we probably won't know. That ignorance of what is going on elsewhere will increase our disquietude and uneasiness. We won't know, so we may become jumpy, and this jumpiness and fear may have rather profound consequences on our national way of living.[75]

The second major implication of a long estimate related not to national mood but to information. One of General Groves's final acts as director of the Manhattan Project was to set up a committee to declassify some atomic information under the directorship of Caltech physicist Richard C. Tolman. The purpose was to decide which data would be of use to a potential enemy and should thus be kept classified, and which would be relatively unimportant and thus could be released so scientists around the world could make use of them for nonmilitary research. There was, however, no bright line between "useful" and "nonuseful" information, because the utility of a fact depended greatly on *when* it was to be used. Oppenheimer, who served on the Tolman Committee, explained: "Our general philosophy was that if we are going to have a long, long period when we are not going to use these things and don't need these things, the more that is open, the better American technology and science will prosper. If the time is kind of short, then the advantages of our secretly developed information will be considerable."[76] That is, an estimated long duration for the monopoly meant more information could and should be declassified—as was in fact put into practice. So various data from the Manhattan Project were released. And the Soviets were paying attention.

THREE
LARGER THAN ENORMOZ

> If the doors of perception were cleansed every thing
> would appear to man as it is, infinite.
> For man has closed himself up, till he sees all
> things thro' narrow chinks of his cavern.
> WILLIAM BLAKE, "THE MARRIAGE OF HEAVEN AND HELL"

The Soviet Union was a black hole to President Harry Truman and his countrymen. From the American point of view, the Soviet Union was a body into which one might send feelers (penetration agents, offers of sharing nuclear information), but nothing ever came out again. The Soviets appeared, as it were, hermetically sealed, and what little leaked out from the edges of the black hole could not be relied upon for information.

For Joseph Stalin and his lieutenants, the situation was not symmetric; for them, the United States was a black box. A black box, as an engineering term, is a device from which a certain input yields a certain output, but whose internal workings either do not matter for the device you are constructing, or of whose detailed microprocesses you are more or less ignorant. Consider an electric alarm clock. Plug it in and it will give you the time—it will give you the *correct* time if you fiddle properly with its buttons—but most of us have no idea what goes on inside the clock. Where does the electricity go? What does it do in there? How many parts are necessary to tell the time? In precisely this sense, the Manhattan Project was a black box to the Soviet Union. If you supplied it with some initial input (say, spies), you would get some defined output (information), but you had to be sure you had tweaked the box sufficiently to get reliable output—that you could *trust* the time your alarm clock was giving you.

Whereas the United States had to speculate about what went on in the Soviet Union with little more to go on than analogy and supposition, the Soviet Union was able to get specific data out of its counterpart. But the information was not complete; Stalin and his advisers did not know exactly how the Manhattan Project operated, but they had access to a good deal of information about it. That information was uncertain, incomplete, and of dubious provenance, but at least it existed. They next had to take the data they obtained and build a bomb. What Western analysts both then and now casually dismiss as "reverse-engineering" would have been no mean feat even if the Soviets had possessed a complete set of plans for the atomic bomb. They actually had far less: no detailed blueprints, no scales on the crude diagrams, no information on the glues and epoxies used, no data on implosion ballistics. To build a plutonium bomb, you needed at least to fill those holes in the picture, among many others.

The Soviets knew a lot, but they did not know everything. In order to evaluate the complexity of the task of turning this data into a working nuclear device, we need to understand the full spectrum of their resources, both domestic and foreign. Stalin's domestic resources, such as the quality of Soviet scientists, local uranium resources, native engineering capacity, were the kinds of elements the American estimators of the duration of the atomic monopoly guessed at (and the same factors that Soviet historians emphasized exclusively).[1] Those domestic resources concerned what the Soviets *did* with their information and is the subject of the following chapter. There were three categories of foreign sources of information: open source, espionage, and German.

These are not mutually exclusive categories—some of the espionage came from German sources, for example—and they do not represent the total resources available to the Soviet Union. But they are the three main types of resources, listed in order of decreasing importance. Indeed, for all the post–cold war ballyhooing about the extent and perfidy of Soviet espionage, the fact remains that the single most important sources of information for the Soviet nuclear project were not those microfilmed and smuggled out of American military bases. They were, rather, those you could pick off the shelf at your public library.

To the Americans in the late 1940s who heard often about "the secret" of the atomic bomb, it might have come as a considerable shock to realize how much one could learn about it just by reading public documents with an educated eye. This quasi-openness of nuclear information was a postwar phenomenon; during World War II, General Leslie Groves had kept a tight hold on any information about the development of the new weapons, both from fear of alerting Nazi Germany and thus spurring them to work harder on their own nuclear deterrent, and to deny such information to the Soviet Union.[2] After the war, this situation changed dramatically.

The impulse to declassify a significant portion, but certainly not all, of the wartime atomic data came from the top: secrecy-obsessed General Groves himself. As he correctly assessed, keeping everything known about the bomb secret might be desirable in the abstract, but it was not possible. The fact that the atomic bombs worked, and that the Americans had erected a large infrastructure to build them, had already been revealed with the destruction of two Japanese cities. Newspapers wanted the story, and some enterprising journalists would get it; Groves wanted to give it to them and thus control what they could say.

He also had a problem with the scientists who had worked on the project. They were going to blab; that was what eggheads did. The great Danish physicist Niels Bohr, who had consulted on some parts of the atomic project (Groves considered him too much of a security risk to take in more deeply), reportedly was in favor of releasing *everything* to the Soviets. Within the bounds of Bohr's typically counterintuitive reasoning, this complete declassification would actually serve to discourage Soviet proliferation: "Giving the Soviet Union all information concerning atomic energy processes including the making of bombs (but not the bombs themselves) would probably so confuse and over-awe them that no net advantage would accrue to them."[3] This was dangerous—*very* dangerous—and Groves here saw the same problem as with the journalists: If you don't solve the problem yourself, someone will do it for you, and do it badly.

Declassification could also bring benefits. A lot of important scientific information was uncovered in the research that led up to the working nuclear devices, and much of it was not crucial or even useful for weapons (such as the properties of radioactive isotopes for medical treatment or biological research). Keeping this information secret was inadvisable, thought Groves, because it would slow scientific progress not just in the Soviet Union but also in the United States, and this progress was central to staying ahead in any superpower competition. As Groves concluded: "Scientific information which can safely be made public should be released as soon as practicable. The possible amount of this information is so great that it cannot all be released at once but the process of release will extend over the next year or so. It includes information on medical research and other scientific matters not related to bomb production."[4] And so Groves, as he wound down the army's Manhattan Project in preparation for transfer to the civilian Atomic Energy Commission, released a good deal of this "scientific information." The scientists were delighted.

Others thought the releases of information had gone quite far enough. For some, there was already sufficient data released to enable the Soviets to build a bomb rapidly. As Air Force Brigadier General R. B. Landry noted in April 1949, "It is my considered judgment that a great amount of the information made public to date is detrimental to our future security . . . It is interesting to note, as a matter of comparison, the scarcity of information of any kind on Russian activities in the field of atomic energy."[5] This same point was made by advocates of nuclear openness, like the *Bulletin of the Atomic Scientists* in early 1946, but the polarities of the fact were reversed. An editorial in that periodical noted that "so much has already been told that, if we gave other nations all our remaining 'secrets,' we would probably shorten their work by only about six months."[6] Landry and the *Bulletin* agreed about exceedingly little, but they spoke with one voice about the quality and quantity of nuclear information that was openly available.

How was such disagreement possible? How could Groves, universally acknowledged as tremendously security-conscious, have let so much information, and such damaging information, go? After all, the Manhattan District not only had released "basic science" about the physics of uranium; its publications had also explained the necessity for isotope separation and many of the methods the Americans had actually used during the war. The difference lay in what Groves and his opponents considered to be useful for building an atomic bomb. Groves emphasized the most technical, most advanced secrets, while his opponents stressed the time-saving utility of knowing the general outlines of the American program: which stages were time-intensive, which were not; which order the various stages of uranium purification needed to be in; and so on. Groves was thinking like a bomb designer, his critics like potential proliferators. In the context of the late 1940s, his critics were more right than wrong.

The best place to see this conflict over the status of "useful" information in action is also the most significant: the official history of the Manhattan Project by the Princeton University physicist Henry DeWolf Smyth, released on August 12, 1945, universally known as the Smyth Report. McGeorge Bundy, Henry

Stimson's postwar amanuensis and later national security adviser to Presidents John F. Kennedy and Lyndon Johnson, later noted that the original idea behind releasing this report at all, and releasing it so quickly (before World War II was over, in fact), was to serve as "both revelation and security fence."[7] That is, the Smyth Report was supposed to include everything that could be safely released about the Manhattan Project, and no more. As Groves put it in his preface to the report: "All pertinent scientific information which can be released to the public at this time without violating the needs of national security is contained in this volume."[8] It then formed the primary basis of declassification and structured what people were allowed to say publicly about the Manhattan Project.

Of course, the safest thing to do for counterproliferation would be to reveal absolutely nothing. But holding on to the monopoly was only one of the constraints working on Groves, Smyth, and their peers. They were also members of a democratic polity, and Smyth was explicit that "the principal reason for [the report's] preparation was to inform the public."[9] Although Smyth believed the secrecy surrounding nuclear weapons was necessary to some extent, he also felt it would be fundamentally antidemocratic "to leave these decisions [about the future of nuclear weapons] in the hands of a small number of men without informing the people of the country what the significance of the discoveries was."[10] Later on, J. Robert Oppenheimer and David Lilienthal would call this stance of comparative nuclear openness "a policy of candor," but Smyth perhaps articulated it best in the conclusion to the 1945 report: "In a free country like ours, such questions should be debated by the people and decisions must be made by the people through their representatives. This is one reason for the release of this report. It is a semi-technical report which it is hoped men of science in this country can use to help their fellow citizens in reaching wise decisions."[11]

Smyth's characterization of his report is apt: It was "semi-technical," no more and no less. Starting from an elementary primer on nuclear physics (what are neutrons, what is fission, etc.), Smyth then included a dry and somewhat elliptical history of the administration of the project. By page 100, the reader had already left the basics of physics and administration and was now learning about the creation of the first reactor at the University of Chicago in 1942, plutonium production (two chapters), separation of isotopes (three chapters), and a very fragmentary chapter titled "The Work on the Atomic Bomb" (which obviously left out much sensitive information, such as the necessity of an implosion trigger for a plutonium device). The paragraphs are numbered, and the text contains all of the excitement of the instructions for filling out income-tax returns—except, of course, that it was about the production of nuclear weapons. Here is an example, from a chapter on isotope separation:

9.32. In all the statistical methods of separating isotopes many successive stages of separation are necessary to get material that is 90 per cent or more U-235 or deuterium. Such a series of successive separating stages is called a cascade if the flow is continuous from one stage to the next. (A fractionating tower of separate plates such as has been described is an example of a simple cascade of separating units.) A complete analysis of the problems of a cascade might be presented in general terms . . .

9.33. The first point is that there must be recycling . . . [Uranium that has gone through one stage of the cascade] must be returned to an earlier stage and recycled. Even the impoverished material from the first (least enriched) stage may be worth recycling; some of the U-235 it contains may be recovered (stripped).

9.34. The second point is that the recycling problem changes greatly at the higher (more enriched) stages . . .

9.35. We mention these points to illustrate a phase of the separation problem that is not always obvious, namely, that the separation process which is best for an early stage of separation is not necessarily best for a later stage.[12]

This extract is simultaneously vague (for example, no numbers are given for how much purification of U 235 or deuterium you need) and helpful (you ought to use several separation methods in sequence). Almost every page of the Smyth Report provides similar instances of both properties.

Smyth was a scientist and thus a member of a professional group inclined toward openness and publication. His composition of the report is thus perhaps not surprising. The more intriguing issue was General Groves's defense of the Smyth Report. His motivations appear to have been several: a sincere belief that the report did not reveal any dangerous information, a desire to give credit to the scientists and engineers who had worked so hard on the project, a bureaucratic defense of how he had spent his money, and a security perimeter to guide declassification in the future. He had authorized Smyth to write his history, and as the bombs were readied for use on Japan, Groves needed higher authorization to release it.

Secretary of War Henry Stimson was reluctant in early August 1945 to release the report, afraid that it set the security barrier too low, that it revealed too much. What finally swayed him, he made clear in his diary, was the commitment of the Atomic General: "Groves, who is a very conservative man, had reached the conclusion that the lesser evil would be for us to make a statement carefully prepared so as not to give away anything vital and thus try to take the stage away from the others." He had to take Groves's word on it, because "the subject was so vast and the scientists' report was so voluminous that it was impossible for a layman like the President or [Secretary of State James] Byrnes or myself to determine this question and we had to rely upon the opinions of our scientific advisers."[13] (For the record, the British were initially opposed to the report's publication, both because they feared it revealed too much and because it did not give the British enough credit.)[14] In the end, Stimson signed off.

Complaints that the Americans had given away the farm came almost immediately and were just as immediately countered. Leo

Szilard—a physicist whom, ironically, Groves considered a serious security risk in his own right—testified before Congress in October 1945 that "knowing that such a bomb can be made is half of the secret. I believe that the other half of the remaining secret was given away when the War Department released the Smyth report, because that report clearly indicates the road along which any other nations will have to travel." A Soviet physicist wanting to make a bomb "would not have all the information by reading the Smyth report, but he would have all the information which he needs to know how to go about to find that information which he still lacks."[15] Szilard was not arguing against the report's publication; he was instead supporting the civilian control of atomic energy in the McMahon Act by attacking the presumption that the military would be more security-conscious. They had released the Smyth Report, after all; that was no mean security breach.

Politicians from the fairly conservative to the avowedly liberal disagreed about the wisdom of the Smyth Report—the former thought it a grave security error, the latter tended to consider it a gesture of goodwill that would mollify the Soviets—but they agreed that the report left little to the imagination. Bernard Baruch, not a man associated with lax views on nuclear matters, certainly felt that way.[16] In strange accord with Baruch (strange because of his public attacks on the financier) was Secretary of Commerce Henry Wallace, a man who stood as far to the left as was viable in contemporary American politics:

At the present time, with the publication of the Smyth report and other published information, there are no substantial scientific secrets that would serve as obstacles to the production of atomic bombs by other nations . . . We have not only already made public much of the scientific information about the atomic bomb, but above all with the authorization of the War Department we have indicated the road others must travel in order to reach the results that we have obtained.[17]

Not as far left as Wallace, David Lilienthal triggered headlines at his confirmation hearing to become the first AEC chairman by testifying, "Yes; the Smyth report is the principal breach of security since the beginning of the atomic energy project."[18] Lilienthal's primary point, like Szilard's, was that the military (which had released the report) was not necessarily more security-conscious than a civilian AEC would be. Significantly, he used the Smyth Report to make this argument.

Lilienthal's statement immediately produced a broad spectrum of defenses of the Smyth Report as "a gesture of good will."[19] Its most important defender was its initial advocate, General Groves, who informed Congress in October 1945 that the "extent of that information which, in fact, was public knowledge to the scientists of the world, is the limit of the Smyth report which you have heard so much about. In other words, nothing in that report discloses any secrets to the world."[20] Or, in the words of leading science administrator Vannevar Bush, the report "contained nothing that the Russians did not already know."[21] Even Lilienthal eventually came around in 1947. Central for him was negotiating the tension between the necessity of having some information to make decisions and the danger of having too much: "Weighted as a whole, the Smyth report is an example of the release of information that is in our own interest; without which not only would our own technical progress have been hampered, but the formulation of intelligent public policies rendered well-nigh impossible."[22]

The Smyth Report controversies resurrect a familiar conundrum: People thought they were talking about the same issue, but they were not. Those who defended the Smyth Report, such as the physicists Frederick Seitz and Hans Bethe, argued that the most important information to keep secret was the most detailed, most specific, most relevant to building actual nuclear devices. As they wrote in 1946: "The Smyth report, valuable mainly because it states that certain processes that would naturally occur to other scientists were actually successful, will be a considerable help in their program. The most important fact, however, is that our entire program was successful . . . Much of the most relevant information in the Smyth report could thus have been deduced from other evidence."[23]

But what if detailed information was not what the Soviets needed? Bethe, Seitz, Groves, and Smyth were thinking like individuals who knew what went into a functioning nuclear bomb. The Soviets, on the other hand, used the Smyth Report as a general guide to the problems of building nuclear weapons. What Groves et al. did not realize was that such a road map would accelerate the Soviet nuclear program.

The Smyth Report is not as sexy as espionage and so does not get a great deal of attention from historians and journalists interested in the development of the Soviet atomic bomb. But there is no question that the report was crucial for the Soviet project— perhaps the most important single source of American information (although it is undeniably true that individual segments of the spy data proved vital for specific aspects of bomb development, such as plutonium implosion). The report went a long way toward unpacking the black box of the Manhattan Project.

Lavrentii Beria, head of the Soviet secret police and the overall director of the Soviet nuclear program, at once recognized the value of the Smyth Report. Draft versions of the report nicked by spies had arrived in Moscow in the first half of 1945—well before Potsdam—and the publicly released edition was of course sent on to Moscow immediately in August. The NKVD had confirmation of the reliability of the Smyth Report from no less a source than Niels Bohr himself. The physicist Ia. P. Terletskii was sent to Copenhagen in November 1945 to interview Bohr for any information he might be willing to reveal. Bohr was up front about his very limited access to the secrets of the Manhattan Project: "I should warn you, that, being in the USA, I did not participate in the engineering elaboration of this problem, and thus I do not know either the construction details or the scale of these apparatuses or even of any part of them . . . During my time in the USA I didn't visit even a single factory." He told Terletskii everything he could, but at only one point did he provide information exceeding what was already in the Smyth Report: that the number of stray neutrons following each fission of a uranium nucleus was greater than two, whereas the report (quite deliberately) left the number floating vaguely between one and three.[24] Upon leaving, Bohr's son Aage handed the Soviet scientist a copy of the Smyth Report, saying that it would answer a lot of their questions. As Terletskii recalled in 1973, "That Bohr factually did not tell us anything essentially new became clear to me after reading Smyth's book and studying the photocopies preserved in the safes of Department S," the division of Soviet intelligence assigned to gathering material about the American atomic bomb.[25]

The report was fully translated into Russian by the middle of November and was published in early 1946 with a print run of thirty thousand copies, an astronomical number for Soviet books in general, and especially ones of a technical nature. The number of copies was set by the Scientific and Technical Committee of the First Chief Directorate (the administrative body for the nuclear project), and the book's sale was carefully choreographed. Sixty percent were to be directed for sale to scientists and to the libraries of the scientific institutes of the Academy of Sciences. The remaining 40 percent would be divided with half on sale at universities and the other half in bookstores. The price was also set by the committee at a very affordable five rubles a copy.[26]

The Soviet Smyth Report superficially looked very much like the American one: unobtrusive title, technical in tone, and supposedly published as a public service to alert Soviet citizens to general information about the atomic bomb. But the sales plan tells us something different: Specific sectors of Soviet society, primarily the scientific and technical elite, were the target audience. Just as the sales were planned, so was the appearance. The translation was supposedly edited by G. N. Ivanov with Iu. V. Naidyshev as technical director. In fact it was produced in Department S of the NKVD, although this was of course not revealed on the title page; the paperback listed the State Transport Railroad Publishers instead. Such dissembling was intended to minimize the perceived attention the NKVD was paying to the problem of nuclear fission and misdirect foreigners who were interested in how seriously the Soviets were taking the nuclear issue.

For the most part, the translation was straightforward and faithful. But a close reading indicates some slight but telling modifications. This might be attributable to sloppiness in translation, given the rush to print the Russian-language Smyth Report, except the errors always went in the same direction: minimizing the terror of atomic weapons. For example, what reads in Section 13.2 of the original report as "A weapon has been developed that is potentially destructive beyond the wildest nightmares of the imagination—" reads in the Russian, "A weapon is created that by its destructive action exceeds everything that one can imagine." No nightmares here. The original continues: "We have an initial advantage in time because, so far as we know, other countries have not been able to carry out parallel developments during the war period. We also have a general advantage in scientific and particularly in industrial strength, but such an advantage can easily be thrown away." In translation, this became: "We enjoy an initial advantage in terms of time, since, as far as we know, other countries were not in a position to carry out analogous work during wartime. We have also a general advantage in scientific forces and especially in industrial development, but such an advantage is not decisive."[27] None of the German, French, and Czech translations, all produced in short order, change the sense of the report in this way.[28] The NKVD and the First Chief Directorate did not want anyone to become panicky about the destructiveness of nuclear weapons or the inevitability of an American lead.

This indicates some of the ways the rationale for the Russian translation was quite different from the American original. After all, Soviet citizens did not live in a democracy, and there was no political reason to keep them informed about nuclear weapons. This Soviet Smyth Report was not a manual for an educated populace; it was a textbook for the rapid training of Soviet nuclear weapons designers. As one historian has noted, the report played "the role in Soviet institutes of a widely used handbook."[29] Interestingly, the British physicist James Chadwick, point man on deliberations with the Americans over whether to release the Smyth Report, anticipated just such an eventuality when he gave his (grudging) consent to its publication:

> I believe that this report, although it conforms to the [security] rules, does nevertheless divulge information which will be useful to foreign governments or others interested in T.A. [Tube Alloys, i.e., atomic bomb] development, not because any one item of information is particularly important but from the illuminating effect of a well-arranged, coherent and well-written presentation of the development of the many aspects of this project.[30]

At first, Soviet physicists picked up the Smyth Report out of curiosity. The transformation of the obscure process of uranium fission into a weapon, and a weapon on such a scale, was surely one of the great scientific stories of the twentieth century, and physical scientists were no less fascinated by the event than was the general public (and substantially more interested in just the kind of details the dry Smyth Report offered). Andrei Sakharov, who began work on the Soviet atomic project only in 1948, recalled that after the war he read the serialization of the Smyth Report in the journal *British Ally*: "I would snatch up each new issue of the *Ally* and scrutinize it minutely with an interest that was purely scientific."[31]

For the administrators who had to transform that scientific talent and curiosity into a workable weapon in short order, the Smyth Report served different functions. Mikhail Pervukhin, one of the leaders of the First Chief Directorate, called the physicist Valerii F. Kalinin into his office. "Do you read English?" Pervukhin asked, as he showed Kalinin the Smyth Report. Kalinin said he did and began to shove the report into his briefcase.

"Stop! Stop!" Pervukhin said. "You can read it only here."

"When? It's already late, 10 p.m.," Kalinin answered.

Pervukhin summoned his secretary: "Serve him tea—both now and later. Let him sit and read in this office as long as he needs to." By morning, Kalinin "had read the whole thing and understood that horrible, enormous, unbearable work awaited."[32]

And that was the chief function of the Smyth Report for the Soviet nuclear project: It candidly revealed the scale of the effort and the sheer quantity of resources, and also hinted at some of the paths that might work and, by omission, some that probably would not. (It also, of course, as in the case of plutonium implosion, omitted crucial paths that did work.) As Anatolii Aleksandrov, later president of the Soviet Academy of Sciences and the Soviet Union's leading reactor designer, recalled years later, "The book did not contain new materials in science and technology for us. However, what we had already worked out in the course of researches, such as, for example, the possibility of a chain reaction in a water-cooled uranium-graphite system, or the very existence of an atomic explosion, were confirmed in Smyth's book."[33] N. M. Sinev, another physicist, concurred: "The report of H. D. Smyth decidedly and irrevocably confirmed our position for the choice of gaseous diffusion method [of isotope separation]. The book was very important for us and quite timely."[34] One could multiply such statements many times over—simply on the issue of the help the Smyth Report gave in terms of its manifest content just for uranium isotope separation. But, as the imported German specialist Heinz Barwich noted, what the report did not say was as important as what it said:

The specialist was no less informed by what [Smyth] was silent about as what was openly presented . . . I forget when we encountered the first photocopies, but it ought to have been about two months after [we had arrived]. Our first reaction upon reading it was shattering. Compared with the giant army of scientific powers, the capacity that had occupied laboratories for five years, we found ourselves like a handful of the shipwrecked who could save their lives only by building an ocean liner.[35]

The critics of Groves and the Smyth Report in the United States were correct. The Soviets *did* find the report useful—and admitted its utility even during the darkest years of censorship when any hint of foreign involvement in the Soviet bomb project, whether espionage or German, was entirely absent. Groves assumed that any foreign power would want to use the Smyth Report as a blueprint for developing its own bomb, and he designed his security rules to forestall this. The report was vague or silent about so many details that no one could conceivably have used it as a playbook. But they could—and did—use it as a general guide to methods of isotope separation, as a checklist of problems that needed to be solved to make separation work, and as a primer in nuclear engineering for the thousands upon thousands of engineers and workers who were drafted into the project without any knowledge of what a neutron or a chain reaction was. If the report did not exist, the Soviets would have had to write a guidebook of their own. Smyth saved them the trouble and a considerable amount of guesswork.

The Smyth Report was the most important open source feeding into the Soviet nuclear project, but it was not the only one. While declassification procedures in the United States continued to hold certain technical information secret, a great deal of useful material that was either considered irrelevant for building an atomic bomb or was cleared by scientifically ignorant censors appeared in specialist journal literature. The Soviet First Chief Directorate placed specific orders for "the necessary number of foreign physical, chemical, and technical journals."[36] This material was assiduously collected by Soviet agents, both open and clandestine. Soviet research institutes had maintained full subscriptions to American and British scientific journals during the war, and NKVD agents considered obtaining more obscure—but still public—scientific reports to be one of their major tasks. Testimony from within the Soviet project attests to the significance of this contact with the Western technical literature for the development of the Soviet bomb.[37]

In addition to journals, the Soviets bought precision equipment from Western suppliers, to the tune of at least $250,000, a very large sum for the impoverished postwar Soviet Union. The scientific director of the Soviet project, Igor Kurchatov, ordered particular machines through the NKVD, and some of them actually made it to the Soviet Union. Some, but not all, for the Americans were conscious that one of the factors slowing Soviet proliferation was their less advanced machining industry, and export controls were heavily discussed behind closed doors. As late as 1950, Bernard Baruch wrote to FBI Director J. Edgar Hoover asserting that this technology leakage was responsible for the Soviet proliferation, and that he had urged restrictions while serving on the United Nations Atomic Energy Commission.[38] Such worries, and the explicit lists of what should not be exported to the Soviet Union, were necessarily top secret. After all, if you told the Soviet Union what you were not going to give them, they would have a list of some of the technical specifics that had been deliberately excluded from the Smyth Report. These layers of classified export controls, however, themselves hindered the effective cessation of such shipments; individuals in certain offices just did not know—because they did not have the clearance—which orders they were not supposed to fill. Most Americans knew only what they read in the papers.

Although journalistic accounts of the atomic bomb in the United States hewed very closely to the security parameters set by the Smyth Report—meaning the Soviets could not obtain any more information from most popular articles than they already had in August 1945—foreign sources were not constrained by the strictures of the McMahon Act. The most significant alternative to the Smyth Report in offering a general picture of the atomic bomb was Hans Thirring's *Die Geschichte der Atombombe* (*The History of the*

Atom Bomb), which appeared in Vienna in 1946. Thirring was a physicist with no access to the internal story of the Manhattan Project, but his volume fulfilled a similar "training-manual" function for German-speaking workers on the Soviet bomb project. Thirring also offered something most important for the would-be proliferators: encouragement. The task was not impossible:

> The fundamental way is through physical facts that are known to all specialists and will be brought closer to the nonspecialists through extracts in this report. Nevertheless, there are still hundreds of details that the official report is silent on and that only through very serious research must be worked out before one can develop a usable bomb . . . On the other hand, it is certain that any large state that meets these prerequisites, on the basis of the already generally known facts alone without any betrayals [i.e., espionage], can within a few years be in the position to construct atomic bombs.[39]

Thirring may not have thought espionage necessary, but the Soviets certainly did.

The extent of espionage derived from the Manhattan Project for the development of the first Soviet nuclear device was one of the great revelations of the Soviet archives when they were opened to both Western and Russian scholars after the cold war. Western sources had long noted the existence of an extensive atomic espionage network, but—this being clandestine work—many of the details remained vague.[40] Behind the Iron Curtain, however, those claims from American intelligence officials and politicians were routinely dismissed as propaganda with the goal of diminishing the power of the Soviet scientific establishment. Yet we now have a fairly clear picture of the range, activities, and implications of Soviet espionage in the Manhattan Project, and although this "spy data" clearly complemented the open sources in crucial ways, it by no means displaced them utterly, nor would it have been sufficient on its own for building a nuclear weapon. Unlike the open sources, however, this spy data was hard won.[41]

Before World War II, Soviet spies found the United States rough going. Counterintelligence in America was fairly advanced, and the FBI knew who most of the Soviet agents were and kept very close watch over them.[42] Then America entered the war, and everything changed. First, many of the American agents tailing their Soviet counterparts were reassigned to monitor suspected Axis targets. (Despite substantial fears, by 1943 the Military Policy Committee of the Manhattan Project had determined that "no espionage activities by the Axis nations with respect to this project have been developed by our counterintelligence, although there have been suspicious indications.")[43] Then came a general acceleration of the American atomic program, which meant there were more employees and thus more security risks. The most significant change, however, was the exponential growth in the Soviet presence on U.S. soil.

Soviet stations (each known as a *rezidentura*) formed the backbone of the espionage infrastructure, and despite their extent and size, they were radically understaffed for the scale of work they would do in the war, even taking into account the doubling of effort through the NKGB (the foreign intelligence wing of the NKVD, detached and renamed in 1943) and GRU (military intelligence) networks. At the start of the war, the Soviet consulate and the Amtorg (Soviet trade delegation) in New York City had only thirteen intelligence officers combined, and the FBI knew most of them. Communist Party members in the United States were also useless, because the FBI knew who they were too, and, besides, they would never be assigned to really secret military work. In late 1941 and early 1942, the trickle of Soviet officials into America grew into a torrent as the Soviet Union qualified for Lend-Lease aid and the Soviet Purchasing Commission was erected. According to New York *rezidentura* agent Aleksandr Feklisov, by 1944 the staff of Amtorg and the Purchasing Committee in the city had reached twenty-five hundred, with an equal number in Washington, D.C.[44] Not all of these officials were spies, of course, but many were.

The Manhattan Project posed only one target for these agents, albeit a target of particular interest. At first no one knew exactly what it was; basing their cryptonym for the project on size alone, they evocatively dubbed it Enormoz.[45] They noticed that physicists and engineers were disappearing from their academic jobs, that funds were being redirected, that new factories and buildings were being erected and heavily guarded—without sharing any hint of what was going on with their Soviet ally. This seemed suspicious and demanded further investigation. At the end of 1941, the NKGB administration established a special priority to atomic matters based on agents' reports that significant scientific and monetary resources of England and the United States were being devoted to the solution of the newest problem, "the use of the internal energy of the atomic nucleus of uranium."[46]

What did your run-of-the-mill Soviet spy know about uranium? Next to nothing. Not only did the GRU request more spies in March 1944, they wanted spies who knew something—*anything*—about physics and engineering, "a minimum of two people who know the language and the topic or subject." "This is an enormous task," A. A. Adams (a cryptonym) noted. "It is only the beginning. I am going to receive material from [my source] several times. On the first occasion, around 1,000 pages." Correctly guessing that Moscow would suspect disinformation, Adams was careful to defend both his source and the quality of the information. First, the source and his motivation: "He does not want such a weapon to be launched at the territory of our country. One can project the complete destruction of Japan, but there is no guarantee that our allies will not try to exert influence also on us when they have such a weapon in their arsenal." So maybe the source was legitimate— but Moscow insisted on paying spies, even volunteers, out of suspicion that self-professed idealists might be agents provocateurs. What about the quality of the information? Adams believed that "the practical Americans, with all their extravagance, would not expend such enormous human resources of the highest qualifications and gigantic means on work whose results were not guaranteed."[47] Still, bona fides were not enough, and all of this information would be checked in Moscow.

That amounted to a lot of double-checking. The scale of what Soviet agents obtained fit the cryptonym Enormoz like a glove. NKGB calculations indicate that up to November 1944 they had gathered 1,167 documents on nuclear research, of which 88 from the United States and 79 from Britain appeared to be of particular importance.[48] Months before Trinity, the American nuclear test of July 16, 1945, spymasters back in Moscow had a fairly good idea of the plutonium bomb's construction.

This much spy data posed its own set of problems. How does one actually transport this material back to the Soviet Union? Of course the Americans suspected, even knew, that some espionage was taking place, but it would not do to confirm those suspicions by openly carting around crates of classified atomic documents. The transportation problem was not trivial. There were four main ways to export information from the United States. The most secure was a sealed diplomatic pouch, but only a small amount of information could be smuggled out this way. (It is a testament to the perceived importance of the atomic project that quite a bit of the above material was so moved.) When that was unavailable, documents or microfilms could be carried by someone with a diplomatic passport, which made clearing customs less risky. Easier but much slower was shipment by boat, carried by an agent posing as a sailor; rarer was shipment by plane.[49]

Getting it back to Soviet territory was only part of the process, and not necessarily the most onerous. Movies have given us too glamorous and clean a sense of what spies obtain. This information was not neat. Most of it arrived as carbon copies or microfilms, hastily made, and often selected at random by the source while hurrying to avoid detection. Pages were not collated, documents were not complete, and many were illegible. And they were in English. Even if Beria wanted his physicists to know that this material was Anglo-American in origin—and he did *not*—he would still have to translate the material into Russian for the benefit of those who did not read the language. (The more common foreign language for Soviet scientists before World War II was German.) The information needed to be cataloged, collated, organized, and translated, and its origins carefully obscured.

All of this was done back in Moscow. In his post–cold war memoirs, spymaster Pavel Sudoplatov claimed that Beria summoned him in February 1944 to head a new Department S to deal exclusively with atomic espionage, thus integrating the material obtained separately by the NKGB and the GRU. This much of Sudoplatov's account appears reliable: He was assigned the task of putting this information in order (although his "revelations" about the identities of the American sources seem much more suspect).[50] With a team of six translators, two editors, two technical advisers, and a crew of helpers, Sudoplatov worked with copies (not handwritten documents, which Beria kept to himself) and was never shown the names of the sources of information.[51]

For those names, we have to turn to the British, Canadians, and Americans, who slowly began pulling at threads of the massive web of Enormoz shortly after the war ended. It is extremely difficult, even today, to obtain a comprehensive picture of Enormoz—not because it was planned so well, but because it wasn't. When the spying network was set up in Britain, Canada, and the United States, it was not erected to look for atomic secrets. Of course not: No one yet knew whether an atomic bomb would be feasible, and in any case it was not then a pressing issue (compared to, say, radar). Yet nuclear matters began to absorb a larger and larger share of the attention of different tendrils of the Soviet intelligence apparatus. We have already seen one segmentation of that apparatus (that between the NKGB and the GRU), but in truth that segmentation went much deeper, with different stations working in different countries and cities with little or no communication between them. Almost all interaction was coordinated through Moscow. The purpose of this multiplication of effort was twofold:

so that the findings from each station could be checked independently against the findings of another; and so that if one station was blown, it would not take down the whole network.

This makes sense in terms of the basic rules of spycraft, but it complicates history writing. There was no organizational chart—not even in Moscow, not even in Beria's head—that mapped out who had which job and who was in charge of obtaining which information. Instead, there was duplication and cross networking, all of which was unintentional in construction but recognized after the fact as beneficial. If different networks obtained the same information, then you could use one to cross-check the validity of the other. Since espionage observations are hard to replicate precisely—it is difficult to get the same agent to go back to look at the same files twice—more observers work better than fewer, and better still to hold them in isolation from each other to avoid contaminating the data. As a result, the historian has to feel his or her way through the network analytically, breaking it apart into groups and studying them sequentially. One needs to remember that all these networks and agents were working simultaneously and often in unknown competition with each other.

The first spy ring involved in obtaining nuclear secrets was also the most notorious: the Cambridge Five (Kim Philby, Donald Maclean, John Cairncross, Guy Burgess, and Anthony Blunt). Mostly upper-middle-class Cambridge men, they were all recruited by Soviet intelligence in the 1930s, whether because of ideology, the frisson of danger, or simply for the money. (Motives are hard to determine even after all these years and clearly differed for each individual, and even within the same individual over time.) Because of their credentials and their unquestionable competence, each found himself in an important post both during and after the war, posts they exploited to pass information to their Soviet handlers.

Even here, with a network deliberately established to wheedle secrets out of various levels of British military and diplomatic circles (such as the Foreign Office), spying on atomic matters began fitfully, which should serve to remind us that not everyone was yet convinced of the feasibility or centrality of nuclear weapons. In the fall of 1941, the Soviet station chief in New York, Pavel Pastelniak (code name Luka), cabled Moscow that three American scientists had traveled to London to work on an explosive (actually to discuss the findings in the British Maud Report, which argued for the feasibility of nuclear weapons). Moscow instructed Anatolii Gorskii (code name Vadim), an NKVD *resident* in London, to obtain information about the meeting from Cairncross. The lanky Scotsman, who possessed degrees from both Germany and France before entering Cambridge on scholarship to study modern languages, was recruited into the spy ring by Blunt and Burgess, and provided perhaps the most important early piece of nuclear espionage: He passed the Maud Report to his handlers. By this time, the Americans had already returned to the States.[52] But the report alone did its job, by alerting the Soviets that uranium fission weapons were something the Allies were interested in pursuing—*without* notifying the Soviet Union. Knowing that you are not supposed to know something is often as valuable as knowing what it is.

The Cambridge Five continued feeding nuclear information back to Moscow. Yuri Modin, the recruiter and chief handler for the Five, would later brag, "Without fear of exaggeration, I can confirm that we in the USSR knew absolutely everything about the technical and political aspects of atomic bomb development."[53] That was surely true as far as it went; it seems unlikely that any of the Five withheld information from Moscow. But as the Americans (and especially General Groves) asserted increasing control over the weapon project, there was simply less to pass on, at least during the war.

After the war was another matter. Donald Maclean was almost certainly the most damaging of the Cambridge spies in the atomic arena during the monopoly. Conventionally handsome and endowed with British public-school charm and extraordinary social and political access (through his father, the Liberal politician Sir Donald Maclean), Maclean had been recruited by Blunt in his last year at Cambridge. The American passage of the McMahon Act, which forbade nuclear cooperation with the British—who had kick-started the American project by sharing the Maud Report—alienated Maclean even further and increased his willingness to assist the Soviets, a willingness already fairly sharpened by ideological commitment. Assistance was relatively easy for him to provide in his postwar assignment as liaison for atomic energy at the British embassy in Washington, giving him restricted access to AEC headquarters and almost certainly keeping him in the loop on the Murray Hill Area Project, as well as on the size of the U.S. atomic stockpile (or at least how much uranium the United States had required for 1947–1948: 2,547 tons).[54]

Maclean was not blown until 1950, and he was the third atomic spy to be revealed. The first came within a month of the bombing of Hiroshima, in Ottawa, Canada, of all places. On the night of September 5, 1945, a cipher clerk named Igor Gouzenko left the Soviet embassy in Ottawa carrying a number of documents from his office and approached Canadian authorities as a defector. Gouzenko had worked in the cipher department at the Embassy in room 12, one of eight rooms in the second floor of a wing of the building. There were iron bars on the window, a steel door, and steel shutters for secrecy at nighttime. The cipher books were kept in a sealed bag handed to an official each night, and the documents stored in a safe.[55] This much was normal: Embassies routinely communicated with their governments in code.

But these documents included secret information concerning atomic reactor work under way at Chalk River in Canada.[56] Soviet-Canadian relations had been nonexistent until the Spring of 1943—Canada had been slow to recognize the Soviet Union—but a Soviet trading presence soon arrived in Ottawa, and with them, apparently, a host of important NKVD agents. Not the ambassador, who was involved in the typical interactions proper to a wartime alliance, but members of the embassy staff. In charge was Colonel Nikolai Zabotin, military attaché of the embassy. He was actively assisted by Lieutenant Colonel Petr Motinov, chief assistant military attaché; Lieutenant Colonel Viktor Rogov, assistant military attaché air; Major Vsevelod Sokolov, of the staff of the commercial counselor of the embassy; Lieutenant Pavel Anfelov, secretary of the military attaché; and several others.[57]

Gouzenko's defection represented one of the few significant breaks in nuclear intelligence during the monopoly; now the West had a view, if not of the interior of the Soviet atomic project, at least of which kinds of documents were being ferried overseas. These spy materials were typically sealed in a bag and sent by diplomatic mail, accompanied by two armed carriers (one on duty and one sleeping or resting), who traveled "only by steamer," according to Gouzenko, usually about twice a month, for a journey of two weeks to one month to arrive in the Soviet Union. (During the war, the trip sometimes took as long as five months.)[58] This in itself indicates that the material was not considered of such urgency that it had to be rushed back.

As a cipher clerk, Gouzenko was reasonably small-fry, and his testimony could not be overly revealing in and of itself. The documents made this case unusual, since they provided a smoking gun of Soviet espionage for the first time, although they proved not to be as revealing as hoped. The roughly 250 documents Gouzenko had lifted from the embassy did not expose too much of the Manhattan Project. The research in Canada was not vital to weaponizing uranium. But Gouzenko's documents and testimony uncovered a scientist-spy, and this was a matter of the highest importance, for he would form the template by which all later scientist-spies— including those much more damaging—were judged.

His name was Alan Nunn May, code-named Alek, a talented physicist working at the Chalk River reactor. May had many of the marks that characterized scientist-spies uncovered at the end of the monopoly: physicists, foreigners, British subjects, left leaning, and often (although not always) Jewish.[59] May had already returned to England by the time the Gouzenko case broke, and he was apprehended there. May of course passed documents to his handlers, but he was most noteworthy for transmitting 162 micrograms (a fantastically small amount) of uranium 235 in the form of an oxide to Soviet agents. The official investigation of the Gouzenko ring (more properly, it should be called the Zabotin ring) found that "these samples were considered so important by the Russians that upon their receipt, Motinov [Zabotin's assistant] flew to Moscow with them."[60] Available Russian archival documents do not indicate that these samples proved terribly useful for the Soviet project, but the sensation of smuggled uranium would make headlines.

The Royal Canadian Mounted Police contacted the FBI and British intelligence and began to roll up the spy ring, which included a significant portion of the leadership of the Communist Party of Canada. For about six months, the Gouzenko revelations remained quiet, then broke in February 1946 (as it happens, a week before George F. Kennan set forth the framework for the cold war policy of containment in his "Long Telegram," published the next year as "Sources of Soviet Conduct" by X). In this case, and in this case alone, the Soviet Union admitted to having received the information (and the uranium samples) from Soviet agents but immediately discounted their relevance.[61]

So would American and British scientists. While the shock at the espionage was heartfelt, physicists in particular were quick to minimize the potential damage wrought by the May materials. Harold Urey, the 1934 Nobel laureate in chemistry for his work on isotopes, took perhaps the most common line: "The biggest secret about the bomb was whether it would work. That secret is out."[62] At the hearing investigating Gouzenko, on the other hand, John Cockcroft, one of the leading scientists on the British nuclear project, dismissed the uranium specifically in terms that highlighted the importance of open sources: "Since so much was disclosed in the Smyth report, in the class of basic scientific information, the importance of passing over these samples was substantially reduced. I think they are of some value, but I would not say they were of tremendous value."[63] Those hearings were closed, however, and no one was interested in closing the barn door the Smyth Report had opened after the horses had already fled.

The problem was far worse than even the most vociferous pundits imagined. The most important spy, both in terms of the quantity and the quality of the information he produced, was Emil Julius Klaus Fuchs: German-born, a British subject, and the single greatest security breach in the Manhattan Project, "Nunn May magnified a hundred times."[64] Klaus Fuchs was born into a Lutheran family, to a father who eventually abandoned his religious calling and joined the Communist Party, and a mother, Else, who suffered from depression and committed suicide in October 1931 by drinking hydrochloric acid, an excruciating way to end one's life.[65] Fuchs trained as a physicist, but his left-wing politics caused him to be a target of National Socialist purges, and he fled to Britain, where he was promptly apprehended as an enemy alien and sent off to an internment camp in Canada. Upon ascertaining that he was not a Nazi agent, the Canadians released him and shipped him back to England. His fragile-seeming frame, topped by wisps of dark hair, and his dreamy eyes framed by large, circular spectacles, endowed him with the aura that exactly suited the popular image of the "theoretical physicist." Rudolf Peierls, the author along with Otto Frisch of the Frisch-Peierls memorandum that calculated the critical mass of uranium 235 for the Maud Report, hired Fuchs to help him with his new work on the weaponization of fission. Fuchs, a left-wing German in Britain, was thus inducted into what would become the Manhattan Project.[66]

From the moment he was involved with nuclear weapons, he was also involved with espionage. While visiting London in late 1941 from his post at the University of Birmingham, Fuchs looked up the German historian Jürgen Kuczynski, a Communist contact (who also happened to be working with the American OSS), and told him that he had some important information for the Soviet Union. Kuczynski in turn put him in contact with the GRU agent "Alexander," actually Simon Davidovich Kremer, who served on the military attaché's staff in London.[67] The information he transmitted at this time almost certainly duplicated what the Soviets were already receiving through Cairncross, although of course Fuchs had no way of knowing that.

Fuchs's real importance, and the root of his dangerousness, was his participation in the British delegation sent to Los Alamos to assist in bomb design in December 1943. As a naturalized British scientist, he was not subject to General Groves's security clearance, which almost certainly would have rejected someone with his Communist past. He worked in the theory group and thus at the epicenter of discussions about how to engineer a plutonium-implosion bomb. (In the next chapter, we will see how this implosion information proved to be the single most important aspect of the Manhattan Project that was revealed solely through espionage, as it was completely suppressed in open sources.) The Americans liked the gentle German. "He would never want to be off in a corner with you alone," one veteran of Los Alamos recalled. "He liked to be in a group where there was small talk."[68] Norris Bradbury, postwar director of Los Alamos, recalled Fuchs as a "very popular, very reticent bachelor, who was welcome at parties because of his nice manners. He worked very hard; worked very hard for us, for this country. His trouble was that he worked very hard for Russia too."[69] Not that anyone knew this at the time. By virtue of the physics colloquium at Los Alamos where scientists shared problems they were having with their work, Fuchs was well placed to learn many different aspects of the weapons work. His courier, Harry Gold (through a mistake in spycraft Gold also served as the courier for David Greenglass, a GI stationed at Los Alamos, and thus provided the link to his brother-in-law, Julius Rosenberg), knew him only as "Raymond," and in secret cables back to Moscow he was identified as "Charles" or "Rest."

After the war, Fuchs returned to Britain, where he worked in the theory division at Harwell, helping to construct the first British atomic device. He renewed his acquaintance with Aleksandr Feklisov, his Soviet contact, in England—their last meeting in the

United States, on September 19, 1945, consisted of Fuchs describing the Trinity test—and this time Feklisov had a scientific aide who assisted him in posing the right questions.[70] This was a long way from the random selection of documents and samples that Alan Nunn May had provided. Fuchs was more like a telescope: You pointed the instrument where you wanted, and it helped you see things more clearly. Fuchs operated for the Soviets like a scientific instrument, helping them to see inside the Manhattan Project, but, like all instruments, Fuchs needed to be calibrated. He and Donald Maclean attended some nuclear meetings together in 1947, completely ignorant of the espionage activities of the other.[71] Their dual reports would serve to check each other, making sure both telescopes were in focus.

Fuchs was so highly placed in Britain, so essential to their nuclear project, that it was surprising he was even suspected of espionage, let alone caught. He was first detected through a simple error of duplication, a mistake that would crack the now famous Venona cables. Venona was a code word assigned only later, in 1961, to a set of nearly three thousand decoded cables intercepted from Soviet offices in the United States back to the Soviet Union from 1940 to 1948. These cables were all encrypted using the method of onetime pads, an essentially unbreakable code. Each agent was provided with a booklet with sixty randomly generated numbers per page, and each page in each booklet was unique, forming a pair with only a single copy in Moscow. The agent would take the plaintext, transform it into a series of five-digit numbers, and add numbers from the onetime pad to produce a coded series of digits. Unless you had the solitary other copy of the pad, you would not know which numbers to subtract and thus could not recover the plaintext.

That is how it was supposed to work. Whether due to a manufacturing error, or because Soviet cryptographers figured the risk of cracking the code was still minuscule, the massive demand for new onetime pads was met by replicating thirty-five thousand pages of the additive numbers. The whole point of the onetime pad—the reason that it was unbreakable—was the uniqueness of each page in each pad. If you had two coded messages that used the same additive, a gifted cryptographer could triangulate the common numbers even without a copy of the code and thus crack the (now poorly named) onetime pad. Meredith Gardner was just such a talented cryptolinguist and, working with FBI agent Robert Lamphere starting in 1947, managed to decipher a large number of secret cables (although many more resisted decryption). The most shocking revelations in Venona concerned the extent of espionage penetration in the Manhattan Project, and especially at Los Alamos.[72]

The Americans and the British now had a stable of atomic spies in their grip, but in order to prosecute them, the authorities needed the spies to confess. Cracking the coded cables was a major intelligence coup, but the advantage it granted would be eliminated if the Soviets knew that the Americans were able to read their secret mail. The project was so secret that not even President Truman was ever briefed on Venona. So although the Americans had hard evidence of Fuchs's espionage, they could not publicize the cables. (In any event, William Weisband, a clerk at the Armed Forces Security Agency, sold the Soviets the information that the Americans had the key to their codebook. On October 29, 1948—a date still known as "Black Friday" at the National Security Agency—the Soviet Union initiated a simultaneous change of all of their codebooks, ending the Venona leverage.)[73]

When the cables were finally declassified in 1995, one surprising finding was the atomic espionage of Theodore "Ted" Hall, known in the cables as "Mlad" ("Young One," in Russian). Hall was the youngest physicist at Los Alamos, a Harvard prodigy who was assigned to work on the implosion experiments for the Fat Man plutonium device before he was even twenty years of age. (It is possible that Hall, not Fuchs, was the first to reveal the implosion method to the Soviets, but in any case the two were used to check each other.[74]) Hall and his Harvard friend Saville Sax, who served as his courier, worked out a code using Walt Whitman's *Leaves of Grass*, which was actually rather primitive and could have been deciphered easily had anyone bothered to check his mail. Hall's manuscripts were written with milk (a makeshift form of invisible ink) on newspaper, but this method proved less than ideal for his Soviet contact, Aleksandr Iatskov (alias Iakovlev) in New York: "With our workload, this method of conveying material is extremely undesirable. We couldn't discern several words in the report, but there were not many such words; the material is generally highly valuable."[75] In 1949, Hall and Sax came to the FBI's attention through a partially decrypted Venona message, and the two were interviewed in 1951 (*after* Soviet proliferation), but since neither cracked under interrogation, the only evidence against them was the Venona cables, which could not be produced in open court for secrecy reasons. The men had to be released.[76]

Fuchs was interrogated by the British beginning in the fall of 1949, just after news of the detection of the Soviet atomic test became known in official circles, and his interrogator, William Skardon, finally got a confession on January 26, 1950. Fuchs gave Skardon only a general overview of his espionage, briefly outlining his six meetings with Soviet agents in the United Kingdom before his move to Los Alamos, ironically because he did not feel Skardon had sufficiently high security clearance to hear the details.[77] He gave the detailed confession a little later to Michael Perrin, who met Fuchs's high standards. Significantly, Fuchs had stopped spying for the Soviets in 1948, as he explained to Skardon:

> It became more and more evident that the time when Russia would expand her influence over Europe was far away, and that, therefore, I had to decide for myself whether I could go on for many years to continue handing over information without being sure in my own mind whether I was doing right. I decided that I could not do so. I did not go to one rendezvous because I was ill at the time. I decided not to go to the following one.[78]

His scruples came too late to save him. Fuchs was sentenced to eighteen years in prison—capital punishment was off the table because his spying was not for an "enemy" power but for a wartime ally—but was released in 1959 and deported to East Germany, where he lived and worked as a physicist until his death in 1988. The trail of Soviet sources to the inside of the Manhattan Project led to Germany.

Even before the war had ended, Stalin was very clear with his British and American allies that he sought significant economic reparations from Germany to compensate for the ravages the Wehrmacht had wrought. And he meant it. While communizing Germany was no doubt one goal of the Soviet authorities, it was subsidiary to appropriating economic resources, to the point of uprooting industrial plants and shipping them wholesale back to Soviet territory. (It should be noted that the Western powers performed similar extractions as well. German coal, for example, was taken from a freezing German population and transferred by Truman to other European powers also suffering from the harsh winter.) The Potsdam Conference was largely convened to deal with issues of the postwar European settlement, and discussion of reparations occupied a good deal of the agenda. Not explicitly mentioned, but certainly on Stalin and Molotov's minds, were the demands of Soviet scientists to extract scientific material as a reparations category.[79]

In parallel with the American Alsos mission, sent into liberated Europe to determine the state of the Nazi nuclear program, the Soviets dispatched a team of scientists into their sectors of the former Axis powers. Samuel Goudsmit, the scientific director of Alsos, sought to assuage fears of a German atomic bomb, to establish that the Americans were in fact in the lead in fission weapons. The Soviets, on the other hand, felt certain that they were behind even the German program and raked Germany and Austria for clues that would further their project—although of course they did not tell the Americans this. Ambassador Averell Harriman noted of his conversation with Stalin immediately after the announcement of the bombing of Hiroshima (a conversation also attended by George F. Kennan): "He added that Soviet scientists had also tried to do it [make an atomic bomb] but had not succeeded. They had found one laboratory in Germany where the Germans had evidently been working on the same problem but the Russians could not find that they had come to any results."[80] The findings of the Soviets and the Americans were the same, and so were their practices: Both appropriated documents, seized materials, and abducted scientists.

Austria fell first, and so it was there that the Soviets dispatched their first team of what eventually amounted to roughly forty leading Soviet physicists, chemists, and engineers to accompany the Red Army and look for nuclear materials. Although the yield from Vienna was eventually overshadowed by the prizes of Berlin, the Soviets obtained much from the capital on the Danube. The NKVD dispatched Vladimir Shevchenko, accompanied by the physicist Igor Golovin (later the biographer of Igor Kurchatov), to Vienna on April 13, and they remained there until May 10, debriefing scientists from the Radium Institute of the Vienna Academy of Sciences and the Second Physical Institute of Vienna University. Besides learning a great deal about cyclotrons and the distribution of atomic sites in Germany, they seized 750 pounds of metallic uranium.[81]

And, indeed, the most important thing the Soviet Union obtained from the Germans was not information at all, whether in document form or, as Oppenheimer once put it, wrapped up in a person; it was uranium itself. The entire American strategy both during and after the war to prevent proliferation hinged on seizing uranium supplies, and this approach made a great deal of sense, for at the end of the war uranium was in fact rare in the Soviet Union. The first Soviet atomic effort, the so-called Uranium Commission, had a hard enough time obtaining sufficient uranium for basic experiments.[82] Uranium needed to be found, and quickly.

The most intense Soviet efforts, understandably, focused on locating domestic ores and setting up an autarkic uranium industry. Given the size of the Soviet Union (one-sixth of Earth's land surface), locating raw ores proved a daunting task. The quest for Soviet uranium was conducted at various times by A. E. Fersman, Avraami Zaveniagin, and especially Petr A. Antropov, who was eventually placed in charge of the entire effort when it was later established as the Second Chief Directorate (the first was in charge of building a Soviet bomb). Antropov was born into a peasant family in late October 1905 and represented one of those success stories of social mobility in the early Soviet years, graduating as a geological engineer in 1932. In gratitude to the regime that had enabled his advancement, he joined the Communist Party that same year. Loyal, determined, and extremely competent, he organized massive expeditions to Central Asia, the Caucasus Mountains, and Siberia, looking beyond the conventional search sites of the so-called five-metal formation: uranium, nickel, cobalt, bismuth, and silver. Antropov's eclecticism proved a great benefit.[83]

From 1948 to 1954 there were 164 expeditions divided into 222 specially designated parties within the Soviet Union, and they covered 55,000 square miles of 102 sites. In the Far East, there were 6,008 active miners as early as 1949, 79 percent of whom were prisoners. (Prison labor was not rare in the Soviet mining industry, and the uranium miners experienced better living conditions and food than their compatriots in the gold or iron industries—although, presumably, also more severe health risks.)[84] E. P. Slavskii, deputy to Boris Vannikov, the director of the Soviet atomic industry, recalled the sheer magnitude of the effort:

I have kept some photographs. In one of them workers are driving donkeys in pairs, one after the other joined together by logs, which served like shafts as bonds between them. And in another photograph, the same donkeys are returning. On each of them hang bags, and in the bags is uranium ore. An ore is considered good if it has 0.1 percent uranium, the rest is just plain rocks. Thus imagine, how much uranium did a donkey carry in a bag?[85]

With so much effort to procure even low-grade ore domestically, the Austrian uranium, already processed into pure metallic form, was greatly appreciated.

It was not, however, the only foreign source to be exploited for the Soviet program. Stalin and Beria had few scruples about where they obtained the requisite fissionable material. Some of the earliest samples for Kurchatov's initial experiments came from the United States itself. Kurchatov's staff asked the Soviet Purchasing Commission to requisition eight tons of uranium oxide and eight tons of uranyl salts from the American War Production Board under the terms of Lend-Lease. The request arrived at the desk of General Groves, as did anything having to do with uranium, and he found himself trapped by his own webs of intelligence and counterintelligence. On the one hand, he knew that the request would facilitate a Soviet nuclear program; on the other, if he denied the request, then the Soviets would know that the Americans were themselves devoted to making an atomic bomb. (Espionage had already revealed this fact to Stalin, but Groves did not yet know that.) After some stalling, Groves agreed in 1944 to send one thousand pounds of uranium salts and two pounds of unenriched uranium metal, ostensibly to smoke out the extent of the Soviet program. The Soviets thanked him and said no more.[86]

But by far the most important source for the full-fledged Soviet nuclear program, especially in the early years, was the already mined material seized in occupied Germany. Iulii B. Khariton, the chief designer of the first Soviet bomb, and his colleague Isaak Kikoin decided that the shortage was so severe that they would have to go to Germany personally with the invading Red Army to seek uranium. (The Americans were doing the same. As General Groves wrote Secretary of War Henry Stimson in June 1945: "The uranium compounds captured in Germany have been shipped to the United Kingdom. This material is urgently needed in our project to increase our margin of safety of raw material. It should be shipped to the United States and made use of in our project.")[87] Zaveniagin authorized Khariton and Kikoin's search, granting them a car, a driver, and the necessary documents. They found the relevant records in a six-story building on the banks of the Spree River in Berlin, near Hitler's working residence. By digging through a haphazard card catalog, two of the century's most talented physicists unearthed a promising reference, and with the help of some military forces in the Soviet zone they found about one hundred tons of uranium ore in a leather factory in the town of Neustadt-Gleve.[88] This fuel powered the first Soviet reactor.

By the summer of 1949, when the Soviet Union detonated its first atomic bomb, a Communist-bloc uranium economy had already started to emerge. Whereas the Americans obtained their uranium from sub-Saharan Africa, Canada, or Brazil, as well as domestically mining it, the Soviets supplemented their growing domestic uranium industry with ore from two satellite states: Czechoslovakia and East Germany. The Czechoslovakian ore was the more immediate concern because the Joachimsthal (now Jáchymov) mines in the newly liberated country had been the primary source of the pitchblende for the Nazi uranium program, and were some of the richest uranium deposits in the world. The Soviets demanded 100 percent of the Joachimsthal production even before the March 1948 Communist coup made such transfers a matter of course. At first, President Edvard Beneš tried to hold on to at least half of the production, but he had to yield it up, and in such secrecy that even the foreign minister was unaware of the transaction. (Not so the U.S. State Department, which kept close watch on such matters.)[89]

Less mercenary, but no less thorough, was Soviet appropriation of uranium ores from their occupied sector of Germany, soon to become the German Democratic Republic. General Ivan Aleksandrovich Serov of the NKGB brought prominent Soviet geologists to the occupied zone in June 1945 and established them in a central office of the Freiberg mining academy. Their task: to evaluate the local environment and initiate mining operations for the benefit of the Soviet nuclear project. Deposits were located at Scheeberg, Zwickau, Aue, Oberschlema, Schwarzenberg, Annaberg, Johanngeorgenstadt, Marienberg, Freiberg, and Freital. Economically speaking, mines that contained less than 6 percent uranium oxide ore were not worth exploiting, and these sites ranged from 4 to 17 percent in content. Now that the spectrum of operations was mapped, the mining began.

Organization of mining was placed under Beria's deputy, Andrei Mikhailovich Mal'tsev, in June 1946. The mining concern, named "Wismut" (bismuth) to mask its actual nuclear function, offered higher wages than most other East German industries in order to attract workers (men and women) in a wartorn labor market. Even so, conditions were gruesome. When the German Democratic Republic was founded in October 1949, Wismut AG became one of many Soviet-German stock companies, but it was not turned over to the Germans in the mid-1950s like so many of its kind. Indeed, until the beginning of the 1990s, the Soviet Union still owned up to 50 percent of the uranium-mining industries in the GDR.[90] The American press occasionally noted that something was happening with German uranium in the Soviet sector, but little was done about it; in 1954, Groves would admit at the Oppenheimer hearings that he had completely underestimated the value of the German uranium to the Soviet atomic effort.[91]

The raw materials may have been the most important single contribution of occupied Germany to the development of the Soviet nuclear bomb, but it was not the feature that garnered the most attention or provoked the most anxiety in the West. The source of deepest concern was "the specialists": the German scientists and engineers who were recruited at war's end to work in Soviet industry. It was a commonplace during the cold war, especially immediately after news of Soviet proliferation hit the West, that these German specialists were responsible for the speed of the Soviet achievement—even for there being a Soviet nuclear bomb at all.[92] This picture was inverted in official Soviet histories, where any German contribution to the Soviet nuclear bomb was omitted.[93]

Most of the historical attention to the issue of German specialists in Stalin's Soviet Union has focused, understandably, on the Soviet rocket program.[94] That program, after all, in 1957 produced Sputnik 1, an orbiting Earth satellite, before the Americans did, and the equivalent German specialists in the United States (especially Wernher von Braun) sparked broad media coverage. While many postwar armament programs (radar, jet engines, etc.) in the Soviet Union followed a pattern similar to rocketry, the nuclear program was different.

The German rocket engineers were assisting the Soviets in reverse-engineering an existing technology: the V-2. The Germans had built such a weapon, and the specialists the Soviets imported had actually worked on that project. There was no such analogy for the atomic bomb. The Nazis had famously failed to make a working nuclear device, and in any case the leading lights of that program were not available for Soviet recruitment. While the Soviets offered substantial cash packages to nuclear scientists who remained in Soviet-occupied sectors of Germany at the end of the war, those in the Western sectors found themselves scooped up by Samuel Goudsmit's Alsos team and whisked off to a lovely country manor in England named Farm Hall.

Unlike the Cecilienhof Palace at Potsdam, where historians desperately wish we had recorded transcripts of certain conversations—especially that between Truman and Stalin—we do know what was said among the German scientists interned at Farm Hall, because the Americans and British had seeded the whole place with hidden microphones and recording devices. (The original German transcript has been lost, but an English translation has survived and was declassified in the 1990s.) Conversations among the ten scientists—including Werner Heisenberg, the theoretical physicist who was one of the architects of quantum mechanics, and Otto Hahn, the discoverer of uranium fission—ranged from their emotions about the defeat of Germany, their hopes and fears for the future, and the status of their own uranium project. Perhaps most revealing were the scientists' reactions to the announcement of the devastation of Hiroshima: a mixture of horror at the extent of the destruction, disbelief that the Americans could actually have produced a bomb, and shame that they themselves had not succeeded in making such a weapon. But although those conversations naturally attract the modern reader, the internees were far more concerned with their own future, and that future was going to lie with the West. As Heisenberg recognized, these ten internees "are now far more bound up with the Anglo-Saxons than we were before as we have no possibility of switching over to the Russians even if we wanted to."[95] So much the worse for them, because the Americans had no need for these nuclear scientists— they already knew far more about nuclear weapons than the Germans did—and the Americans took great pains to make sure that the pinnacle of German nuclear science remained in the West (which did not stop newspaper reports and even highly classified rumors that the Soviets were trying either to abduct Heisenberg or lure him to the Soviet Union with a handsome salary).[96]

The German nuclear scientists who were located in the Soviet sector at the end of the war were beyond the reach of Alsos kidnapers; those who then emigrated to the Soviet Union did so voluntarily. (This was not true for their aeronautical engineer or chemist peers.) There were three significant waves of "recruitment" of German experts after the war: the first between May and November 1945, which was essentially all atomic; the second (Operation Osoaviakhim) took place on the night of October 21–22, 1946, when about twenty-three hundred Germans who had worked in various war industries were rounded up with their families and deported east, comprising about 84 percent of the Germans who worked for the Soviets; the third wave consisted of only thirty to forty Germans, imported between February 1947 and February 1948. The Germans numbered only about three thousand scientists and technicians, coming to a total of eight thousand including their dependents, a far cry from the inflated thirty thousand touted in the Western media.[97] Very few of these worked on the atomic project—about two hundred in 1947, including thirty-three doctor-level scientists, seventy-seven engineers, and eighty lab assistants; by the end of 1948 the number was about three hundred, and it would decline afterward.[98]

The Germans who worked on the Soviet atomic project actively sought out the possibility. Manfred von Ardenne, Gustav Hertz, and several others agreed informally as the siege of Berlin was coming to an end that they should meet the Soviet Army—or at least not evacuate to the West—and offer their services.[99] The reasons for this were multiple and persuasive. The first calculation was financial: The Soviets were paying good and reliable salaries for this kind of work, much more than the equivalent offers from the British or Americans. As Heinz Barwich, who had also committed on June 10, 1945, to going east partially from Socialist principles, put it, "Of course a job in Russia was also materially rewarding. Overnight we had all lost our positions. In Germany there were no longer any possibilities."[100]

It was more than just the money; it was also the status. For any nuclear physicist, a job offer from the United States or Britain would be simply charity. As they would learn shortly, the Western allies knew more than the Germans about the bomb, and so the only reason to offer anything at all to these refugees would be to deny them to the Soviets. Being a pawn—and a disrespected pawn, at that—was distinctly unpalatable to these often proud and distinguished scientists. This was especially true for Gustav Hertz, the only Nobel laureate (for physics in 1925) to accept a Soviet offer. (Curiously, he had shared the prize with James Franck for their eponymous experiment to determine the discontinuous energy levels in atoms, and Franck was in turn a central figure at the Manhattan Project's Metallurgical Laboratory and the namesake of the famous Franck Report.) A specialist on isotope diffusion, Hertz had consulted with Heisenberg on the possibilities for separating uranium, but he was blackballed under the Third Reich's civil-service regulations (he was partly Jewish) and was pushed to work for the Siemens Corporation instead. One of the German nuclear physicists later stated, "I believe that if Gustav Hertz had a leading position in this group the first working reactor in the world would have been built in Germany."[101] But Germany did not take him, and he felt that a job from the Americans would be insulting, so, as Hans Thirring's booklet (that German alternative to the Smyth Report) noted in 1946, "at the moment he is located in Russia."[102] Hertz himself remained mostly tight-lipped about his experiences there even after repatriation (to Communist East Germany), maintaining little more than platitudes: "I think back very happily on this time of successful cooperation in our collective of Soviet and German scientists of different disciplines."[103]

There was in reality very little cooperation, for the German atomic scientists were kept mostly isolated from their Russian counterparts, working in parallel instead of together. As Max Steenbeck, one of these scientists, correctly observed, "Of course it meant a risk for the Soviet Union to let German scientists contribute to this politically and militarily absolutely highest-priority task."[104] A few months earlier, these people had been the citizens of an enemy belligerent, and—with the solitary exception of Russian-born, bilingual uranium chemist Nikolaus Riehl—Beria was not about to integrate them into the heart of the single most important project then under way in the Soviet Union.[105]

Yet the presence of the German specialists, however marginal their contribution may have been, still rankles in Western minds. Much like the espionage, something about it stinks: How can one speak of any "Soviet" creation of a nuclear bomb if the plans were American (and stolen) and the skill was German (and bought)? Such accusations undervalue how complicated it is, even with espionage and foreign consultants, actually to build an atomic bomb and overestimate the relatively limited German contribution to the Soviet effort.

A step back into a comparative perspective reveals something else. One might presume, given the indignation of American pundits in the 1940s and later about the German contribution to the Soviet atomic effort, that the Manhattan Project had been staffed entirely with Americans, salted lightly perhaps with a few Brits—and the latter had been a mistake, since they were riddled with spies. An *American* atomic project? Hardly. A large number of foreign-born scientists worked on the Manhattan Project, albeit many of them became naturalized U.S. citizens. The United States in the 1930s had proved substantially more friendly than the Soviet Union to European refugee scientists, and the Manhattan Project benefited significantly from this fact. Besides many of German origin (such as Hans Bethe), there were also native Hungarians (Edward Teller), Danes (Niels Bohr), Italians (Enrico Fermi), French (Bertrand Goldschmidt), and many others. These were no small fry, either, but some of the seminal figures in the American atomic effort. The main difference, such Soviet writers retorted, was that the Americans took their European specialists before the war, and the Soviet Union afterward. As an unpublished Soviet official history of their own program—perhaps an intended counterpart to the Smyth Report?—noted circa 1953, "The knowledge and experience of the greatest physicists of the world were concentrated in the USA and thrown at the solution of the atomic problem."[106]

The American (and British) use of German specialists was not a prewar peculiarity, either. After the war, the Western Allies also conducted selective hiring raids in the former Axis countries, enticing various coveted German experts to enter America's service. (This was after the initial abductions of Heisenberg and his colleagues on the German uranium project for debriefing in England.) The case of the rocket scientists, while the most famous, was hardly unique. The initial American program to recruit German technical experts was dubbed Overcast, but when that code name was blown by a careless mailing error, the name was changed to Paperclip, after the paper clips recruiters put on the denazification files of those they wanted to enroll. Although Paperclip was officially terminated on September 30, 1947, having brought more than 457 scientists and 453 dependents to the United States, the same process of cherry picking German experts was continued by a new program, National Interest.[107] The difference between the American and Soviet programs is twofold: First, the Americans were looking not only for expertise, but also for "denial" (to keep certain individuals out of Soviet hands), a practice not reciprocated by the Communists; and the Soviets were simply better than the Western powers at offering attractive jobs and salaries. Everyone was playing realpolitik.

But the Soviets were playing for higher stakes. For the problem that this rummaging through the open literature, spy data, and the various matériel and personnel from Germany was designed to solve remained acute: The Americans had an atomic bomb and the Soviet Union did not. The black box was no longer closed; Soviet scientists now had several vantage points to peek inside, even if they did not have a complete blueprint. The new task was to transform their limited knowledge of the American black box into a bomb of their own—and to do so without letting the Americans know what was happening. That would take four years and one of the most staggering organizational feats in the history of science.

FOUR

FIRST LIGHTNING

And it grew both day and night,
Till it bore an apple bright;
And my foe beheld it shine,
And he knew that it was mine.
WILLIAM BLAKE, "A POISON TREE"

The only way to be absolutely certain that you have a working atomic weapon is to set it off. Short of actually destroying your bomb in a nuclear inferno of its own creation, there will always remain doubts that this specific device truly works. This was certainly how General Leslie Groves and the scientists working for the U.S. Army's Manhattan Project reasoned; too much sweat and treasure had been expended in the effort to build a working fission bomb since the full-scale effort had begun in early 1942 not to be positive that at least the plutonium implosion bomb (Fat Man) would actually function as specified: that is, explode in a fiery blast that would destroy the greater part of a Japanese city, its infrastructure, and its population. The uranium gun-assembly bomb (Little Boy) seemed to be so simple, and the fuel so difficult to obtain, that Groves decided to risk shipping its components out to the Pacific so it could be dropped in early August on a Japanese city without prior testing. But the implosion bomb was trickier. Before the mechanism for scaling up the production of these bombs—not to mention sending the first exemplar over to the assembly team at Project Alberta on the Pacific island of Tinian so it could be assembled for its eventual target of Nagasaki—Groves and Oppenheimer knew they needed a test.

More than that, even: There needed to be a test before the test. The world's first nuclear explosion, the Trinity test, was actually the second test conducted by Los Alamos scientists. Since none of the participants in the American project had ever experienced an explosion of the anticipated size of Trinity (radically underestimated in advance as the equivalent of four thousand to five thousand tons of TNT), Kenneth Bainbridge, to whom Oppenheimer had delegated the testing procedure, opted to conduct a scale model of the forthcoming atomic test by detonating one hundred tons of TNT off a thirty-eight-foot-high tower. (The size of the tower was meant to mimic Trinity's one-hundred-foot tower by providing a scale model of the much larger test.) The test, which also served as a dry run of the wiring and instrumentation, was conducted on May 7, 1945. Some fission products were placed in the explosive so that radioactive traces could be measured. This was as close to a practice run as the Americans had.[1]

In retrospect, many American scientists understandably considered the Trinity test of July 16, 1945, as the watershed of their involvement in weapons design. Yet during the preceding months, it was by no means clear that the explosion would work, and Groves authorized the construction of a twenty-five-by-ten-foot, two-hundred-ton vessel (code-named "Jumbo") to contain the explosion in case of a misfire, so as to recover the valuable plutonium. It was eventually decided to proceed without Jumbo, but the very consideration of it reveals how uncertain the Manhattan Project seemed even at that late date.[2]

Yet Trinity was a success. The observation and instrument stations were set up in a circle of just about one hundred square miles inside an 18-by-25-mile rectangle of an air base just outside Alamogordo, New Mexico. The plutonium implosion device was set atop a one-hundred-foot tower, 9.5 miles north of Base Camp, and surrounded by instrumentation and experimental devices.[3] The explosion yielded roughly twenty thousand tons of TNT equivalent in blast, and the fireball and consequent mushroom cloud left an extremely vivid impression on the observing scientists. Consider the handwritten notes of Harvard president James Bryant Conant, not a man given to effusive hyperbole: "My first impression remains the most vivid, a cosmic phenomenon like an eclipse."[4] This was relatively mild among the transformational, world-changing talk characteristic of the Americans at their test. Within a few months, on October 1, the new director of Los Alamos, Norris Bradbury, spoke of testing to the project's Coordinating Council in a very different vein:

> The occasional demonstration of an atomic bomb—not weapon—may have a salutary psychological effect on the world, quite apart from our scientific and technical interest in it . . . It may also be pointed out that I believe that further TR[inity]'s may be a goal which will provide some intellectual stimulus for people working here. Answers can be found; work is not stopped short of completion; and lacking the weapon aspect directly, another TR might even be FUN.[5]

What did the Soviets make of such talk, much of which was reproduced endlessly in newspapers and published interviews? By the time their own test approached, in 1949, they were accustomed to American tests, being well aware of the subsequent American test series of 1946 and 1948. Simon Aleksandrov, a Soviet member of the United Nations delegation invited to the American Bikini tests in the summer of 1946, explicitly analogized any future Soviet test to these public demonstrations:

I went to the Bikini test because the Soviet government wishes to know how such a test should be organized and conducted, so that in the event Russia prepared a bomb, she would know how it should be demonstrated.

If the Soviet prepares this bomb, it would hold such a test somewhere in Russia where it would not endanger the population.[6]

The Soviets knew, as administrator Avraami Zaveniagin put it, "that only the explosion of a bomb would give a final answer to all questions."[7] The Americans expected a Soviet test. "If, or when she is able to build one, however," wrote Hanson Baldwin in the *New York Times* in November 1947, "she will almost certainly have to test her construction by detonating a bomb, as we did with our first experimental one at New Mexico."[8]

Many Americans anticipated that the Soviet program would thus follow, almost step by step, the Manhattan Project's development of a nuclear weapon, and Soviet scientists and administrators often spoke in an analogous fashion, as if they were deliberating "copying" the American effort. This impression of the Soviet project is more apparent than real, however. Although there were many similarities between the Soviet process and the prior American one, and the Soviets used a great deal of information from that model, we should avoid thinking of this as a "Soviet Manhattan Project." The two projects started from similar information (even without the spy data and the public information, the physics of uranium is the same regardless of where one happens to be) and produced devices that look remarkably similar, but the process of getting from start to end was completely different. A whale might look like a fish, but their internal biology diverges enormously. The American experience provided a background and a series of benchmarks, but it did not translate directly or unproblematically into the Soviet context.

The history of the construction of the first Soviet atomic device (and the simultaneous erection of a nuclear industry) was long and complicated, and this book cannot offer a comprehensive account.[9] Instead, this chapter emphasizes specific features of that development, exploring what happened after a particular (incomplete) set of ingredients—uranium (stolen and purchased), scientists (domestic and imported), and information (public and espionage)—were assembled within the Soviet Union. How did the assembled knowledge become an assembled bomb, and one that "worked" (i.e., detonated) in 1949? How did Soviet scientists, administrators, and military officers turn that morass of resources into a working explosive device? This is the biography of a nuclear test.

The Soviets had a tremendous advantage that was not available to the Americans: They knew that a nuclear bomb was feasible. They had the additional advantage of both public and inside information as to how the Americans had accomplished the task. Deciding that you have some knowledge, what the status of that knowledge is, and what one can do with it is not just a scientific problem, it is also a problem of organization. Problems of knowledge in such contexts are often bureaucratic problems, and so it proved with the first Soviet bomb. The dual solutions to problems of knowledge and organization were conspicuous at the very pinnacle of the project. The man Stalin chose to put in charge of the project as it entered its hectic phase after Hiroshima not only exemplified brutal efficiency in organizing individuals, but also was at the apex of the Stalinist state's mechanism for assembling knowledge: the head of the secret police, NKVD chief Lavrentii Beria.[10] His gleaming bald pate rimmed by a cropped penumbra of dark hair, accompanied by his rigid gaze and Georgian-accented Russian, made Beria an instantly recognizable and universally feared figure for Soviet citizens—the number-two man in Stalin's regime. In Stalin's selection of Beria, and in Beria's practice, we see an attention to the flow and elaboration of information that was distinctive of the Soviet project in comparison with either the American or the German projects.

Atomic energy was possibly the highest priority of the Soviet state and the primary reason why physics was stressed in the first postwar five-year plan.[11] Beria epitomized that priority in his person. The very presence of Stalin's fellow Georgian—widely loathed and feared both within and without the generalissimo's inner circle—served to keep all other parts of the bureaucracy out of the nuclear project, providing the program with an integrity and unity of purpose. There were no material limits to procurement.[12] All things considered, the architect of the last and final wave of the Great Purges—and also the man whom elites credited with having to some extent stanched the bloodshed unleashed by his predecessors—received positive reviews from the scientists; they liked that he did not meddle with scientific questions.[13] But Beria ensured that the scientific decision-making process was as centralized as the political and economic choices that he controlled directly. As Max Steenbeck, one of the German nuclear specialists recruited to the Soviet project, later recalled, "All suggestions were carefully examined in Moscow, and then it was decided whether an idea should be pursued further or should be entirely given up."[14]

Beria instituted this centralization partly from habit (this was simply how things were done), but also in order to remedy defects he had observed in the organization of the nuclear project in its early stages, before he was given control. There were actually three separate decisions to initiate an atomic project in the Soviet Union, and each should be understood not as an evolutionary development but more as an attempt to restart the organizational process from scratch. The first was the Academy of Sciences' decision in 1940 *not* to seek more money from the government to develop the "uranium problem," a reasonable decision given the paucity of Soviet-controlled uranium resources and the more pressing military situation in Europe.[15] In 1942, at perhaps the lowest point in the war for the Soviets, the State Defense Committee initiated a small project to explore the military potential of fission. Underline the word "small": As of January 1944, Laboratory No. 2, the epicenter of the project under scientific director Igor Kurchatov, employed only sixty-five people.[16] Yet this was a pivotal period, and Kurchatov's memoranda of March 1943 indicate that some of the crucial compartmentalization decisions, especially with respect to isotope separation, were made then.[17] Only after the meeting at Potsdam and the atomic bombings of Hiroshima and Nagasaki was the project fully reorganized under Beria's direct control and scaled up to what we may now consider an all-out effort to build an atomic bomb, and build it soon.

To do this, Beria needed someone who could understand the scientific data, who could command the loyalty and respect of the technical experts indispensable to the project, and who was himself politically reliable. That was Igor Vasil'evich Kurchatov, the scientific director of the project, and it is perhaps best to understand Kurchatov as Beria's representative in the world of science. (This pattern was replicated at each local site of the Soviet project; a political/military director was doubled with a scientific director.) It would thus be a mistake to analogize the Kurchatov-Beria relationship in terms of the relationship between General Leslie R. Groves of the Manhattan Project and the scientific director of Los Alamos, J. Robert Oppenheimer. While Beria and Groves were in some sense parallel figures in their national contexts, Oppenheimer directed only the bomb-designing facility of the Manhattan Project, not the science of the whole endeavor. Thus, his counterpart was more properly Iulii Khariton (whom we meet shortly). Kurchatov remained without parallel.

His peers thought of him that way too—a great deal of the memoir and historical literature in Russian on the Soviet bomb relates tales of Kurchatov's brilliance and moral uprightness, almost as though it were a one-man show.[18] Kurchatov, with his flowing beard and aristocratic bearing, possessed impeccable Soviet credentials (even becoming a member of the Communist Party in August 1948). As the leading Soviet experimentalist in the 1930s in the then backwater of nuclear physics (he had switched from studies of piezoelectricity in 1932), he was a logical selection for Stalin. He also benefited from being not too famous. Stalin reportedly opted for Kurchatov over the internationally renowned chemist Nikolai N. Semenov because the latter was too well known in the scientific world.[19] (Indeed, Semenov would eventually be awarded the 1956 Nobel Prize in chemistry.) Kurchatov managed to rally his troops effectively, and he was often lauded by his collaborators for his deep intuition and cleverness in solving problems that cropped up in the bomb work: "Precisely the most important parts of his creativity were an unusually powerful logical analysis of all possibilities and a brilliant physical intuition."[20] He even gave a series of lectures to bureaucrats and administrators on the principles of nuclear physics so that they would understand the scope of the task, a presentation several of them recalled afterward as approaching genius.[21] Later, some would sneer that there was no great mystery here; Kurchatov had all of the spy data and passed off as his own insights secret information locked in his office safe.[22] This judgment tempers some of the adoration of Kurchatov, but it is overly harsh, for it ignores the sheer difficulty of the task at hand.

Before addressing those issues of organization and information, however, there remains a linked question about the ethical and moral issues involved. Consider, by contrast, the heavily studied case of the scientists who worked on the applications of uranium physics in Nazi Germany in the Second World War. Those who worked on these projects, and especially Werner Heisenberg, have been subjected to unrelenting scrutiny for their apparent willingness to provide the weapon to Adolf Hitler. The same kind of moral attention has not been directed at the Soviet bomb makers who were, after all, building a nuclear bomb for the cruel and brutal regime of Joseph Stalin. This omission is especially surprising because those who provided the atomic bomb to Stalin were *successful* and thus unable to invoke similar excuses to the Germans about their inability (or lack of desire, depending on whom you believe) to create a bomb. As the leading historian of the Soviet nuclear project David Holloway has put it, these scientists "were, in this sense, complicit in the Soviet regime."[23] What were the moral implications of being a Soviet atomic weaponeer?

Combing through the mountains of available evidence—memoirs, archives, reports, histories—about the Soviet atomic project, it is by no means clear that such a question was particularly important for the Soviet scientists who were actually confronted with the issue.[24] This might not be surprising. Essentially no participant in the American wartime nuclear program, whether U.S. citizen, British subject, or European refugee, questioned the morality of building a very large bomb that would almost certainly target civilians. They saw a race against a Nazi atomic bomb—a race in which they perceived themselves to be far behind and desperate to catch up—as justified and thus did not raise any moral questions, at least publicly but probably also privately, until the end of the war in Europe on May 8, 1945. (Here I am referring to questions about the *creation* of the weapons, and not their *use*, which constituted a different and more complicated question, and one that has no analogy for the Soviet context.) Only one scientist, Joseph Rotblat, left the Manhattan Project for moral reasons because he believed that there was no credible threat of a Nazi bomb, a conclusion he deduced from intelligence data in late 1944. Several scientists who would eventually develop very strong moral qualms about their work on nuclear weapons did so only *after* the atomic destruction of Hiroshima and Nagasaki in early August. The apparent counterexample to this, the July 1945 Franck Report, did not oppose the use of nuclear weapons on Japan; it recommended a demonstration and explicit warning before use and did not object to the bomb's deployment as a military weapon per se. It also raised no qualms about the building of the weapons in the first place. The antinuclear interpretation of the document came only later. To Robert Wilson, one of the most prominent of the later self-critics, this delay in moral questioning remained his personal shame.[25]

There are two features of this very brief recounting of the American reaction—better put: lack of reaction—to the moral valences of nuclear weapons work that bear upon any analysis of the Soviet case. First, the American moral reflections almost all came after the fact, often long after the fact; in the heat of the project, few paused to ponder the rightness of their actions. The Soviet case was no less pressured and hectic, and thus one should not expect moral reflections until much later, which is in fact what one finds.

The second feature is more relevant to the content of that moral reflection when it finally came. American questioning of the moral justification of the creation of weapons of mass destruction remained absent while there was a strong sense of chasing the Nazis for the bomb.[26] For the Soviets, the feeling of a race was even more real: The Americans actually *did* have an atomic bomb, and the Soviet scientists knew it. The repressive effect on introspection was strong. And the Americans possessed not one atomic bomb, they possessed several; they not only had them, but they had used them; and they had used them against a nonnuclear adversary—*twice*.

When we find traces of Soviet physicists examining the moral justification of their weapons work, we see that Stalin occupied a very small place in their reasoning and the Americans a massive one. For Igor Kurchatov, the scientific director of the Soviet nuclear program, the Americans, by building the bomb, had obviated the question of the morality of a Soviet nuclear project. Once the Soviet project became public knowledge (after the second Soviet nuclear test), Kurchatov redirected all rebukes to the Americans: "You should not address [this question of morality] to us but to those who released these forces. The physics is not frightening, but [the Americans'] adventuristic game is not science but the exploitation of it by scoundrels."[27] For Vasilii S. Emel'ianov, a nuclear physicist who in the 1960s assumed the role of Soviet international envoy on nuclear matters, the central issue was American priority and American threat: "It wasn't we who started the arms race. The United States did that, surrounding our country with a ring of military bases, posing a deadly danger."[28] The Americans had not asked any questions about the aggressive or dangerous potential of their own leaders—present or future—and so their decision to weaponize nuclear fission gave everyone else a free pass.

The nuclear threat to the Soviet homeland from the Americans in the monopoly period made morality irrelevant for most nuclear physicists. As one put it, "In this situation one can come to only one conclusion"—build a bomb, protect the homeland.[29] For many of these scientists, and for the soldiers and bureaucrats who worked with them, the budding cold war was a continuation of World War II (the Great Patriotic War, in Soviet parlance), and the American atomic bombers who threatened the homeland were no different from Hitler's Wehrmacht.[30] To the extent that one finds any moral discussion in the memoirs of Soviet scientists, it centers on the barbarity of the destruction of Hiroshima and Nagasaki.[31] It is not difficult to imagine them seeing an image of the ravished postblockade Leningrad and projecting that to a nuclear-devastated Moscow. "We thought that this was necessary. That was our internal conviction," wrote V. B. Adamskii.[32] For L. V. Al'tshuler, it was even a "categorical imperative."[33]

Yet defense of homeland could come in multiple forms. The above comments mostly focused on the Soviets' perception that they needed a nuclear bomb to deter an immediate attack by the atomic jingoists in Washington, who were at that moment busy reconstructing Western Europe in order to sow it with bomber bases to burn the Soviet Union to cinders. The development of a Soviet atomic bomb, and even more a Soviet atomic stockpile, could also be seen—especially with the crystal clarity of hindsight—as creating a stable mutual-deterrence structure that would eliminate global war. This rhetoric obviously played a central role in the political justification of obscenely large nuclear stockpiles during the cold war, but it also provided even the dissident Andrei D. Sakharov, in his earlier guise as the chief developer of the Soviet thermonuclear bomb, with his personal justification for working on such weapons.[34] From the perspective of his later life as a human-rights activist and disarmament advocate, the creation of nuclear bombs had at least the temporary benefit of discouraging their use. By his own account in his memoirs, however, his entry into the project was less reflective: "In 1948, no one asked whether or not I *wanted* to take part in such work. I had no real choice in the matter, but the concentration, total absorption, and energy that I brought to the task were my own . . . Our initial zeal, however, was inspired more by emotion than by intellect."[35] Feeling as he must have at the end of a war that left the Soviet Union mired in horrific destruction, who could blame him?

The same set of justifications, however, were not so easily deployed by the German specialists who had been brought in to assist the Soviet atomic project. Their moral position was more tenuous, and German moral excuses for their willingness to serve dictators usually undergo intense examination—as we can easily see from the renewed recriminations about the moral turpitude of German nuclear physicists in the wake of the critical and commercial success of Michael Frayn's Heisenberg-centric drama *Copenhagen*.[36] Yet the Soviet-employed German specialists have mostly been excluded from the heat that surrounds their contemporaries.

Every German who has left an account of his experience on the Soviet project addressed the moral issue. Max Steenbeck, who worked at Sukhumi on isotope separation, cited as pivotal a conversation he had with his Soviet counterpart Lev Artsimovich, in which the latter insisted that the morality of working on the Soviet bomb was already resolved by the American destruction of Hiroshima. The German émigrés to the United States, Steenbeck noted, seemed to have had no reservations about working for hire on a foreign nuclear program, and so neither should he.[37] The obvious asymmetry between the case of Jewish refugees and the threat of Hitler was left unspoken here.

Steenbeck, however, had it relatively easy, because he had been essentially uninvolved in the German nuclear program. The same cannot be said of two other participants who have left their moral justifications in the historical record. The first, Nikolaus Riehl, who was the most highly placed German in the Soviet project and whose uranium purification work proved vital for the launching of the first Soviet production reactor, had in fact participated in the Nazi project, although in a limited fashion. Despite his Russian-Jewish mother (which was why he was excluded from later German research), he notified the German army about the military possibilities of fission in 1939. (They were relatively uninterested.)[38] Yet Riehl seemed to have felt greater moral qualms in working for Stalin:

> The lack of any requirement on the part of the government caused many of us not to expect any significant results from the uranium project before the collapse of Hitler's government. As a result, we never felt any compulsion to bring the matter to the attention of our consciences.
>
> The atmosphere was completely different when we entered the Soviet Union. There we felt a strong undertow, stemming from the government, that reflected a brutally driven concern about the uranium program.[39]

It was only at this point that Riehl invoked the usual arguments about deterrence and how the Americans had started the whole mess. Very interesting in his account is how the Nazi bomb seems to be the least morally troubling, with the American the most. And for both Riehl and those others who had worked on both projects, their *additional* work on the Soviet bomb seems to have cleansed their prior efforts for Hitler—as if the two canceled each other out, leaving these scientists in a position of moral neutrality.

Along the same lines, Manfred von Ardenne, who had sponsored some Nazi atomic work, would claim after the war from the comfort of his exalted position in East Germany that he had opposed the bombing of Hiroshima from the moment he had heard of it: "Why do that?" he recalled having thought. (Leave aside the fact that he had enrolled in the Soviet project about two months *before* Hiroshima.) His version of nuclear morality drew a blanket defense for all Germans working in the Soviet Union: "It was our hope that through the rapid achievement of a nuclear stalemate, the outbreak of a nuclear third world war would be delayed. This conception formed for all of us the moral justification for our participation in the achievement of the technical prerequisites for the construction of nuclear weapons."[40] Von Ardenne thus managed to encompass most of the major arguments in favor of working on the bomb in two sentences: It was only technical work; it was construction, not use; it was in response to the Americans; and it was to prevent a nuclear war.

While the Germans—understandably in view of the delicacy of their legal and moral culpability—tended toward one voice, it would be truly surprising if there were no voices from within the Soviet program who questioned the legitimacy of this activity. And, indeed, such doubts existed, although expressed only after Stalin's death in May 1953. On one level, the doubts centered on the idea of making bombs at all, specifically, making thermonuclear (hydrogen) bombs, with their seemingly infinite potential for destructive power. Such misgivings about thermonuclear bombs (not fission bombs) also seem to have existed for Sakharov and even Kurchatov, but most clearly of all for Lev Landau, the best-known Soviet theoretical physicist in the post-Stalin years.[41]

But for Landau, there seemed to be the additional dimension not just of making bombs but of making bombs for *Stalin*. This was the same regime, after all, that had in 1938 imprisoned him for a year for making anti-Stalin protests (he was released upon the intervention of the physicist Peter Kapitza), and that had the potential to seize him again at any moment as a former enemy of the state, as a "cosmopolitan" (read: Jew), and as an independent-minded misfit. While Landau had told Sakharov that he disliked nuclear weapons work because it was "too much noise," comments he made to a set of close scientist friends in 1952 or 1953 perhaps summed it up more accurately: "I have been reduced to the level of a 'scientist slave' and this defines it all."[42]

Nonetheless, Landau did not quit the project until after Stalin's death. Understandably, he felt he needed the insurance it provided him against additional run-ins with the NKVD. Vitalii Ginzburg, a physicist with similar liabilities to Stalinist persecution, also believed that the bomb project "possibly saved my life."[43] (Not only was he at risk for being Jewish, but his wife had been arrested earlier, and thus the physicist was vulnerable as a "spouse of an enemy of the people.") Now, after the collapse of the Soviet Union, one finds some who declared that "the creation of the atomic weapon would only strengthen the Stalinist regime, which, as I already understood then, even without this [weapon], was a tragedy for our country," and thus claimed they refused to work on the project.[44] No such records or recollections exist in earlier sources. Iulii Khariton, the chief bomb designer for the Soviet fission project, recalled that the first refusal to work on nuclear weapons took place only on October 19, 1954, well over a year after Stalin's death.[45] Moral qualms were rare, and it was hazardous to express them even when they did exist.

It is important to emphasize that the vast majority of Soviet physicists involved with the construction of "Stalin's bomb" saw absolutely nothing morally problematic about the venture, and the few who did kept silent. Even those who did have doubts about the justice of the nuclear venture may have continued to work on it not just to protect themselves but to protect their discipline, physics, from undergoing the same kind of sanitization and evisceration to which Stalin had lately subjected genetics through his functionary Trofim D. Lysenko. In August 1948, at the Lenin All-Union Academy of Agricultural Sciences, Lysenko read a long speech (which had been edited and approved by Stalin) rejecting Mendelian genetics as "bourgeois" and installing in its stead "creative Soviet Darwinism" in the form of neo-Lamarckian inheritance of acquired characteristics. Not until the mid-1960s was Lysenko's hold on Soviet biology broken, and physicists had some reason to worry that perhaps some level of ideological interference—although almost certainly nothing so drastic as what happened in biology—would be presented in an upcoming scheduled conference on philosophical conflicts in contemporary physics. Although we do not know exactly what happened behind the scenes, we do know that the physics meeting was canceled, almost certainly with the intervention of either Kurchatov, Beria, or Stalin, and that the bomb project provided at least implicit (and possibly explicit) defense of the discipline as a whole. Lev Landau famously quipped that the cancellation of the projected 1949 physics session and the unhampered survival of Soviet physics was the first successful example of nuclear deterrence.[46]

It was against the background of these personal and disciplinary reflections, then, that Igor Kurchatov had a job to do. Simply put, his job was to build a nuclear bomb for the Soviet Union in the shortest possible time. But how does one do that? The decision was made to follow some of the engineering choices of the American bomb makers. Even this restricted form of "copying" was easier said than done, for converting the limited information obtained from the West into a nuclear device was a very tall order. To understand the scale of complexity involved, it is worth examining briefly the alternative available to Beria and Stalin.

That alternative was articulated forcefully in a letter to Stalin from Peter Kapitza, the most famous Soviet physicist of the day. Kapitza had earned an international reputation at the Cavendish Laboratory in Cambridge, England, for his low-temperature experiments, and was lured back to the Soviet Union in the mid-1930s and then denied exit so he could work for the glory of the fatherland. Kapitza's status was thus highly anomalous (not typically a good thing in Stalin's Soviet Union) and allowed him some degree of freedom to criticize his superiors—although not, as we shall see, without cost. He occasionally expressed his criticisms and suggestions in letters to Stalin, and one in particular stands out for bearing directly on this question of the wisdom of copying the American plutonium bomb.

From the archival documents available to us, it seems there was never any question that the Soviets would attempt to build a plutonium bomb, analogous to the Fat Man device that destroyed Nagasaki, as opposed to a Hiroshima-style Little Boy, which worked with uranium 235. In making this selection, Kurchatov and Beria made perhaps the most significant change from the "Manhattan model," which would have suggested building a Little Boy first. The logical chain is nowhere explicitly spelled out, but is fairly straightforward to reconstruct. From one perspective, Little Boy was a lot easier to build. If you had two subcritical masses of uranium 235, you could simply place one piece at the end of a pipe, and then launch the other piece toward it using a conventional explosive—hence the designation "gun assembly." The problem was the fuel: Uranium 235 is highly fissionable (which is why this system works at all) but it is very rare, comprising less than 1 percent of naturally occurring uranium, which is mostly the less fissionable, heavier isotope, uranium 238. The Soviets had access to relatively little high-grade ore (meaning that there was very little uranium oxide in a given amount of ore) as a result of General Groves's efforts to monopolize the world's supply of the heavy metal, and would have had to engage in a much more elaborate separation operation than even the Americans had in order to isolate enough fuel for such a bomb. Kurchatov was thus basically precluded from building a gun assembly.

The other fuel, plutonium, had to be manufactured from uranium, so it was less straightforward to obtain, but it was manufactured from U 238, and the Soviets had much more of that. Some separation work was still necessary to obtain enough U 235 to power a reactor, but the stray neutrons from that reactor could irradiate U 238 and produce plutonium to be separated chemically. This approach not only made the best use of the available resources in the Soviet Union; it also implied an assembly line of fuel production: Once you had the reactor setup working, you could make as much plutonium as you had unenriched uranium. Stalin clearly wanted a production line of these bombs, if only because the Americans already had one set up in Hanford, Washington, and so again Kurchatov and Beria seemed to be making an easy decision.

Except for the design problem—and it was a big problem. If you attempt to build a gun assembly for plutonium, the fuel begins to spontaneously predetonate before the entire assembly goes critical. This property of plutonium is precisely what killed Thin Man, Los Alamos's first plutonium gun design, and shifted the entire project toward an implosion assembly.[47] The implosion design was elegant: Several subcritical pieces of plutonium were simultaneously propelled by conventional charges into an extremely dense core, which then detonated. The rapidity of the assembly obviated the predetonation problem. This was the only feasible way to assemble a plutonium bomb, and Kurchatov and Beria adopted it.

They learned about this—all of it, both the failure of the plutonium gun and the basic mechanics of the implosion design—however, from the spy data sent along by Klaus Fuchs. After beginning his work in Los Alamos, Fuchs first met with a Soviet agent in February 1945, in Boston, where the physicist was visiting his sister. At that time he turned over a report of several pages he had written summarizing the problems of making an atomic bomb. Crucially, he noted that a plutonium device would not work by the gun-assembly method; an implosion assembly was required. In his second report, of June 1945, he more fully described the implosion method and informed the Soviets about the upcoming test at Alamogordo.[48] Igor Kurchatov, after evaluating the quality of this information back in Moscow, recognized that knowing that the spontaneous fission of plutonium necessitated a more rapid assembly system was uniquely valuable and would save quite a bit of time.[49] These specifics about implosion, any mention of which was studiously omitted from the Smyth Report, are the major contribution of espionage to the design of the first Soviet nuclear bomb. And so the spy material was intimately linked with the decision to use plutonium as a fuel, which was a decision in turn generated by the conditions imposed by the Combined Development Trust's uranium monopoly. Beria and Kurchatov followed the trail of reasoning and opted for a plutonium bomb with an implosion configuration.

Kaptiza questioned this entire line of reasoning. A letter to Stalin dated November 25, 1945, already several months after the acceleration of the project to its grand scale and after Beria had instituted many of the organizational decisions that would structure it, made clear that Kapitza was not pleased: "In the organization of work on the A[tomic] B[omb], it seems to me, there is much that is abnormal. In any case, what is being done right now is not the shortest and cheapest path to its creation." Kaptiza made these claims in full knowledge that there was espionage data in play, although he almost certainly did not know the full extent of it: "The secret of the A.B. is unknown to us. The secret to key questions is very delicately guarded and seems to be the most important state secret of America alone. The information received so far is inadequate to create an A.B., but often it gives us, without doubt, something to hit on the correct path." At times, in fact, Kapitza's critique of Beria's organizational acumen veered very close to the cocky American dismissals of Soviet potential to proliferate:

In resolving these problems we have only one advantage—we know that the A.B. problem has a solution; the Americans took a chance, we won't have to. We have several disadvantages:

1. The Americans were supported by a more powerful industry; ours is weaker, corrupted by war, and destroyed.

2. The Americans brought to the work the greatest scientists of the entire world. Our scientists are fewer and they live in poor conditions, overburdened by too many jobs, and thus they work less well.

3. The Americans have strong scientific bases; we have very limited ones and they are wrecked by the war . . .

4. America has a good industry for scientific apparatus; here, this field is scattered among different ministries, is found in a neglected and chaotic condition.

According to Kapitza, copying was thus out of the question: "We want to redo everything that the Americans did, and are not trying to go our own way. We forget that we can't afford to go by the American path, and it would take a long time." So a new path needed to be found, even if Kapitza could not say at the moment what it would be. By structuring their own program in imitation of the Americans, the Soviets risked ratcheting up costs and wasting time with redundancies. Originality would pay dividends in the end. In closing, Kapitza took a swipe at Beria: "Comrade Beria has the fundamental weakness in that the director should not only wave the baton, but should understand the score."[50] Scientific ignorance was squandering time and treasure.

For his pains, Kapitza was removed from all association with the atomic project and sent into a kind of quasi limbo of administrative irrelevance for the next several years. The decision to copy had already been made—and it had been made, unbeknownst to Kapitza, taking into account all of the problems that he had invoked. As Khariton would note after the cold war had ended, copying was selected precisely because it was considered by Stalin to be fastest: "It became clear that it would be best for us to test precisely this [American] schema. The fastest and most reliable means was necessary to show that we also had nuclear weapons."[51] It was considered fastest through somewhat dubious logic: Since it had worked for the Americans, it was able to produce a guaranteed result. And, of course, Kapitza was at least partially correct—the overwhelming dominance of the American approach meant that some of Beria's choices, such as displacing the ultracentrifuge for the much less efficient electromagnetic approach to isotope separation, may have slowed the Soviet project.[52] This is not to say that proposed changes to the American template were dismissed out of hand, but the presumption was to follow the path laid out in the

Smyth Report; those who argued to the contrary had to fight an uphill battle.

Yet Kapitza had a point, for in the end it is not clear that using American espionage data saved any time for the Soviets, although it surely saved much uncertainty. For at every stage of information flow through the atomic bomb project, every single piece of data obtained from the American project needed to be subjected to critical analysis, deconstruction, and wholesale reverification, which amounted in some cases to consciously reinventing the wheel. This included the Smyth Report. The spymasters in Moscow were so astonished by the extent of the information presented in the report that they sent an agent to investigate whether the whole effort was simply disinformation on a massive scale. The agent, posing innocuously as an interested member of the public, found that at least American scientists thought the report was genuine.[53] It could be safely relied on. Why so much vetting, so much cross-checking? The reasons were several, and all had to do with problems about the instability of information.

The first worry concerned the reliability of intelligence data in general. The sheer quantity and variety of spy data raised the specter of disinformation. As future Soviet leader Nikita S. Khrushchev put it with his customary directness, "When you buy stolen property, you don't always get exactly what you need, and a thief sometimes is a stooge. Sometimes what he thinks he is stealing has actually been sold to him by order of an intelligence agency."[54] Beria and Stalin were not sure that the information that had arrived from Fuchs and others was not disinformation, either consciously fed to them by Fuchs or passed along without his knowledge through the machinations of General Groves.[55] Those who trade in secret information and the techniques of counterespionage can never escape the sense that they are being duped. "Of course, we couldn't quietly trust this information," said Khariton. "It could contain elements of disinformation; after all, we had no idea how this information was obtained—and therefore it required painstaking verification and supplementary studies." Every experiment, every physical value needed to be rechecked.[56] Although these doubts were never fully laid to rest, Kurchatov vetted all of the information, and his assessments from 1943 onward were designed specifically to assuage this concern:

> Of course the question arises whether the received information reflects the actual course of scientific research work in England and is not an invention, the goal of which would be to disorient our science . . .
>
> On the basis of careful examination with the material, I have the impression that *it reflects the true position of things.*
>
> Certain results, even in very important areas of the work, seem to me doubtful, some of them poorly based, but the English scientists are responsible for those, not the good quality of the information.[57]

The second threat to the integrity of the foreign intelligence was more routine for scientific work and less corrupted by the vagaries of the spymaster's suspicions: basic incompleteness. Even considering the large volume of information pouring into the project from Fuchs, Ted Hall, and the piles of public sources, crucial information, such as the scale of the drawings, was never passed on. Basic industrial processes were omitted. Considering the vast scope of the Manhattan Project, it would have been impossible to transmit *every* piece of information that was relevant to the Soviets, and not only did the scientists not have the complete information, they had no idea how much was missing and how important that absent data might be (although they did know that they lacked crucial information on gaseous dynamics, nuclear processes, properties of materials, and the physics of explosions). And when they had experimental data, it often proved contradictory or possibly outdated. They had to redo everything just to know where the gaps were.[58] And not just gaps. The basic building materials—epoxies, washers, solder—were different in the Soviet Union and the United States, so the physical properties of the Soviet materials had to be established precisely even in those few cases where the Soviets had access to full American details.

The third problem of knowledge concerned not *what* the Soviet physicists knew but *which* physicists knew it. Beria mirrored the attitude toward knowledge that General Groves dubbed "compartmentalization" and that he considered "the very heart of security. My rule was simple and not capable of misinterpretation—each man should know everything he needed to know to do his job and nothing else."[59] The technique in the United States was inspired by counterespionage, not efficiency, and it had the additional effect of amplifying Groves's authority in the Manhattan Project by making him the central hub through which all vital communications flowed. For these reasons, this practice was well adapted not only to the secrecy demanded for producing a nuclear weapon but also to the prevalent practices of Soviet society. Beria and Kurchatov compartmentalized all the aspects of the Soviet project, and the American information most of all.

Compartmentalization was also the reason that most Soviet physicists who were involved in nuclear weapons work in the late 1940s did not learn until the final days of the Soviet Union that much of their information had originated in the United States and Great Britain, and that the device detonated at the August 1949 test was a replica of the Fat Man core exploded in the Trinity test of 1945. Even for matters less sensitive than intelligence information, most Soviet scientists were unaware of the tremendous redundancies built into the organization of the project and learned of competing laboratories working out the same problems only when they were confronted with alternative results in the case of a conflict. Kurchatov occasionally used the spy information in a similar fashion, to check up on the accuracy of the work his own men were doing, thus using American physicists as benchmarks for the quality of Soviet physicists.[60] Similarly, code words for crucial elements of nuclear research (such as "zero points" for neutrons or "sediment" for plasma), and especially multiple words for the same thing, created an effect the physicists dubbed "pigeon language" and further muddied the waters of transparent knowledge transmission.[61] Which was, of course, the point.

Occasionally, scientists working on parts of the project would suddenly become aware of the extent of the deliberate obfuscation caused by all this compartmentalization and parallelism. For example, Veniamin Tsukerman recalled an incident when he and V. V. Sof'ina were working on the problem of measuring the detonation pressure of explosives, a property that depends on their efficiency and is absolutely central to the workability of a plutonium implosion bomb. Theoretical computations produced two competing results—one from the Germans and one from Lev Landau and K. P. Staniukovich—of either 200,000 or 250,000 atmospheres, a very wide discrepancy. (An atmosphere is a unit of pressure, with one atmosphere representing the pressure of air at sea level.) Tsukerman and Sof'ina used flash radiography—essentially an X-ray strobe light—to register the path of detonations on multiple trials, starting with small charges and then gradually increasing the blast power. At first, they obtained no results at all, but when they increased the charges *and* replaced the steel balls they were originally trying to implode with bits of thin foil, they obtained values close to those estimated by Landau and Staniukovich. In the spring of 1948 Tsukerman realized there was further confirmation, using two different methods, from Lev Al'tshuler's laboratory, again confirming the 250,000-atmosphere prediction.

A few months later, however, in September, Kurchatov chaired a meeting that announced that E. K. Zavoiskii's laboratory, using an electromagnetic measurement method, had obtained much lower values. Al'tshuler, Zavoiskii, and Tsukerman had to argue the point out, and eventually flaws were found in Zavoiskii's experiments.[62] Iulii Khariton later would use this incident of two parallel theoretical tracks matched with three parallel experimental tracks, none of which knew about the others until their results disagreed, to point to the extreme difficulties of "copying" the American path:

The work was tense and nerve-racking. In order to reckon out all the processes that happen in an atomic bomb, it was necessary to calculate all the pressures well. For they are varied and, after all, this is a detonation in an explosive . . . Since this was very delicate work, I decided to create two groups of measurements, so that the work would go in parallel. The first gives the conclusion: the device will work! The second: it won't work! A commission was created, and [leading atomic administrator Boris] Vannikov himself came to the meeting . . . It turned out that the first group was correct . . . I produce this example as an illustration of the nervous situation, and also the tension of the work.[63]

Spy data was closely rationed as well as compartmentalized, much more so than the greater amount of information obtained from open sources. Kurchatov, as scientific director, was the only physicist Beria permitted to access all of the espionage data, and he had to submit an affidavit to the NKVD to authorize selected individuals to look at segments of it. The paper trail was unavoidable and meant that Kurchatov seldom exerted this power.[64] Khariton described the process thus:

The fact is that this material was shown in its entirety only to the scientific director of the entire problem—academician I. V. Kurchatov. Kurchatov transmitted to the directors of the fundamental divisions of the work only those materials which immediately concerned the problems they were working out then. Kurchatov had to receive corresponding permission for each such transmission. Thus, I. K. Kikoin received materials concerning the separation of isotopes, and I received information concerning only those questions immediately connected with the working out of the construction of an atomic bomb, and I could share that in its entirety only with my first deputy K. I. Shchelkin.[65]

And that was where the information trail stopped. As Khariton noted later, "The prohibition against publicizing the very fact of the receipt of such information was severe."[66] No one ever forgot he was working for Beria.

Much like the information, the organization of the Soviet atomic bomb project was physically compartmentalized, the various tasks involved in assembling a nuclear device literally embedded in concrete and distributed across the thousands of miles of the nuclear archipelago.

Functionally, of course, the structure was a pyramid, with Beria at the top, closely followed—but *always* followed, never preceded—by Kurchatov. Even though the administration followed this personal command path (as, for example, did the Soviet Union as a whole under Stalin's control), nominally a ministry was established to provide for delegation of responsibility (again, much like the Soviet system as a whole). This pseudoministry was called the First Chief Directorate (PGU, *Pervoe glavnoe upravlenie*), subordinate to the highest governing body, the Council of Ministers—and that meant Stalin and Beria. On August 20, 1945, immediately after the end of the Pacific war, a scientific-technical committee was created under the authority of Boris L. Vannikov, with deputies Kurchatov and Mikhail G. Pervukhin to handle the daily administration.[67] (A Second Chief Directorate was created on December 27, 1949, after the first Soviet test, under Petr A. Antropov to coordinate the uranium search.)[68] Vannikov also sat at the apex of the atomic industry, with deputy Avraami Zaveniagin.

Vannikov was born in Baku in 1897 and had joined the Bolshevik Party in 1919, making him one of the select set of early Communists to survive the first two decades of the Soviet Union and the ravages of the purges and the war. Trained as an engineer, and appointed as director of the defense industrial plant at Tula in 1926, he was well placed to become deputy people's commissar of the defense industry in 1937. When that commissariat was broken into four separate new ones two years later, he became people's commissar of armament.[69] He was thus an ideal liaison between the military establishment and the intelligence-scientific complex that composed the bomb project.

That complex tended to be young, much like the Manhattan Project had been, although since the Great Patriotic War had more than decimated the young population of the Soviet Union and disrupted scientific education, the scientists on the Soviet project tended to be slightly older on average than their wartime American equivalents. Except at the very peaks of administration, the Soviets were usually no older than thirty to thirty-five.[70] And these people were spread far and wide across the vast expanse of the country, across at least ten closed cities, with a greater concentration of these latter (five) in the Ural Mountains, which had the benefit of being in Russia proper, close to hydroelectric power stations, and far from any border—and foreign spies.[71]

This being the Soviet Union, however, the center for most things was still Moscow. Not only was Beria based there, but so was Kurchatov, whose official post was director of Laboratory No. 2 of the Academy of Sciences. As noted earlier, this installation grew slowly at first but experienced a rapid burst at the end of the war, as Kurchatov obtained both more official passes to allow physicists to live in Moscow and the right to demobilize individuals from the Red Army. At first located at the Seismological Institute on Pyzhevskii Lane in the center of the city, he moved it in April 1944 (for reasons of space and security) to the northwest of the city, close to the Moscow River, at Pokrovskoe-Streshenev.[72] Laboratory No. 2 performed work on the basic physics of fission as well as preliminary investigations on ballistics. It was clear, however, from the sum of American public information, especially the Smyth Report, that the full development of a nuclear device would require three things: (a) an isotope-separation facility, to produce enough high-grade uranium fuel for (b) a reactor, which would in turn produce greater amounts of plutonium from low-grade uranium, which would then be shipped to (c) a bomb-design center.

Kurchatov ensured that all these facilities were built, and built apart from each other along the rationale of compartmentalization.

Isotope separation and reactor construction were the parts of the project that were most straightforwardly reverse-engineered from the Smyth Report and the espionage material, although one should not understate either the scale of the construction of each of these facilities or the technical complexity of the details *not* found in the available information and that thus had to be reinvented by the Soviet scientists and engineers. The goal of isotope separation is just what it sounds like: to separate out the slightly lighter uranium 235 from the most common isotope, uranium 238. The three methods employed for separating isotopes discussed in the Smyth Report were established in the Soviet Union: thermal diffusion under Anatolii Aleksandrov, which relied on the fact that the slightly heavier molecules of U 238 move less rapidly than lighter ones; gaseous diffusion under Isaak Kikoin and Ia. A. Smorodinskii, exploiting a similar set of properties; and electromagnetic diffusion under Lev Artsimovich with Igor Golovin and G. Ia. Shchepkin, shooting charged ions of uranium through a magnetic field in order to exploit the difference of deflection between the masses.[73] Most of this work was focused on two goals: a long-term goal of separating enough U 235 to produce a uranium-only fission bomb, similar to Little Boy dropped on Hiroshima; and a short-term goal of producing uranium with enough enrichment to power a reactor, which could in turn produce plutonium for a Fat Man–style implosion bomb.

The first Soviet experimental reactor, F-1 (for "Physical-1"), went critical on Christmas Day 1946, in Kurchatov's Laboratory No. 2. Its purpose was not only to measure various nuclear properties and constants that were essential to bomb design but also to prove different reactor designs so one could be scaled up into a production reactor. The first plutonium production reactor, following a design by Nikolai Dollezhal' and dubbed Anniushka (or A reactor), located at Maiak in the Urals, went online within eighteen months. This reactor produced plutonium, and lots of it.

Moderated by graphite (to slow the flow of neutrons and increase the probability of reaction), it passed slugs of uranium 238 through 1,168 channels so they could absorb neutrons and beta-decay into plutonium 239. It also produced energy, upgraded to 500 MW from its initial capacity of 100 MW. It was loaded with all the uranium then available in the country—including what was left of the 100 tons of German uranium acquired in Berlin, which "allowed us to shorten the time for the creation of the first industrial reactor by a year," and powered up on June 19, 1948.[74] By February 1949, radiochemists were able to isolate fifteen milligrams of plutonium per liter of solution produced from Anniushka. By the end of June, there was enough for the first bomb.[75]

That bomb was designed and built at Arzamas-16, later known affectionately (and ironically) by the Soviet physicists as Los Arzamas, in tribute to its American counterpart, Los Alamos, in New Mexico. Arzamas-16 was built at the small monastery town of Sarov, and the name, like all these word-number combinations, was designed to obfuscate as much as to enlighten: Ostensibly, the name stood for a town, and the number for a post office box, but Arzamas-16 was not in Arzamas (where Leo Tolstoi had had a famous vision of death in 1869), but about forty miles south, and it was not a post office box. The name for the bomb design center had already rotated through several incarnations, including Base-112, KB-11, Kremlev, Arzamas-75, Installation (*ob"ekt*) No. 550, Moskva, Center-300, and the Volga Office (*Privolzhskaia kontora*). Experiments on the implosion model were begun in the middle of 1947. To let off steam (again much like Los Alamos), the scientists—but not the political prisoners who built the infrastructure—put on theatrical shows and skits, and the general tenor of the memoir literature reflects a fondness for an idyllic time.[76]

Much of that affection is directed toward the birdlike Iulii Borisovich Khariton, the chief bomb designer and the scientific director of this site, placing him in the equivalent position to Oppenheimer in the American project. (Khariton did not officially control Arzamas-16; just as Kurchatov had Beria, Khariton had

Pavel Mikhailovich Zernov.) Whereas most of the other Soviet physicists and administrators introduced above sported impeccable Soviet credentials, Khariton (like Lev Landau) had a more checkered past, and it is likely that his devotion to the atomic project—and his unquestioned mastery of the craft of weapons design—saved him from a worse fate.

His father had been expelled from Soviet Russia before the war and spent time in Berlin before moving to Riga, where he was arrested by the NKVD in October 1940 after the Soviet Union annexed Latvia. He was condemned to seven years in the camps and was subsequently killed. Khariton's mother was by then living in Palestine. As a Jew and a son of two émigrés and enemies of the people, and with a stint abroad himself at Cambridge, he was in a precarious position. He was also unquestionably gifted, and Beria's son claims in his memoirs that his father had to exert himself to save Khariton (surely on Kurchatov's bona fides).[77] Like the other scientific leaders of the project, Khariton was shadowed by his NKVD "secretaries," assigned to the scientists to make sure no wrecking or sabotage took place. (Reactions to them varied. Iakov Zel'dovich would not let his secretaries into his apartment, and they had to sleep in the stairwell. Landau threatened suicide if they came too close.)[78] It was Khariton, more than any other single scientist on the project, who bore the task of building a workable nuclear device in the shortest time, although to be sure he was assisted by many individuals in his own lab and in the fuel production centers, and watched over by Kurchatov.

It is certain from the documentary record that it was the Soviet physicists—among them overwhelmingly men of Russian or Russian-Jewish origin and not the German "specialists" imported from the wreckage of Nazi Germany—who built and constructed the first device. Even Max Steenbeck, one of those specialists, called allegations that the Germans had built the Soviet bomb "entirely false."[79] The Germans were located at two major sites in the Soviet project: Nikolaus Riehl's group at Elektrostal near Noginsk (formerly known as Bogorodsk), forty miles east of

Moscow, which worked on purifying metallic uranium for the reactors; and the multiple laboratories at Sukhumi on the Black Sea coast. Riehl's plant (with its eight German members) was vital, and his uranium went into the first Soviet reactors. Being bilingual (he was born in St. Petersburg to a German Siemens engineer and a Russian-Jewish mother), he was the only German specialist to be integrated at all into the major thrust of Soviet bomb development.

The Germans in Sukhumi worked differently.[80] They were involved mostly in uranium isotope separation and thus by definition were excluded from the plutonium track of the first Soviet bomb. The work was divided into several institutes, labeled according to the initial of the director's last name. In Institute A, located in the Sinop sanatorium, thirty Germans worked on isotope separation (mostly electromagnetic) for Manfred von Ardenne, assisted by Peter Adolf Thiessen (diffusion diaphragms) and Max Steenbeck (centrifuges). In Institute G (the Cyrillic letter that substitutes for H), at the Agudzeri sanatorium at Sukhumi, roughly fifteen scientists and laboratory technicians from the fall of 1945 worked for Gustav Hertz on gaseous diffusion, assisted by Justus Mühlenpford (condensation pumps) and Gustav Barwich (theory of the stability of the separation cascade).[81] By February 1958, all the German specialists had been repatriated.

This work was significant, but it was also redundant. The Germans at Sukhumi created their devices in parallel with and in complete isolation from the other PGU laboratories. Although it is unclear what Beria and Kurchatov had in mind for them, it seems likely that they functioned as a check on the accuracy of the work of the Soviets—a form of quality control similar to the spy data so Beria could be sure that his own scientists were not deceiving him.[82] Thus, although the Germans were not vital for developing or even probably speeding up the Soviet bomb, they played a crucial role in the information flows within the project. They checked (unwittingly) the accuracy of the spy data and the work of the Soviet physicists, mostly about the properties of uranium and the techniques for isotope separation, as can be seen by the allocation of responsibilities at Sukhumi. That checking certainly increased Stalin's and Beria's confidence in the final product: RDS-1.

RDS-1 was the Soviet code name for their first nuclear device. No one is really sure what the initials mean. Or, rather, lots of people are sure—they just don't agree with each other. Khariton claimed that General V. A. Makhnev named it "Stalin's rocket engine" (*reaktivnyi dvigatel' Stalina* = RDS).[83] Others claim that variant is a myth.[84] Still others believe the letters meant "Russia Does It Itself" (*Rossiia delaet sama*); ironic, to say the least. As a matter of record we know that the original report where the name is first mentioned calls it "Rocket Engine S," without specifying the meaning, and at other times it was called "device 501" or "1-200."[85] In another instance, it was called "Rocket Engine Special." All of these variants come with multiple, and contested, claims of authorship.[86]

They are also all misleading. For no matter what you think of the first Soviet bomb, it was certainly not a rocket engine (these were being developed elsewhere in the Soviet Union at the same time). A glance at the model for RDS-1 (figure 1), shown with bomb designer Iulii Khariton, reveals nothing that looks like a rocket engine but instead something that looks an *awful lot* like a Nagasaki-style Fat Man. This device also had very little to do with Stalin, for all of his reputed despotic control over every feature of Soviet life. Beria and Kurchatov were present for all stages of the nuclear test; Stalin was, as we shall see, aware of the impending explosion but was never present. In fact, he never saw the bomb. Khariton would later recall that Stalin had summoned him (Khariton remembered the date as summer 1949 although it probably actually took place in 1947) and asked, "Would it be possible instead of one large [bomb] to make several small ones?" (presumably, with the idea that some would be in reserve after the test).[87] The answer, of course, was no: One needs a critical mass in order to have any nuclear explosion, and Khariton told this to Stalin. So much for his rocket engine.

FIGURE 1 | Khariton sitting with a replica of RDS-1. Visually, the device appears almost identical to the American Fat Man. *Source: V. P. Vizgin, Istoriia Sovetskogo Atomnogo Proekta: Dokumenty, Vospominaniia, Issledovaniia, vyp. 2 (St. Petersburg: Izd. Russkogo Khristianskogo Gumanitarnogo Instituta, 2002), figure 2.*

Stalin, of course, had his suspicions about the reliability of the scientists, but he would have insisted on a test even if he had the utmost confidence in them. For the only way to be sure that RDS-1 was a functioning atomic bomb was to detonate it. It was one thing to cross-check Soviet labs with each other, and again against the Germans, and yet again against the intelligence data and public sources. It was another to see a mushroom cloud. From very early on in the Soviet project, voices from above made it clear that there would have to be a nuclear explosion to verify the years of effort.

The Soviet test dwarfed the Trinity test in terms of preparations and scale. Unlike the Alamogordo explosion, which was conducted by the army under the extreme time pressures of the late stages of the war, Beria and Kurchatov began preparing for the test a full *three years* before it happened. Construction of the Soviet experimental "polygon"—known variously as Mountain Seismic Station, Object 905, Training Proving Ground No. 2 of the Defense Ministry, the country of Limonia, the Semipalatinsk Experimental Proving Ground, or most commonly as Polygon No. 2—began by late 1946, and the Ministry of Defense, which directed the effort, had spent 185 million rubles by 1949.[88] There was even a miniature copy of the polygon at Arzamas-16, so that small-scale replicas of the eventual test could be modeled with conventional explosions (analogous to the American one-hundred-ton test). It was, at the time, one of the most highly instrumented and well-prepared scientific experiments ever performed.

Consider, for a moment, the scope of the polygon's proving grounds, which spanned more than 6,000 square miles. Lieutenant General Nikolai Timofeev directed the construction of a massive series of installations, under the central command of General S. G. Kolesnikov. In the center there stood a 104-foot tower (figure 2), almost an exact analogue to the 100-foot tower of Trinity, except that this tower was equipped with a freight elevator to lift the nuclear device, as well as a reinforced concrete base to allow for calibration and final verification of instruments.[89]

Timofeev erected multiple structures along various radii emanating from ground zero, in order to gain as much data as possible about not just the success of the explosion but also the effect of a nuclear attack on Soviet urban spaces. (Americans would not undertake analogous blast-effects tests until the 1950s; earlier American estimates were derived from the results of the actual combat damage from Hiroshima and Nagasaki.) At 2,600 feet from ground zero, Soviet military engineers built two three-story houses; at 3,200 feet, they placed a section of railroad, complete with a metal bridge and two rail cars; at 3,900 feet, they erected a section of highway with a reinforced concrete bridge, stationing trucks and automobiles upon it. Those construction projects were among the less elaborate ones. At 5,000 feet, the engineers built an electric power station running two diesel generators; at 600–1,000 feet, a subway tunnel 50–100 feet deep; and, finally, two Petliakov-2

FIGURE 2 | The test tower for First Lightning.   *Source*: V. Zhuchikhin, *Pervaia atomnaia: Zapiski inzhenera-issledovatelia* (Moscow: IzdAT, 1993), 85.

bombers were placed 6 miles away from the tower, one positioned as if taking off, the other as if in a steep turn. After two years of round-the-clock construction, animals provided the final touch: dogs, pigs, rats, mice, and even two camels were staked out in the open or inside military equipment (to test the shielding) at various distances. As one of the scientists assigned to measuring the effects recalled:

On the naked spot, far from inhabited areas in two radii from the center at distances of 500, 600, 800, 1,200, 1,800, 3,000, 5,000, and 10,000 meters, instrument arrays were set up in the form of so-called "geese" [V-shaped arrays] of 20-meter size and four-story towers with a casemate inside and underground. Five hundred kilometers of coaxial cable were expended for equipping the experimental field (in a year when only 300 kilometers of it were produced in the entire country). In the rest of the space, in order to test the shock factors of a nuclear explosion, they had placed multiple forms of military equipment, fortifications, and even civilian equipment: bridges, industrial and residential buildings, electric power lines, underground constructions, and a sewage grid. On the ground of the experimental field and inside the military equipment, over a thousand animals were also placed (a quarter of them died during the blast, another quarter within ten days).[90]

Fifteen thousand workers had been very busy.

In addition to the scientific equipment, they had to construct living quarters for the large number of military personnel who were involved in the three years of preparation. A village on the Irtysh River was displaced and the engineers erected a military post in its stead. There was a building for the staff of the military unit, a house for officers, a two-story hotel for temporary visitors, and two eight-apartment homes (one for the command staff and the other a hotel for generals). There was also a two-story canteen and several apartment houses for officers. All of this was designated site "M"; the scientific-production center, "O," was a mile away—and more sites followed. These were supplemented by storage sheds, machining shops, and laboratories for calibrating and verifying measuring devices.[91] This complex was built in essentially the middle of nowhere, backwoods Kazakhstan. M. A. El'iashevich, who directed the optical measurements of the atomic fireball for the State Optical Institute, recalled nothing so much as the distance: "We rode by train [from Moscow] to Novosibirsk (five and a half days), and then to Semipalatinsk and from there by car to the military village of the polygon."[92]

All of these features of the Soviet construction—the enormous

labor, the vast distances, the nuclear topography of the desert—
invite comparison to the Alamogordo test site for Trinity. The contrast is stark. The American test site, located in the desert expanse
of the Jornada del Muerto (Journey of the Dead Man) in New
Mexico, was acquired in the fall of 1944, well under a year before
the July 16, 1945, test date. The land was leased from several
ranchers (principally the McDonald family), contained within
twelve miles of circumference. By April 1945, construction teams
had transformed the landscape, wiring the test site for electricity,
diverting antelope herds, and housing the construction workers
(and, later, the scientists and military personnel). The personnel
never exceeded a few hundred at the peak, and military discipline
was noticeably lax (a fact which infuriated Groves). The expense
for the construction and instrumentation of the ramshackle village
of fewer than three dozen buildings was a bare fraction of that for
the transformation of the former boys' school on the mesa at Los
Alamos.[93] In either case, the costs were *far* below that for the
wholesale metamorphosis of Semipalatinsk-21.

For all the differences between Alamogordo and Semipalatinsk-
21 (the final code name for the site), there was one strong analogy,
which held true for almost every person present in the summer of
1949 for the event dubbed First Lightning (*Pervaia Molniia*): They
had never witnessed the detonation of a nuclear device. (The
exception, on the side of the Soviets, were the few scientists who
had witnessed the atomic tests at Bikini, like Simon Aleksandrov.)
Just as for the people in Alamogordo, this was a real and true test,
in multiple senses. Different people at different layers of the
Soviet atomic project were testing different things at the polygon.
For Khariton and his coworkers from Arzamas-16, this was a test of
the device they had constructed. For Kurchatov, who knew the
quality of his scientists and the scale of the problem, First Lightning was a test of the intelligence material: If that data were truly
reliable, then the bomb would go off. Since he trusted the competence of his people, he thought the variable was the quality of the
information Beria fed him. For Beria and Stalin, who had confi-

dence in their methods of intelligence gathering (more or less; fears of American disinformation never completely subsided), First Lightning tested not only RDS-1; it also tested Soviet *scientists*. Were they reliable? Were they competent? By late August 1949, a great many expectations were projected onto a hunk of metallic plutonium and its attached circuitry.

Although the Americans would later lament how early the Soviet Union managed to explode its first nuclear device, as far as Beria was concerned, the test was already running late. The original schedule of 1946 had projected a test for RDS-1 (the plutonium device) on January 1, 1948, and RDS-2 (the uranium device) on June 1, 1948. Obviously, time had gotten a bit away from them, and the schedule for RDS-1 was moved to February 8, 1948, and then to March 1, 1949. By the spring of 1949, Kurchatov knew that he could stage a test for the summer, and preparations were made accordingly.[94] On August 26, 1949, Stalin issued the final order for the test of the atomic bomb. Among its major points:

2. The test of the atomic bomb is to take place *on August 29– 30*, 1949, at polygon No. 2 (170 km west of Semipalatinsk), built and equipped in accordance with the Decree of the Council of Ministers of the USSR of June 19, 1947, No. 2142-564ss/op.

In order to secure the possibility of conducting the necessary researches and measurements, the test of the atomic bomb is to take place in a stationary position via exploding it on a metallic tower, at a height of 33 m above the ground (without a ballistic casing and instruments necessary for the use of an atomic bomb from an airplane).

3. To ascertain that the task of the test is the achievement of an atomic explosion via the incitement of a rapid chain nuclear reaction in the plutonium charge.

The atomic explosion should be fixed with the help of observations and special instruments and apparatus.[95]

Tasks were allocated accordingly to the various groups. And, in early August, four planes brought the parts of the bombs to Semipalatinsk, where scientists, engineers, and soldiers waited in the hundred-degree heat and blinding dust.

Final preparations for the test took into account the multiple layers of testing. Physicists gave lectures to military officers about the functioning and aftereffects of the bomb, so that the latter would know what to expect when the explosion took place. Since the polygon was equally compartmentalized, only the highest echelons received the benefit of such briefing; most of the people there knew nothing about the bomb's construction and even less about the risks involved.[96] Beyond the possibility of radiation exposure or heat stroke, upper-level scientists like Kurchatov faced more severe penalties in case of failure. A. I. Alikhanov, the director of Laboratory No. 3 and the creator of the first Soviet heavy-water reactor, was asked by Beria to be Kurchatov's "understudy," with the implication that if the test failed, Kurchatov would be shot, and Alikhanov would take over. He refused (and told Kurchatov about it), but that meant only that Beria probably found someone else.[97] These were veterans of the Great Terror of the 1930s and they fully understood the importance Stalin placed on the project. Unemployment and internal exile were the least severe penalties imaginable for failure; imprisonment and death were more likely.

For all the attention lavished on the American scientists' impressions at Trinity, no one has examined in detail the reactions of the Soviet physicists at the polygon to the first Soviet nuclear test. This was, for almost all of them, their first exposure to the power of an explosive fission chain reaction, and one would expect to find analogous expressions of awe and wonder. One would be disappointed. Much as the Soviets spent less time after the fact agonizing over the moral implications of what they had done, they spent less time expressing wonder at the power of their handicraft. The tone of the surviving reports is almost uniformly unemotional and descriptive.

This demonstrates eloquently the attitude of most of the scientists that the polygon was the site of a scientific experiment—a dramatic and geopolitically crucial experiment, to be sure, but first and foremost an experiment to be handled with scientific decorum. The pacing to prepare for the test was strict but allowed for everything to be triple-checked. On August 26 from 8 a.m. until midnight, the explosive charge was fixed in building MAIa-1 and then temporarily moved to building 32P. The next day, from 1 a.m. to 7 a.m., the charge was moved to the central testing zone, where the physicists spent the rest of the day adding instrumentation and testing the connections on the charge. On August 28, the day before the scheduled test, all personnel were granted a rest from midnight to 10 a.m., but then activities resumed. From 10 to 4 in the afternoon, the charge was prepared for priming and the neutron initiators set in place in building FAS. By 9 p.m., the plutonium was added to the central core, at which point the official Soviet commission in charge of the test (Beria, Kurchatov, Khariton, Zaveniagin, and Zernov—Vannikov was ill in Moscow) authorized arming the device. This took A. Fishman and N. A. Terletskii until the wee hours of August 29. At 4:30 a.m. they brought the device over to the tower, and by 5 a.m. Shchelkin and engineer G. G. Lominskii had attached the detonator capsules, and Zernov brought it up on the elevator. By 5:40 a.m. the work was completed, and by 6:20 a.m. everyone had evacuated ground zero. The test was scheduled for 7 a.m., local time.[98]

The description of what happened is best left to those who were there. Veniamin Tsukerman:

> An explosion. A bright flash of light. A column of flame, dragging clouds of dusts and sand with it, formed the "foot" of an atomic mushroom. Kurchatov said only two words: "It worked."
> Half a minute later the shock wave rocked the casemate.

Even before it came, it was clear to everyone that "it had worked." What remarkable words these are: "It had worked! It had worked!"[99]

V. Zhuchikhin:

Two to three seconds after the word "zero," a sharp bump occurred under the feet, a weak movement of the building—and everything went silent. How long the silence lasted, it is hard to recall; it was characteristic that everyone forgot about clocks, no one looked at them, although the sound of them continued; everyone hiding, as if they were waiting for something. Suddenly there followed a deafening blow of force, a crash, and the sound of some kind of turning and grating things. Only then we understood that these sounds were coming from outside. An unimaginable din continued for several seconds, and then everything went silent. People continued to stand in silence, literally hypnotized. And suddenly everyone stirred at once, opened the door and poured out of building KP to see what had happened out there on the field.

At the place where the tower had been, an enormous dust-gas pillar rose as a cloud. The blinding rays of the sun fell to the earth through the enormous expanses of the hole that was forming into clouds. It was already above our heads. Some kind of unknown force continued to shove aside the rain clouds. The gaseous pillar above the place of the explosion achieved enormous extent and height.[100]

A. I. Burnazian:

In the incinerating light we saw how the shock wave thrust off and licked away the clouds from the sky above the site of the nuclear explosion. Tanks were flung about like feathers . . . For a few minutes we observed from the hill the formation of the radioactive cloud. In binoculars one could see the ominously sparkling glassy crust in the center of the explosion from the "frying pan" of the rays of a rising sun.[101]

V. S. Komel'kov:

At the top of the tower an unbearably bright light flared up. For an instant it weakened and then began to grow quickly with new strength. The fiery white sphere swallowed the tower and structure and, rapidly expanding, changing color, strove upward. The basis wave, pushing layers, stone houses, cars out of its path, as a wave, coursing from the center, displacing stones, logs, pieces of metal, dust in one chaotic mass. The fiery sphere, rising and rotating, turned orange, red. Then the dark streaks appeared. After them, as in a funnel, bits of dust, chunks of brick and boards were drawn in. Outstripping the fiery vortex, the shock wave, having hit the upper layers of the atmosphere, went through several layers of inversion, and there, as in a Wilson [cloud] chamber, began the condensation of water vapor.

It was possible to track how the hazy lenses, spreading out in a radial direction from the axis of the explosion, gradually lost their frontal speed and, becoming thinner and thinner, slipped away into nothing. The strong wind weakened the sound, and it reported to us as the din of an avalanche. Above the proving ground rose a gray cloud of sand, smoke, and fog with a cupola-shaped, puffed top, having desiccated two tiers of clouds and layers of inversion. The upper part of this structure, having reached a height of 6–8 km, recalled a cupola of clumps of storm clouds. The atomic mushroom drifted to the south, losing its characteristics, transforming into a formless pile of clouds from a gigantic fire.[102]

There are other accounts of the explosion, the successful detonation of RDS-1 that marked the conclusion of First Lightning.[103] They are all in the same descriptive, mostly dispassionate tone.

This was reasonable, for despite all the links and parallels with

FIGURE 3 | Mushroom cloud of First Lightning, taken one minute after detonation. *Source:* V. Zhuchikhin, *Pervaia atomnaia: Zapiski inzhenera-issledovatelia* (Moscow: IzdAT, 1993), 97.

the American project, we cannot forget that the Soviet test was fundamentally *unlike* its predecessor, which had donated (even if unwittingly) so much information and guidance to Stalin's bomb designers. The Americans witnessed at Trinity something no human being had seen before: a nuclear blast. The Soviets knew that such a blast was possible, knew, in fact, that eight such blasts had taken place already under American auspices. What they found out at First Lightning was not that a nuclear explosion was feasible, but that *they* could produce one. The object of awe was less the explosion than themselves, and they were far too professional, too focused, to expend much effort on self-admiration.

Beria would not grant even that much. Immediately after the explosion, after the shock wave had rocked the command post and the mushroom was forming, he began to worry about whether it really was an atomic blast. Was this what the Americans did? Was the Soviet one just as big? Perhaps bigger? It had better not be smaller! He called M. G. Meshcheriakov, who was observing the test from another post, since Meshcheriakov had been at the Bikini test along with D. B. Skobel'tsyn and Simon Aleksandrov (the only Soviets to witness any previous atomic blasts). He asked, "Was it similar to the American one? Very? We didn't muff it? Kurchatov didn't steal our glasses? Everything was the same? Good. That means we can inform Stalin that the test took place successfully? Good, good."[104] He called Stalin in Moscow immediately, several time zones earlier, and even the famously late-working dictator had gone to bed. Beria enthusiastically told Stalin that RDS-1 had gone off. Stalin, perhaps to put Beria in his place, casually retorted that he already knew, and hung up.[105] Beria was humbled, then furious, but at no one in particular.

Beria's job at the test site was far from over—not to mention the tasks that awaited him as he returned to Moscow and began to organize the production of these weapons and the preparation for tests of future RDS models. The first item on the agenda was to assess the scale of the destruction. Striking clouds of flame were one thing, but this was an experiment, and it was supposed to produce concrete data about the physical consequences of an atomic explosion.

The day after the test, Beria and Kurchatov sent a report to Stalin from the polygon: "On August 29, 1949, at 4 a.m. Moscow time and 7 a.m. local time in the distant steppe region of the Kazakh SSR, 170 km west of Semipalatinsk, the first explosion of an atomic bomb in the USSR, exceptional in the destructive and striking force of its power, was achieved at a specially constructed and equipped experimental polygon." The blast damage to brick buildings showed complete destruction within a radius of 5,000 feet, or 2.5 square miles, and negative conditions for living or working within 4 to 8 square miles (radius of 1.25 to 1.75 miles). Preliminary results indicated no less than 10,000 tons of TNT equivalent.[106] Beria's final report to Stalin noted that the three subway shafts, each 170 feet from the point of destruction, at 30, 60, and 90 feet deep, were all destroyed.[107] Later analysis produced more data points, none of them publicized to individuals below the highest echelon of the nuclear project: Within 10^{-6} second, the fireball had reached about 50 feet in diameter, with a temperature (derived from optical measurements) as high as 540,000°F. Within the next 0.015 second, the range was 325 feet, and the temperature had dropped to 9,000–13,000°F. In 1 second, the fireball reached its maximum range of 500 feet. The bomb had exploded with 15 percent efficiency, which was a full 50 percent higher than anticipated.[108]

The Soviet science system functioned in part through a disbursement of state rewards for a job well done. First Lightning was unquestionably a job well done, and within two months of the test, Stalin had approved an elaborate list that gave different levels of recognition depending on one's estimated level of contribution. The historian David Holloway characterizes the reasoning:

> In deciding on who was to receive which award, Beria is said to have adopted a simple principle: those who were to be shot in case of failure were now to become Heroes of Socialist Labor; those who would have received maximum prison terms were to be given the Order of Lenin, and so on down the list. This story may well be apocryphal, but it nevertheless conveys the feeling of those in the project that their fate hinged on the success of the test.[109]

Not that the list was ever made public; only recently was its full text released from the archives. The awards were given in secret, and they included free housing, free summer dachas, free cars, monetary gifts, and medals. Kurchatov was placed in the highest category all by himself. Among the Germans, who all also received honors, Nikolaus Riehl was by far the most highly rewarded for his work on producing metallic uranium. The other Germans were compensated much like the proletariat of the project—handsomely, but not overly so.[110]

The greatest reward, however, judging from the memoirs of those involved, was that the test had succeeded—that the test of the *scientific competence of the Soviet Union* had succeeded. Anatolii Aleksandrov expressed a common sentiment: "The success of Soviet scientists had once again demonstrated the great power of the socialist system."[111] The reactor engineer Nikolai Dollezhal' echoed this sentiment, with a twist: "And our triumph was great. The country received a mighty sword and with calm satisfaction sheathed it, not drawing it, not threatening; by the very fact of its existence it served as a shield—a sword, created by the talent and industriousness of Soviet people."[112]

For, as Dollezhal' noted, the weapon was sheathed. Very little changed overtly. Soviet scientists now knew that they could make a working nuclear device, and they continued, as before, producing plutonium, separating uranium isotopes, and designing bombs. Beria continued administering the project. Stalin knew that he had a nuclear device—or, more exactly, that he *had* had one, before it exploded on the plains of Kazakhstan. It would be some months before he would have another. For now, he would stay silent, not announce the successful test, and wait. The Americans, across the ocean, greeted the morning of August 29 as they had the morning of the 28th. Nothing in particular was unusual, nothing had changed. Until the winds blowing out of Asia changed everything.

FIVE

MAKING VERMONT

> At last to the east, distant about three degrees appear'd a
> fiery crest above the waves; slowly it reared like a ridge of
> golden rocks, till we discover'd two globes of crimson fire,
> from which the sea fled away in clouds of smoke; and now
> we saw it was the head of Leviathan.
>
> WILLIAM BLAKE, "THE MARRIAGE OF HEAVEN AND HELL"

There is a peculiar symmetry between the first Soviet atomic test of August 29, 1949, and the first American test of July 16, 1945, even beyond the basic fact that the devices exploded were almost identical in fuel, in mechanism, and in test conditions. Only a few hundred Americans were aware of their nuclear blast, and it was not announced for about three weeks, after the destruction of Hiroshima on August 6. Truman's public release was designed to achieve certain political goals, chiefly the ending of the Pacific war. The same was true of the Soviet test: only a few hundred in the know (the vast majority of those who had contributed to the project, as in the American case, were deliberately excluded), and the announcement did not come until several weeks later.

There is another asymmetry. It was not Joseph Stalin or Lavrentii Beria who announced the successful Soviet test. It was no citizen of the Soviet Union or representative of any Communist Party or Soviet bloc state. It was the same man who announced Trinity: President Harry S. Truman issued a release on September 23, 1949. How did this happen? We now know that Stalin was aware of the American test through espionage reports both before and after the fact, but we also know that the United States did not possess any significant agents in the Soviet atomic project. How did the Americans come to know of the Soviet test? This question is most usefully split in two: How did they obtain data related to the Soviet test? and How did that raw data get interpreted in a manner that provided convincing evidence of a Soviet nuclear test?

In short, how do you solve a problem—a deeply complicated, technically difficult problem—that a few years before would never have even occurred to you as existing? Before 1945, very few American politicians, soldiers, or scientists thought about how one might detect a nuclear blast at a very great distance; before 1939, scarcely anyone had even thought about the idea of nuclear blasts. As for how to detect them, the three major proposed systems exploited the features most obviously associated with nuclear explosions: the tremendous power of their blasts (detected either seismically, like earthquakes, or acoustically, like sonic booms), or the radioactive residues they left behind (the radiological method). From the starting line, within ten years from the point of complete ignorance, American decision makers had enough confidence to restructure the cold war on the basis of scientific claims about the long-range detection of atomic explosions. For this to happen, several problems had to be solved: technical, political, and bureaucratic. Only a satisfactory total solution—an outcome that was in much doubt throughout the atomic monopoly—would make nuclear knowledge convincing. Most important in this story, as in the stories that have preceded it, is the central issue of time; only when you have persuaded someone that this is a problem that both can and should be solved, and solved *soon*, can such knowledge be built. And it was built out of wisps of wind, air both hot and cold.

As we have already seen, a cursory glance at the American intelligence structure in late 1945 would have revealed little that reflected either structure or intelligence. In September 1945, Truman had abolished the Office of Strategic Services and then had only slowly begun the tedious process of inventing a national intelligence infrastructure, the first time such an organization had existed in the United States in peacetime. By 1947, the Central Intelligence Agency had been erected, but the agency itself was a newborn foundling in a rapidly expanding Washington bureaucracy, and it was by no means obvious that nuclear intelligence should fall under its purview. In the end, it did not.

The crux of the problem was too many concerned parties and too little sense of urgency to act on those concerns. A partial list of the organizations potentially interested in this problem includes, besides the CIA, the National Security Council (NSC), the Atomic Energy Commission, the State Department, the Joint Chiefs of Staff, the Strategic Air Command (SAC), the Joint Research and Development Board, the Armed Forces Special Weapons Group, the Department of War, the Department of the Navy, the Army Air Forces, and, after their 1947 unification, the National Military Establishment (renamed the Department of Defense in summer 1949); and the separate military intelligence agencies associated with each branch. It was precisely this plurality that worried those, such as William T. Golden, most nervous about the potential for Soviet progress: "In the long run, by being everyone's concern, this will become Mr. Nobody's responsibility."[1] Or, in the view of AEC Commissioner Lewis L. Strauss: "It was nobody's child for over two years after Hiroshima."[2]

Yet the problem of how to acquire hard intelligence about foreign (especially Soviet) atomic developments—in particular the recognition that this was a problem that needed to be solved—was not ignored in the aftermath of Hiroshima. When General Curtis E. LeMay was appointed the deputy chief of staff for research and development in the Army Air Forces (later the U.S. Air Force) in 1946, he quickly initiated work on an airborne nuclear-monitoring system, although with limited technical success.[3] More significantly, Admiral William Leahy, Franklin Roosevelt's wartime chief of staff and thus Truman's at war's end, in 1946 wrote to the president with a request to give authority for atomic intelligence to the newly created director of central intelligence: "The Director of Central Intelligence . . . is hereby authorized and directed to coordinate the collection by agencies subject to coordination by N[ational] I[ntelligence] A[gency] of all intelligence information related to foreign atomic energy developments and potentialities which may affect the national security, and to accomplish the correlation, evaluation, and appropriate dissemination within the Government of the resulting intelligence."[4] And then, after Leahy's order, nothing much happened. Any information that came in was supposed to go to the DCI, but there was no mechanism to acquire such information, particularly since the Soviets were trying to conceal it. The kind of information that grew on trees was not worth much more than the compost it eventually became. Valuable information demanded effort.

The first of the many organizations to notice the lack of notice and act on the lack of activity was the AEC. Credit for solving the problem of long-range detection has usually been assigned to Lewis Strauss, who was certainly the squeakiest wheel in the efforts to get the detection system operational (and also the loudest sounder of his own accolades on this score).[5] As Edward Teller, one of the very few physicists who would remain an admirer of Strauss after the latter engineered the disgrace of J. Robert Oppenheimer in 1954 (and who himself served as the primary weapon in that affair), put it after the end of the cold war, "In the AEC, it seemed that only Lewis Strauss was seriously worried about the Soviets."[6]

In April 1947, Strauss wrote a memo to the other four AEC commissioners, opining that "it would be interesting to know whether the intelligence arrangements of the Manhattan District made any provision in the past for continuous monitoring of radioactivity in the upper atmosphere."[7] Strauss would later deploy this query to several ends, pitting conservative Republican prudence versus liberal Democratic nonchalance (especially with respect to AEC Chairman David E. Lilienthal and his ally Oppenheimer, chairman of the AEC's General Advisory Committee), and also the merits of civilian control of atomic-energy policy against the military incompetence of the Manhattan District. But these shoots grew only in certain soil. Notice that Strauss was *not* calling for a global nuclear-monitoring system. He was calling for monitoring of radioactivity in the upper atmosphere. True, this was one conceivable method for detecting foreign atomic activities, but it was certainly not the only one, and not necessarily the best.[8] In any case, Strauss had no evidence in early 1947 even to know whether such a system was feasible. But this was the system he wanted, and he would not rest until it was created.

The son of a Virginia shoe wholesaler, Strauss resembled Bernard Baruch in being a Southern, Jewish, self-made Wall Street millionaire. That was where the resemblance ended. Strauss was a dyed-in-the-wool Republican compared to Baruch's conservative Democratic credentials, and Strauss's most prominent features were his bald dome and spectacles. (Baruch was proud of his own full head of hair and his unadorned profile.) With little more than a high school education, Strauss convinced future president Herbert Hoover to take him on as a research assistant for the Food Administration in 1917, and within a month had so impressed the practical engineer that he became his private secretary. In 1919, he joined the prestigious Wall Street law firm of Kuhn, Loeb; married the daughter of a partner; and achieved partner status himself in 1929. Long an admirer of the navy, he had obtained a commission as a naval reserve officer in 1925 and went on active duty in 1941 as the assistant to Secretary of the Navy James V. Forrestal, to whom he remained close up to the latter's suicide in May 1949. Although he never went to college, Strauss had a sharp mind and a deep interest in science (especially nuclear physics), and during the war served as the navy's wartime representative on matters concerning atomic energy, which proved a good training ground for his future career.[9]

In an effort to keep the infant AEC bipartisan (in correspondence with his foreign policy), President Truman nominated Strauss to it in 1946. One of the first issues he raised concerned atmospheric detection. Although he was not the only person interested in nuclear monitoring, he was one of the most persistent, and his dogged insistence on a solution to the problem of atmospheric radiological detection was certainly one of the principal reasons this particular method was later implemented.

Strauss's April 1947 memorandum to the AEC was forwarded to the various loops of intelligence and military circles, and the responses were not satisfactory, either to Strauss or to the rest of the AEC. "Although two years have passed since Alamogordo, the United States still has no systematic monitoring system to determine whether and where atomic bombs are exploded in other parts of the world," William Golden, assigned to sound out the status of any existing monitoring programs, wrote Strauss in May. "The real problem is not one of technique but of organization. Primary responsibility for the establishment and operation of a detection system must be placed with a single organization." He concluded with a prediction of progress: "It was stated at the conference that *two years would be required, from the date of starting* (i.e., four years after Hiroshima) to have a comprehensive monitoring system functioning on a dependable basis." Strauss scrawled in the margin of Golden's memorandum: "Too long!!"[10] The GAC was of like mind, as Oppenheimer wrote to Lilienthal in October 1947: "The Advisory Committee has as its primary concern, not that it be informed about progress in this work, but that the progress be adequate and the work in competent hands."[11] The other members of the AEC agreed, but they also knew that their organization had neither the resources nor the status to foster such a program.[12] Who could?

Strauss turned to his closest ally in the Truman cabinet: James Forrestal, then secretary of the navy and from September 17, 1947, the first secretary of defense. According to Strauss's (admittedly self-serving) memoir account, Forrestal was positive someone in the military must have already begun this program, exclaiming, "Hell! We must be doing it!" Strauss responded logically that the navy was not doing it, or Forrestal would already know, and he would find from inquiries to the Pentagon that neither army ground forces nor army air forces were either. Demonstrating how much of the solution to this problem was bureaucratic-organizational as well as technical, he subtly threatened Forrestal that if the military did not undertake this project, the AEC would. The AEC, however, was underfunded and would have to go to Congress to ask for additional appropriations. "When we ask for the money," he told Forrestal, "that will be the first time Congress will know that monitoring hasn't been going on all this time."[13]

Forrestal's diary account of this meeting differs in important respects—not about the facts of the matter, but about the emphasis. According to Forrestal, Strauss attempted to link the orphaning of the detection project with the AEC-military debate over custody of nuclear weapons, which he knew was a sore spot with Forrestal. The secretary refused to take the bait:

> In connection with his discussion of readiness he mentioned the fact that in September of last year the question of monitoring the atmosphere for evidences of radioactive disturbance had been assigned to the Armed Forces but that no steps had been taken to discharge this responsibility until roughly three months later when the Commission had a visit from General Spaatz. I said I did not think this was analogous because it was a much more abstract question than the very hard and realistic one provided by the matter of custody.[14]

For Strauss, the lethargy about long-range detection stemmed from a typical military complacency that should be remedied by hard-headed civilian accountability. The military's casual attitude, he was convinced, hinged on its belief that Soviet proliferation was in the far distant future, relying on Leslie Groves's assessment that this would be a problem for their grandchildren rather than for themselves. But for Strauss, Soviet proliferation was only one reason for the utility of the program; he was equally worried about *false* claims of proliferation used for atomic blackmail. He believed an effective monitoring system could debunk those claims: "Any delay in the establishment of thoroughgoing air monitoring will incur the hazard that a test of a spurious weapon may be made by another power (accompanied by effects for observers) which, unless its true character can be ascertained, would have unpredictable but important repercussions on our international relations."[15]

In 1948, Strauss committed his version of this history to paper as part of a campaign of memoranda to nudge the program into operation: "It will be noted that the subject was dormant until the Atomic Energy Commission pressed for its activation in the Spring of 1947 after taking office and discovering its status."[16] Supposedly, Strauss put his money where his mouth was, for when it seemed in January 1948 that the funds for the prototype system's instrumentation during the upcoming Sandstone tests were insufficient, "Mr. Strauss said that he had informed them that because of the urgency of the subject, he would be personally responsible to see that funds were provided although it was late in the day. The Commission approved proposals by Mr. Strauss that it consider transfer of the required funds, estimated at $1,000,000 [just under $9 million in 2009 dollars], upon receipt of a formal request from the Air Force, in view of the urgency of the matter." The AEC authorized the transfer of $1.5 million on January 13 to cover Strauss's bets.[17] With the passage of a year, one finds the rarest of documents penned by Strauss—an enthusiastic expression of satisfaction.[18] He had succeeded.

Strauss's hot potato had landed in the lap of the U.S. Air Force.

Of all the victories the Army Air Forces accomplished in the Second World War, perhaps none was greater than the public-relations victory that persuaded Congress and a good portion of the American electorate that strategic bombing was and would continue to be the crucial edge to military victory—especially against the Soviet Union. Thus, when unification of the army and navy into a single National Military Establishment came in the autumn of 1947, the two branches were accompanied by a third: the United States Air Force.[19] Given the disparity of manpower in conventional forces, the Soviet Union's negligible navy, and the tremendous distance to the Soviet heartland, bombing from American bases in European and Middle Eastern countries provided one of the only means of threatening (and thus, in principle, deterring) the Soviet Union. The atomic bomb was the central ingredient of this strategy, and this gave the USAF reason enough to be concerned about the status of the American atomic monopoly.

General Hoyt Vandenberg, then recently retired as head of the CIA, was awarded the dubious honor of responsibility for long-range nuclear detection by the chief of staff, General Dwight Eisenhower, on September 16, 1947—two days before the AAF achieved autonomy as the USAF: "The Commanding General, Army Air Forces, is hereby charged with the over-all responsibility for detecting atomic explosions anywhere in the world. This responsibility is to include the collection, analysis and evaluation of the required scientific data and the appropriate dissemination of the resulting intelligence."[20] This was intended to include only *technical* monitoring, however, not human intelligence. Lest he be misunderstood, Eisenhower requested on November 5 that the phrase "long-range detection devices" be inserted into the above order, because "it is possible the original wording could be misinterpreted to include espionage activities."[21] Since USAF intelligence (A-2) had a reputation for being more technically savvy than the other military intelligence agencies, this allocation made some sense.[22] It also intrinsically biased the program toward airborne radiological monitoring.

So far, as Strauss and the AEC well understood, the responsibility existed only on paper, and some specific (and, they hoped, competent) individual needed to be entrusted with this task—which, one must recall, was regarded as not urgent by most military brass and political elites throughout the late 1940s.[23] Major General Albert F. Hegenberger returned to the United States from his service in occupied Japan shortly after Eisenhower's order, and on December 5, 1947, was assigned to the Armed Forces Special Weapons Group, the military counterpart to the civilian AEC. Nine days later, the group's commander, Major General William Kepner, placed Hegenberger in charge of a new section within his group to be dubbed AFMSW-1 (Air Force Deputy Chief of Staff for Materiel, Special Weapons Group, Section 1).[24] Other branches of the military and intelligence communities, unwilling to see the air force absorb yet more resources and prestige, wanted in, and on December 31, 1947, the navy and the CIA joined with the USAF to form the Joint Nuclear Energy Intelligence Committee (JNEIC). The process of bureaucratic mutation continued apace. In July 1948, AFMSW-1 was transferred to the Office of the Deputy Chief of Staff for Operations of the USAF, and Hegenberger's organization was rechristened AFOAT-1 (Air Force Deputy Chief of Staff for Operations, Atomic Energy Office, Section 1).[25]

Eisenhower's mandate had come with no additional funds, and certainly the USAF—the most expensive of the three forces under the cost-cutting Truman ax—was unwilling to divert resources from its commitments. The costs would be significant. Strauss's one-track lobbying, to the extent that it produced a result, had managed to force the National Military Establishment to at least attempt to solve this problem through some device attached to aircraft. The air force did not want to divert any crews from priority missions for seemingly pointless reconnaissance flights over the Bering Sea—the probable path of air masses from the Soviet heartland. The Air Weather Service, however, seeing detection as an opportunity to enhance their profile, offered to carry the necessary equipment on their routine flights, thus doubling the utility of their prioritized meteorological missions. This not only solved a budget problem but also helped solidify the Air Weather Service's identity at the moment when it had just been downgraded from an independent command to a submerged position within the Air Transport Command.[26]

Strauss had reason to be satisfied. He had gotten what he wanted: bureaucratic delegation of responsibility, the personal satisfaction that *he* had moved mountains, and the promise of an airborne system. But what exactly was this system to be? Strauss certainly did not know (and there is little evidence that he cared for the details). Yet one finds that this problem had been tackled by many people before Lewis Strauss grappled with it. Solutions— or at least hints of approximations of approaches to potential solutions—began to crop up even before the atomic bomb was developed.

The quest for the Holy Grail of long-range detection began, as Strauss's had, with fear of a nuclear enemy, although the enemy was Nazi Germany and the time was 1943. General Leslie Groves would in time turn sanguine about the possibility of other nations obtaining nuclear weapons, but during the war he was obsessed with the possibility of a German bomb. He recruited the young experimental physicist Luis Alvarez (later to fly in the instruments plane during the bombing of Nagasaki and then to win the 1968 Nobel Prize in physics) to design some device to detect whether or not the Germans had managed to produce a working reactor. (Unlike the British, Groves refused to accept the indications of signals and human intelligence that the Germans had not prioritized their atomic-energy program.) Alvarez moved his office to the University of Chicago campus so he could be nearer to the physics library, and he concluded that perhaps the best indicator of a working reactor would be the emission of the telltale noble gas isotope, xenon 133.

Hitting upon xenon was a good idea, but it was a far cry from a working device. Alvarez traveled to the General Electric plant in Cleveland, where lightbulb manufacture had resulted in considerable experience handling argon (another noble gas). He then contracted with General Electric to build a device that would fit in the bombardier's compartment of a Douglas A-26.

In essence, the device was an elaborate activated-charcoal air filter. When air passed over the filter, the charcoal would trap atmospheric xenon and radon gases but not the much more copious oxygen or nitrogen. The captured gases were chemically inert, and the radon needed to be eliminated before the xenon could be analyzed for the telltale variant. The charcoal was heated, and the resultant gases passed into a stream of helium, then over charcoal again, but at a temperature that would freeze out the radon (which has a higher boiling point) and isolate the xenon. With the helium pumped out, the xenon could be analyzed. Test runs over Cleveland proved that it could work, and three planes flew sorties over selected sites in Germany in 1944 and found nothing.[27] Although they produced no positive signal, Alvarez's (and Groves's) efforts demonstrate that the question of how to do airborne detection (or any detection at all) was not the simple product of Strauss's 1947 memo.

Fearing that the Germans might use radiological warfare (radioactive isotopes mixed with drinking water, foodstuffs, or conventional explosives) during the Normandy invasion and after, Groves authorized Operation Peppermint, an effort to equip invading forces with photographic film, Geiger counters, and basic information about radiological warfare.[28] Likewise, the Alsos mission to track down the personnel and data from the German project did not rely only on interviews and archival gathering but also sampled water from sites like the lower Rhine in order to ascertain whether nuclear activities were occurring along its tributaries.[29] This was a long way from atomic test detection, but it did demonstrate an awareness of the basic features of radiation that might leave environmental traces for the prepared sleuth.

The only way to make sure that you were actually detecting a nuclear explosion, however—to ascertain that instruments were properly calibrated and not registering false positives or negatives—was to set off a nuclear explosion of your own (creating a signal whose place and time you know) and use it to focus your equipment. Obviously, the only people who could set off such explosions for calibration purposes before 1949, and thus the only ones who could set the baseline for the instrumentation of long-range detection, were the Americans, monopolists of the bomb. In fact, a major factor in slowing the development of a viable detection system was the limited number of nuclear explosions—eight—produced by the United States in the monopoly period.[30]

During the Trinity test, the emphasis was on speed, and there was little time to set up instrumentation at the site to evaluate long-distance effects. The measurements done at Trinity, ranging from seismographic work to short-distance examination of fallout patterns—itself a completely new problem drawn from studies of Saharan sand dunes, Chemical Warfare Service cloud-drift data, air pollution analysis, and the physics of airplane vapor trails—were ordered by Groves only to forestall potential future lawsuits about radiation damage that might be filed after the news of the test was publicly released.[31] As for the bombings of Hiroshima and Nagasaki, the Manhattan Engineering District was so caught up in the endgame of the Second World War—and the possible production of more bombs for further atomic bombing—that no one bothered taking measurements of the radioactive cloud as it drifted across the Pacific.[32]

The military was not the only one watching, though. After the war had ended and limited information about Trinity was released, scientists began to reinterpret anomalous results obtained from routine measurements and found a plausible link to the test bombing: Sites in the Midwest and on the East Coast had unwittingly "detected" the Trinity test in Alamogordo, New Mexico. Not only does this spate of articles demonstrate the convergence of a scattered array of scientists on an interesting problem, but the fact that they were published in the open scientific literature indicates that this problem of long-range detection was seen as too minor to trigger military censorship until 1947.

It turns out that the first atomic test was caught on film, although thousands of miles away, thanks to copious rainfall. In an article published only in August 1949 in *Physical Review*, the premier journal of the American physics community—and in the postwar era, the most prominent physics journal in the world—a group of scientists reported experimental observations of September and December 1945, demonstrating another way the flow of knowledge was intimately tied to the flow of material products. They had noticed, in examining their stock of green 14" x 17" film used for industrial X-rays, that tiny pinhole-sized dots and minuscule thin lines corrupted the newly unpacked sheets. Tracing back to the source of the film, Eastman Kodak in Rochester, New York, they found the problem came from the strawboard in which the film was packed, which proved to be mildly radioactive. *That* material had come from two paper mills, one in Vincennes, Indiana, which drew the water for the production of its cardboard from the Wabash River, and another five hundred miles to the west in Tama, Iowa, which drew from the Iowa River. Deducing that the source of the contamination was the water in the rivers, recently swelled by rainfall, by factoring in wind velocities and dates of precipitation they concluded that fission products from Trinity "were detected by photographic means on paper stock derived from raw products and manufactured in a paper mill at a location approximately 1000 miles from the point of detonation."[33]

This September 1945 observation was the first long-range detection (though not reported for some years). It was not, however, the only one. In late November 1945, more radioactive-rainfall results were reported from Annapolis.[34] (Seismic results from Alamogordo published in the open literature in 1946 demonstrated that it was still difficult to obtain good measurements of the tremors induced by the shockwave of an atomic blast—at least at great distances.[35])

Given the failure to obtain *any* significant long-range data from the atomic bombings of Hiroshima and Nagasaki, the next nuclear explosions that could be used to calibrate instruments were the Able and Baker test shots of Operation Crossroads, detonated at the Bikini atoll in the South Pacific on July 1 and 25, 1946, respectively. Billed in its official history as "perhaps the most elaborate scientific tests ever conducted," the test series was authorized by the Joint Chiefs of Staff ostensibly to evaluate the effects of atomic blasts on naval hardware (the weapons were modified Fat Men of World War II vintage), but more plausibly to demonstrate the navy's involvement in atomic decisions to their rivals in the AAF and to showcase American might to assembled observers from the United Nations (including two Soviet scientists).[36] The grander political objectives did not obviate the need for careful instrumentation, a problem that Los Alamos director Norris Bradbury would later characterize as "beyond belief; the logistics were fantastic."[37] A segment of the government's instrumentation array—a small and low-priority segment—concerned long-range detection.

The results were disappointing, at least those produced at short to medium range, the only distances able to be monitored by Los Alamos on the short notice the intramilitary infighting over schedules provided. Seismographs were able to register the underwater Baker test of July 25, but not the July 1 airburst, indicating that this mechanism of long-range detection could easily be subverted by countermeasures.[38] Radiological detection fared a little better. Planes with oil-bathed air filters gathered samples at increasing distances from Bikini: Guam (1,600 miles), Okinawa (1,900 miles), Hawaii (2,100 miles), Spokane, Washington (4,500 miles), Tucson, Arizona (4,700 miles), Tampa, Florida (6,500 miles), and Panama (8,000 miles). The filters for each flight were tested in Berkeley, California, at an Army Corps of Engineers laboratory, and indicated some limited capacity to record the tests at significant distances, although the results were far from unequivocal.[39]

The unofficial reports—the data produced by independent scientists analyzing their routine observations—were less encouraging. All of the results of the various methods were either inconclusive or downright negative. In Houston, Texas (among other places), laboratories indicated a mild anomaly in the frequency of detected gamma rays, which appeared to be correlated with the Bikini blasts.[40] Once again seismic results—published like the gamma-ray anomalies in the open literature—were inconclusive.[41] Official radiation filter results (classified, of course) might have suggested the tentative feasibility of the radiological method of long-range detection when the filters were mounted on airplanes, but ground-based radiation detection was a dud. An analysis of the Baker results published in September 1946 left no room for doubt: "No general correlation of the total radioactive intensity with the explosion of the bomb was obtained."[42] Others agreed: "From the evidence presented here it is practically certain that no effects from the Bikini test were in evidence in the North Atlantic states, more than 7000 miles from the Bikini Islands."[43]

A classified report written in October 1946 cited much of this publicly available literature and discussed the options for seismic, sonic (measuring pressure differences in the atmosphere using microbarographs), and radiological testing, with an emphasis on detecting an atomic *test* at a distance. (The unquestioned assumption was that any nuclear program would necessarily test the devices before attempting to use them militarily, reasoning from the experience of the Manhattan Project.) The report noted that seismometers in Australia, sensitive to earth displacements of up to one-thousandth of an inch, failed to register anything from Bikini, three thousand miles away.[44] With seismic detection ruled out at present, the authors even discussed more outlandish detection options, such as looking for effects on the opposite point on Earth's surface—which was Ascension Island in the Atlantic Ocean for the Bikini tests—similar to the antipodal depressions caused by the 1883 Krakatoa volcanic eruption. Unfortunately, no nuclear blast then conceivable would come even close to the violence of Krakatoa, and so this option was quietly shelved.[45] The authors likewise dismissed the possibility of ground-based air filtration for radiological monitoring: "The above reported increases in radioactivity are isolated reports in which the observed effects are rather small and could easily have been in error."[46] The secret report's conclusion from Crossroads: No form of long-distance monitoring was ready to be deployed and, pending further nuclear tests, one could know no more.

But what if the whole approach were wrongheaded? As noted above, almost all the then current detection methods were geared toward detecting a nuclear *test*. Edward Teller, the bushy-eye-browed physicist who consistently voiced the alarmist view of the nuclear future, thought the Soviet Union would refrain from detonating a nuclear bomb, being far too clever to repeat what the Americans did: "One reason that may deter them is the fact that detonation of a bomb is not easily kept secret. Firing of a Russian bomb would inform us of the progress they are making. The Russians might wish to delay a bomb test in order not to give us premature warning of their strength."[47] Instead, Teller worried that the Soviets might simply develop nuclear reactors and use the waste products to conduct radiological warfare (analogous to Groves's fears in Operation Peppermint). In that case, all the detection mechanisms then proposed would be inadequate. William Golden wrote to AEC commissioner Robert Bacher suggesting a different approach: "It may be more timely to devise methods for detecting pile operations (and, if ingenuity can devise the technique, U-235 separation activities) than the detection of an atomic bomb test."[48] No one questioned, however, that the solution to this problem—whichever problem it was—was going to have to be technical and laboratory based.[49]

The situation, in brief, at the time of Strauss's 1947 mobilization, was the following: There was no mechanism that was sure to detect a test that might never be conducted, and was not expected for a great many years, if ever. There was no pressure, no target, no mechanism, and no point.

Then, in 1948, came Sandstone.

Conducted at the Eniwetok atoll in the Marshall Islands in the South Pacific, this series of three nuclear tests (X-Ray, Yoke, and

Zebra) comprised the first nuclear tests under the jurisdiction and control of the AEC.[50] The undisputed success of Sandstone verified the first major innovations in nuclear weapons design since the end of the war, including levitated cores and plutonium-uranium hybrids, both of which allowed for the minimization of warheads and hence ended the age of nuclear scarcity through more efficient use of fuel. The Sandstone tests were in several senses the inverse of Crossroads: Tests exceeded expectations, instead of the relative disappointments of Bikini; interservice cooperation reached new levels of amity; and long-range detection scored its first, though preliminary, successes.[51]

The announcement of the test, which was not performed with any of the international observers or public-relations fanfare that had surrounded Crossroads, emphasized the scientific, not the military, features of the detonations: "The tests of Operation Sandstone were literally and truly field laboratory tests."[52] It should be noted that even this very limited public announcement was a bone of contention in an administration that had grown wary of releasing *any* information about nuclear matters for fear of repeating the controversy around the Smyth Report. AEC chairman David Lilienthal fumed about this reflexive taciturnity in his diary: "It is not feasible to have a test without some public statement; and a test is essential to the present program."[53] As he reiterated in April 1948 in the face of military resistance to announcing the test: "I object on the ground that the Russians will know, and so will everyone except the American people."[54]

One of the reasons the Sandstone tests were initially delayed, and the laconic announcement as well, was fear that the Soviets would use long-range detection methods such as airborne filters to pick up residues from the bombs and hence reverse-engineer the Los Alamos innovations.[55] Ironically, such an airborne system was precisely one of the methods that the Americans were trying to test. In any case, Lilienthal got his wish, and his announcement, which revealed little about what had happened on the ground. (Even today, information about long-range detection constitutes one of the few features of these tests that the historian is permitted to access.)

Strauss, who claimed he was almost forced to front his own money for the instrumentation, understood that these tests would be crucial for solving the calibration difficulty of long-range detection.[56] The project for testing the proposed detection methods (Operation Fitzwilliam) was directed by Dr. Ellis A. Johnson, the scientific director of AFMSW-1. Johnson, an MIT graduate, had taken a post at the Carnegie Institution in 1935, and worked at the Naval Ordnance Laboratory during the war. (By chance, he had been present at Pearl Harbor during the attack of December 7, 1941.) He organized 466 air-sampling sorties for a total of 4,944 hours in the air, as well as seismic teams from the Coast and Geodetic Survey for short-range work on Runit, Parry, and Aniyaaii atolls near Eniwetok. Naval Ordnance Laboratory seismographs were distributed at eight sites in the Pacific, including Kwajalein and Eniwetok. These methods had all been tried before at Crossroads, though not with instruments of such sensitivity.

New methods were tested as well. The Signal Corps and the Naval Ordnance Laboratory established sonic sensors of various sorts. The army erected an array of more than twenty acoustical sensors, while the USAF sent theirs up attached to a series of Project Mogul balloons. These high-altitude balloons were launched from Kwajalein (450 miles from ground zero), Guam (1,200 miles), Hawaii (2,750 miles), and even from as far away as New Mexico and Alabama. Two Army Signal Corps teams, led by D. M. Crenshaw and D. J. Southard, made efforts to detect any light from the test that might be reflected off the surface of the moon— one of the more far-fetched detection attempts—through telescopes attached to photoelectric devices at Guam and Eniwetok.[57] Naval Ordnance Laboratory magnetometers to measure post-atomic electromagnetic disturbances were placed at Eniwetok and Kwajalein. A hypothesized "ionospheric dimple" above the point of detonation (theoretically detectable through radio-wave interference) was searched for from an installation on Kwajalein. As far away as Los Alamos (5,000 miles), scientists sought minute changes in the sky's illumination. Even if long-range detection happened to be only a subsidiary priority of the tests of the new devices at Sandstone, it cannot be said it was neglected.

Most of the results for the three tower bursts were terrible. The Yoke shot (forty-nine kilotons of TNT equivalent) was the largest nuclear explosion the world had yet seen and still could not be detected by seismometers at distances of more than 500 miles away. Ellis Johnson evaluated the program: "In connection with the seismic program . . . in the present state of the art, there is only about a one to one chance of success in distinguishing between an earthquake and a major explosion. Furthermore, [Johnson] did not think there was much chance by seismic methods of distinguishing a deep underground atomic explosion from a similar explosion of an appropriate quantity of chemical explosives."[58] Sonic measurements were slightly (but only slightly) better, detecting Yoke at 1,700 miles, but the eighteen-kiloton explosion at only 1,000 miles. This was woefully inadequate if one wanted to detect a supposed test in the center of the Soviet heartland.[59]

Among the three major detection methods available, this left the radiological method, collected by airborne filters. For this method, the results were better; Flight C of the 373rd Reconnaissance Squadron, Very Long Range Weather, based in Lagens in the Azores (halfway around the world), had definitely registered the tests.[60] Partisans of long-range detection optimistically interpreted the data as a qualified success, making it seem that a tower or ground burst might be detectable at the requisite ranges (although it appeared as though a burst in midair might provide an adequate countermeasure by minimizing fallout production).[61] Lilienthal chose to ally with the optimists: "With the system working, everything except an explosion in a cave, etc., would hardly go undetected, and even some idea of its force at given distances. The travels of the radioactive clouds, dispersed to a width of several miles, around the globe, was fascinating."[62]

Thus the only viable system was an airborne radiological-monitoring network. The tests, with their mildly positive results, mostly concerned gathering the radioactive fallout for analysis; the physics and chemistry of how to analyze it was by 1948 straightforward. The extremely hot fireball from the atomic blast would scoop up dust and earth into the column of the mushroom cloud, where molten fission products would condense around the dust particles and then rise on the hot winds into the upper atmosphere, where they would be carried on prevailing winds. Assuming the particles were carried far enough and were present in a density large enough to be collected, they could be filtered out of the air and presented for isotopic analysis.

This is precisely what it sounds like: an analysis of isotopes—differently weighted variants of atoms of particular elements—of the radioactive material present in the sample. One cannot, however, simply read back the content of the original fission isotopes from the isotopic mix, because each of the radioactive atoms decays according to a characteristic rate (its half-life), different for each isotope. By measuring the intensity of the so-called beta radiation (the emission of stray electrons from radioactive atoms), one could extrapolate from the current mix of short-lived and long-lived isotopes, climbing backward along the decay chains of the isotopes. If the net result of this retrospective clambering was a single "birthday" that made sense of all of the isotopes present, then the radioactive particles were probably the result of an explosion (volcanic or atomic). If the results produced no consistent single birthday, one was probably dealing with something continuous: a reactor or natural emissions of radioactivity. Naturally, this worked only because physicists around the world had already measured half-lives of the relevant isotopes to a high degree of accuracy over the half century of research into radioactivity.[63]

So much for the theory. Actually filtering the fallout, decomposing it into its constituent particles, measuring the half-lives, and analyzing the mix required a specialist. Enter Tracerlab. This company was founded in March 1946 by veterans of the MIT-based Rad Lab, which had developed radar during the Second World

War (and, despite the name, had absolutely nothing to do with radioactivity or nuclear-related radiation). William Barbour, age thirty-seven at the time, an MIT graduate and a major in the AAF, gathered former colleagues, like the young MIT physicist Wendell Peacock, to build an electronics firm that would capitalize on the budding AEC-sponsored research area of radioisotopes (mostly for biological research or medical treatment). Tracerlab was an exciting young company in 1946, and in 1948 it became the only civilian organization brought into Fitzwilliam, where it accomplished tasks as varied as assessing data and training military personnel in the handling of Geiger counters. It soon emerged as the sole subcontractor for analyzing any radiological findings from the long-range-monitoring system.[64]

Tracerlab formed, with an initial military contract of $1,107,000, the civilian edge of a military detection system erected under the auspices of the air force with the cooperation of the CIA at the instigation of the AEC. Fitzwilliam turned into Whitesmith, and then in a standard change of name to preserve security, Whitesmith in February 1949 became Bequeath: the official name of the *interim* long-range-monitoring system.[65] It was interim because no one was especially enthusiastic about airborne radiological monitoring, which was expensive, time-consuming, unreliable, and prone to countermeasures—such as artificial dispersals from conventional bombs laced with radioactive isotopes, exploding the bomb at a high altitude to minimize fallout, or simply detonating it underground. On the other hand, the theoretically more reliable seismic and acoustic monitoring proved operational failures. No one had any better ideas.

The Joint Chiefs of Staff resolved on March 28, 1948, that they would back an interim radiological system although the Joint Research and Development Board (RDB), under the leadership of Vannevar Bush, advised against it. But the JCS insisted that a system be operational by mid-1950, and since it was unlikely that a better system could be introduced by then, they authorized a flawed system rather than none at all.[66]

Flawed and expensive. Original program requirements were set at $30 million: $4.7 million for "nuclear" ($41.4 million in 2009 dollars), $6.4 million ($56.3 million) for seismic, $8.9 million ($78.4 million) for sonic, $3.6 million ($31.7 million) for "surveillance," and $6.4 million ($56.4 million) for contingencies and repayment of advances; the cost of the flights was not included in these figures. This total was cut to $12 million and then $6 million, mostly because the RDB thought that the $8 million already spent on the radiological approach sufficed and they wanted to shift the rest to the other possible long-range-detection methods.[67] These numbers might appear a bit counterintuitive, since the RDB seemed to be denying funding to the only mechanism that worked. Strauss thought so, too. Yet Bush and his peers believed strongly that the countermeasures to the airborne system were so simple and obvious that the money already spent on it was more than enough—and likely to have been wasted. Nonetheless, money continued to be spent. In March 1949, shortly after the erection of the interim system, building on the same nagging worry that something must be afoot in Siberia, Congress authorized $85.5 million ($762.3 million in 2009) for a radar early-warning system for bombers and missiles to be placed across the Canadian north.[68]

Strauss was delighted, writing in February 1949, "I did think that under the present system, a test of a bomb in air would have nine chances out of ten of detection."[69] Those figures seem to be based on little more than conjecture, but optimism was the order of the day (unless you happened to serve on the RDB). The few leaks in the media about the erection of a long-range detection network gave the public a misleading impression that such detection would be relatively straightforward and that it would be easy to sift out true nuclear explosions from accidents, volcanic eruptions, chemical explosions, and other false positives.[70]

The actual interim system was a Rube Goldberg contraption held together by spit, sealing wax, and immense effort and ingenuity. Reading through popular accounts of atomic-test detection both at the time and since, one might walk away with the impression that finding out if there had been a nuclear test in the Soviet Union was much like checking one's answering machine: a light beeps, you press a button, and you learn the news. In reality, it was much more like dusting the entirety of the Empire State Building for fingerprints *every day*, on the off chance that the fingerprints of a specific individual might show up, someone you do not expect to arrive for roughly a decade. Except it was even more complicated than that; for "Empire State Building," substitute "atmosphere of the northern hemisphere."

The fingerprint kit was soon dubbed by Arctic flight crews the "bug-catcher." It was not a term of affection. The instrument for airborne detection consisted of a 9" x 22" filter pressed between two layers of open-mesh wire screen, which was then pushed through the fuselage so the air at 18,500 feet could wash over it. The bug-catcher was located in an unpressurized section of the Air Weather Service B-29s and had to be changed during the flight, which meant the crew was routinely exposed to −60°F temperatures every few hours.[71] This only exacerbated the general hazards of flying in the Arctic, which included malfunctioning carburetors due to poor heating capacity, icing fog, inadequate polar charts, and navigation complications due to the proximity of the magnetic north pole.[72] Upon landing, the several filters from the bug-catcher were quickly scanned with a Geiger counter. If they registered more than 100 counts per minute (cpm)—lowered on August 1, 1949, to 50 cpm (both levels set by Sandstone and operational experience)—they were whisked to Tracerlab for analysis.[73]

Parallel to Bequeath, and running at just over 10 percent of the cost ($150,000 [$1.34 million in 2009]), was the Naval Research Laboratory's Project Rainbarrel, following the hint of the original Kodak results to examine radioactivity levels in rainwater, which brought dust particles down from the troposphere without having to fly up to fetch them. (The disadvantage, obviously, was that it required good—or poor, depending on your perspective—weather conditions involving lots of precipitation.) The brainchild of Roger Revelle in the spring of 1947, Rainbarrel was another installment in the navy's struggle not to be shut out of nuclear matters by the air force. Seventy-five counters, each consisting of a nest of seven large Geiger counters hooked up in anticoincidence (to eliminate the natural background from cosmic rays) and mostly constructed in-house, were operational by the time of Sandstone. In June 1948, following the three nuclear tests, NRL scientists obtained water from the Virgin Islands (whose entire water supply was provided by rainwater trapped in tremendous cisterns), and using five-hundred-gallon decontamination trucks from the Chemical Weapons Service, treated the water to settle the flocculent and siphon off the clear water. After treating two thousand five hundred gallons, they obtained about five gallons of "floc," which was found to contain the fission products yttrium 91, cerium 141, and cerium 144 in ratios indicating origins in Sandstone. The navy passed this information on to AFOAT-1, as decreed in the original Eisenhower order, but (perhaps not surprisingly) received little information in return.[74] It was a longshot and an iffy solution to a problem that not everyone was certain needed to be resolved, but at least it was in place.

And so, several times a week, on multiple routine flights between Alaska and the Soviet Pacific coast, and whenever it rained at NRL stations in Alaska or Washington, D.C., scientists and soldiers dusted the world for fingerprints. By the beginning of September, alert levels of 50 cpm had been exceeded 111 times. One hundred and eleven false alarms, each explicable by natural causes.

The 112th was Vermont, which proved to be something completely different.

On Saturday, September 3, 1949, Lieutenant Robert Johnson flew his B-29 weather plane at eighteen thousand feet on the Loon Charlie route between Japan and Alaska, his crew exposing and changing the bug-catchers as usual. Several filter papers were exposed on this flight, and two were somewhat out of the ordinary. The first, exposed to the winds wafting across the fuselage for three hours, had a Geiger counter rate of 85 cpm—enough to trigger Alert 112, but only because the count rate had been lowered from 100 to 50 cpm on August 1. The second filter registered 153 cpm (over 300 percent of the alert rate). As per standard operating procedure, more planes were sent up over the next two days to gather additional samples, and the filters were sent to Tracerlab's facilities at Berkeley for isotopic analysis.[75]

Doyle Northrup and his team assembled at AFOAT-1's Data Analysis Center at 1712 G Street NW in Washington, D.C., to await Tracerlab's report. Meanwhile, data flowed in from other bug-catching flights in the Pacific. On Monday, a plane originating from Guam registered 1,000 cpm at ten thousand feet over the North Pacific. By the time all the data was gathered—a period that lasted less than two weeks—ninety-two special, previously unscheduled flights had been flown by the Americans, not counting the standard routes, which continued to be monitored and analyzed as before. Alert 112 was now given a code name: Vermont.

At 3:30 a.m. on Wednesday, September 7, Tracerlab got in touch. Barium and cerium were found in the samples. Before 9 a.m. the phone rang again. They had identified molybdenum. All three of these elements are by-products of plutonium fission and were present in levels far too high to be explained by a natural event. Between September 3 and 16, more than 500 radioactive samples had been gathered, 167 of them above 1,000 cpm. By September 9, even ground-based units started registering elevated gamma rays. This did not look like another false alarm. It was time to phone upstairs.

On Thursday, September 8, William Webster, deputy secretary of defense for atomic energy under the new and imperious Secretary Louis Johnson, decided that this might in fact have been what they had been searching for all this time: a Soviet nuclear detonation. Webster called the AEC's general manager, Carroll Wilson, and informed him of AFOAT-1's tentative conclusions. Wilson in turn called in the radiochemist Spofford G. English and the AEC's new director of intelligence, Walter F. Colby, to examine the data Webster had sent along.[76]

By this time, the radioactive air mass had traveled over the United States and was somewhere over the mid-Atlantic. The Americans had to let the British in on the alert if they wanted any more data. On September 10, Alex Longair, assistant scientific attaché at the British embassy in Washington, was rushed into the telex room and informed about the ongoing investigation. He contacted London, where British atomic-energy officials were beginning to intensify their investigation of allegations of espionage of the head of the theory division at the Harwell establishment, one Klaus Fuchs.[77] As the British report on Vermont recalled, "A conference was held by teletype in the American Embassy in London and the British were informed that a mass of air containing activity was about to pass north of Scotland. It was estimated that the activity would be approximately 1/4 of a disintegration per minute per cubic foot." Temporarily putting the Fuchs investigation on hold, they scrambled more planes and intensified their sampling efforts along two routes, Bismuth and Nocturnal, which had their own bug-catching flights (figure 4). The report continued: "If the Americans had not alerted the British the first evidence of activity would have been obtained by the British on the Nocturnal flight from Gibraltar on Saturday the 10th of September, and results would not have been obtained before Wednesday the 14th of September, as there is a delay of approximately three to four days in getting the filters from Gibraltar into the laboratory at Harwell." Their conclusion was no less dreary than the Americans', if colored by a touch of classic British understatement: "It is perhaps worth noting that the maximum activity collected by the British filters, for flights of equal duration at similar altitudes, was roughly 20 times that obtained for any of the Sandstone tests."[78]

Back in the United States, Rainbarrel also had something to report. The air monitor at the Washington NRL site received elevated readings on September 10, and the rain of Tuesday, Septem-

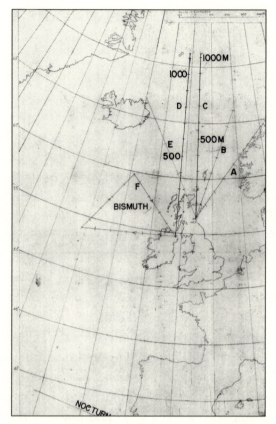

FIGURE 4 | Paths of Nocturnal and Bismuth flights from the United Kingdom. *Source:* W. Penney, "An Interim Report of British Work on Joe," September 22, 1949, PSF, Subject File 1940–1953, National Security Council—Atomic Files, Box 173, Folder: "Atomic Bomb: Reports."

ber 13, was collected and filtered. The full data from August 15 to September 23, 1949, was plotted and a clear peak emerged (figure 5). Reports from Kodiak, Alaska, registered intense readings for both September 6–12 and 13–17, and the rainwater was floc'ed and sent to the NRL. In their final report of September 22, they noted that the "birthday" of the activity ratios in the sample was "probably not earlier than 24 August." And the isotopic mix indicated that the explosion was not just a bomb, but probably a plutonium one, a conclusion derived from radium and thorium compounds (RaB and ThB, with 30-minute and 10.6-hour half-

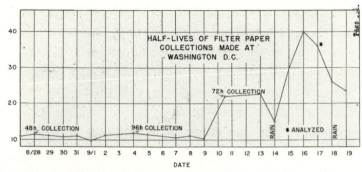

FIGURE 5 | Graph of radiation data collected by the NRL in Washington, D.C., area in September 1949. *Source:* Peter King and H. Friedman, "Part I: Collection and Identification of Fission Products of Foreign Origin," Naval Research Laboratory Report CN 3536, NRL RD Serial Number 21, PSF: Subject File 1940–1953, National Security Council—Atomic Files, Box 173, Folder: "Atomic Bomb: Reports," p. 3.

lives, respectively). The NRL's conclusions were directly based on the Sandstone calibration benchmark:

When fission products from the Sandstone test fell out in the Washington area, the NRL filter unit detected their presence by indicating an apparent half life of 20 hours on the filter paper, rather than the normal 10.6 hrs. of ThB. From June of 1948 until 9 September 1949, all filter collections at NRL yielded different apparent half lives less than 12 hours (apparent half life at 10 hours after removal from collector). Beginning on 9 September, the apparent half life of the filtered radioactivity rose rapidly to a peak of fifty [*sic*] hours on 16 September. The activity has fallen since then but not yet returned to normal.[79]

AFOAT-1, however, based its conclusions not on rainwater analysis or the British data (both rather cavalierly appended to the conclusions) but instead on Tracerlab and the fruits of the interim system. For the analysts at AFOAT-1 and Tracerlab, the main question to be resolved at this point was not whether an explosion had happened—they had no doubt on that score—but *when* it had happened. They had to find the birthday. To determine this, one had to factor in two different variables: the isotopic mix (which fixed the times of origin and quantities of the fission products) and the wind speed of the cloud of radioactive debris (in order to fix the location of origin from the samples collected between Japan and Western Europe). Ascertaining a birthday was necessarily linked to a judgment of birthplace.

The isotopic mix was relatively unproblematic. Tracerlab had found barium 140, molybdenum 99, zirconium 95, and protactinium 144, and in quantities sufficient to produce a single birthday.[80] Unfortunately, there was no reliable data—often no data at all—for the wind speed and direction over the first few days of the cloud's trajectory, for the obvious reason that the Soviets did not make a habit of releasing this kind of sensitive information. In the absence of exact values, AFOAT-1 had to guess, and the only approximation they could make was a bad one—and they knew it. Since most of the flights were done on a pressure surface of 500 millibars (18,500 feet above mean sea level), the analysts decided to substitute the geostrophic wind for actual wind for large portions of the data. The geostrophic wind is the theoretical wind that would result from the exact balance of the pressure gradient (the natural flow of air from regions of high pressure to regions of low pressure) and the Coriolis force (attributed to Earth's rotation):

> Since the wind observations are insufficient to show speeds at all points along the trajectories, it becomes necessary to employ the geostrophic wind computed from the pressure field, as the best approximation to the true wind. It is well known that the geostrophic wind is at times a poor approximation to the actual wind, giving results as much as 25% in error. For this reason, trajectories based on 25% less than and 25% greater than the geostrophic wind were computed to give the minimum and maximum air transport.[81]

Using the geostrophic wind for backtracking, they also tracked forward, using known values from Spitzbergen, as well as the

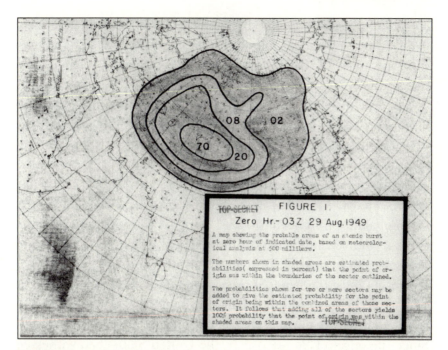

FIGURE 6 | Map predicting where the Soviet explosion might have happened if it took place on August 29, the numbers indicating percentage probability. This was the actual date of the explosion, although U.S. officials believed at the time that it was more likely to have happened on August 27. *Source:* Figure 3 in "U.S. Weather Bureau Report on Alert Number 112 of the Atomic Detection System," September 29, 1949, PSF: Subject File 1940–1953, National Security Council—Atomic Files, Box 173, Folder: "Atomic Bomb: Reports."

products from a seismic disturbance north of the Black Sea on August 30 (at 4 p.m. GMT).[82] In the end, they produced probability maps of the Soviet Union, coloring in with crayon the different probabilities of location across the enormous span of 35° and 170° east longitude (figure 6). Factoring in all the uncertainties, they concluded that the probable date for the Soviet explosion was August 27, 1949, although with enough error factored in to place it almost any time between August 26 and 29 (the latter being the correct date).[83]

AFOAT-1 had the result it had been created to obtain: There was evidence that a fission device had been detonated somewhere in the Soviet heartland. But what did this information mean? As long as it was in the hands of AFOAT-1 (and them alone), the answer is: not much. What existed so far were some graphs, some maps, some tables, and some verbiage buried in technical reports. First this mass of material had to be vouchsafed as reliable; only then could anyone decide what to do with it.

The military and intelligence personnel who had worked so hard to produce the Vermont results knew better than anyone that the data by itself could be dismissed. There had already been 111 recognized false alarms. What was to say that this wasn't the 112th? After all, reliable estimates had predicted the *earliest* possible Soviet explosion in 1951 and even assigned that estimate a very low probability compared to 1953. To make Vermont actionable, to make it literally intelligible to the political figures who needed to recognize it—primarily President Harry S. Truman, Secretary of Defense Louis Johnson, Secretary of State Dean Acheson, and AEC Chairman David Lilienthal—the material needed to be translated from the realm of the laboratory to the realm of politics. Since the onset of World War II, the United States had witnessed the growth of just such a stratum of translators; scientists who could communicate in the language of politics. They were summoned now, not to reanalyze the data but to digest it and validate it so a finding could be passed on to the civilian leadership.

Robert F. Bacher had resigned as commissioner of the AEC in early 1949, returning to his physics post at Caltech. Since both he and Lilienthal agreed that it was important to have a physicist on the commission, the two consulted about possible candidates and eventually resolved on Henry DeWolf Smyth, sometime chair of the Physics Department at Princeton University and author of the eponymous report. Smyth accepted, and Bacher focused his attention on academia—though as a member of the GAC, he still had to attend the few required meetings a year. He was looking forward to getting on with research.

In the first week of September, he received a phone call from Doyle Northrup. Northrup began by saying that Bacher would not know who he was, but that he worked for General Hegenberger (although Bacher would misremember the name in the early 1980s as "Hergenrother"). Bacher knew this meant long-range detection and AFOAT-1, so he waited. Northrup stated: "We have some positive information." Bacher replied: "Positive information?" Northrup continued: "Yes, and we'd like you to come to Washington to participate in a committee that's being set up to evaluate what we've found and make a report to the President on what the situation is."[84] Well, this was it, Bacher thought and agreed to come, but he hoped the meeting could be timed for the third week of September, when he was already scheduled to meet with the GAC and attend conferences with the British about exchange of nuclear materials and information. Northrup obliged.

On September 19, Bacher walked into "one of those rooms where, when you went out through the door, they locked it up, like a big safe," he recalled. "Yet the meeting had thirty people in it, or something like that. I've forgotten who all was on the committee, but Van [Vannevar] Bush, I think, was the chairman of it. Robert Oppenheimer was on it, Arthur Compton, Admiral [William S.] Parsons, and I guess I don't remember who else was on it."[85] (Or who was not: Arthur Holly Compton was not in fact present.) Although there were many observers in the room, the panel was small, being chaired by Vannevar Bush, and comprised of Bacher, Oppenheimer, and Parsons (who had armed Little Boy in midair on board the *Enola Gay* on August 6, 1945).[86]

Everyone had been assembled on short notice and was equally grave. The Department of Defense had tapped Bush to chair the panel. As he recalled in 1954, "I remember saying to him [General Morris R. Nelson], 'But wouldn't it be more reasonable for Dr. Oppenheimer to be chairman, since he is chairman of the General Advisory Committee,' and he said to me something to the effect that they would prefer it the way it was."[87] Bush, however, made sure that Oppenheimer would serve on the panel.[88] The latter had been hard to reach. He had just returned to Princeton's Institute of Advanced Study from a week vacationing at Perro Caliente.[89] (The job of director of the institute, incidentally, had been offered to him in November 1946 by the trustee who chaired the search committee: Lewis L. Strauss.)

The mood in the large, safelike room was somber. None of the participants on the panel (with the possible exception of Bacher) had expected something quite so definitive so soon. Bush had, for example, just received the page proofs of his forthcoming book, *Modern Arms and Free Men*, and had time (and inside information) enough to cut the now-embarrassing prediction of a further ten years before the Soviets would detonate their first test explosion.[90]

The AFOAT-1, British, NRL, and Tracerlab reports were convincing. A member of the committee (probably Oppenheimer) told journalists in 1950 about the data: "The chances are nine hundred and ninety-nine to one that it was a bomb that went off, and if it was not a bomb, neither I nor any of my colleagues can think of what it might have been."[91] Given the tremendous spread of estimates about the date of Soviet proliferation we have already seen, such sudden unanimity might appear surprising. The nature of the evidence produced by Tracerlab, Rainbarrell, and the British, however, was qualitatively light-years better than the spurious guesses and assumptions that had dogged the Americans during the monopoly. This was evidence of an entirely different order. Bacher recalled, "It was absolutely completely clear from the evidence that they had atomic bomb material. There just wasn't any doubt about this whatever; it could only have come, at such an altitude and in such density, from an atomic bomb explosion. So we wrote a report."[92] And that, of course, had been the point: to produce a report above the signatures of these venerable wartime and postwar atomic personalities—part politician, part scientist. Bush was offhand about the importance of this document: "When we came to the report, we wrote the report around the table. It was a very brief report."[93] It was forwarded up the bureaucratic food chain.

At this point, Vermont was an established fact: There had been an atomic explosion in the Soviet Union. A few hundred Ameri-

cans—scientists, technicians, pilots, diplomats, military officers—
had learned this and believed it. But it was still a secret, a fact held
in the utmost confidence, barred behind the highest walls security
clearances could offer. And there it would remain, unless someone
decided to make it public. Eventually, someone would.

SIX

DRAMATIZING THE SITUATION

I found them blind: I taught them how to see;
And now they know neither themselves nor me.
WILLIAM BLAKE, "TO F—— AND S——"

For a president who had been battered and besieged in the wake of Roosevelt's death, the end of the war, and the subsequent economic woes (not to mention the Republican-dominated 80th Congress), 1949 started out as a very good year for Harry S. Truman. He had just been elected in his own right in one of the most hard-fought presidential elections in American history, coming from behind against Republican Thomas E. Dewey while overcoming the fracturing of his own party into Henry Wallace's Progressive Party on the left and Strom Thurmond's Dixiecrats on the right.

Triumphant domestically, Truman was also experiencing a good year internationally. The Soviets lifted the blockade of Berlin in May 1949, retreating in the face of Truman's determination to hold on to West Berlin through the stunningly successful airlift. That stand also promoted the signing of the North Atlantic Treaty in April, securing Western Europe's place in the American camp. Truman's foreign policy team was reengineered as well. Dean Acheson, the perpetual undersecretary of state for James F. Byrnes and George C. Marshall, returned as secretary on January 21, 1949, winning approval from a usually cool Senate by eighty-three to six. (He had resigned as Marshall's undersecretary in June 1947. Marshall had in turn moved on, taking over from Basil O'Connor as director of the Red Cross.) And in mid-August, General Omar Bradley became chairman of the Joint Chiefs of Staff. Here was a brand-new national-security team for a new and more confident Truman.[1] To be sure, there were crises on the international front, but Truman was certain they could be met with resolve. On August 31, 1949, Truman told his staff that the split of Tito's Yugoslavia from the Soviet Union brought the world "nearer to war than we have been at any time."[2] But he was ready for it.

Vermont—the data on the Soviet test that would later be dubbed Joe-1 by the Americans in homage to Joseph Stalin— would shake that confidence quite a bit.[3] From the moment the information from Vermont entered Truman's purview, the finding that the Soviet Union had detonated a fission device within its borders provoked heated debate about what this fact meant: Was it a bomb? Should the United States announce it? If so, who should make the announcement? When? Would announcing it compromise national security or enhance it? Truman's ultimate decision to make public the knowledge of Joe-1 on September 23, 1949, merits at most a paragraph in histories of the cold war, marking the break from atomic monopoly to arms race. The historian John Lewis Gaddis pithily relates the result: "The Truman administration responded to the Soviet bomb test in much the same way that Stalin had absorbed the news from Alamogordo, Hiroshima and Nagasaki four years earlier."[4]

That is true as far as it goes, but while in fact Stalin did not make much of announcing the American accomplishments (the bombing of Nagasaki was not reported in *Pravda*, and Stalin never even considered announcing Trinity), Truman did go public. Indeed, the announcement itself should not be taken for granted, for the situation could have been handled in many different ways.

Looking back from the perspective of the cold war (and our current post–cold war era), it is easy to overstress the shock that Joe-1 produced in the American establishment and public. Shock there was, to be sure. But it was not as though this event had never been contemplated. Even the act of predicting (erroneously, as it turned out) a distant future date for the first Soviet test implicitly involved considering what the United States would do when it came.

It would take us too far afield to explore every such blueprint for action, but one stands out, both for its proximity to the actual news of Vermont and its author: George F. Kennan's analysis of such an event for the State Department's Policy Planning Staff (PPS), which he directed, produced on August 16, 1949. Kennan, the State Department's resident Soviet expert, considered it vital for the United States to acquire accurate information about any Soviet test and then to announce it:

Definite knowledge by the Government of the explosion by the U.S.S.R. of its first bomb is considered by the Department to be important for the following reasons:

(1) It would have a steadying effect on the American people and give them a sense of security if this Government could give assurance that the U.S.S.R. probably could not, without our knowledge, have a bomb or bombs for any length of time. With this knowledge, the Government would be able to combat intelligently defeatist or irrational attitudes arising from uncertainty as to whether the U.S.S.R. was capable of using atomic bombs, and would be in a position to refute with conviction false claims or rumors.

(2) It would be of the utmost importance for us to know when

the U.S.S.R. has successfully tested a bomb in order to antici-
pate and counter possible changes in Soviet foreign policy which
might result therefrom, and to know whether a shift in its foreign policy was the result of the possession of atomic bombs.
We cannot know whether the U.S.S.R. would make the knowledge public if it did possess the atomic bomb; however, we
would be in a position to know the truth of what the U.S.S.R.
said publicly.

(3) The Soviet possession of a bomb or bombs may require a
reevaluation of U.S. policy in the United Nations in our efforts
to obtain effective international control.[5]

Knowledge was important because it structured American responses. The more that people knew, the more rationally they
could act, and rationality was vital. This view seemed to be the
pre-Vermont consensus among Truman's cabinet—or at least those
who had the clearance to see the PPS memorandum. Kennan's
missive circulated up to Acheson, and presumably to other members of the National Security Council. Principal among those
would be Louis Johnson, secretary of defense.

September 3, the day Alert 112 was discovered, was the Saturday of Labor Day weekend in the United States, and no one
wanted to be in the office. The Senate assembled and adjourned in
a record forty seconds, to head home for the sultry late summer
holiday. Only on Wednesday, September 7, did William Webster,
Johnson's undersecretary for atomic matters and the chair of the
Military Liaison Committee to the AEC, receive the report on the
elevated radiation findings from AFOAT-1, and he presented them
to the secretary. Johnson initially refused to believe it.

Louis Johnson had made a habit of doing things his own way. A
wealthy attorney with impeccable Democratic credentials, Johnson had been a crusader for American military preparedness in the
1930s, a time when the default position in the United States was
isolationism. He was a founder of the American Legion, had acted
as its national president in the 1930s, and from 1937 to 1940 had

served in Franklin Roosevelt's War Department as assistant secretary to the isolationist Harry H. Woodring. Fighting almost every step of the way, he pressed on to lay the groundwork for the American mobilization that would prove so effective after Pearl Harbor. When Roosevelt released Woodring as war clouds loomed on the horizon, Johnson was convinced that he would receive the cabinet post. Instead, Henry L. Stimson was appointed, and Johnson was fired. A bear of a man—tall, bald, and muscular—Johnson was crushed but not undaunted, hoping to regain the prized post of secretary of war someday.

It certainly would not happen under FDR, that much he knew. But when Harry Truman became president, the political landscape looked different. The National Military Establishment unified the services under a single Department of Defense in September 1947, and Secretary James Forrestal seemed to be stumbling in the execution of his duties. When Truman seemed certain to lose the 1948 election, Johnson stepped in and ably managed the campaign's finances, playing a pivotal role in Truman's narrow victory. Johnson expected a reward, and he wanted to be secretary of defense; Forrestal was the major obstacle in his way. Selectively leaking damaging information to conservative hatchet journalist Drew Pearson, Johnson managed to tarnish Forrestal's reputation, only exacerbating Truman's frustration with the latter. Forrestal was let go on March 2, 1949, and by March 28 Johnson had taken his place. (Forrestal was quickly hospitalized for mental exhaustion; in May, he leaped from his hospital window to his death.) Johnson would hold the job until September 1950, when Truman fired him—a second and this time final blow at the hands of a Democratic president—in the wake of hostilities in Korea. Replaced by George Marshall, his hopes for the 1952 Democratic nomination for the presidency dashed, Johnson retired from the limelight.[6]

The North Atlantic Treaty—exactly the kind of entanglement that he had opposed at the American Legion—was agreed upon the same day Johnson assumed office, and he had not only to cease his former criticism but also reverse himself to support Truman's agenda. The treaty's path was leisurely: It was not submitted to the Senate until April 12, was not approved until July 21, and not signed by Truman until July 25. Johnson displayed no equivalent leisure in his own domain. On his first day, he moved into a more lavish office that Forrestal had eschewed, and required almost all twenty-seven thousand employees in the Pentagon to move their offices *on the same day*, ostensibly in order to reorganize the military into a more efficient and unified organization (but at least in part also to demonstrate that he had the power to do so).[7] Johnson was not well loved at the Department of Defense (so renamed in August 1949), but not solely for his imperial demeanor.

The main reason was money, and the primary cause of the money woes was not Johnson but Harry Truman himself. Although he may not always have commanded the details of foreign policy, Truman understood budgets and enjoyed the intricacy of balancing them. Since the Republicans in Congress would not let him raise taxes, the only way he had to balance the country's finances was to cut spending—and he did, running surpluses almost every year.[8] The U.S. economy was by far the world's largest and richest in the postwar years, but it was also beset by labor unrest, inflation (combated through price controls), and recessions. In the first half of 1949, unemployment rose, peaking at almost 6 percent in July. Consumer prices inched up, and farm income began to slide.[9] Truman had reason to fear a recession and thought to fight it by cutting spending.

The military budget was the perpetual target, and Truman repeatedly lowered its budget ceilings, down as low as $13 billion in 1949 to stave off a business recession.[10] (This amounts to $114.5 billion in 2009 dollars. For comparison, the 2008 defense budget, excluding special funds for ongoing wars in Iraq and Afghanistan, came to $481.4 billion.) Granted, Truman's allocation was much higher than prewar American defense budgets, but the United States had assumed many more—and more expensive— obligations for world leadership. The military was costly. In mid-

1949, the United States had 1,591,232 men under arms. The army fielded 10 divisions, but only one of them was ready for combat; the navy had 331 combat ships; and the air force had 48 groups, with strategic-bombing advocates pushing for many more. Truman slightly upped the fiscal 1950 defense budget ceiling to $14.4 billion ($128.3 billion in 2009 dollars).[11] It was up to Louis Johnson to make this work, and he wielded his ax, hoping to ride the reputation as a cost cutter to the presidency after Truman retired.

It so happened that Vermont hit Johnson at a bad time. On September 8, the day after he heard the news, he authorized cuts in the services for fiscal 1950, not waiting for fiscal 1951, amounting to $929 million ($8.3 billion in 2009 dollars). The air force lost $196 million, the army $357 million, and the navy $376 million. The navy, in particular, was incensed, seeing this as only the latest of Johnson's insults to their service.[12] On April 23, because of Johnson, Secretary of the Navy John L. Sullivan resigned. Part of the problem was Johnson's stifling of any public criticism of his actions; but mostly it was money.[13]

The navy rebelled. The so-called Revolt of the Admirals broke out publicly on September 10, when the naval aviation hero John G. Crommelin publicly attacked Johnson. For the rest of this month and the next, Johnson had to quell the dissent in his own department.[14] He was already having a bad enough time even without the navy because of Vermont. As General Omar Bradley remembered it: "This news came as a terrible shock to Louis Johnson. It caught him with economy ax poised in midair for yet another blow. He swung and continued to swing for some months, but it was almost immediately obvious that he was embarked on the wrong course; the balance of power had profoundly shifted."[15] Johnson at first refused to believe the data, but upon assurance from advisers such as Vannevar Bush, he quickly not only recognized the results but also began to lobby Truman for a public announcement, instead of keeping it secret or leaking it quietly. (Although, privately, Johnson continued to believe that the explosion had been a reactor accident and not the detonation of a bomb.)[16]

Convincing Truman was an uphill battle. We are able to reconstruct the path of this information through the administration because of detailed notes, assembled by Truman's aide, George Elsey, beginning on September 23, on the genesis of the decision to release the announcement. Although it would be preferable to have a real-time chronicle of the course of the flow, nothing like this survives in Truman's files. Elsey began his reconstruction only after the public announcement. As he noted at the top of his copy of Truman's bulletin: "This was so well kept a secret that I knew nothing of it until the announcement was made at 11:10 a.m. this date."[17] Elsey's reconstruction was nonetheless meticulous.

On Friday, September 9, NSC Chairman Sidney Souers (an old friend of Truman's from Missouri) handed the president and CIA Director Roscoe Hillenkoetter a memorandum about the elevated AFOAT-1 results. "Thereafter," Elsey reported in his notes on an interview with Souers, "as additional info came, Souers gave Pres informal verbal reports."[18] In his interview with Truman, Elsey recorded a slightly different account: The president claimed he had first heard around the 13th, and Souers had been accompanied to Blair House (the White House was under renovation) with Louis Johnson, Omar Bradley, and Steven Early.[19] (Souers's account seems more probable, as it was unlikely that anyone would have waited four unnecessary days before informing the president.)

On the next Friday, September 16, "convinced it was man-made explosion," Souers returned to see Truman at about 5:30 p.m. He reported that State and Defense both thought a statement should be prepared in case there was a leak of the information—after all, roughly three hundred people knew this information, and it was hard to keep a lid on that kind of secret in Washington. The military prepared a draft, and Souers said James Webb, undersecretary of state (Acheson was in New York City), would revise the statement and return it to Truman by 10:15 a.m. on the 17th. The president approved the draft that day, and Souers held on to it, in case a leak made release necessary.[20]

Truman was not pleased at the news and certainly initially did not want to make it known, even though he acquiesced to Souers's prudent suggestion that he be prepared. As we have seen, Truman had on multiple occasions taken the opportunity to publicly deny reports that the Soviet Union had already conducted an atomic test or possessed a nuclear bomb. In fact, in a press conference on July 28, 1949, he had to refute rumors that a nuclear test had just happened in Siberia.[21] And even as late as September 20, 1949, the CIA's Office of Reports and Estimates (ORE)—apparently unaware of the news from AFOAT-1—sent Truman a memorandum declaring that "the earliest possible date by which the USSR might be expected to produce an atomic bomb is mid-1950 and the most probable date is mid-1953."[22] So if Truman wanted to interpret this evidence as yet another false alarm, he had plenty of ammunition to do so.

In his memoirs, Truman emphasized the certainty of the data and his resolve in taking quick action:

> Then the scientists went to work and analyzed the data. The Air Force specialists, the AEC's experts, and consultants called in from universities went over the available information. Then a special committee, composed of Vannevar Bush, J. Robert Oppenheimer, Robert F. Bacher, and W. S. Parsons, reviewed the findings. There was no room for doubt. Between August 26 and 29 an atomic explosion had been set off somewhere on the Asiatic mainland.
>
> General Hoyt Vandenberg, who as Chief of Staff of the Air Force was directly responsible for the long-range detection program, reported these facts to me on September 21. I was surprised, of course, that the Russians had made progress at a more rapid rate than was anticipated.[23]

According to his recollections, he then began to consider announcing it, and did so two days later. As we have seen, however, Truman learned about the facts almost two weeks earlier than September 21 and had dallied on the report of the Bush panel and other findings. Concealed within Truman's quick retrospective narrative lay a complicated debate about the relative values of open and secret knowledge in nuclear matters.

Should the United States announce the news of a Soviet test? It had already been several weeks and the Soviets had said nothing. Why do it for them? In what might seem to be a counterintuitive alignment of forces from the perspective of the twenty-first century, the military "advocated instant release," according to Elsey's notes, while Acheson at the State Department (as well as Ernest Bevin, his British counterpart) "didn't like the idea of release" because they felt it would compromise their tough diplomatic stance.[24] (Soon afterward, disagreement over the issue of release at the State Department became yet another bone of contention between pro-publicity Kennan and his boss, Acheson. Kennan would resign by the end of the year.) Acheson, who was at that very moment negotiating with the British about revising the Modus Vivendi nuclear exchange agreements and attending sessions of the United Nations, received the news in New York City through a special courier. He had meetings all day at his suite at the Waldorf on the 22nd debating the issue of release and concluded it would be a bad idea, even taking into account the inevitability of leaks.[25]

Truman's press secretary, Charles Ross, agreed, advising against release "on grounds Pres couldn't let Acheson down."[26] Or, as Carlton Savage of Kennan's PPS reported, "[Ross] felt the President should not yet make the announcement as Secretary Acheson and Foreign Minister Bevin of Great Britain were recommending against it at this time; an announcement by the President would dramatize the situation too much; and the American people had about all the bad news they could stand with the current possibility of labor strikes."[27] The British advised quietly leaking the information, hoping to avoid mass panic at the news that the monopoly had ended.[28] There was, after all, a serious security issue here. As *Time* magazine noted after the September 23 release, "Disclosure might give away the workings of the U.S. atomic detection network; it might be better if the Russians did not know the U.S. knew."[29]

Yet Truman eventually did decide to release the information, despite the security issue, the fear of panic, and his own frustration and embarrassment at this event which General Leslie Groves had assured him would not happen on his watch. What was he thinking? And whom was he talking to?

Not his AEC chairman, that much was clear. David Lilienthal recorded his interactions with Truman on the issue of Joe-1 in a lengthy, almost expressionist diary entry of September 21, begun with extended prosy description and eventually collapsing into telegraphic, clipped sentences. He began with the night of the 20th: "These are the notes of a remarkable twenty-four hours in the life of a vacationer." Chronically fatigued and frustrated by his job at the AEC—and in particular his dealings with Lewis Strauss—Lilienthal and his wife had left for Martha's Vineyard on August 18.[30] Thus, he knew nothing of Vermont. The man in charge of atomic-energy policy was not informed for almost three weeks about the most momentous potential change in America's atomic situation since Trinity.

The circumstances were unusual. He was driving home from dinner at 11 p.m. on September 19 through a "heavy ground-fog." Just as he turned into his lane (he made a reference to Emily Brontë's *Wuthering Heights* here, and this was not the only time in this extended entry), he noticed General James McCormack, director of the Division of Military Applications of the AEC, standing at his gate. At 11:30, after sending his wife out of the room, Lilienthal finally heard the story of Vermont. He had to go to Washington.

At 6 a.m. Lilienthal woke up, and by 8:20 he was on a plane. He made up for lost time and had a day full of meetings. At 12:35 he met with Robert Bacher and J. Robert Oppenheimer, both of whom had been on Bush's panel, and fellow AEC commissioner Sumner Pike: "The possibilities that this is something else disposed of flatly—Robert Oppenheimer positive, unequivocal; even Bob Bacher almost without a 'qualification.' The feeling in the abdomen—here it is." The mood was somber, Lilienthal finding Oppenheimer "frantic, drawn," and Bacher "deeply worried." Bacher "felt it should be announced and right away: let's not muff the duty to initiate the facts, rather than shore up a 'leak' (inevitable with 300 people knowing it) or have the other fellow say it." At 12:50, Lilienthal had lunch with Bacher's replacement at the AEC, Henry D. Smyth, and at 2:15 he spoke with Souers and at 2:20 with Strauss—the latter presumably gratified that his push for long-range detection had borne some fruit.

At 3:45 p.m. he was ushered into the president's office. Lilienthal's description of this meeting almost reduces to the terse prose of a hard-boiled crime novel:

He said: want to talk about this detection report—knew about it—knew it would probably come—German scientists in Russia did it, probably something like that. Be glad to call in Joint Committee chairman, ranking minority member, tell them just what I'm telling you now; don't want you to be in trouble with them. Not going to say anything myself now; later, when this (pointing to news reports re sterling devaluation troubles) quiets down, maybe in a week; realize may leak, lots people know—still take that chance, meet it when it comes.

I said: may I have permission to state views, despite fact you have reached conclusion? He took off glasses, first time I saw him without them, large, fine eyes. Considerate, fine air of patience and interest. I tried to set out affirmative view of making it [announcement] now and initiating matter rather than plugging leaks. Advantages would be three in number. First, would show Pres. knows what is going on in Vermont [Russia]; that would reassure auto mechanic in Vineyard Haven, etc. Second, Pres. knowing and saying so would show him not scared, hence others needn't be; third, would show Pres. will tell people when things come along they need to know that won't hurt being told.

These comments clearly echo Kennan's recommendations from mid-August. Nonetheless, Truman was not going to budge. He said he "can't be sure anyway" that the Soviets have the bomb.

Lilienthal had said his piece. He met with Oppenheimer and Bacher again at 4:44 and described the former as "feeling badly" and "badly upset." He saw James Webb at 4:50, and held an extraordinary session with the AEC—Sumner Pike, Lewis Strauss, Joseph Volpe, Henry Smyth, Gordon Dean, and general manager Carroll Wilson—at 5:10.[31] At 6:55 he was already off the ground, penning segments of this diary entry in midair, and was back home with his wife on Martha's Vineyard at 10:30, "the wind blowing like mad, the Wuthering Heights touch again as it goes through the loose house; to bed."[32] Not that the trip had done any good as far as Lilienthal knew. Truman wasn't going to make an announcement right away. And apparently because of the sterling devaluation, of all reasons!

What Truman told Lilienthal seems well established through multiple other sources. Hoyt Vandenberg, the second director of the CIA and in 1949 chief of staff of the air force, noted in his desk diary on September 21 that "the President made decision not to make any release at present due to the English pound situation."[33] Admittedly, this situation was not good in September 1949. At the end of the war, the United Kingdom was the world's leading debtor country, owing more than £3 billion to wartime creditors, many of whom were in the sterling zone, and possessed a balance of payments deficit of £1.35 billion between 1945 and 1950.[34] Even the Marshall Plan's easing of currency pressures could not stave off the coming crisis.

Britain's Labour government had nationalized the Bank of England in 1946, not out of socialist principles but merely in recognition of the role the bank had been playing in Britain's economy for some time. The bank thus had the power to take an active part in forming monetary policy; it also had a strong motivation. Although British exports had risen in 1946 and 1948, an energy crisis in 1947—coupled with an unusually harsh winter, unemployment rising to over six million, and rations falling to below wartime levels—caused a severe setback and demonstrated how sensitive the British situation was to random shocks, including the 1949 American recession.[35]

Stafford Cripps, the chancellor of the exchequer, had resisted devaluing the pound, even though it was fairly clear that this would provide a quick and, it was hoped, durable fix to the balance-of-payments crisis. (In simplest terms, devaluation causes exports to become cheaper and imports more expensive, thus improving the balance of payments.) In the middle of July 1949, however, Cripps took leave in a Swiss sanatorium, and within two days of his departure, the junior ministers entrusted with the economy (Hugh Gaitskell, Douglas Jay, and Harold Wilson) pressed for devaluation. In August, Prime Minister Clement Attlee informed Cripps by letter about the upcoming devaluation, which the British scheduled for September 18. The pound dropped from $4.03 to $2.80, a 30 percent adjustment. (Since other sterling countries were tied to the same rate and other European countries took the British move as an excuse to devalue their own currencies, the trade-weighted devaluation was only 9 percent.) Unquestionably, the devaluation significantly ameliorated British economic worries.[36]

Politically, the failure of the British to warn other European countries caused some damage to continental relations. The British did not neglect, however, to notify the Americans that devaluation was coming, and discussed the geopolitical implications (especially for Europe) with the State Department's point man on the matter, George F. Kennan.[37] Truman, having learned of both Joe-1 and the pound situation at roughly the same time, thought that "2 shocks too much."[38] As Elsey generously interpreted the president's version of events:

> The President decided against releasing information on the Soviet atomic explosion prior to that date [the 18th], fearing that the impact of the two announcements would be too great a shock to the western nations, and—since there was no connection between sterling devaluation and the Soviet atomic explosion—the former should be announced first. If the atomic news were made public first, followed by announcement of a sharp cut in the value of the pound, the British public especially might well become panicky.[39]

Eisenhower, then president of Columbia University and ignorant of the internal wrangles over Joe-1, was delighted by devaluation: "If they are successful in this regard, we may come to look upon this month of September, 1949, as the real beginning of effective results in our strenuous efforts to restore Britain and Western Europe to the status of efficient economic and military partners."[40] In any case, Eisenhower had more reason to be pleased than Lilienthal, who feared that Truman would leap at almost any excuse to delay or possibly forever postpone making Vermont public.

And yet Truman would announce it on Friday, September 23, just five days after the Sunday devaluation. What changed his mind? Although the meeting with Lilienthal clearly did not, Truman did ask Webb to send a message to Acheson that day to ask about a release, and on September 22 asked Ross to write a new and fuller statement building on the previous "flash" announcements that were designed to respond to leaks—"even though no decision yet." After a press conference that day, Truman approved the statement, and then Souers sent it to Webb and British envoy Sir Oliver Franks to take it up to Acheson in New York to get his opinion.

Acheson, although still reluctant, realized—given how many

people knew already—that Truman was probably going to release the news anyway, and he and Bevin amended the statement somewhat and sent it back on the morning of the 23rd. At 9:30 that morning, Truman met with Souers, Webb, and Ross, and then he approved Acheson's corrections to the statement. Even though he was still not in favor of a release, Acheson appreciated the gesture: "This action of the President in keeping me fully informed and in consulting with me even though we were separated was typical of his consideration."[41] As was done with the text of Truman's announcement of the bombing of Hiroshima, many eyes had gone over the text of this address.[42]

The announcement was a public-relations offensive because it had to be; Truman had reason to think a leak was imminent, and if the news of the Soviet test had to be publicized, he would rather *he* decided the time and the place, and not the Soviets or anyone else. Before he had made any decision, he invited two members of the Congressional Joint Committee on Atomic Energy to the White House. As Truman recalled later:

> The first persons [outside the administration] I wanted to be informed about the Russian atomic explosion, even before I made a public statement, were the members of the Congressional Joint Committee on Atomic Energy. I therefore asked Senator [Brien] McMahon, the chairman, and Senator [Bourke] Hickenlooper, the ranking Republican member, to join me in my office at the White House the following day, September 22. Hickenlooper was out of town, however, and so McMahon came alone.[43]

McMahon in turn told Hickenlooper at 10:30 on the 23rd, when he summoned a special JCAE meeting: "The meeting is to deal with an extremely important and confidential matter and I would appreciate it if you would not divulge the fact that the meeting is going to be held."[44]

Truman did not particularly trust McMahon. Having seized the issue of atomic energy from the end of the war as his special purview, McMahon had come to relish his reputation as the "Atomic Senator" and had occasionally taken the opportunity to leak when it suited him. There was no way around informing him, however. More to the point, Truman knew that the new Soviet foreign minister, Andrei Vyshinsky, was due to address the General Assembly of the United Nations in the afternoon of the 23rd, and Truman expected that a Soviet announcement was planned for then. As Elsey reconstructed it: "Vishinsky news & McMahon decided the hour."[45]

Truman called a cabinet meeting for 10 a.m. on the 23rd and informed them about the AFOAT-1 reports—although the president incorrectly related the substance of the Bush panel's assessment, placing the Siberian explosion during August 18–21.[46] Truman took a straw poll to see who was in favor of announcement, although it seems pretty clear that he had already reconciled himself to publicizing the news and was merely taking the temperature of the room, as he had with the Stimson Plan in September 1945. Everyone was in favor of release except for Acheson and Ross. The mood was somber. Alben Barkley, the vice president, recalled feeling "terribly depressed."[47] Not so Lilienthal when he was informed about the announcement on Martha's Vineyard (having been unable to attend the cabinet meeting). He wrote to Oppenheimer immediately:

> I know you must feel much better, as I do, now that the President has made the announcement, and made it in a timely fashion. I felt pretty much ears-pinned-backish, having tried every argument I knew with so little apparent headway; but it may have helped a bit for all I know; the lesson for me is, nothing that is right is ever too hopeless to try . . . We mustn't muff it this time; this could be an end of the miasma of secrecy.[48]

The public statement—again like Truman's Hiroshima announcement—was not delivered by the president himself. At

10:30 on September 23, immediately after the cabinet meeting, Charles Ross conducted his regular press conference, making no mention of any upcoming news. At 11:00, however, he invited the correspondents into his office. There he handed out a mimeographed sheet of the text Truman had approved scarcely ninety minutes before. The statement was very carefully crafted:

I believe the American people, to the fullest extent consistent with national security, are entitled to be informed of all developments in the field of atomic energy. That is my reason for making public the following information.

We have evidence that within recent weeks an atomic explosion occurred in the U.S.S.R.

Ever since atomic energy was first released by man, the eventual development of this new force by other nations was to be expected. The probability has always been taken into account by us.

Nearly four years ago I pointed out that "Scientific opinion appears to be practically unanimous that the essential theoretical knowledge upon which the discovery is based is already widely known. There is also substantial agreement that foreign research can come abreast of our present theoretical knowledge in time." And, in the Three-Nation Declaration of the President of the United States and the Prime Ministers of the United Kingdom and of Canada, dated November 15, 1945, it was emphasized that no single nation could in fact have a monopoly of atomic weapons.

This recent development emphasizes once again, if indeed such emphasis were needed, the necessity for that truly effective enforceable international control of atomic energy which this Government and the large majority of the members of the United Nations support.[49]

Across the Atlantic, Downing Street simultaneously issued a similarly worded announcement. Pressed for further comment in the following weeks, Truman demurred, retorting, "I made all the statement that I intend to make, on the subject, in that statement that was made on the 23rd of September."[50]

The news was out. This was how the world learned that the atomic monopoly had ended, that the Soviet Union had cracked "the secret" of nuclear weapons. Given the tremendous importance later laid on the qualitative difference between preannouncement and postannouncement worlds by both the political actors and historians, it is worth taking a closer look at the statement to observe what it said—and what it did not say.

In the first paragraph, Truman declared a general principle of atomic policy, and one that he had not invariably held to so far, as his resistance to announcing Sandstone made clear. Clearly, Lilienthal thought that this single sentence was the most important one of the entire announcement, even more so than news of the "explosion." As he related at a dinner two weeks later:

> In my opinion, the President's statement to the country concerning Russian progress was a shining demonstration of the best in American democracy, and the best in the American temperament. He didn't keep the news from the people, on the ground that it was an important piece of military intelligence, which it most certainly was. The President showed, in his brief statement that he does not share the view that atomic secrecy requires the abandonment of the very fundamental of democracy: the need of the people to essential information by which they may steer their own course.[51]

Walter Lippmann, the most respected newspaper columnist of the day, agreed: "Short of a public demonstration by the Russians themselves, like our own at Bikini, the fact that our atomic monopoly has ended could not have been established more conclusively."[52] In 1952, Oppenheimer was appointed by Truman to chair a panel to rethink nuclear policies for a postmonopoly world, and in January 1953 his report would reformulate this openness into a policy of "Candor": "The United States Government should adopt a policy of candor toward the American people . . . in presenting the meaning of the arms race . . . We are wholly persuaded that this country does better when it knows the truth, and we would not want to be in the shoes of a government which had to deal with a nation which awoke to reality after a long period of concealment and deception."[53] Truman's September 23 announcement was thus, in one respect, a victory for those who wanted an end to a reflexive attitude of secrecy, a return to the same spirit that had called for the release of the Smyth Report.

The very next sentence, however—"We have evidence that within recent weeks an atomic explosion occurred in the U.S.S.R."—demonstrated to the discerning eye that the dialectical dance of secrecy and revelation was not yet over. These fourteen words, the most newsworthy, actually gave away very little. First of all, there is absolutely no indication *how* this information was obtained, although silence did not restrain the press from extended speculation on probable mechanisms. Most guessed correctly that some form of radiological monitoring was involved, although there were still ardent adherents to theories of espionage, drunken diplomats, or human intelligence.[54]

But the most interesting word among the fourteen was "explosion." Not "bomb." Kenneth Nichols, who had been Groves's assistant during World War II and served on the Military Liaison Committee to the AEC in this period (later he would become general manager), believed that he was responsible for this word choice. Even though he personally was convinced that this was a test of a weapon, when asked in mid-September by James Lay of the NSC staff whether the device had been dropped as a bomb from a plane, he responded that he expected that it had been a tower burst, like Trinity. This, he would later recall, likely prompted them to exclude the word "bomb" as possibly inaccurate and certainly inflammatory.[55] Not that many were deluded by word choice into underestimating the seriousness of what had occurred. *Life* magazine argued, "It seems probable that the blast was caused by a bomb."[56] And Acheson, at a press conference, seemed of like mind: "Now, your next question was whether this means that the Soviet Union has the atomic bomb, by which I suppose you mean that they have made a weapon and the weapon has gone off. That, again, gets out of the technical sphere of which I am competent to speak. For my own purposes, I am assuming that they have made a weapon which has exploded."[57]

Ironically, one of the few people who were not convinced that "explosion" was a synonym for "bomb" was the man responsible for the announcement itself: President Truman. Upon leaving office on January 26, 1953, Truman told a reporter, "I am not convinced Russia has the bomb. I am not convinced the Russians have achieved the know-how to put the complicated mechanism together to make an A-bomb work."[58] In this, he was in a minority of Americans, although a growing minority. In August 1950, 73 percent of the public believed that the Soviet Union in fact had atomic bombs, and in February 1953, that number had dropped slightly to 69 percent.[59] Truman's position, however, was by no means adopted by most in the administration.

In fact, those individuals, echoing the third and fourth paragraphs of the September 23 announcement, not only admitted that the Soviet bomb was a fact, but—in contrast to the wide array of estimates during the monopoly—also claimed that it was a minor fact, one that the Americans had always expected and were completely prepared for. Whereas Lilienthal saw the main message of the announcement as candor, and most of the public took the distillation of the message to be the terse "explosion" information, from the perspective of the AEC, the Department of Defense, and the State Department, it was this point—that the Soviet bomb was no real news at all—that was crucial.

Louis Johnson, leaving the cabinet meeting and encountering reporters, was the only cabinet secretary to give an immediate statement, and it was to this very point: "I warn you: don't overplay this."[60] General Groves, who had so confidently basked in the comfort of his twenty-years-or-more prediction, now completely reversed himself: "I see no need to become unduly alarmed over the President's announcement. We have all known since before August, 1945, that it could be anticipated. It was provided for in our planning."[61] In brief: "I'm not losing any sleep over it."[62] Oppenheimer, somewhat disingenuously telegraphing a prior sagacity on this issue, followed Groves: "I think I'm one of the few people who didn't say anything about Russia's A-bomb development. I'm very glad we know the facts."[63]

The organized campaign to spin the announcement centered on this message of calm. JCS chairman Omar Bradley was immediately called upon to produce an article for the *Saturday Evening Post* to smooth troubled waters. "Actually, such an event is no occasion for hysteria," he wrote. "Our plans have contemplated this for the past five years. It need not seriously affect the stable equilibrium of force or our strategy for peace."[64] In this article, Bradley introduced a clever rhetorical maneuver that would become American conventional wisdom on this question. Instead of discussing *possession* of the bomb, which had been the dominant form for earlier discourse on estimates, he emphasized *stockpiles* and delivery systems. Clearly, since the Soviet Union had only just tested, he argued, they had few bombs and no means to send them over the United States. There was thus no need to fear any immediate change in international relations. George Kennan was also commissioned to write an article for the *Reader's Digest* with a similar message.[65]

Reporters attempted to corral Ross and Acheson into explaining more about the origins of the information or to speculate about the significance of the timing of the announcement. Acheson, hoping to dispel images of a Machiavellian manipulation on Truman's part, claimed that there was no story here. "No, there is no significance except the very central and important significance which, I think, is that the President announced this as soon as he was completely sure of the ground on which he stood," Acheson averred. "It was not timed in any tricky way. It has no significance to any other events."[66] This was, strictly speaking, false, and on two counts.

First, as we have already seen, the timing was certainly correlated with the British devaluation of the pound. And second, as discussed in the following chapter, it had direct implications for national-security bills pending in Congress.

Neither military officers nor scientists had been brought into the loop in large numbers before the announcement. To a surprising degree, many of the most central figures in later atomic policy learned of Joe-1 the same way the average citizen did: through the news. They also were told in no uncertain terms not to editorialize on the matter. Immediately after Truman's announcement was read on the radio, General Lauris Norstad telephoned Curtis LeMay and alerted him not to make any comment, an order LeMay passed down the chain of command at the air staff.[67] Likewise, the General Advisory Committee of the AEC was having one of its yearly meetings that very week, and was in its second day of sessions when the Truman announcement was released. The Berkeley chemist Glenn Seaborg noted in his diary on September 23 that "our meeting was interrupted at 11:30 a.m. when Morse Salisbury brought in a copy of this morning's Presidential statement, announcing the Russian atomic bomb explosion. All of us were relieved that this information has been made public."[68] Placing the issue on their agenda, they contemplated making a statement: "If the Committee were to make any comment on the effect of the detection of the Russian explosion, it would be to express the hope that one outcome of the release of this information would be the achievement of a more rational security policy for the United States."[69] In other words, they were going to adhere to the fifth paragraph of Truman's statement.

The reaction of policy makers and consultants was this disciplined in part because the control of information was so tight. Even this event, which was ostensibly about the release of information to inform the public, can more accurately be described as a controlled management of information in order to produce a specific reaction: absence of panic and the public's trust in the leadership. Immediately after the announcement, a memorandum was circulated in the executive branch of the U.S. government to control the kind of information that could be discussed. This document was compiled by the PPS and cleared with Ross on *September 21*, that is, at the very moment that Truman was telling Lilienthal that no announcement was forthcoming.[70] A selection of its talking points—with its prescribed answers—is illuminating:

1. Does this mean that the Russians have the bomb? [We know that there was an atomic explosion. That is all we can say.]

2. How do we know that there was an atomic explosion? [It would not be compatible with national security to give further information on this subject.]

3. Do you know where and when it took place, and whether on the ground or water? [We have a pretty good idea.]

4. Is this the first atomic explosion in Russia? [So far as we know.]

5. Does our information indicate that the Russians may have a number of bombs? [No.] . . .

12. In what way has this development been taken into account in our basic policy? [As stated in the President's announcement, we have always known that efforts would be made to develop this weapon, and it has been no secret that such efforts were in progress in the Soviet Union. It has been for this reason, among others, that we have laid such great emphasis on the necessity for a firm and durable system of peaceful relationships between the nations of the world and that we have made such effort and such sacrifices to this end. We have consistently refrained from basing our own policies on a monopoly of the weapon and have endeavored to frame them throughout with a view to their validity in a period when that monopoly would no longer exist. We have tried to make our military posture one which would be an effective deterrent to aggression whether or not others had the atomic weapon. The atomic bomb must always be judged not as an isolated weapon but in the general framework of the relative military capabilities of countries.

> United States policies in helping strengthen the economies of
> European countries, in particular in the Atlantic Pact, and in
> considering a program of military assistance to other nations
> have all tended to increase the strength of this country.][71]

The last point essentially reprises the scope of Harry Truman's policy for the waging of the cold war as it would be implemented for
the duration of his administration.

The immediate reactions to the announcement were as good as the
inner circle of the Truman administration could have hoped—
better, even. It is true that an occasional frantic citizen wrote a
letter to the president urging that the time had come to wage a
preventive war against the Soviets, but such voices were few and
far between.[72] For the most part, private and public discourse mirrored the "official" interpretation. The only significant addition was
a reassessment of previous dismissive attitudes to Soviet science.
Despite all the harsh words about "backward Russians," the veteran journalist Joseph C. Harsch expressed the new consensus
recognizing the egg on American faces: "It would seem that there
has been a slight underrating of Russian atomic scientists."[73] Or, as
Samuel K. Allison, the director of the University of Chicago's Institute of Nuclear Studies, put it, "We must at least say that some
recent estimates of Russian scientific and technological efficiency
need to be revised radically upward."[74]

British reactions were more somber, and for good reason. First,
given the limited long-range bombing capacity known to be in the
Soviet Union's possession, the United Kingdom was a far more
likely target for a Soviet attack than America. The British also, significantly, did not have a nuclear deterrent of their own. From
being the world leaders in the weaponization of nuclear fission in
1941—the time of the Maud Report that triggered the American
and Soviet programs—Great Britain had fallen behind not only the
upstart Americans but even the *Russians*. Winston Churchill, now

leader of the Tory opposition in Parliament, saw this as insult added to the injury of sterling devaluation, holding forth on September 28: "Finally over all there looms and broods the atomic bomb which the Russian Soviet, for reasons not yet explained, have got before the British though happily not before the Americans . . . The hour is grave."[75]

Other European nations, and the rest of the world, seemed more sanguine about it all. Admiral William S. Parsons noted in a letter to Oppenheimer that the Europeans "appeared to be more interested in our motives in announcing it than in the fact itself."[76] Indeed, press and official reactions in other countries indicate that there was more concern about the pound devaluation than the Joe-1 news, as there had been a general sense that the monopoly had to end sometime, so it might as well be now as later.[77] In this, they were following the American interpretation fairly closely.

To some other foreign audiences, Joe-1 was more good news than bad. Otto Hahn, who was awarded the 1944 Nobel Prize in chemistry for his work on the discovery of fission, told reporters that he had not expected so quick an end to the monopoly, but he was relieved because he believed—in an explicit analogy to chemical weapons—that the dual possession of atomic weapons meant no one would ever use them.[78] As a German living in the likely future atomic battlefield, this was no mean assurance. Likewise, in Japan, the news of the Soviet bomb marked the beginning of the end of American occupation censorship of unfavorable coverage of nuclear weapons.[79] Not everyone was as morose as Churchill.

This leaves the most interesting reaction of all: the Soviet Union's. Obviously, the announcement that the first Soviet nuclear test was successful was not news to Joseph Stalin or the Soviet leadership. What was new, however, was the publicizing of the fact—and by the Americans, of all people. Why did the Soviets not announce First Lightning? And how did they react to the news not of Joe-1 but of the American detection of Joe-1?

We do not have direct evidence from Stalin as to why he did not announce his test, but we are able to make some fairly plausible guesses. The major reason for Soviet silence on the matter was a fear of American preemptive attack. The point Omar Bradley raised about the absence of a Soviet stockpile was surely more present to Stalin than to anyone else: If the Americans knew in late August 1949 that the Soviet Union had detonated its entire supply of plutonium, would they not certainly mount an attack before the Soviet Union could properly arm itself? According to this interpretation, the Soviets mainly wanted to keep their success quiet to avoid triggering a rearmament overreaction in the West.[80] (Which is, of course, what did happen.) Stalin was so worried about preemption that he kept news of milestone successes in the Soviet project—such as the launching of the F-1 reactor—secret from even most of the people in his inner circle.[81]

Fear of an American preventive strike was surely one reason to keep news of the test quiet, but almost certainly not the only one. Even dismissing American speculation at the time that the reason the Soviets did not announce their test is that the Vermont data was really evidence of an accident, not an intentional explosion—which we know now for certain was not true—the Soviet downplaying of First Lightning was overdetermined.[82] Stalin's consistent position on nuclear weapons before Joe-1, which he publicly maintained until his death in 1953, was that these were not decisive weapons in combat and would always remain subservient to the so-called permanently operating factors. Therefore, we should not have expected Stalin to treat the nuclear test any differently from any other weapons innovation.[83] But even that explanation might be interpreting too much. For the general stance of the Soviet state to *anything* nuclear (and much else) was to keep it secret— espionage data, Soviet achievements, war-fighting doctrine. Nikolaus Riehl, the most highly placed German specialist in the Soviet nuclear project, did not even know there was a scheduled test, and learned of the explosion of Joe-1 only after hearing the news broadcast on BBC Radio![84] Stalin may indeed have made the announcement himself once he had more bombs in his stockpile, or when the geopolitical scene made such a sudden revelation advantageous—but not before. The presumption was for secrecy, and First Lightning was no different.

So the Soviets found themselves on September 23, 1949, in a bit of a bind. Stalin and his advisers had not known that the Americans knew about the test. Decision makers had to scramble to produce an appropriate response to this Western intelligence coup. As Soviet spymaster Pavel Sudoplatov recalled, "Our immediate reaction was that there had been an American agent penetration of our test; but in a week our scientists reported that nuclear explosions in the atmosphere could be easily detected by planes sampling air around Soviet borders."[85] That would truly have been the last straw: a Klaus Fuchs of their own! But once this fear was dismissed (and fears of internal wrecking and sabotage died hard with Stalin), there was still the problem of how to address it. The American ambassador to the Soviet Union, Alan G. Kirk, reported to Acheson in early October what by then was obvious to all intelligent observers: "Some evidence here that Soviet Government caught flat-footed by our tripartite announcement."[86]

The best evidence of this was the official Soviet response, issued by the TASS news agency on September 25. As it was produced for foreign consumption more than to inform Soviet citizens, I reproduce here the official translation in its entirety:

In the Soviet Union, as is known, large-scale construction works are under way—construction of hydro-electric power stations, mines, canals and roads—which necessitate much blasting with the application of the most up-to-date technical means.

Since this blasting work has taken place and is taking place rather frequently in various parts of the country, it is possible that this might attract attention beyond the boundaries of the Soviet Union.

As for the production of atomic energy, *TASS* deems it necessary to recall the fact that already on November 6, 1947, the Minister of Foreign Affairs of the U.S.S.R., V. M. Molotov, made a statement concerning the secret of the atomic bomb, saying that "this secret ceased to exist long ago."

This statement signified that the Soviet Union had already discovered the secret of the atomic weapons and had this weapon at its disposal.

Scientific circles of the United States of America regarded this statement by V. M. Molotov as [a] bluff, considering that the Russians would not be able to master the atomic weapon earlier than the year 1952.

They were mistaken, however, since the Soviet Union had found out the secret of the atomic weapon as early as 1947.

As for the alarm that is being spread in this connection by certain foreign circles, there are not the slightest grounds for alarm.

It should be pointed out that, although the Soviet Government has the atomic weapon at its disposal, it adheres and intends to adhere hereafter to its old position in favour of the unconditional prohibition of the use of the atomic weapon.

Concerning control over the atomic weapon, it has to be said that this control will be essential in order to check up on the fulfilment of the decision on the prohibition of the atomic weapon.[87]

The impact of Truman's announcement on the Soviet leadership was so strong that Soviet-era histories tended to periodize their account unconsciously around it. Several historians, including some who were involved in the atomic project, erroneously dated First Lightning on September 23, 1949, as if Truman had announced it immediately.[88] Others protested too much and ignored Truman altogether, reproducing only the TASS statement.[89] Either option represents a tacit admission that the American response induced the Soviet one.

That response was both superficially ridiculous and extremely clever. The ridiculous part was the assertion that any "explosion" the West might believe happened was simply the result of normal large-scale construction of a sort common in the postwar Soviet Union. Either the Soviets were ignorant of any potential for long-range detection (which is unlikely) or they thought a seismic or sonic method (or even possibly human intelligence at a distance) was responsible for Truman's announcement, as there was simply no way radiological detection could be mistaken in this manner.

As with Truman's announcement, the clever part had to do with what was said—and even more with what was not said. Notice that there is no admission in this statement that the Soviet Union had in fact detonated an atomic device, in parallel to Truman's omitting mention of anything about the method of long-range detection. (The Soviet Union would not explicitly admit possession of nuclear weapons until 1951.) If the Americans wanted to start a preventive war, they would find no casus belli here. On the other hand, the explicit reference to Molotov's 1947 announcement that there was no longer a secret to the atomic bomb—again a parallel to the invocation of history in Truman's statement—was also designed to forestall any preemptive attack. For while Stalin would not admit that they had just acquired any nuclear weapons, he would imply that there just *might* have been a Soviet stock-pile accruing since 1947, an implication American intelligence was quick to apprehend.[90] Although the dismissal of Truman's announcement was facile, the coded signals to deter the Americans were just plausible enough that they might indeed have acted as a brake on hotter heads in the United States.

The renewed call for total abolition of nuclear weapons reiterated the single note that the Soviets had been hitting since the introduction of the Gromyko Plan in 1946. And, as in 1946, the Soviet delegation to the United Nations was at the forefront of responding to Truman's announcement. Recall that one of the reasons Truman released his announcement on the morning of the 23rd was that that very afternoon there was to be a public address to the General Assembly by the newly appointed Soviet foreign minister, Andrei Vyshinsky.

Vyshinsky had replaced V. M. Molotov as foreign minister only in March 1949, but he was not new to American Kremlin watchers, having served as the chief prosecutor during the grotesque show trials of the Bolshevik elite in the late 1930s. Soviet watchers in the West were apprehensive about this appointment. The last time Stalin had suddenly replaced foreign ministers—substituting Molotov for Maksim Litvinov—it heralded the signing of the Nazi-Soviet nonaggression pact, a dramatic shift in Soviet foreign policy that boded very ill indeed.[91] Vyshinsky certainly instituted changes in the running of his ministry; one diplomat later recalled that what had been Molotov's "strict regime [now] became cruel and inhuman."[92] But did Vyshinsky's appointment presage a radical shift in policy? The news of Joe-1 lent weight to the possibility, and that afternoon of the 23rd, all eyes were on the General Assembly.

It was a disappointing performance. Mostly, Vyshinsky reiterated Soviet platitudes on international relations and nuclear arms control, making no direct reference to Truman's announcement from the morning. He came closest with an echo of Molotov's 1947 remarks: "The secret of atomic energy has been completely discovered and harnessed by us. Nevertheless, we maintain that atomic weapons must be prohibited internationally and control of atomic energy established."[93] Outside the United Nations, there was more of the same. Vyshinsky slightly escalated the Communist-led Peace Offensive in anticipation of the November 1949 meeting of the Cominform in Budapest. But this was mostly a continuation of the late August formation in Moscow of a Soviet Committee for the Defense of Peace at the All-Union Conference of Partisans of Peace.[94] If Soviet foreign policy was going to change because of a successful Soviet test (and the successful American detection of that test), the world would have to wait a while longer.

Within the Soviet Union, there seemed to be little excitement in response to TASS's statement (the Truman announcement was not publicized domestically). American intelligence analysts came to the conclusion that the Soviet public in general believed that Molotov had been telling the truth in 1947 when he had implied their military already had the atomic bomb.[95] And, truly, the same discourse about American atomic coercion and belligerence and Soviet preparedness (since 1947) remained prevalent throughout the Stalin years. A propaganda article from 1950 provides a typical reaction: "The skirmishers of America atomic diplomacy, deploying their misanthropic campaign of atomic blackmail and extortion, issued from the illusion that American was and for a long time would still be a monopolist in the production of atomic weapons. But in 1947 the Soviet government released a general announcement that the secret of the atomic bomb no longer existed."[96] Ambassador Kirk confirmed as much to Acheson: "Samples correspond to our guess about general attitude of Soviet citizens: Little excitement, some pride in Soviet achievement, perhaps slightly greater sense security due to diminution American atomic 'threat.' "[97]

The cat was out of the bag, the milk was spilled, the horses had fled the stable. Any number of clichés and adages were mobilized in the United States to confront this new fact, vouchsafed at the highest level possible through Truman's imprimatur. The Soviets had the atomic bomb. But what did this event mean? Was it the case, as Senator Arthur Vandenberg intoned after a "very solemn" meeting of JCAE, that "this is now a different world"?[98] Or perhaps it was more as a newspaper wag put it: "The excitement over the President's statement is something like that at the birth of a child. The event had been expected for quite a while, but yet—."[99] Was it really *news*?

There were a number of paths the reaction to Joe-1 could take, but everyone was certain that there would be changes. For both Vandenberg and the columnist were correct: This was expected, yet it was still a different world. As so often was the case, the *Washington Post* cartoonist Herblock captured the moment perfectly (figure 7). The cartoon harkened back to a time when one could expect casual newspaper readers to be familiar with Daniel Defoe's *Robinson Crusoe*. The hero of the novel, having been stranded alone on his tropical island for years, on an otherwise ordinary walk "was exceedingly surprised with the print of a man's naked foot on the shore, which was very plain to be seen in the sand. I stood like one thunderstruck, or as if I had seen an apparition." The American atomic bomb in Herblock's cartoon, coming across the footprint of another, was no less shocked and no less at a loss for what to do. Crusoe returned to his fortified abode, drew up his ladder, and slept poorly. The United States, it would turn out, acted much the same.

FIGURE 7 | September 1949 cartoon following Truman's announcement of the first Soviet atomic explosion. *Source:* Herbert Block, *The Herblock Book* (Boston: Beacon Press, 1952), 132. Copyright by The Herb Block Foundation.

SEVEN
THE YEAR OF JOE

These are the Gods of the Kingdoms of the Earth: in contrarious
And cruel opposition: Element against Element, opposed in War
Not Mental, as the Wars of Eternity, but a Corporeal Strife.
WILLIAM BLAKE, "MILTON"

The atomic monopoly was over, and everyone knew it. The Soviet Union had tested their first atomic device, indicating at the very least that it had the potential to set off more atomic explosions, possibly in an American city. Lewis Strauss, not content to see the glass as half empty, worried that the United States was in even worse straits. What if the Soviet atomic explosion had not been their first? "An atomic explosion which occurred in Russian territory was detected in August, 1949," Strauss wrote in 1952. "It is regularly referred to as the 'first' but there is *no evidence* that it was actually the first Russian test."[1] Strauss was almost a lone skeptic on this point; even the CIA dismissed this claim as unlikely.[2] Soviet archives indicate that the CIA was correct.

Although we now know a great deal about what happened after Joe-1, we should resist the temptation to read back from the end of the cold war to the waning days of September 1949. True, there was an arms race, and we live today in a world populated with a large number of nuclear powers (and nuclear warheads), but it was by no means obvious to American (or Soviet) decision makers what their reactions to the Soviet explosion should be. For J. Robert Oppenheimer, Joe-1 served as a wake-up call, an invitation to reconsider fundamental policy:

> "Operation Joe" is simply the fulfillment of an expectation that we have long attempted to take into account. Until now we had evaluated the situation by reasonable guesses. Today we have a fact, and we can be grateful to the many men and women whose hard work and imagination have uncovered it. But now that we have a certainty instead of a conjecture, it is inevitable and healthy that we take a fresh look at the many deep problems of policy that confront us.[3]

Given the rapid pace of events in the year following Joe-1, one is struck by the comparative calm expressed by Oppenheimer and other important actors in its immediate aftermath. The CIA, for example, advised against any hasty moves: "With the announcement of an atomic explosion in the USSR, Soviet capabilities for fighting the cold war have increased. No immediate change in Soviet policy or tactics is expected"—although they also noted that "the USSR has seriously weakened the psychological advantage until now held by the US as a result of monopoly of atomic weapons."[4]

On the Soviet side, as we have seen, the success of First Lightning did not alter very much at all; Beria and his scientists simply continued to build more nuclear weapons. At first, the American public reacted to Truman's announcement the way the president had wanted them to: with calm and trust in their leaders. But very shortly, especially among political, military, and scientific decision makers, panic began to set in. It was not instant, but when it came it arrived in full force. For these Americans, Joe-1 soon came to mean change, and fast. "While Soviet possession of an atomic weapon was to be expected," opined Bernard Baruch from his armchair position, "let no one be deceived that it does not necessitate revaluing our strategy for peace."[5] Vested with greater responsibility, AEC Chairman David Lilienthal was also rather more frank: "The Russian bomb has changed the situation drastically, and . . . the talk about our having anticipated everything and following the same program as we had before is the bunk."[6]

Oppenheimer felt he knew what needed to be done. He wrote to Lilienthal immediately after Truman's announcement: "We [the GAC] felt quite strongly that the real impact of the news of Operation Joe lay not in the fact itself, but in the response of public opinion and public policy to the fact." That is, he wanted more transparency with respect to nuclear weapons, and he saw Soviet proliferation as the fulcrum around which the "miasma" of nuclear secrecy would finally be overcome.[7] After the initial passive response to Truman's announcement, rethinking had suddenly become the order of the day, as the contrarian commentator William Reuben sarcastically noted: "The Soviet's atom bomb had repercussive effects into well-nigh every aspect of American political life. It was the sort of issue, like death, taxes or sex, on which all public figures were expected to express a firm opinion on at least some aspect of the question."[8]

Clearly, the American program had to change. But change how? American policy toward nuclear weapons was a mixed bag by 1949. Officially, the United States still pushed for the modified Baruch Plan at the United Nations, but it was also building more nuclear weapons after the Sandstone test had verified more efficient nuclear designs, and it was also negotiating the North Atlantic Treaty to provide for the conventional defense of Europe. Which aspect (or aspects) of this motley assortment—nuclear disarmament, nuclear rearmament, or conventional mobilization—needed to be reevaluated, exactly?

In the event, essentially everything was rethought, but not as Oppenheimer, Baruch, Lilienthal, or the CIA had initially imagined. Immediately after Truman's announcement of the American detection of the first Soviet nuclear test, a series of options were openly and sincerely discussed. Within a few months, the possibilities had been whittled down to a precious few that shaped—to the historical actors' eyes, even *compelled*—an intensification of hostility. Within a year of Joe-1, certain tendencies of America's approach to the cold war had hardened into permanent features of the geopolitical landscape: nuclear and conventional arms races, spy hunts and anticommunist paranoia, and proxy wars outside of Europe. Each of these three dominant reactions was interpreted after the fact as "caused" by Joe-1. This oversimplifies the situation. A number of politicians, military officers, and scientists mobilized the event of Joe-1 into a reason for moving the cold war along these paths. But this transformation was not inevitable at noon on September 23, 1949, and it was not easily accomplished.

The Red Army lifted the Berlin blockade on May 12, 1949, implicitly recognizing the success of the Anglo-American airlift in supplying the beleaguered city without caving to Soviet demands. The summer of 1949 was thus a high time of scorn for the "appeasement" that had ostensibly led to the tragedy of World War II; the Americans would not make the same mistake again. After the announcement of Joe-1, the U.S. State Department worried that the world might slip into a mind-set of appeasement once again, that they would cede to Soviet demands out of fears of a nuclear retaliation.[9] Hartley Rowe, a member of the General Advisory Committee to the AEC, feared the same: "For a very considerable time the general public considered the A-bomb an absolute weapon, and therefore was lulled into a false sense of security. This condition was completely reversed by the announcement of the Russian explosion."[10] To prevent a lapse into appeasement, the Americans needed a response, one that suited the magnitude of the provocation.

As the stimulus was nuclear, so the response should be nuclear.

Gordon Dean, newly appointed to the AEC, noted in a memo to his fellow commissioners that playing down the significance of the Soviet success was all well and good, but "nevertheless, I think we must be prepared to demonstrate that we have in light of this knowledge taken or considered taking certain definite steps."[11] The most obvious and direct reaction to the nuclearization of the Soviet Union was to make America even more nuclear by expanding the enrichment of fissile material and the production of atomic weapons. This response was also the easiest, since it had been in the planning stages for months before any radioactive debris was lifted from the troposphere over the Pacific. Once Sandstone had demonstrated the possibility of making more (and more efficient) bombs from the same amount of nuclear fuel and the Modus Vivendi agreement with the United Kingdom had granted the Americans a greater share of the world's uranium ore, the AEC developed concrete proposals for expanded production. Immediately after Joe-1, Truman approved the requests and asked Congress for $1.4 billion ($12.5 billion in 2009 dollars) for another gaseous diffusion plant for uranium enrichment and three additional heavy-water reactors. Peacetime AEC financing now finally eclipsed that of the wartime Manhattan Project.[12]

The expansion of AEC facilities would certainly have happened without the provocation of Joe-1. Not so, however, other escalations of the incipient arms race. It was one thing to take the resources one already had (uranium) and turn them into a particular end product (bombs). It was something else entirely to conceive of the Soviet explosion as a move in a competition, one that demanded a response in multiple areas. The Princeton physicist Eugene Wigner, in a talk at Oak Ridge, Tennessee, in October 1949 called explicitly for more competition—in this case in nuclear reactor design:

It is to be hoped that now, after the September 23 news of developments in the U.S.S.R., the sense of disorientation will soon be replaced by an objective and well-founded appraisal of the situation based on an adequate knowledge of the conditions and on common agreement among all.

The announcement of September 23 will also make clear to us that we are in competition, that we must work hard if we are not to be outpaced hopelessly. We will stop glorifying our past, forget about the unique abilities and accomplishments of ourselves and our industrial organizations, and get back to work.[13]

Was this an obvious response to detecting a Soviet weapon? In any case, the nuclear physicists quickly embraced the framework of competition.

This competitive mind-set lay behind even apparently counter-intuitive responses to the Soviet test by scientists, such as calls to alleviate or eliminate atomic secrecy. One might think that news of Joe-1 would encourage those who were critical of the publication of the Smyth Report, prompting them to intensify the rapidly growing classification apparatus around nuclear information. Instead, AEC commissioner William Waymack (no liberal) virtually delighted in the news as a way to silence this reflexive clampdown response: "Nothing could shake them loose from the monopoly concept and therefore the secrecy obsession. As simple, as irrefutable and as fundamental a fact as the fact that our real security rested on progress was perhaps nominally accepted but in effect rejected . . . Not instantly but perhaps rather rapidly the Russian achievement will destroy this illusory and dangerous attitude . . . of fearful ostrichism."[14] Even Edward Teller, a prominent hawk and the leading scientific advocate of intensifying research on thermonuclear (hydrogen fusion) weapons, wanted less secrecy, *precisely* because openness favored the United States in an atomic competition with the Soviet Union: "Rather, our safety depends upon the rapid conception and utilization of ideas . . . Because free discussion encourages progress and usually improves ideas, I believe less secrecy would mean more speed in our race for new and useful ideas. And the United States needs more speed in the races which vitally concern our freedom and survival."[15] These calls were generally not heeded, for the national-security state that had emerged over the recent past had already made control of information its most important security measure. The congressmen who had the power to amend the McMahon Act and the military men who controlled declassification protocols were not interested in carefully exploring alternatives, especially when the hour seemed so grave. Competition would have to flourish within security strictures.

Another possibility for relaxing the tense policies of the monopoly years lay in reinvigorating the approach to arms control at the United Nations Atomic Energy Commission. By the time Joe-1 was announced, a slightly modified Baruch Plan—now known as the "majority plan"—had been sent to the UN General Assembly, where it languished. Perhaps, now that they had a nuclear weapon of their own, the Soviet Union would be more flexible? Chester Barnard, one of the members of the Acheson-Lilienthal Committee and a staunch critic of Baruch's version of its proposals, certainly hoped so: "My immediate reaction was that the chances of attaining the international control of atomic energy under the aegis of the United Nations had increased rather than decreased."[16]

This tendency to translate the impact of Joe-1 into a call for deescalating the cold war and reviving arms control and mutual cooperation appeared not only among the left-leaning or dovish. It seemed to as cautious a body as the CIA's ORE a logical consequence of Soviet proliferation: "Moscow's current campaign to prohibit the use of atomic weapons and to attach a moral and legal stigma to their use is enhanced by the fact that the USSR can pose as willing to accept the same restrictions that it demands of other countries."[17] Of course, the Americans would likely still be unwilling to give up any weapons without a strict verification regime, and shortly the climate in the Senate would become so hostile to any notion of arms control that even had the plan been endorsed by the Soviets, it would have failed to be ratified. If this were so, if the majority plan proved inappropriate, optimists believed that perhaps the world situation had changed enough—with two nuclear pow-

ers instead of one—to justify reconvening the UNAEC and renegotiating an interim arms-control agreement, if not Baruch's 1946
call for total disarmament.[18]

Perhaps not surprisingly, the Baruch of 1950 no longer called for
any such thing: "If we are to presume that more than one nation
knows how to make an atomic weapon, that fact argues all the
more forcefully for really effective control as against an illusory
control which would penalize those nations which observed their
agreements to the advantage of those which might not."[19] That is,
the inspection protocols needed to be at least as strict as he had
argued for in the past, almost certainly even stricter now that
Stalin had demonstrated that it was possible to build a nuclear
bomb in secret—and in the past the Soviets had seemed unwilling
to entertain the possibility. And now, two atomic-policy specialists
noted, "the Russians were, if anything, even stiffer than before."[20]
It seemed highly unlikely that either side would agree even to the
Gromyko alternative, which required total disarmament before
inspection, because now both sides had the atomic potential to
strike at each other. The majority proposal gathered dust in the
General Assembly, increasingly moot in the wake of Joe-1.

Were the Soviets going to remain content with a bomb or two, or
was there going to be an actual arms race? Norris Bradbury, the
director of Los Alamos, later interpreted the race metaphor literally:

> It was clear at that time [after Joe-1] that—I am now only quot-
> ing my own thinking and opinion in this matter—it seemed to
> me that we were in the position of 2 runners in the race, where
> it was quite clear that your opponent was running and running
> quite fast. It was probabl[e] you were ahead of him in actual
> distance. It was not obvious that he was not running faster
> than you were. Our own objectives at that time had to be as far
> as we could make them to be sure we were running as fast as he
> was.[21]

But no one knew the actual status of Soviet armaments.

The fact remained, despite the success of the long-range detection system, that American nuclear intelligence was still riddled with the same old systemic problems: uncertain, incomplete, and corrupted information, with no human agents on the ground to provide direct corroboration. The only difference in late 1949 was that now the government *knew* that it had egregiously underestimated Soviet capabilities. The Joint Chiefs of Staff, for one, were going to take CIA estimates of Soviet atomic progress with several grains of salt.[22]

Joe-1 became a pretext for an overhaul of the American intelligence infrastructure, the second such restructuring in the four years since the end of the war. Former ambassador to the Soviet Union Walter Bedell Smith replaced Roscoe Hillenkoetter as director of central intelligence in late 1950 and by November had abolished ORE, the scapegoat for a series of general intelligence failures, including Joe-1. ORE was replaced with three units, designed to eliminate confusion: the Office of National Estimates, the Office of Research and Reports, and the Office of Current Intelligence.[23] Whether this would produce any better intelligence was an open question.

Certainly the American methods of obtaining intelligence had improved, and not just because of the cracking of the Venona codes and continued long-range detection flights. In late 1949, the British obtained their first Soviet defector, code-named "Gong," who provided some valuable data. Gong was soon eclipsed by larger quarry. Between September 19 and December 31 of the next year, 610 German specialists and 1,078 members of their families were returned from the Soviet Union to Frankfurt on the Oder, in East Germany. The Soviets had extracted all the knowledge they needed from these people, and keeping the Germans around as the Soviet Union explored further advances was poor security. Few of these early repatriates were connected with the Soviet atomic project, but they were also only the tip of the iceberg. By 1952, 31.2 percent of the specialists had been repatriated; by the end of

1954, 91.4 percent were back. The atomic specialists were almost all living in one of the two Germanys by March 1955. The British and the Americans collaborated on operations Dragon Return and Wringer to milk as much atomic information out of this cohort as possible. Although all the German specialists in the atomic project had been cycled out of their nuclear research into a mandatory "cooling-off" period beginning in roughly 1950, during which they were isolated from classified research and thus were unable to provide any current data about the status of Soviet developments, they did offer rich historical information on the early years of the program, even considering their relative isolation in Sukhumi. For years, these Germans supplied the most detailed account of the engineering and scientific aspects of the early Soviet project available in the West, rendered all the more credible by their honesty about their limited role in the Soviet achievement.[24]

The Americans now had some information; transforming it into actionable intelligence, intelligence that could somehow influence policy decisions, turned out to be much trickier. If the atomic monopoly was beset with anxiety, the dominant emotion in the duopoly was flat-out fear. The first two Hollywood movies overtly about the atomic arms race appeared in 1951, *The Day the Earth Stood Still* and *Five*, the latter being America's first postapocalypse nuclear film. Stories of the United States after nuclear war leapt out of the realm of science fiction and hit mainstream culture. The apprehension of a Soviet attack was not confined to overly imaginative screenwriters. Stuart Symington, secretary of the air force, believed that since the sanguine predictions of Soviet proliferation underestimated Soviet competence in nuclear physics, they may perhaps have lowballed the Soviets in other areas as well:

The recent atomic explosion in Russia indicates that the Soviets can have a militarily significant number of atomic bombs by a date two or three years earlier than was expected from original estimates.

In addition, should Russia use the relatively simple and completely proven process of refueling in flight, she would now have the capacity to deliver the bomb against the country without resorting to suicide missions.[25]

This, indeed, was the great worry: that the Soviet Union, even without atomic bombers in nearby bases, could somehow launch a catastrophic first strike against America. (Silently understood here was the fact that Americans *did* have such striking power against Moscow from Europe, although they did not yet station atomic weapons on the continent. Until the mid-1950s, atomic bombs would first have to be flown to Europe from American bases, the planes refueled, and then launched against the Soviet heartland.) In 1948, the Joint Intelligence Committee believed that the Soviets possessed two hundred Tu-4 aircraft, a plane copied from the B-29 and thus capable of a three-thousand-mile striking range. With refueling, these could be devastating. These kinds of first-strike fears mushroomed during the first eighteen months after Joe-1.[26]

Delivery systems were only part of the worry. How many bombs did the Soviets actually have? The intelligence services were in the unenviable position of being forced by Joe-1 to revise their estimates of the Soviet stockpile up from zero but without necessarily having any more accurate information on which to base their new numbers. Immediately after Joe-1, CIA analysts predicted that the Kremlin would command 10 to 20 atomic bombs by mid-1950, 25 to 45 in 1951, 45 to 90 in 1952, and 120 to 200 by mid-1954, "if the simplest type of atomic bombs developing roughly 20 kilotons explosive power are assumed for calculation."[27] In June 1950, stockpile estimates went up; analysts now predicted 70 to 135 by mid-1953. By November 1950, that estimate hit 165.[28] The ORE, in one of its last estimates, admitted that its predictions were fragile:

Special attention is called to the fact that estimates of the Soviet atomic stockpile are tentative and uncertain because:

(a) The number and/or size of the production facilities postulated as a basis for this estimate may be incorrect. The minimum program, which is not inconsistent with the information available, would provide a stockpile of about one-half the number of weapons indicated. On the other hand, from the information available at the present time, the possibility that additional or expanded production facilities will be constructed during the period under consideration cannot be precluded.

(b) The type of weapon postulated for calculating the stockpile figures may be incorrect. It is possible by changing the weapon design to substantially increase or decrease the number of weapons in the stockpile, given a certain quantity of fissionable material. Such changes, however, alter the kilotonnage of the individual weapons accordingly.[29]

But what to do? Estimates, however unreliable, were necessary. Even the criteria for evaluating the spotty data emanating from the Soviet Union had changed. Whereas before Joe-1, the tendency had been to deflate Soviet claims as propaganda, by the mid-1950s, the air-policy expert Thomas K. Finletter strongly argued that "we should make our plans on the assumption that within the range of probable error the Russians will do substantially better than the average prediction. They have in the past—in atomic bombs, in electronics, and in aircraft."[30]

As might be expected, the pendulum swung too far the other way. Actual stockpile data from the Soviet archives—insofar as we have them—indicate that American predictions now grossly *over*-estimated the extent of Soviet progress. Although the first model of a Soviet nuclear device (RDS-1) was proved at Semipalatinsk in August 1949, it was not placed into mass production; only the second model (RDS-2), based on an indigenous design, was serially produced as of December 1951. In 1949 there were only two Soviet bombs besides the test model of RDS-1 (which was, of course, detonated and thus destroyed); and by 1950 overfulfillment of the quota had yielded nine weapons instead of the seven Beria had anticipated—still a long way from the CIA's predictions.

By Stalin's death in May 1953, the Soviet stockpile probably numbered no more than fifty bombs—the limiting reagent was still a relatively constrained uranium supply.[31] Had you told that to an intelligence officer in the West in the early 1950s, he would not have believed it and accused you of willfully deflating your figures. Soviet delivery capability was no more impressive.[32]

Yet the actual numbers could not matter to American decision making, for Truman and his advisers had no access to them. All they could go on were their guesses, and hope for the best. In short, they tended to agree with Gordon Dean: "The precise number doesn't matter. They have enough, if delivered on target, to hurt this country badly."[33] America simply had to become better prepared. Given that much of the problem centered on a lack of information, the American data deficit had to be managed so as to leave the United States at less of a disadvantage against the black hole of Stalin's Soviet Union.

The first and most obvious way to gain more information was to continue to intensify and exploit the only path that had proved reliable: long-range detection. Not only were the Loon Charlie and Ptarmigan flights from Alaska continued, but new routes were added. By May 1951, the United States Air Force sent a sampling flight once every seventy-two hours from Saudi Arabia to Pakistan. And in 1954 high-altitude planes began flying over the USSR to measure krypton 85 levels. This noble gas isotope was the only consistent method employed during the height of the cold war to estimate Soviet plutonium (and thus warhead) production.[34]

But who would alert the public? Long-range detection informed only the highest echelons of the military and intelligence communities, those with both the security clearance and technical competence to evaluate the isotopic mix. The public needed to be educated about what to do in the event of a Soviet strike, and the information in this case came in the form of civil-defense training. Joe-1 had made some level of awareness and training of the civilian population essential. "The recent atomic explosion in Russia brings closer the time when decisions must be made on major issues of civilian defense," David Lilienthal wrote to Sidney Souers, "including the matter of dispersal out from congested urban areas of facilities such as those of Government in Washington."[35] Now that Washington could be directly hit, perhaps the centralization of government was inadvisable. What about the people? Civil defense had been assigned in March 1949 to the Office of Civil Defense Planning in the office of the secretary of defense, but it was not intensified until Congress passed the Civil Defense Act of 1950, which created a Federal Civil Defense Administration (a civilian agency) to organize the population: planning evacuations, providing instructions for the construction and provisioning of bomb shelters, and erecting the CONELRAD radio-alert system in 1951.[36] The deluge of civil-defense announcements and activities—duck and cover, Bert the Turtle, and so on—were thus a direct product of the fear generated by Truman's announcement of Joe-1.

The third form of information management blossomed into the school of thought that made use of the principles of the social sciences, mathematical game theory, and the limited data about the Soviet nuclear program in order to formulate a strategy for dealing with the Communist enemy. Nuclear strategy, that child born in the aftermath of Hiroshima and Nagasaki, passed into adolescence with the end of the atomic monopoly. When nuclear parity was achieved by the late 1950s, it reached maturity.

One of the first actions of the unified Department of Defense in 1947 was to create a joint war plan in the event of an outbreak of hostilities against the Soviet Union. Given the reliance on nuclear weapons during the monopoly to offset the massive Red Army deployment in Eastern Europe, it stood to reason that these plans would rely on prompt and extensive utilization of nuclear weapons. Broiler, the earliest of these full-scale plans, was first briefed on November 8, 1947, but it relied on completely fictitious values for the number of available bombs. In the middle of 1947, not even Truman was fully aware of how many American bombs were actually ready, and nothing even close to the amount envisioned in Broiler or its successor Bushwhacker would be produced until after the expansion of AEC facilities in 1949–1950. These early plans were characterized by two features: obliviousness to nuclear scarcity and the presumed existence of a monopoly.[37] The coming of Joe-1 changed both.

The first post-Joe plan for the course of military engagement in the event of a hot war with the Soviet Union, briefed in October 1949 and dubbed Offtackle, called for 220 atomic bombs to be delivered on 104 urban Soviet targets, with a reserve of 72 weapons. That kind of plan required accelerating production of bombs and also bombers, as well as increasing the number of air force groups and trained pilots to get them there. After Joe-1, the Strategic Air Command under General Curtis E. LeMay began to provide the delivery systems that the AEC expansion required. W. Stuart Symington, the first secretary of the air force, insisted on more funds from Louis Johnson six weeks after Truman's announcement: "It now appears that even this gloomy hypothesis [of 1952 or 1953 for Soviet proliferation] was too optimistic; and by a substantial period . . . Therefore the planned build-up of the Air Force—which comprises two elements: (a) Increase in group strength, and (b) modernization of equipment, now proves to be inadequate in the light of demonstrated Soviet technical and industrial capabilities."[38] Even the maniacally frugal Johnson began to loosen his purse strings. By December 31, 1949, SAC had 521 aircraft (out of 837 total planes) modified to deliver atomic bombs; two years later they had 658 atomic-capable out of 1,165 (though the United States had nowhere near 658 bombs to put on those planes). SAC consistently assumed that only 70–85 percent of the modified bombers would make it through to their targets, which necessitated overkill.[39]

The term "overkill" was no exaggeration. Government secrecy on nuclear matters meant that many of the individuals involved with war planning were not informed enough about the specific details necessary to make a coordinated strategy. As the historian David Rosenberg has astutely observed, the fact that the air force did not know in advance how many bombs would be ready, or the AEC how many ships and planes, or the secretary of defense the extent of our atomic cooperation with allies, all made for a situation where instead of building up enough weapons and delivery systems to suit American strategy, American strategy instead conformed itself to the capabilities available.[40] The more bombs we built, the more we should throw at the Soviet Union, no matter whether or not they were necessary to destroy Moscow—did one really need to incinerate it two hundred times over? The assumption of nuclear scarcity, evident in early nuclear strategists from Bernard Brodie onward, coupled with the skittish paranoia induced by Joe-1, led to a situation where the elimination of scarcity did not change the axioms of strategy. What was more, the Americans began to assume that the Soviets thought as the Americans did. In the words of Herman Kahn, eventually the most salient and hawkish of these atomic mandarins: "It *is* important that the United States and Russia have certain views in common about strategic military problems."[41] For Kahn, one of the beauties of game theory—the science of conflict and strategy—was that it articulated the way any "rational actor" would behave when faced with similar situations. Given the post-Joe symmetry of the arms race, game theory's postulates now might obtain, which in turn pushed with a seemingly iron logic for the further armament of America.

This extreme fear about falling behind the Soviet Union, coupled with an assumption of symmetry (that is, that the Soviets would reason about nuclear matters in precisely the same way the Americans did, and that their reasoning would drive them to escalation), led in the United States to the most famous, and at the time most controversial, consequence of Joe-1: the crash program to develop the hydrogen bomb. Nuclear bombs release the energy stored in the nucleus of atoms. There are two ways of releasing this energy. The first—breaking apart large, heavy nuclei—is exploited in fission bombs such as the uranium and plutonium weapons used on Hiroshima and Nagasaki. During the entire period of the atomic monopoly (up to and including RDS-1, the Soviet bomb whose explosion ended it), fission bombs were the only nuclear bombs able to be constructed.

At Los Alamos during World War II, Edward Teller, a Hungarian émigré theoretical physicist, insisted to Oppenheimer on exploring the other path to releasing atomic energy: fusing light nuclei, such as those of hydrogen, its isotopes deuterium (one extra neutron) or tritium (two extra neutrons), helium, or lithium, into a larger nucleus. This process, which releases vastly more energy than a fission bomb, can be accomplished only under intense heat, hence its alternative designation: thermonuclear. (More commonly, these are known as hydrogen bombs.) Fission bombs are technically limited in their scope; though you can make them increasingly more efficient, there is a limit to the net amount of nuclear fuel you can deploy per bomb. If you exceed the so-called critical mass, you predetonate—they blow up before they are delivered to the target, presumably killing your own people, an outcome to be avoided at all costs. The critical mass does not limit only the maximum bomb size; it also limits the maximum size of the components for a larger bomb, so that while large fission bombs are indeed possible, there are engineering as well as physical limits to how large. The hydrogen in thermonuclear weapons, on the other hand, has no critical mass and so could theoretically reach any destructive magnitude one wished once it is ignited. The reason these superweapons— throughout the Truman administration, the potential hydrogen bomb was almost universally referred to as the "Super"—were not built was that the only thing that could ignite the fusion process was a fission bomb, and linking the fission and fusion reactions together proved to be an exceptionally tricky process.[42] Teller, still associated with Los Alamos, continued to pursue the Super at a moderate pace, but with little success.

Joe-1 seemed to change all that. Now that the Soviet Union had a fission bomb, they could also start to work on mastering the complicated linkage necessary for thermonuclear devices. The fact that Klaus Fuchs had been present at previous discussions of models for the Super (soon discarded because they were technically unworkable) only intensified the anxiety of Teller and others. As Stanislaw Ulam, the Polish-born mathematician who together with Teller later designed the first successful thermonuclear trigger, recalled his arrival at Los Alamos immediately after Truman's announcement: "The general question was 'What now?' At once I said that work should be pushed on the 'super.' Teller nodded."[43] Although he would eventually fall on the opposite side of the debate over the new weapon, Oppenheimer concurred at his 1954 security-clearance hearings on the link between Joe-1 and the Super: "No serious controversy arose about the super until the Soviet explosion of an atomic bomb in the autumn of 1949."[44] There is no question that there was a temporal link between the two: The controversy on the Super immediately followed the news of Joe-1. It took significant lobbying by Edward Teller and his ally Lewis Strauss to make the linkage seem logical: that Joe-1 necessitated the Super. The Soviet test became a rhetorical resource for certain scientific and political figures in the Truman administration to escalate the arms race.

The story began with Teller, who happened to be in Washington, D.C., at the time of Truman's announcement. Since that also coincided with one of the scheduled GAC meetings (Teller was not a member), that meant that he had access at this very tense moment to essentially all the major science advisers to the Truman administration on nuclear matters. "Almost instinctively, I thought of Oppenheimer," Teller later recalled. "With his prediction about the rate of Soviet progress proved wrong, I imagined he would be working on some appropriate new effort. I called him to ask, 'What do we do now?' His answer was abrupt: 'Keep your shirt on.' With great reluctance, I did."[45] Keeping his shirt on did not mean keeping silent about the Super, and Teller began to urge his allies on the AEC, principally Strauss, that a crash program was needed. Los Alamos had never stopped working on the Super, but progress had been slow; Teller wanted the same kind of mobilization and attention to solving the problem of how to ignite the thermonuclear fuel that had been unleashed on the problem of fission weapons during the war. Indeed, on September 29, the JCAE began to hear classified testimony on the possibility of pursuing a Super. The AEC was not far behind: On October 5, Strauss proposed a "quantum jump" in nuclear firepower by devoting more resources to the Super. The logic is not hard to fathom: Joe-1 was a fission event, and so it demanded a nuclear response; since the United States rightfully held the leadership in nuclear matters, it was necessary not just to increase the quantity of nuclear weapons but also to dramatically intensify their quality.

Unfortunately for Teller and for Strauss, they were respectively opposed by the influential leaders of the relevant organizations: J. Robert Oppenheimer, chairman of the GAC, and David Lilienthal, head of the AEC. This opposition was not lightly considered. Recall that at every previous decision about escalation of the arms of the race—to use the weapons on Japan, to test weapons at Bikini, to conduct Sandstone, to abandon the Baruch Plan, to expand AEC facilities—both Oppenheimer and Lilienthal had been in accord with the more hawkish position. And this pattern of endorsing a massive buildup of fission bombs still held when, on October 29, the GAC convened to discuss accelerating development of the Super. Arguments ranged over the utility of the weapon, its relationship to arms-control efforts, its technical feasibility, and its morality. For Oppenheimer, the chief reason not to initiate the crash program remained preventing the Soviets from doing likewise. As he put it later: "I believe that their [Soviet] atomic effort was quite imitative and that made it quite natural for us to think that their thermonuclear work would be quite imitative and that we should not set the pace in this development."[46] If we did nothing, perhaps they would not either. In addition, Oppenheimer argued that a crash program would divert crucial resources from fission-bomb construction—for example, shifting reactors away from plutonium production to tritium production—into a risky venture at a time when stockpiles were low. Agreeing with Oppenheimer, the GAC majority decided not to change the current moderate pace of Super research, in hope of averting an arms race with the Soviet Union in the thermonuclear, as opposed to just the fission, realm—as well as continuing the scaled-up production of proven plutonium and uranium bombs. I. I. Rabi and Enrico Fermi dissented from the majority, arguing that thermonuclear weapons were an evil "in any light," a genocidal weapon with no significant military utility and tremendous risks.[47] Both the (more practical) GAC judgment and the (more moral) minority report were passed on to the AEC and to the various departments and secretaries concerned with nuclear matters.

And then everything went public. On November 1, 1949, Senator Edwin Johnson appeared on a television program in New York and blurted out a series of ventures currently under exploration in response to Joe-1; ironically, he did so while making a point about the need for intensified secrecy about nuclear matters. One of the initiatives he mentioned was the investigation of a new bomb a thousand times more powerful than the Hiroshima device: the Super. (He also revealed that the Soviet test had been of a plutonium device, something that Truman had been very careful *not* to release so as not to alert the Soviets to the mechanism and sensitivity of America's long-range detection apparatus.) On November 18, after the story lay fallow for two and a half weeks, the *Washington Post* decided to turn Johnson's gaffe into a major news story.[48] The news about the Super was out.

This intensified the pressure on Truman to come to a decision, and he asked for advice from the relevant agencies. Predictably, he got plenty of unsolicited advice as well. "Atomic Senator" Brien McMahon was strongly in favor of a crash program. His logic derived directly from the failure to predict Joe-1:

> I do think it important to challenge the complacent attitude toward Soviet progress that pervades the thinking of those against the super. Some of them are the very ones who preached, from 1945 onward, that Russia would soon achieve the atomic bomb through her own independent effort; and yet they now ignore

the logic which led them to this correct conclusion, saying that Soviet achievement of the super may well be a decade away, if not longer. They speak of our taking the initiative in super development—just as though such a weapon has never occurred to Russian scientists, just as though we dare assume that the Soviets are not working toward it with all haste, and just as though American and British intelligence had not lately underestimated Russia to the extent of missing by three years the date of her first fission bomb test.[49]

Here, McMahon executed precisely the logical leap that Teller and Strauss were pushing for: viewing the Super decision as a way of erasing the fact of the end of the monopoly. Lilienthal refused to accept the connection:

> More seriously, the "Campbell" [a code name for the Super, from a pun on Campbell's Soup] discussion in the emotional atmosphere following the President's announcement of the Russian bomb on Sept. 23rd confirms my feeling that we are all giving far too high a value to atomic weapons, little, big, or biggest; that just as the A-bomb obscured our view and gave a false sense of security, we are in danger of falling into the same error again in discussion of "Campbell"—some cheap, easy way out.[50]

Truman took the decision about the hydrogen bomb more seriously than he had taken any atomic decision since before the bombings on Japan. He appointed a special commission of Secretary of Defense Louis Johnson, AEC Chairman Lilienthal, and Secretary of State Dean Acheson. Johnson, echoing the sentiment of the JCS that Soviet possession of a Super without an American counterpart would be "intolerable," was in favor of a crash program.[51] Lilienthal, as noted above, was opposed. Over the next few months, Acheson had to make up his mind. On January 31, the committee met with Truman; Acheson had decided in favor of a crash program on the Super. That same day, Truman publicly announced his instructions for "the Atomic Energy Commission to continue its work on all forms of atomic weapons, including the so-called hydrogen or super-bomb."[52] (Strauss resigned from the AEC that day, his work accomplished; he would return as President Dwight Eisenhower's AEC chairman.) In 1949, there was still no feasible mechanism for actually building a Super, yet on November 1, 1952, the AEC detonated the first thermonuclear explosion, code-named Mike, measuring 10.4 megatons (650 times more powerful than Trinity). The thermonuclear age had commenced.

Though there was no doubt in the American military that any war between the superpowers would have a nuclear (and later a thermonuclear) component, it was equally clear that the United States could not rely on the threat of nuclear bombardment every time the Soviets acted in a manner contrary to American interests. After all, the Soviet Union could now retaliate in kind, which meant that the balance that underlay the monopoly—American nukes versus Soviet soldiers—was broken. If the Soviets were going to nuclearize, then the Americans had better develop a conventional capacity. Given the resistance to a peacetime draft, America was incapable of deploying a conventional army of American troops to balance the Soviet ones, especially when the Far East was added into the calculus. The only way to offset Soviet conventional forces adequately was by bringing Western Europe into the military equation.

After the Soviet test—more accurately, after the publicizing of that test by Truman on September 23—American diplomats began to interpret typical Soviet recalcitrance as evidence of a new post-Joe-1 stance, even though these particular roadblocks seemed consistent with the pattern of Soviet diplomacy in the wake of the failure of the Berlin blockade. For example, negotiations on the Austrian peace treaty, which was to end the occupation and unify the country, had finally broken through the final impasses in October 1949, as the Americans moved closer to the Soviet negotiating stance. And then, abruptly, the Soviets changed their policy, and within a month the possibility of an agreement vanished, leaving Austria occupied and in limbo for another five years.[53]

Diplomats now read such stonewalling as evidence that the Soviets would flex their newfound nuclear muscle. The JCS was more circumspect, arguing that "the Soviet atomic capability will not alter its objectives or basic concepts and methods for achieving these objectives, although these methods will be developed to an unprecedented degree." The change, so argued the leadership of the American military, was only a matter of perception in the West. That did not mean, however, that those changes were inconsequential, for "the West" was much larger than simply America. What was to happen to Western Europe? The Joint Chiefs worried that the advent of a Soviet nuclear capability, however modest at this stage, would dramatically increase the British sense of vulnerability and possibly induce the United Kingdom to renounce its alliance with the West: "If under these circumstances this objective were not attained, it must be considered possible that the United Kingdom[,] because of its extreme vulnerability, could be detached from alignment with the United States."[54] The problem was more general than just the British and extended across all of Europe. Chip Bohlen, Truman's translator from Potsdam, wrote to his longtime friend and Soviet expert George F. Kennan, director of the State Department's Policy Planning Staff, that the ramifications might be dramatic: "While the initial reaction to the announcement that the Soviets have the atomic bomb has been on the whole calm, I think its long-term effect will be undoubtedly to strengthen those elements in Europe who have always hankered after the policy of neutrality."[55]

One way to prevent the slippage of Western Europe into neutrality—perceived by Bohlen as a step closer to alignment with the Communist bloc—was to reaffirm America's commitment to defend its allies in the face of a nuclear Soviet aggressor. The obvious way to do this was to intensify American involvement with

Europe, specifically through the North Atlantic Treaty. (The organization—the O in NATO—was a product of the Korean War, which led to an even stronger commitment to Europe.) This would alleviate not only the practical problem (how to assemble enough forces to provide an adequate deterrent) but also the perceptual problem. For Western Europeans knew that the kind of protection later promised by NATO was not a guaranteed development in 1949. Ratification of the North Atlantic Treaty on July 25, 1949, had preceded the news of Joe-1 by months, but it had not gone smoothly, and Republican opposition was still fierce. The Mutual Defense Assistance Act, which provided the military funds to bolster collective security in Europe and implemented the paper commitments of Europe, experienced a series of roadblocks before Joe-1. From the $1 billion ($8.9 billion in 2009 dollars) in foreign military assistance originally proposed in the bill, the Senate reserved $400 million until the president had actually provided integrated military plans. As the reduced bill sat in House-Senate conference, Truman made his September 23 announcement. On September 26, the committee not only restored the reserved funding but increased the allocations to $1.3 billion. The Act passed by 223–109 in the House and by voice vote in the Senate, and was signed by Truman on October 6. There is no question that fear induced by Soviet proliferation, and its possible implications for European security, turned the tide. As Dean Acheson would later wryly put it: "An ill wind blows some good."[56]

Collective security—protecting the West against communism— was built from three major components: the international agreements that signaled willingness to defend Europe, the funds and matériel to do it, and a strategy by which both were turned to achieve their goals. The first and the second were now in place. The strategy, however, needed work. Even though, as publicly proclaimed, "everyone had expected" that the Soviet Union would sooner or later (mostly later) develop a nuclear capability, American grand strategy was still anchored in a monopoly mind-set. American defense of Europe from 1945 to 1949 had relied mainly on a "tripwire" strategy: If Soviet forces crossed into Western Europe, America would launch atomic bombers against the Soviet Union. Soviet proliferation not only dulled the willingness of the United States to engage in atomic warfare—which would now be two-sided—it also sped up the clock. The Soviet Union could conceivably launch nuclear bombs against Western Europe, which would devastate the continent, too quickly for any tripwire to produce an Allied response. The tripwire strategy was conceived largely to accommodate Truman's tight budget constraints, but Congress's new generosity with military assistance indicated that those constraints were now lifted.[57]

Within a few weeks of Truman's announcement, both the PPS in the State Department and the interagency National Security Council were engaged in a thorough reevaluation of American strategic posture. Truman assured Senator McMahon in October 1949 that "the State Department's Policy Planning Staff is making a thorough reassessment of the impact of this event, not only on the international control problem but on our foreign policy generally. This survey is being conducted quietly and confidentially, but I am sure you will be pleased to learn that it is under way."[58] In the same letter, Truman also alerted him to the expansion of atomic fuel production at the AEC. Reconsideration of general security meant reconsideration of atomic security.

The NSC, which first met on September 26, 1947, was a relatively new player to national-security policy. It was created along with the unification of the armed services into the Defense Department as an institutionalization of State-Defense consultation. Truman had initially mostly ignored the NSC as a covert attempt by Secretary of Defense James V. Forrestal to assume control over security policy. At first, Truman did not even attend the meetings. This was not because they were rare. In its first full year of operation, the NSC conducted 30 meetings, considered 79 papers, and took 166 actions (although many of these were minor). Louis Johnson's habit of bringing an entourage to dominate NSC meetings tended to diminish the efficiency of consultation and further alienated Truman, despite the best efforts of NSC chairman Sidney Souers, a longtime Missouri friend of the president. Before Joe-1, the NSC worked on a variety of topics, producing eleven major policy studies on Taiwan alone.[59] The end of the atomic monopoly gave it a new mission.

That mission was encoded in a paper the NSC produced on April 14, 1950, titled "United States Objectives and Programs for National Security," known universally by its shorthand moniker: NSC-68. Truman had informed McMahon that "reassessment" of strategy was under way *directly* because of Joe-1; NSC-68 was the result and is eclipsed only by the hydrogen bomb as the most enduring legacy of First Lightning.[60] For the previous few years, this kind of complete overhaul of grand strategy would naturally have taken place within the PPS, an office Dean Acheson established while serving as acting secretary of state under James Byrnes. George Kennan, the intellectual architect of containment—attempting primarily through political and economic means to keep Soviet influence confined within the geographical domain defined by the end of the war—would have been the natural spearhead of the new effort.

His role, however, was supplanted by his deputy, Paul Nitze. Nitze had no diplomatic background (he was an economist) and was not a Soviet expert like Kennan. His first foray into the realm of nuclear policy was as a member of the United States Strategic Bombing Survey, which evaluated the efficacy of the massive bombing campaigns during the war in both Europe and Asia. Nitze concluded that strategic bombing was not worth the resources expended, a claim as controversial then as now, especially given the reliance of the USAF on atomic bombing and the general American perception that the two atomic bombs had ended the war. Nitze, based on his firsthand damage assessments, was not impressed, and thus was less chary of considering strategies that authorized extensive use of nuclear weapons. (By contrast, Kennan, who was growing increasingly friendly with Oppenheimer, was both strategically and ethically more opposed to an atomic strategy.) While Kennan at the PPS had negotiated intra-European cooperation and the Modus Vivendi on exchange of nuclear information with Britain, Nitze took another path to European reconstruction, serving as one of the main administrators of Marshall Plan aid to Europe, and advised Acheson in May and June 1949 on complicated currency deliberations concerning divided Germany and Austria.[61] Up to Joe-1, he had mostly spent his time thinking about money and resources. He was not the most obvious person to conduct the strategic reevaluation.

That would have been Kennan: fluent in Russian, a firm advocate of containment, and well versed through Anglo-American atomic negotiations in the limits and potentials of America's atomic arsenal. Although later critics of NSC-68 would claim that Kennan had been bypassed in the deliberations over the new document, this seems not to have been the case. Kennan had been evolving in an increasingly antinuclear direction and also resisted any attempt to militarize containment (that is, replacing some of the political and economic pressure on the Soviet Union with a conventional or nuclear buildup). Strategic discussions pushed toward militarization, especially nuclear militarization, however, and Kennan felt that Acheson was ignoring the PPS in general and himself in particular. On September 29, 1949, within a week of Truman's announcement, Kennan told Undersecretary of State James Webb that he wanted to be relieved of his job at PPS, and by the end of December Nitze had taken over.[62]

Nitze shared the opinion that a mild response to Soviet proliferation would be viewed by both America's allies and the Soviets as appeasement, and thus he was naturally inclined toward a strategy that emphasized force rather than willingness to negotiate. That said, Nitze insisted that the United States not respond to Joe-1 as if it were a move in a bipolar geopolitical chess game: "We felt the Soviet nuclear detonation signified that they wanted nuclear weapons, not that they were testing us." For him the lack of an announcement by Stalin confirmed this view. Instead of perceiving the Soviet Union's action as a distortion of the natural state of affairs, Nitze saw the *monopoly* as having been the distortion and a nuclear standoff as the more typical case. This had further implications:

> I was also persuaded that, over time, the U.S. atomic monopoly, and the strategic significance thereof, would progressively decline. We would eventually have to move away from primary reliance upon nuclear weapons. But I did not think that we could rebuild our conventional defenses, in conjunction with our allies, in time entirely to avoid a reliance upon our nuclear capability. We would therefore have to try to maintain some margin of nuclear superiority for as long as possible. So the question remained: what should the United States do to avoid complete reliance upon nuclear weapons?[63]

Or, as he stated in 1993: "The detonation of a Soviet nuclear device in late August 1949 gave a sharper focus to the analysis of what might be required to implement the policy of containment, as the Soviet threat acquired a new and more ominous dimension."[64]

American policy toward the Soviet Union had already taken a more aggressive and confrontational stance at least since the 1947 Truman Doctrine announced the support of anticommunist regimes in Greece and Turkey, and especially since the Czechoslovakian coup and the Berlin blockade, and so NSC-68 moved in the same direction—at the same time overestimating and inflating Soviet capabilities and aggressive intentions.[65] It was a radical departure not in goals but in tone and in means. NSC-68 called for a massive conventional buildup of forces to actively militarize containment. The most obvious way it did this was by calling for more money—*lots* more money. The entire thrust of Truman's defense policy had been to keep costs down, and this was in itself one of the original reasons to rely more and more heavily on nuclear weapons. With NSC-68's advocacy of significantly increased conventional forces (although carefully omitting any price tags), the logic of the overweening American reliance on nuclear weapons was somewhat weakened. Yet neither the NSC nor Truman himself suggested substituting conventional forces for nuclear overkill, only using them to supplement each other. Thus, while NATO was in part conceived of as a way of conventionalizing American defense of Europe, the net result proved to be the nuclearization of NATO (deployment of American nuclear weapons in Western Europe) by the mid-1950s.[66]

Conventional and nuclear defense became increasingly intertwined along a variety of fronts. American membership in NATO in 1952 not only brought European conventional forces in line with America's, it also offered the "umbrella" of American nuclear deterrence for Western Europe. In addition, Soviet proliferation jolted Americans out of reflexive hostility to any other nuclear programs. The Acheson-Lilienthal proposals and the Baruch Plan, recall, were premised on preventing *any* foreign power from acquiring nuclear weapons. Now that the Soviets had rendered those plans moot, it was only fitting that Truman and Acheson relax some of their opposition to the British nuclear project. The timing was right in several respects. Not only had Joe-1 provided a shocking demonstration of the feasibility and dangers of unmanaged proliferation, but the Anglo-American Modus Vivendi (providing the British with selected nuclear information in exchange for a larger share of the jointly held uranium stocks) was due for renegotiation in the summer and fall of 1949. Truman had already approved expansion of AEC uranium processing; to get the fuel for it, he had to talk to the British.

The process of renegotiating the Modus Vivendi with an eye to more generous terms for the British had been undertaken while Soviet proliferation was assumed to be years off. On July 14, 1949, Truman called a private conference of key members of the JCAE, Vice President Alben Barkley, General Dwight Eisenhower (acting chairman of the JCS), and three members of the NSC at Blair

House. Truman wanted to reopen negotiations and declared his support for greater interchange. Crucial changes of staffing in the Truman administration increased substantially the possibility for a favorable agreement. Secretary of State George Marshall and Undersecretary Robert A. Lovett were replaced in early 1949 with Anglophiles Dean Acheson and James Webb, respectively. At the same time, secrecy hawk James V. Forrestal was replaced by Louis Johnson at Defense. Johnson was no friend to the British, but he was too busy chopping the military budget to pay much attention to nuclear matters in the summer of 1949. Finally, David Carpenter replaced William Webster on the Military Liaison Committee of the AEC, adding another important player.[67]

Although the public was still hostile to the idea, the consensus among both scientists and politicians was that the intensification of the cold war meant that cooperation with Britain—with the unmentioned expectation that it would shortly proliferate as a result—was increasingly necessary. For their part, the British were so unnerved by the possibility of Soviet bombs raining on London (vastly more likely in the near future than an attack on Washington) that they were eager to compromise.[68] The Berkeley chemist Glenn Seaborg, one of the few members of the GAC to support the hydrogen bomb crash program (and thus no nuclear softie), echoed a general sentiment for cooperation at the GAC meeting immediately before Truman's announcement: "I remarked that I believe the futility of secrecy in certain areas should be considered in order to secure effectiveness of any increase of activity and the desirability of cooperation with the British is indicated."[69]

Opening up more secrets to the British was part of a general program of revisiting the stringent AEC security provisions as stipulated in the McMahon Act. One of the counterintuitive results of Joe-1 was a relaxation of nuclear secrecy essentially across the board. It was almost as though, now that the Soviets had proliferated, the pressure to hold on to every secret was lessened. A major declassification conference, the third of its kind, opened three days after Truman's September announcement, and the fourth in

February 1950. The latter concluded with an agreement to release much (though not all) of the basic nuclear physics information that was still classified. Only nuclear constants for a few selected isotopes (instead of for fifty) were now considered to be vital information. Most significant in British eyes, information on certain low-power reactors was open for exchange.[70]

The result was that the United Kingdom was supposed to slightly curtail its nuclear program, keeping two (instead of three) atomic piles at Windscale and a small diffusion plant for uranium enrichment at Capenhurst. If and when a British nuclear device was developed, it was to be tested at a U.S. site. The Americans backed down from previous more extreme demands, such as requiring that all British bombs be built in North America and that British scientists should be integrated into the American program. In exchange, the British would cede the lion's share of the stockpiled uranium to the Americans. William Penney, the scientific director of the British nuclear program and one of two British physicists who had been present on the island of Tinian when both nuclear bombs were launched against Japan, continued negotiating in December 1949, then tabled the proposals for integration for a month.[71]

A month proved to be just a few days too long, for in early February, the world learned of the most damaging case of nuclear espionage yet revealed: the perfidy and treason of British subject Klaus Fuchs. Although the British and Americans had been interrogating Fuchs since August 1949—following a tip from partially decrypted Venona cables—the FBI established for certain only on September 26, 1949, immediately after Truman's announcement, that the spy named "Charles" or "Rest" in the cable traffic was in fact Fuchs. Yet the story remained quiet until the moment Fuchs, now in the theory division at the British nuclear establishment at Harwell, was arrested on February 2, 1950. Fuchs was charged with four counts of violating the Official Secrets Act for espionage activities conducted in New York, Boston, and Great Britain; Los Alamos was not mentioned.[72] The news spread rapidly across the

United States, leading to, among other things, the elimination of roughly forty Soviet spy sources still active in the Allied countries.[73] (Julius and Ethel Rosenberg were arrested, for example, because Fuchs's courier from Los Alamos, Harry Gold, had also conveyed the information transmitted by David Greenglass, Ethel's brother.)

One week after Fuchs's arrest, the junior senator from Wisconsin, Joseph McCarthy, gave a speech in Wheeling, West Virginia, in which he claimed he had a list of 205 "known" Communists working for the State Department. The impetus for McCarthy was less the arrest of Fuchs than the conclusion of the trial of Alger Hiss. Hiss, a onetime trusted and valued civil servant in the Roosevelt administration (he attended the Yalta Conference) and after the war the director of the Carnegie Endowment for International Peace, was accused in 1948 by Whittaker Chambers before Richard Nixon's House Un-American Activities Committee of having served as a spy for the Soviet Union. Dismissing those accusations publicly, Hiss was tried for perjury in a trial that ran from May 31 to July 7, 1949. The jury deadlocked eight to four in favor of conviction. His second trial began on November 17. This was now a world in which the Soviet Union had detonated an atomic bomb, and the stakes for accusations of Soviet espionage were higher.

The jury returned a guilty verdict on January 21, 1950. Hiss was sentenced to two consecutive five-year sentences, of which he served forty-four months. Ten days after his conviction, Truman announced the crash program to develop thermonuclear weapons, and three days later Fuchs was arrested. And now there was McCarthy, whose anticommunist rampage through the U.S. government climaxed in the well-known red-baiting hysteria of the early 1950s.[74] Thus, though McCarthy was surely capitalizing on Hiss—hence the emphasis on the State Department in his mythical list—the Wheeling speech was injected into a climate saturated with the fallout from Joe-1.

Together, Fuchs and McCarthy scuttled Anglo-American nuclear cooperation for the next several years. Uranium still flowed grudgingly toward the Americans, but very little information flowed back to the United Kingdom. The first British test in 1952 happened without significant help from the Americans on the Australian island of Monte Bello, in contravention of what would have been the revised Modus Vivendi. Only after the British had demonstrated their nuclear competence was the American McMahon Act amended into the Atomic Energy Act of 1954, allowing for greater cooperation, although the payoff was not significant before 1957.[75] Not only did Joe-1 intensify public fear of the Soviet Union "catching up" to the Americans—generating a reflex, contrary to both the scientists' and government officials' desires, to hold on to nuclear secrecy—but it was the *British* who seemed to be precisely the leak that threatened to sink America's atomic ship.

In another spectacular instance of bad judgment linked to bad timing, two of the Cambridge Five spy ring, Donald Maclean and Guy Burgess, defected to the Soviet Union in May 1951, having been alerted by fellow member of the ring Kim Philby, now liaison officer for British intelligence in Washington. Maclean was clearly identified as "Homer" in the Venona cables, and Philby instructed Burgess to abscond with the former atomic-energy liaison only days before Maclean was to be confronted with the evidence. Eight months earlier, in September 1950, Italian-born nuclear physicist Bruno Pontecorvo, an employee at Harwell but never at Los Alamos (he had worked at Chalk River in Canada during the war), defected to the Soviet Union. Thus climaxed the series of what one historian has called Britain's "self-inflicted wounds."[76]

Despite the best efforts of American scientists and politicians after Truman's September 23 announcement to defuse the idea that there were indeed "hot formulas" or "secrets" to the atomic bomb that could be stolen and hidden in the handle of a hunting knife or the heel of a shoe, the shocks of Joe-1, Fuchs, McCarthy, Maclean, and Pontecorvo turned the entire argument around. It was no longer assumed that Soviet proliferation had been inevitable, "a matter of time," but rather that it was possible *only* because of the tremendous perfidy of Soviet espionage, and particularly the lax security practices of the British.[77] Not just the British: The Rosenbergs were arrested, tried, and sentenced to death by Judge Irving Kaufmann on April 5, 1951, for allegedly transmitting atomic secrets to NKVD handlers.[78] Kaufmann's reasoning for the harsh sentence? That the proliferation of the Soviet Union had led to the Soviet-backed North Korean invasion of South Korea, and thus the carnage of the Korean War. Although the place of the Rosenbergs' information in this sequence of events is open to question, the view that Joe-1 led directly to North Korean aggression was less fanciful.

There was no question that Joe-1 had altered the military calculus in Europe. If the Red Army was no longer simply balanced by American atomic bombs, the combination of Red Army plus nuclear weapons was now countered with NATO and the post-Sandstone expansion of American armaments. The sheer scale of destruction now possible in Europe focused diplomatic attention on defusing European crises before they escalated into superpower confrontation. Eugene Rabinowitch, the editor of the *Bulletin of the Atomic Scientists*, predicted in 1950 that this situation would likely push armed conflict off the European continent for the foreseeable future: "It is not unlikely that this period will witness a series of 'small wars' waged by the communist satellites or guerrilla armies in Asia and Europe while the Soviet Union will remain formally at peace with everybody, proclaiming strict adherence to the principle of non-intervention."[79]

The situation in Europe had frozen by 1950 into a tableau of terror, and would remain more or less in the status quo of 1950 until the fall of the Berlin Wall in November 1989. The situation in Asia, on the other hand, was dynamic, and the trends did not favor the West. On October 1, 1949, a week after the news of Joe-1 was publicly announced, Mao Zedong's Chinese Communist

Party declared victory, announcing the creation of the People's Republic of China. The United States would resist recognizing Mao's China until the presidency of Richard Nixon, but the British were quick to recognize the new China, and Stalin signed a friendship pact with Mao to provide for mutual defense on February 14, 1950 (the same week as McCarthy's demarche). If there had been a lot of speculation early in 1949, as the Communists racked up one military victory after another against Chiang Kai-shek's Nationalists, about Titoism in China—Acheson, for one, envisaged an early Sino-Soviet split—the friendship pact scuttled those dreams.[80] The Communist bloc had just enlarged itself enormously. As Communist China loomed, Deputy Assistant Secretary of State Durward V. Sandifer lamented the coincidence with Truman's announcement that very day: "We should consider carefully and realistically the effect of this information concerning atomic energy plus the development in China on the international prestige situation."[81]

The "loss" of China to the Communist camp was a tremendous blow for American diplomacy and prestige, even if it were not intensified by coming on the heels of the end of the monopoly. This was still only a diplomatic blow; it was not militarily disadvantageous—yet. And then, on July 25, 1950, North Korean forces attacked South Korea, invading an American client state. The rickety postwar peace, rocked as it was by tensions in Greece, Berlin, and Czechoslovakia, had been transformed into a full-scale proxy war. The United States and Britain quickly intervened under UN auspices to protect the sovereignty of South Korea, and as General Douglas MacArthur drove the northern forces almost to the Yalu River, Communist China intervened and the Americans were directly at war with not one but two Soviet allies. This pattern of a superpower either fighting a foreign proxy directly (the United States in Vietnam, the Soviet Union in Afghanistan) or two proxies fighting each other with the support of either superpower (numerous cases in Central America and Africa) had been established.

Nuclear weapons indeed seemed to preserve the peace in Europe, but that meant only that hostile impulses would be acted upon elsewhere.

It is possible that nuclear weapons played an even more direct role in the initiation of the Korean War, thus further cementing the link between atomic bombs and proxy wars. Although it is impossible to determine for certain without access to North Korean archives, it appears that North Korean leader Kim Il Sung signaled to Stalin that he was interested in attempting to reunify Korea by force of arms and sought support from his Soviet patron. Our limited evidence indicates that Stalin felt buoyed up enough by the success of Joe-1, coupled with the synergy of the Communist victory in China, to induce him at the very least not to prevent Kim's invasion.[82] Certainly Mao viewed Soviet proliferation as a deterrent to an American nuclear strike in response to Chinese intervention when he sent his forces across the Yalu on November 1, 1950.[83] This did not prevent Truman (to a limited degree) and President-elect Eisenhower (much more forcefully) from threatening nuclear retaliation against the Chinese as the war stagnated. (It also began active theorizing of the concept of limited nuclear war.)[84] Some historians have argued that these American threats were central in bringing all parties to the negotiating table, where they worked out the agreement that has kept Korea divided to the present day. This is certainly possible. The only incontrovertible result of the threats, however, was to convince Mao that he too needed to develop nuclear weapons to forestall such strongarming.[85] The dialectical push of nuclear proliferation moved onward.

The Korean War, aside from the destruction of life, environment, and funds for three years only to produce the status quo ante, marked the end of the early, uncertain phase of the cold war. After the onset of hostilities in Korea, the vacillating, changeable patterns of engagement and conflict that had characterized U.S.-Soviet relations since the end of the Second World War—and the period of the atomic monopoly—hardened into the specific doctrines and behaviors we now associate with the cold war proper.

Just as Joe-1 had sparked the reevaluation of American strategic posture that resulted in NSC-68, the outbreak of a hot war on the Korean peninsula transformed NSC-68 from speculative doctrine into reality. Besides confirming the basic assumptions of NSC-68 about an aggressive Soviet bloc, the new reality meant a great deal more money, for the active military containment envisioned by Nitze would be impossible on Truman's pre-Joe shoestring budgets. On July 19, 1950, less than a month after the outbreak of the war, Truman asked Congress for an additional $10 billion for defense; by August 4 he requested another $4 billion for military assistance, and another $16.8 billion on December 1. The final defense authorization for fiscal year 1951 totaled $48.2 billion ($424.4 billion in 2009 dollars), a 257 percent increase over the original request of $13.5 billion.[86] The real transformation heralded by Joe-1 had arrived. Never again would the American defense budget be so constrained.

At the same time, the Soviet Union jettisoned the Peace Offensive—it was, after all, hard to argue about the pacifist intentions of Communist countries—and began to spend a great deal more money on conventional arms. A new five-year plan was announced in 1950 for 1951–1955, which emphasized conventional rearmament. Some of this was already in the works after the big push for developing a nuclear bomb was accomplished, but the plans were reworked to account for the forceful American intervention in Korea (which took Stalin by surprise). By the end of 1950, the Soviet Union had forced all of its satellites to revise their own plans to supply the North Koreans.[87]

The first year after Truman's announcement of the American detection of the first Soviet nuclear blast—the year of Joe—proved dramatic and, above all, gloomy. Whereas the news had at first been greeted on many sides as opening new potential avenues for arms control, transparency, and scientific exchange, by the end of the year all of that optimism had vanished with the dust from First Lightning. The United States was committed to fission and fusion nuclear arms, an expanded and confrontational conventional presence in Europe and Asia, anticommunist purges at home, and a hot war in Asia. Most scientists, government officials, and military officers had expected that the end of the atomic monopoly would bring changes, but no one had expected those changes to be so negative and to come so quickly. There was little to do but settle in to the cold war.

TRACES AND TAILINGS

So he took his wings and fled;
Then the morn blush'd rosy red;
I dried my tears, & arm'd my fears
With ten thousand shields and spears.
WILLIAM BLAKE, "THE ANGEL"

When Harry Truman assumed the presidency of the United States upon the death of Franklin D. Roosevelt on April 12, 1945, he had never heard of atomic bombs: not what they were, not that they were feasible, not that the Americans were attempting to build one, not that they were about to succeed. By the midterm congressional elections of November 1946, not only had he learned of the existence of the Manhattan Project, but he had authorized the use of its weapons against an enemy, initiated the first nuclear test series, proposed the first multilateral arms-control agreement, and seen that proposal decay into a stalemate. By the presidential election of 1948, which he won by a nose over Thomas E. Dewey, he had already faced the blockade of Berlin and the Czechoslovakian coup, announced the Truman Doctrine, approved the second nuclear test series, and unified the Department of Defense. By the next midterm elections in November 1950, the United States was engaged in a hot war with the Soviet proxies of North Korea and the People's Republic of China, had uncovered several rings of atomic spies, authorized a massive conventional, nuclear, and thermonuclear buildup, and—crucially—seen the end of the atomic monopoly with the first Soviet nuclear test. Just over five years, and the postwar world had transitioned from an anti-Fascist grand alliance into a bipolar cold war. While they were not at the center of each of these developments, nuclear weapons tinged and shaped all of them. The cold war hardened at precisely the period that America (and the world) learned to think about, deal with, and live among nuclear weapons, and both war and weapons would remain linked for the next forty years.

Understandably, given this dismal track record, Truman's advisers on both atomic weapons and science policy were tired and more than a little overwhelmed. For James Bryant Conant, the essential feature of this new atomic world was expansion of the regime of secrecy, to an extent "no one would have imagined possible fifteen years ago." Because the Americans developed their atomic weapons in the context of intense classification—at first to block the Nazis from learning anything about their intentions, and later to forestall the Soviets—much of the information that the public had received was incomplete, misleading, or simply false: "Governments are forced to say things about technical developments that are not necessarily accurate and . . . information that 'leaks' more or less in a planned fashion is even less reliable."[1] Truman's announcement on September 23, 1949, a somewhat deceptive revelation in itself, was the product of this new culture of secrecy in at least two ways: First, the surprise of the announcement stemmed from the skewed interpretation of scattered data about Soviet atomic progress; second, the successful erection of a long-range detection network to sample atmospheric radioactivity became the only way America could generate reliable atomic information about their adversary's progress. The control and interpretation of information was one of the many sinews that linked nuclear weapons to the cold war itself.

The story I have told could be read as a prehistory to the world many already recognize, or at best as a plug filling in a hole between two important historical epochs—World War II and the cold war. But this account is much more than the prologue or epilogue to the "real history." The international narrative of the construction and detection of the first Soviet atomic explosion and the aftershocks that came in its wake is essential to an understanding of the position of nuclear weapons even in our present post–cold war world. For nuclear weapons are bound up today with power, secrecy, and fear. That linkage was built in these first years of living with the bomb, and understanding the origins can provide some tools for living in a new, and somewhat altered, nuclear present.

At the onset of the Korean War, there were fewer than two hundred nuclear weapons on Earth's surface; as of 2002, there were more than twenty thousand.[2] As that relatively small initial number exponentially increased over the following decades, the history to be told expanded with it. I cannot address those developments fully here. Instead, I will explore five points in particular that draw directly from the history of First Lightning, Joe-1, Vermont, or whatever other moniker the first Soviet explosion bore: the superpower arms race, contrasting styles of intelligence gathering, the first limited arms-control treaties, nuclear weapons proliferation, and ecological destruction. Each of these developments built with a steely logic upon patterns of reaction and response that were first established during the atomic monopoly.

David E. Lilienthal—former director of the Tennessee Valley Authority, veteran New Dealer, and the first chairman of the Atomic Energy Commission—played a central role at the dawn of the nuclear age. Often his private diary and public pronouncements provided an optimistic gloss, a hope that perhaps the worst predictable consequences of the nuclear standoff could be averted. By 1963, more than a decade after leaving atomic politics, Lilienthal had no optimism left:

> The story of nuclear weapons is not one of change in a world of change, but essentially one of repetition—a circle in which we and the Russians have gone round and round, chasing each others' tails, year after year after year. This is the source of our despair, of our frustration, of our fear. We seem to remain locked in the same cell of circumstance, the Russians and ourselves together, with what at times seems only a remote hope of ever emerging.[3]

The main indicator of this mirror symmetry, this vicious circle, was the construction of massive stockpiles of nuclear weapons and ever-advancing delivery systems with which to rain them down on the opposing side.

When Truman left office in early 1953, the United States had already built 832 nuclear weapons. Within a year, that number had risen to 1,161; in two years, to 1,630; and in three years, to 2,280.[4] The only viable delivery system for any of these devices was the long-distance bomber, and yet the American nuclear arsenal had already reached a level that can only be described as overkill. President Dwight D. Eisenhower, inaugurated in January 1953 in the waning days of the Korean War, issued with Secretary of State John Foster Dulles a new doctrine of nuclear war fighting: the New Look, or, without euphemism, "massive retaliation." Simply put, America threatened to respond to even limited amounts of conventional aggression with a saturating nuclear strike. The hope was to use America's hydrogen, uranium, and plutonium arsenal to deter conventional war as well as a nuclear attack (and save untold amounts of national treasure in the process). Information about Soviet intentions had not changed, and America was no closer to initiating a global war; the impetus to change the doctrine to one of Mutually Assured Destruction stemmed more from the rise in

American capabilities than from any other source. The frantic desire to respond to a nuclear Soviet enemy after 1949 had produced so many weapons that a doctrine was found to suit them. The cart was leading the horse.[5]

Henry Kissinger, then professor of government at Harvard University and a nuclear strategist (and over a decade away from becoming the architect of President Richard Nixon's realpolitik), believed that this ratcheting effect of American capabilities, which in turn spurred further escalation on the Soviet side, was only the logical outcome of the bipolar nuclear situation. Not only was the seesawing armament race a natural response, it was positively a good thing. "The growth of the Soviet atomic stockpile," Kissinger wrote in 1957, "has merely brought the physical equation into line with the psychological one; it has increased our reluctance to engage in war even more."[6] Indeed, whether or not because of a "nuclear taboo" that psychologically restrained American and Soviet leaders from engaging in nuclear war, the relative rarity of nuclear threats and blackmail during the cold war is remarkable. As we have seen, the Americans made strikingly little political use of the atomic monopoly to extract concessions from the Soviet Union, its allies, American clients, or neutral powers. Even in the atomic duopoly, the Americans issued few nuclear threats—almost always against China and never against a nuclear-armed opponent—and the Soviet Union rattled its atomic saber only once (against the British and French during the 1956 Suez crisis), although many of these were extremely close calls.[7] We all know that no nuclear war—limited or global—broke out in the second half of the twentieth century. We probably shall never know exactly why, but it was not for lack of armament or opportunity.

At the same time that the atom was mobilized for war, it was simultaneously domesticated for peace. The Soviet Union adopted nuclear power more enthusiastically—and in the case of the 1986 Chernobyl meltdown, more destructively—than even the United States did, and aspects of "nuclear culture" were to be seen everywhere, from radioactive decontamination of food to nuclear-powered icebreakers keeping northern sea-lanes open.[8] Despite the publicly acknowledged threat of American nuclear attack during the late 1940s, Soviet civil defense did not begin until 1955, at about the same time that Stalin's death and Nikita Khrushchev's assumption of power allowed an active reconsideration of the role of nuclear weapons in Soviet military policy.[9] As the cold war became a routine fact of life, the balance of power within the Soviet atomic complex shifted as well. On June 26, 1953, immediately after Stalin's death and Beria's arrest, the euphemistically misnamed Ministry of Medium Machine-Building was established to take over the secret atomic complex from the First Chief Directorate. Although this nominally raised the atomic project to a ministry level, it had the effect of a real decline in power for the Soviet project, much as the transition from Manhattan Project to the AEC had had in the United States.[10] In the meantime, whether or not the Soviet Union ever adhered directly to MAD or massive retaliation or limited nuclear war fighting, they continued to build weapons at roughly the same rate as the Americans.

More weapons meant, naturally, more testing, a link that was established at Trinity and reinforced by the successful detonation of First Lightning on August 29, 1949. The world is today in a moratorium on nuclear testing, initiated on the American side by Congress during the presidency of George H. W. Bush in 1992. It was none too soon. According to official data, as of January 1, 1991, there had been 2,059 nuclear tests around the world: 1,085 by the United States (including 205 in the atmosphere) for a total blast yield of 141 megatons of TNT equivalent. The Soviet Union had detonated "only" 715 test bombs, including 215 in the atmosphere, although with a total TNT equivalent of 452 megatons, over three times the American. (These figures do not include so-called peaceful nuclear explosions, or PNEs, which the Soviets deployed for a limited time in order to stimulate gas and oil fields, mine ore, extinguish oil and gas fires, incinerate nuclear and chemical waste, store such waste underground, and mold the geophysical landscape.)[11] The United Kingdom tested 42 times, and France and China (neither of which joined the moratorium at first) exploded 182 and 35, respectively. The test site of Semipalatinsk-21 continued as an active site throughout the cold war, although its importance was significantly diminished by the opening of the test field at Novaia Zemlia archipelago in the Arctic Ocean in the 1950s. The Semipalatinsk fields hosted either 467 or 468 blasts (accounts are uncertain), including 26 on Earth's surface.[12] First Lightning was the first of many.

Both sides continued arming, both sides continued testing, and both sides continued trying to find out as much as possible about what the other was doing. For the Americans, following the pattern set up during the monopoly, this called for more and more extensive long-range detection. After its astonishing success in detecting Joe-1 within the data of Vermont, AFOAT-1 had to wait two years for another chance to test the mettle of its system. The second Soviet nuclear device (RDS-2), a uranium bomb based on indigenous Soviet designs, was tested at Semipalatinsk at 9:19 a.m. (local time) on September 24, 1951, for a yield of 38.3 kilotons, more than twice the yield of the plutonium-fueled First Lightning. This test also took place on a tower, but the detonation signal was transmitted from an airplane instead of a ground-based command center. Less than a month later, on October 18, another bomb was tested, this one dropped from a plane (similar to the Able shot during the American tests at Bikini in 1946), yielding 42 kilotons.[13] The Americans knew nothing of these tests from spies or communications intercepts.

Once again, they sniffed the wind. And not just AFOAT-1: A citizen in Great Falls, Montana, wrote to the AEC on October 1, 1951, that he had detected elevated radiation levels, and he wanted not to let them know but only to hear back from them if he was in fact correct that there had been a recent test in the Soviet Union. What had once been a source of panic was now a bit of a game.[14] Resources had expanded as well: The Norwegian intelligence services became very active collaborators on test detection from 1951 onward, and Tracerlab was cut out on the American side as Los Alamos began conducting isotopic analysis in-house.[15] On October 3, Henry DeWolf Smyth, author of *Atomic Energy for Military Purposes* and now the only scientist among the five AEC commissioners, released a statement to the press:

> Another atomic bomb has recently been exploded within the Soviet Union. In spite of Soviet pretenses that their atomic energy program is being directed exclusively toward peaceful purposes[,] this event confirms again that the Soviet Union is continuing to make atomic weapons.
>
> In accordance with the policy of the President to keep the American people informed to the fullest extent consistent with our National security the President has directed me to make this statement and to stress again the necessity for that effective and enforceable international control of atomic energy which the United States and the large majority of the United Nations support.
>
> Further details cannot be given without adversely affecting our national security interests.[16]

Notice how much has changed from the announcement of September 23, 1949: First, Truman did not announce this one, and neither did the chairman of the AEC, Gordon Dean (who had replaced David Lilienthal from July 11, 1950, to June 30, 1953, when he was in turn succeeded by Lewis Strauss). Instead, an ordinary member of the AEC announced it; by only the second bomb, reporting had become almost a matter of routine. (The flow of the information in the Truman White House was also less hectic and more orderly than the path in 1949.)[17] Second, the shock of Soviet testing was over, and immediately Smyth moved into an attack on the Soviet Union's hypocrisy. This was not a statement for domestic consumption but rather was targeted at international audiences. And third, Smyth, whose name was almost synonymous with nuclear openness, ended with an invocation of secrecy. Two years had passed since Truman's first announcement, and the world had utterly changed.

It had changed for the Soviet Union, too. Stalin and Beria now knew that there was a strong likelihood that the Americans would detect the renewed nuclear testing, and also probably be able to determine quite a bit about the nature and properties of the blast. There was less risk of a preemptive strike this time, and Stalin felt free to announce his test. Nevertheless, he did not do so until October 16, 1951, *after* the Americans had already notified the world about RDS-2: "Actually, not long ago a test of one of the types of the atomic bomb was tested here. The test of atomic bombs of various calibers will be conducted in the future for the purpose of defending our country from an attack of the Anglo-American aggressive bloc."[18] This pattern continued until 1961: The Soviet Union would not admit to a test unless the United States had announced it first, and it was not the AEC's policy to announce every test. Lewis Strauss publicized another test in 1953, and as AEC chairman continued to do so when the president believed it would score valuable propaganda points, a total of thirty-nine times by the spring of 1958.[19] In 1961, the Soviets renewed testing after a moratorium and saw a clear benefit to making the announcements themselves.

The fact that announcements came out regularly did not mean that the decision to release a public statement was automatic. When the Soviet Union detonated its first nuclear explosion that exhibited characteristics of a hydrogen fusion (thermonuclear) reaction—an extensive debate continues to this day over whether this was a test of a true hydrogen bomb or a "boosted" fission device—the discussion within the Eisenhower White House over whether to announce the Soviet achievement was remarkably similar in structure to that in the Truman administration over Vermont.[20] Lewis Strauss, not typically identified with openness in atomic matters (or any other matters), was strongly in favor of release: "He [Strauss] would like to have urged that such information *not* be released to other countries unless arrangements had been completed to release it also to the American people."[21] Although he consistently advised Eisenhower against accommodation or negotiation with the Soviets on nuclear matters, Strauss continued to insist on nuclear openness in this specific area, as he wrote to the president in 1954: "Withholding a statement does not in any way deceive the Russians who know from past experience that we have detected their previous tests and that these tests by the nature in which they were conducted were recorded by the very same indicia."[22] In other words, he wanted to avoid repeating Truman's error at Potsdam: giving away too much by trying to conceal what was no secret.

The Soviets, for their part, were again mirroring the Americans (who thought they were mirroring the Soviet Union) by developing an extensive radiological long-range detection network of their own. The detection of First Lightning was such a shock to the higher leadership, both within the atomic bomb project (Kurchatov) and without (Stalin), that as soon as the higher priority of constructing more atomic bombs was regularized, attention in 1951 turned to developing a long-range detection system of their own. Igor Kurchatov himself directed the radiological project, and G. A. Gaburtsev began investigation of seismic methods. On September 24, 1951, at the test of RDS-2, they registered a distinct seismic footprint, thus initiating their own long-range detection system as primarily seismic in nature. By 1958 it was fully operational.[23]

This time lag is crucial, for it refutes one particular mythology about Soviet long-range detection that has gained some currency with the end of the cold war. In early 1990, Daniel Hirsch and William G. Matthews published an article in the *Bulletin of the Atomic Scientists*, one of the leading journals for nuclear issues, arguing two points: that the Soviet Union did not obtain a design for their hydrogen bomb through espionage, because the data provided by Klaus Fuchs on the "classical Super" were outdated and unworkable; and that Soviet physicists Andrei Sakharov and Igor Tamm *did* derive their hydrogen bomb trigger from the American

Teller-Ulam design by analyzing radioactive debris from the 1952 Mike test.[24] The first part of this argument was definitely correct: The Soviets did not obtain useful espionage data on the Super. It was also clearly possible to interpret the fallout data from a thermonuclear test to deduce some properties of the two-stage trigger; in fact, the British learned much of how to accomplish this for their own hydrogen bomb by analyzing the debris from Joe-19, a Soviet thermonuclear test.[25] Nonetheless, Hirsch and Matthews overstated the case, for the Soviets simply did not have an adequate long-range capacity in 1952 for this kind of analysis. Not that they didn't try: Sakharov and Viktor Davidenko gathered snow after the Mike shot with hopes of obtaining useful data, but a chemist at Arzamas-16 dumped it down the drain by accident.[26] The first Soviet hydrogen bomb was indigenous.

Clarifying this issue is important because the real story reveals something crucial about the different cultures of obtaining and managing intelligence in the Soviet Union and the United States. Repeatedly throughout this book we have seen two different approaches to gaining information from an opponent who was trying very hard not to let you know what he was up to: On the one hand, you could rely on human intelligence; on the other, you could attempt to use scientific and technical apparatus to produce information. The Soviet Union throughout the 1940s depended almost exclusively on a dedicated network of agents who provided valuable information about many aspects of the Manhattan Project. These information sources could exhibit judgment, make selections, and respond intelligently to requests for specific kinds of further information.

The Americans, however, never managed to develop a reliable information network of human informants within the Soviet atomic complex. What information they had was obtained almost exclusively through technical means. The scientist and atomic commentator Ralph Lapp put it particularly well: "Not even the secretive Soviets can keep their tests free from the prying eyes of the West. By this I do not mean that we have agents in their Proving

Grounds. Our 'prying' is done remotely and in a most unconventional manner. Instead of depending upon spies, we now rely upon scientists and instruments."[27] These instruments produced hard data, although that data needed, as we have seen, a lot of interpretation and analysis before politicians could even understand them, let alone act upon them. These technological "agents" never broke ranks, never turned double agent, and could not be arrested.

Each style of intelligence gathering had advantages and drawbacks, and both the Americans and the Soviets understood what was missing from their own methods. Stalin and Beria, for example, were often worried about disinformation, which was not something AFOAT-1 ever had to concern itself with: Machines had no consciousness and so could not willfully deceive (although they could be foiled by countermeasures). On the other hand, it was relatively straightforward to calibrate a human spy—you simply sent in another spy to see the same or similar documents or blueprints. The Americans, however, had to detonate the Sandstone series in order to determine how reliable their instruments were. But just as important as the asymmetries between the two methods is their fundamental *symmetry*. It is helpful in some contexts to think of Klaus Fuchs or Ted Hall as scientific instruments of sorts, each with his own error bars and requiring his own interpretive skills back in Moscow, just as Lapp thought of his Geiger counters as spies.

Obviously, opting for technical or human intelligence mechanisms was not a completely free choice. The United States did attempt to plant (and recruit) human spies within the Soviet Union's atomic project, and failed. The internal security apparatus on the other end was too good at rooting out prospective agents. For their part, the Soviet Union was (significantly) poorer than the United States both in treasure and in electronics know-how, and thus was less effective in developing technical espionage in the early stages of the cold war. Beria and Stalin also benefited from a pool of Western citizens (including Fuchs and Hall) who were willing to pass atomic secrets on to the Soviet Union for their own ideological and personal reasons. An open society on one side and a closed society on the other weighted these decisions.

Weighting the decisions was not the same as *determining* them. Each side did try to complement its own preferred method with the other style, and eventually did erect parallel systems (limited Western spies in the Soviet Union later in the cold war; more extensive Soviet technical intelligence in the Western bloc). But the preferences run deeper than simply meeting the constraints of feasibility. Stalinism was built not just on coercion but most extensively on *voluntary* confessions and denunciations—human-produced information, domestic and foreign, had a track record of reliability (or at least utility, whether or not the denunciations exposed any real counterrevolutionaries). Likewise, the American experience for decades had emphasized technical ingenuity and inventiveness. It seemed obvious to unleash the spirit of Edison to solve the problems of atomic intelligence. Besides, humans were unreliable where communism was concerned: If you could not necessarily trust your most highly placed individuals (such as Alger Hiss) not to have Marxist sympathies, it appeared to J. Edgar Hoover, Harry Truman, and Lewis Strauss simply more prudent to trust cold circuitry. The styles resonated on multiple levels.

Understanding these methods as cultures—that is, as sets of beliefs and practices shared by a group of people—helps explain other features of the nuclear arms race as well. From the 1950s onward, for example, the United States and the Soviet Union had different styles of negotiation in arms-control treaties. The Americans tended to prefer technical solutions to strategic threats: Find a measuring device that can detect violations, one that is objective, and you will solve the problem of the arms race. The Soviets, by contrast, sought political solutions, seeking to create an environment in which both sides would feel less threatened. If you didn't feel a need for this specific weapon, it would be easy to give it up.[28] Once again, we have the contrast between technical and more human, psychological methods of approaching the control of information.

Consider the negotiations over the eventual Limited Test Ban Treaty (LTBT) of May 1963. Every feature of the eventual completion of the LTBT drew on practices and technologies from the monopoly period. On May 7, 1954, Herbert Clark published an analysis in the journal *Science* demonstrating that significant fallout from a recent series of hydrogen bomb tests in the Pacific had been precipitated by rainfall as far away as the city of Troy in upstate New York.[29] Of course, this finding was nothing new: For years, as we have seen, scientists had detected elevated radiation levels in the winds following nuclear tests, and the navy's Project Rainbarrel exploited precipitation for long-range monitoring of Soviet nuclear tests. The novelty here was the intensity of the radiation produced by the much larger thermonuclear explosions. As similar findings were reported from around the world—including the irradiation of the Japanese fishing boat *Lucky Dragon* after the Castle Bravo hydrogen bomb test in 1954—public concern about the long-term environmental and especially genetic consequences of atmospheric nuclear testing rose.[30]

In 1955, during a meeting at the United Nations discussing arms-control and disarmament issues, the Soviet Union introduced a proposal to discontinue nuclear testing altogether. The protracted and painful history of the negotiations among the Soviet Union, the United States, and the United Kingdom (with France playing the role of perpetual spoiler) is a saga beyond the scope of these pages.[31] Suffice it to say that by 1963, after several testing moratoria had failed, the successors of the Big Three from Potsdam signed a treaty in Moscow prohibiting nuclear explosions in the atmosphere, underwater, or in outer space. Instead of a comprehensive ban on nuclear testing, the tests were driven underground. Why?

The United States and the Soviet Union proved unable to agree on a number of issues related to a comprehensive test ban, such as the international status of monitoring stations, limitations on on-site inspections, and the possibility of cheating or circumventing by testing nuclear weapons in secret—all resonances from the failed discussion over the Baruch Plan. This time, however, an agreement proved possible, precisely because there was symmetry between the two powers: Both had nuclear weapons, both had long-distance monitoring systems, and thus both could verify that the other side had not cheated by conducting an open-air test. The debates over the efficacy of airborne testing, and the limitations on seismic testing, occupied a sizable part of the negotiations over the LTBT.

In the end, it was the very success of systems like that erected by AFOAT-1 that made a ban against atmospheric tests feasible. As the CIA noted in December 1957, "The Soviet scientists have a fairly accurate estimate of present US detection capabilities. They would recognize that some types of tests would almost certainly be detected . . . There would be some uncertainty in Soviet calculations of their ability to escape detection and proof of their responsibility."[32] This satisfied the American proclivity for technical means of intelligence gathering; the scientific problem of arms-control verification had been solved in this instance.[33] The Soviets, on the other hand, saw the agreement as a way to ameliorate the arms race (which they needed for political and economic reasons) by establishing a strategic situation in which neither side wanted to cheat. The agreement needed to come first; verification technologies could fill in the holes later.[34] The success of the LTBT hinged on the compromise between the two attitudes to information control, all built on the legacy of radiological detection, the failure of the Baruch Plan, and the inherent limitations of uncertainty in intelligence gathering.

One of the goals of the LTBT was to provide a check against other powers producing nuclear weapons. If one could not test in the atmosphere without being detected, that meant that nonnuclear signatories faced a higher barrier for weapons proliferation: They would have to develop the techniques for testing underground first. In recognition of this aspect of the treaty, France and the People's Republic of China refused to sign. (France, in fact, proliferated during the final negotiations over the treaty, repeatedly testing in the atmosphere in the deserts of Algeria, and later moving their tests to the South Pacific.)[35] By the end of the 1950s, there were three nuclear powers (the United States, the Soviet Union, and the United Kingdom), all armed with both fission and thermonuclear weapons. These powers had a distinct security interest in keeping the number of other nuclear powers down, both because more bombs meant greater risk of accident, and because proliferation limited their freedom to threaten nuclear strikes against nonnuclear powers. Several nonnuclear states were equally eager to keep the nuclear genie as confined as possible. Canada, for example, became in 1945 the first nation to explicitly disavow any intention to build an atomic arsenal—a noteworthy development since they had the domestic uranium resources and the know-how from the war to proliferate relatively easily. Several nations followed this example in the coming decades.[36]

Others did not. Each case of proliferation demands a study at least as detailed—and at least as attentive to the international flows of knowledge and matériel—as that given to the Soviet Union here. There is no general pattern followed by nations that desire to have a nuclear-weapons capability, although there are some commonalities with the Soviet case. All the proliferators after 1945 had to face a world in which the United States already possessed these weapons—and, to stress it once more, had already used them twice. The American nuclear capacity emitted a variety of signals: that nuclear bombs were in fact feasible, that the Manhattan Project provided one template for how to build such weapons, and that the Americans might use these bombs against a nonnuclear power. The Soviet proliferation in 1949 added dimensions to the nuclear calculus: that other countries besides the Anglo-American bloc were able to acquire such weapons, that nuclear tests were detectable at a distance, and that a nuclear capacity offered a deterrent of sorts against American threats.

All of these lessons of the American and Soviet atomic programs were assessed and evaluated by the People's Republic of China as Mao Zedong initiated his nuclear program. The Americans provided the crucial motivation for the Chinese to develop atomic bombs. It seems fairly clear from the limited archival evidence available that Mao was not deeply concerned with nuclear weapons in the 1940s, and that Truman's (and Eisenhower's) threats to drop atomic bombs on the Chinese provided the first spur to his proliferating ambitions. The evidence on the influence of the Korean War on the Chinese nuclear decision is equivocal; that of the two crises in the Taiwan Straits (1955 and 1958), when Eisenhower again rattled his atomic saber, is much clearer. Shortly after the first crisis, the Chinese nuclear program began in earnest.[37]

This is where the Soviets came in, following the Sino-Soviet atomic cooperation treaty of April 29, 1955. Recall that no country has ever succeeded in building a nuclear bomb without foreign assistance; China was no exception. Nikita Khrushchev's government provided important early aid to the Chinese program, ranging from training scientists to supplying experimental reactors for the Beijing plant and for the Peking Institute, in exchange for access to Chinese uranium ores. (There are clear echoes here of the Modus Vivendi and Anglo-American atomic cooperation.) At the last moment, the Soviets withheld a promised working nuclear bomb.[38] Cooperation ceased entirely with the Sino-Soviet split following 1959, yet the Chinese nuclear program proceeded apace.

On October 16, 1964, the Chinese detonated a sophisticated uranium fission bomb from a four-hundred-foot tower in the Xinjiang desert near the oasis of Huangyanggou, ninety miles northwest of Lop Nur. The yield was twenty kilotons of TNT equivalent, slightly greater than Trinity or First Lightning. In the apotheosis of long-range detection, with a foresight completely absent from American assessments of Soviet proliferation, Secretary of State

Dean Rusk publicly announced that the Chinese test was imminent *two weeks beforehand*. This might not seem so striking; after all, the Soviets knew about the first American test a few weeks before it happened also. But that Soviet foresight was obtained through human intelligence, and the Americans learned everything they knew about the Chinese program through signals intelligence, high-altitude flights, and radiological monitoring of uranium mining.[39] Once again, it was all technical intelligence. And, once again, the Americans failed to prevent another nation from joining the "nuclear club."

Like the traces of fission decay products floating in the stratosphere, traces of the story told in these pages drift through the decades down to the present. Some of the reasons nuclear proliferation extended beyond the original nuclear club—the United States, the Soviet Union, the United Kingdom, France, and the People's Republic of China—to nations like India, Pakistan, Israel, and North Korea, and why it might still spread further, stem from policies America began in the monopoly. For example, the Truman administration, irritated at having to negotiate with the British time and again to release more uranium from the Combined Development Trust for the construction of yet more warheads, initiated an extensive domestic search for uranium ore. By the end of the 1950s, America was largely able to supply its own needs and terminated its monopoly agreements with South Africa and Canada. The world's largest consumer had dropped out, which flooded the world market with cheap uranium.[40] More uranium made it easier to proliferate.

This connection was not obvious at the time, but it should have been. The main insight of the Acheson-Lilienthal Report—an insight preserved in the Baruch Plan—was the paramount importance of controlling raw material if one wanted to control the spread of nuclear weapons. The price to be paid for monopolizing the raw material was to weaken the American monopoly on atomic information. With the failure of the Baruch Plan, these materials-centric nonproliferation policies suffered, as can be seen with the 1968 Nuclear Non-Proliferation Treaty. Instead, the United States and the Soviet Union emphasized plugging leaks and stopping spies; in other words, controlling the flow of nuclear information. At the same time, as the A. Q. Khan smuggling network run out of Pakistan indicates, the flow of material and technology continued, which directly assisted the North Korean, Libyan, and Iranian programs. The very situation the Americans strove to avoid came to pass.

For today's Russians, as well, the legacies of the atomic monopoly and the consequent arms race continue to be felt literally in their bones. It is certainly true that the nuclear arms race produced significant environmental destruction and health damage in the United States, especially among soldiers and Native American tribes such as the Navajo, who were exposed to uranium-mining operations or nuclear tests with nothing close to the adequate level of precautions—to say nothing about the South Sea Islanders exposed to the first generation of open-air testing.[41] Yet the effects in the Soviet Union were more extensive, have lasted longer, and were preceded by an even more cavalier attitude to the human consequences than in the American context. The environmental destruction wrought by the Soviet atomic complex has left the post-Soviet landscape strewn with tailings from uranium mines, deserts pocked with nuclear craters, and multiple dead zones of radioactive contamination. Devastation of the natural environment and disregard for the health costs to workers were systemic in the Soviet regime, but in the atomic industries this cavalier attitude to long-term consequences was raised to new heights, due at least in part to the tremendous haste to develop an atomic bomb. During 1949, workers at the Anniushka reactor received routine doses of 96.3 rem, which was three times the standard officially set by the Soviet government (and those were already far too high for reasonable safety). The cancer rates among atomic workers immediately following First Lightning were dramatic.[42]

To a certain extent, those workers knew what they were doing. They received higher salaries than average, and they knew those salaries were linked with the secrecy, the importance, and the dangers of their work. Not so the political prisoners who were forced to mine uranium. And not so Soviet citizens living in the Ural Mountains in the vicinity of the Mayak plutonium-production plant. Although the practice was soon stopped, for a few years radioactive waste from the Cheliabinsk-70 plant was dumped into the Techka River. Worse was yet to come. On the afternoon of September 29, 1957, one of the storage tanks for nuclear waste at the plant exploded, with a magnitude of seventy to one hundred tons of TNT equivalent, blowing roughly eighty tons of radioactive waste into the environment. It has proved almost impossible to calculate the human and ecological costs of this disaster—and it was not the only one.[43] Decades before Chernobyl, ordinary Russians suffered terribly for their regime's desire to proliferate.

The stories of ecological disaster and bureaucratic disregard for human consequences can be multiplied for both the American and the Soviet cases, and researchers have begun to uncover many of these buried tales. Special attention might be directed to one of these contaminated places: the site of the central event of this narrative, the testing polygon at Semipalatinsk-21 where First Lightning burst on the morning of August 29, 1949. Although local residents had been evacuated from the site during construction in 1948, no one had anticipated the scale nuclear explosions—and their subsequent fallout—would eventually reach. This meant that roughly half a million people were exposed to the tests in Kazakhstan. About ten thousand of those experienced exposure problems, locally dubbed "Semipalatinsk AIDS," with symptoms including hair loss, miscarriage, cancer, infant mortality, skin disorders, depression, and suicide. In the spring of 1991, as if to prove a point, the Soviet government conducted three underground tests at the Semipalatinsk site (two of 20 kiloton magnitude, and one 0.05-kiloton explosion), before the site was permanently shut down in 1992.[44] A moratorium on nuclear testing was emerging around the world, and the Soviet Union was no more, having passed out of existence on Christmas Day, 1991. The people around Semipalatinsk-21, however, have to live with the aftereffects of decades of nuclear competition between the superpowers, even as one of those superpowers no longer exists.

This all seems rather removed from the Potsdam Conference of July 1945, but in fact it is directly tied to the main subject of that meeting: the postwar settlement in Europe. Only with the reunification of Germany, the withering of the Warsaw Pact, and the dissolution of the Soviet Union did the postwar stalemate in Europe—how to balance the bipolar striving for spheres of influence with the even greater desire to avoid a third world war on the European continent—reach a conclusion of sorts. The exchange between Truman and Stalin, however, never really ended. We are still dancing between the poles of concealment and revelation.

For there were two basic approaches, formulated in those concluding days of World War II, to both the development of nuclear weapons and their control: material approaches (embodied in the uranium monopoly, the Acheson-Lilienthal proposal, and the Baruch Plan), and informational ones (represented in classification and secrecy protocols on both sides). Truman's approach to Stalin at Potsdam fell solidly into the second variant, and, once the Baruch Plan failed, it was the only option apparently remaining. Learning about other nations' nuclear programs, and disciplining one's own, came to be seen as almost exclusively problems of information. The situation has not changed very much in the past sixty years: The ambiguities of information hovered over the debates about the American invasion of Iraq in 2003 and still dominate discussions of Iran's potential to develop nuclear weapons. There were, as we have seen, a lot of fairly good reasons that highly placed individuals in both the United States and the Soviet Union thought informational control would be the best solution to the problem of weapons proliferation. But all of those individuals substantially underrated the difficulties posed by the rampant *uncertainty* in these kinds of data. And so the control of nuclear weapons based on the informational approach has generally failed, and the material consequences of the spread of nuclear weapons and uranium mining linger to remind us of the road not taken. The Soviet Union is gone, but the problems of nuclear weapons and information are still with us. Of the triad of geopolitics, intelligence, and the atomic bomb, only the geopolitics have changed. It was not supposed to happen this way.

NOTES

ABBREVIATIONS USED IN THE NOTES

APSSSR	*Atomnyi proekt SSSR: Dokumenty i materialy*
BAS	*Bulletin of the Atomic Scientists*
CDT	*Chicago Daily Tribune*
CSM	*Christian Science Monitor*
FRUS	*Foreign Relations of the United States*
LAT	*Los Angeles Times*
NYT	*New York Times*
OF	Official File
PSF	President's Secretary's Files
VIET	*Voprosy Istorii Estestvoznaniia i Tekhniki*
WHCF	White House Confidential File
WP	*Washington Post*

INTRODUCTION: WHAT HAPPENED AT POTSDAM

1. Charles L. Mee, Jr., *Meeting at Potsdam* (New York: M. Evans, 1975); Marc Trachtenberg, *A Constructed Peace: The Making of the European Settlement, 1945–1963* (Princeton: Princeton University Press, 1999), 23.

2. David Holloway, "Jockeying for Position in the Postwar World: Soviet Entry into the War with Japan in August 1945," in Tsuyoshi Hasegawa, ed., *The End of the Pacific War: Reappraisals* (Palo Alto: Stanford University Press, 2007), 145–88.

3. On the exclusion of the Soviet Union from the atomic alliance, see Barton J. Bernstein, "The Quest for Security: American Foreign Policy and International Control of Atomic Energy, 1942–1946," *Journal of*

American History 60 (1974): 1003–44; and Joseph I. Lieberman, *The Scorpion and the Tarantula: The Struggle to Control Atomic Weapons, 1945–1949* (Boston: Houghton Mifflin, 1970), 20. For a detailed discussion of wartime policies toward the Soviet Union and atomic energy, see Martin J. Sherwin, *A World Destroyed: Hiroshima and the Origins of the Arms Race* (New York: Vintage, 1987 [1975]).

4. Minutes of Meeting of Combined Policy Committee [extracts], July 4, 1945, *FRUS* 1945, 2:13.

5. "Notes of the Interim Committee Meeting," June 21, 1945, Harrison-Bundy Files, Roll 8, Target 14, File 100: "Interim Committee—Minutes of Meeting," 7.

6. Stimson, diary entry of July 22, 1945.

7. Charles E. Bohlen, *Witness to History, 1929–1969* (New York: Norton, 1973), 237.

8. James F. Byrnes, *Speaking Frankly* (New York: Harper, 1947), 263.

9. James F. Byrnes, *All in One Lifetime* (New York: Harper, 1958), 300–301.

10. In Felix Chuev, *Molotov Remembers: Inside Kremlin Politics. Conversations with Felix Chuev*, ed. Albert Resis (Chicago: Ivan R. Dee, 1993), 55–56.

11. G. K. Zhukov, *Vospominaniia i razmyshleniia*, 2 vols., 13th ed. (Moscow: Olma Press, 2002), 2:375. See the similar account in Anatolii Gromyko, *Andrei Gromyko. V labarintakh Kremlia: Vospominaniia i razmyshleniia syna* (Moscow: Avtor, 1997), 64.

12. Truman, interviews of October 23 and November 17, 1959, reproduced in Ralph E. Weber, ed., *Talking with Harry: Candid Conversations with President Harry S. Truman* (Wilmington, DE: Scholarly Resources, 2001), 3. See also the speculations in Herbert Feis, *The Atomic Bomb and the End of World War II* (Princeton: Princeton University Press, 1966), 101–103.

13. Memorandum of conversation between Averell Harriman and Molotov, August 7, 1945, Harriman Papers, Public Service Special File, World War II, Moscow Files, Box 181, File: "Chron. File, Aug. 5–9, 1945."

14. W. Averell Harriman and Elie Abel, *Special Envoy to Churchill and Stalin, 1941–1946* (New York: Random House, 1975), 491.

15. Zhukov, *Vospominaniia i razmyshleniia*, 2:375.

16. Merkulov to Beria, February 29, 1945, quoted in Vladislav Zubok and Constantine Pleshakov, *Inside the Kremlin's Cold War: From Stalin to Khrushchev* (Cambridge: Harvard University Press, 1996), 41.

17. Stalin, "Otvety na voprosy zadannye moskovskim korrespondentom

'Sandei Taims,' g-nom A. Vert poluchennye 17-go sentiabria 1946 g.," in Joseph Stalin, *Sochineniia*, 3 vols., ed. Robert H. McNeal (Stanford: Hoover Institution, 1967), 3:56.

18. See, for example, O. V. Trakhtenberg, " 'Sotsiologiia' atomnoi bomby," *Voprosy filosofii*, no. 3 (1948): 294–300. For Western analysis, see David Holloway, *Stalin and the Bomb: The Soviet Union and Atomic Energy, 1939–1956* (New Haven: Yale University Press, 1994), 117; Adam B. Ulam, *Expansion and Coexistence: Soviet Foreign Policy, 1917–1973*, 2d ed. (New York: Holt, 1974 [1968]), 414; Vojtech Mastny, *Russia's Road to the Cold War: Diplomacy, Warfare, and the Politics of Communism, 1941–1945* (New York: Columbia University Press, 1979), 298; Thomas W. Wolfe, *Soviet Power and Europe, 1945–1970* (Baltimore: Johns Hopkins Press, 1970), 37; and McGeorge Bundy, "The Unimpressive Record of Atomic Diplomacy," in Gwyn Prins, ed., *The Choice: Nuclear Weapons Versus Security* (London: Chatto & Windus, 1984), 42–54, esp. 44.

19. Svetlana Allilueva, *Dvadtsat' pisem k drugu* (New York: Russkaia kniga, 1981), 175.

20. Michael D. Gordin, *Five Days in August: How World War II Became a Nuclear War* (Princeton: Princeton University Press, 2007), 34–36.

21. Quoted in George McKee Elsey, *An Unplanned Life: A Memoir* (Columbia: University of Missouri Press, 2005), 90.

22. Press and Radio Conference #148, May 27, 1948, PSF: Press Conference File, Box 52, Folder: "January–December, 1948 (Nos. 132–162)," 5.

23. Henry Wallace, diary entry of October 19, 1945, in John Morton Blum, ed., *The Price of Vision: The Diary of Henry A. Wallace, 1942–1946* (Boston: Houghton Mifflin, 1973), 497. On the implications of Potsdam, see also Daniel Yergin, *Shattered Peace: The Origins of the Cold War and the National Security State* (Boston: Houghton Mifflin, 1977), 121; and Lisle A. Rose, *Dubious Victory: The United States and the End of World War II* (Kent, OH: Kent State University Press, 1973), 354.

24. Tsuyoshi Hasegawa, *Racing the Enemy: Stalin, Truman, and the Surrender of Japan* (Cambridge, MA: Belknap Press, 2005), 155.

25. Walter Laqueur, *A World of Secrets: The Uses and Limits of Intelligence* (New York: Basic Books, 1985), 255.

26. I am deeply indebted to the pioneering work of several historians who have focused on the same events in a more national-centric manner: Holloway, *Stalin and the Bomb*; Thomas B. Cochran, Robert S. Norris, and Oleg A. Bukharin, *Making the Russian Bomb: From Stalin to Yeltsin*

(Boulder, CO: Westview Press, 1995); Jeffrey T. Richelson, *Spying on the Bomb: American Nuclear Intelligence from Nazi Germany to Iran and North Korea* (New York: Norton, 2006); and Charles A. Ziegler and David Jacobson, *Spying Without Spies: Origins of America's Secret Nuclear Surveillance System* (Westport, CT: Praeger, 1995).

27. John Lewis Gaddis, "Intelligence, Espionage, and Cold War Origins," *Diplomatic History* 13 (1989): 191–212; John Ferris, "The Intelligence-Deception Complex: An Anatomy," *Intelligence and National Security* 4 (1989): 719–34; Isaac Ben-Israel, "Philosophy and the Methodology of Intelligence: The Logic of Estimate Process," *Intelligence and National Security* 4 (1989): 660–718; Abram N. Shulsky, *Silent Warfare: Understanding the World of Intelligence*, 2d rev. ed. (Washington, D.C.: Brassey's, 1993); Raymond L. Garthoff, "Worst-Case Assumptions: Uses, Abuses and Consequences," in Prins, *The Choice*, 98–108; and Mark M. Lowenthal, "Intelligence Epistemology: Dealing with the Unbelievable," *International Journal of Intelligence and Counterintelligence* 6 (1993): 319–25.

28. H. H. Arnold, "Air Force in the Atomic Age," in Dexter Masters and Katharine Way, eds., *One World or None* (New York: Whittlesey House, 1946), 31. See also Paul Boyer, *By the Bomb's Early Light: American Thought and Culture at the Dawn of the Atomic Age* (Chapel Hill: University of North Carolina Press, 1994 [1985]), 15.

29. These messy features of intelligence are not unique to nuclear information, or to the high-stakes game of international logrolling—they are intrinsic to the process of obtaining reliable knowledge in general. Here I am inspired by the sociological approach to nuclear weapons by Donald MacKenzie and Graham Spinardi, "Tacit Knowledge, Nuclear Weapons Design, and the Uninvention of Nuclear Weapons," *American Journal of Sociology* 101 (1995): 44–99.

30. William Langwiesche, *The Atomic Bazaar: The Rise of the Nuclear Poor* (New York: Farrar, Straus and Giroux, 2007).

31. Holloway, *Stalin and the Bomb*; Paul R. Josephson, *Red Atom: Russia's Nuclear Power Program from Stalin to Today* (New York: W. H. Freeman, 2000); John Wilson Lewis and Xue Litai, *China Builds the Bomb* (Palo Alto: Stanford University Press, 1988); Margaret Gowing, *Britain and Atomic Energy, 1939–1945* (New York: St. Martin's Press, 1964); Margaret Gowing with Lorna Arnold, *Independence and Deterrence: Britain and Atomic Energy, 1945–1952*, 2 vols. (New York: St. Martin's Press, 1974); Gabrielle Hecht, *The Radiance of France: Nuclear Power and National Identity after World War II* (Cambridge, MA: MIT Press,

1998); Spencer R. Weart, *Scientists in Power* (Cambridge, MA: Harvard University Press, 1979); George Perkovich, *India's Nuclear Bomb: The Impact on Global Proliferation* (Berkeley: University of California Press, 1999); Itty Abraham, *The Making of the Indian Atomic Bomb: Science, Secrecy and the Postcolonial State* (New York: Zed Books, 1998); and Avner Cohen, *Israel and the Bomb* (New York: Columbia University Press, 1998). This list can be significantly extended. The only case that is not explicitly labeled as a national history, but nonetheless represents the archetype, is the American one, most notably Richard Rhodes, *The Making of the Atomic Bomb* (New York: Simon & Schuster, 1986). All of these histories, of course, acknowledge some of the international transfers of information, matériel, and personnel but almost never make it a central feature of the story. A welcome recent exception is Andrew J. Rotter, *Hiroshima: The World's Bomb* (New York: Oxford University Press, 2008).

32. See Itty Abraham, "The Ambivalence of Nuclear Histories," *Osiris* 21 (2006): 50.

33. David Kaiser, "The Atomic Secret in Red Hands? American Suspicions of Theoretical Physicists During the Early Cold War," *Representations* 90 (Spring 2005): 49. Yet the comparison of time scales still pulls powerfully on the historian's imagination, as in Lorna Arnold with Katherine Pyne, *Britain and the H-Bomb* (New York: St. Martin's Press, 2001), 30–31.

34. We should be wary of projecting our assumptions of "proper" state behavior on any nation that seeks nuclear weapons. See the analysis in Scott D. Sagan, "Why Do States Build Nuclear Weapons? Three Models in Search of a Bomb," *International Security* 21 (1996–1997): 54–86.

35. Further important sources about the intricacies of the Soviet atomic program are the by-product of an internal post-Soviet Russian debate about who deserves "credit" for creating the Soviet bomb: the spies who provided the American information or the scientists and engineers who built it. See Sergei Leskov, "Dividing the Glory of the Fathers," *BAS* 49 (May 1993): 37–39; Roald Sagdeev, "Russian Scientists Save American Secrets," *BAS* 49 (May 1993): 32; Aleksandr Feklisov, *Za okeanom i na ostrove: Zapiski razvedchika* (Moscow: DEM, 1994), 176; Vladimir Chikov, *Razvedchiki-Nelegaly* (Moscow: Eksmo, 2003), 322–23; and Stanislav Pestov, *Bomba: Tainy i strasti atomnoi preispodnei* (St. Petersburg: Shans, 1995). To a great degree, the impetus behind these claims of credit for the spies was part of a strategy deployed by the

Federal Security Service—the successor to the KGB—to improve its public image. Scientists' responses, in turn, were at least in part an argument for continued state support of Russian science.

ONE: ATOMIC MONOPOLY

1. On the status of atomic weapons at the end of the war, see Gordin, *Five Days in August*. The Soviet reaction to the bombings was famously muted, especially publicly. Interestingly, underplaying of the bomb took place among Soviet decision makers as well. See the internal report on the bombings in Nikita Moiseyev, ed., "The Hiroshima and Nagasaki Tragedy in Documents," *International Affairs* 8 (1990): 122–39.

2. On American and Soviet capabilities, see, respectively, Robert Gregory Joseph, "Commitments and Capabilities: United States Foreign and Defense Policy Coordination, 1945 to the Korean War" (Ph.D. dissertation, Columbia University, 1978), 151; and Melvyn P. Leffler, *A Preponderance of Power: National Security, the Truman Administration, and the Cold War* (Palo Alto: Stanford University Press, 1992), 306. Soviet troop levels may have been exaggerated by Western observers (see, for example, the high estimates in Malcolm Mackintosh, *Juggernaut: A History of the Soviet Armed Forces* [New York: Macmillan, 1967]), as argued in Matthew A. Evangelista, "Stalin's Postwar Army Reappraised," *International Security* 7 (1982–1983): 110–38.

3. "Spaatz Board Report," October 23, 1945, Spaatz Papers, Box 22, File: "Personal, October 1945," 1. See Lauris Norstad to Leslie Groves, September 15, 1945, Top Secret Files, Roll 1, Target 4, File 3: "Stockpile, Storage, and Military Characteristics," 4, 7.

4. Leffler, *A Preponderance of Power*, 2. On the Soviet economy, see N. S. Simonov, *Voenno-promyshlennyi kompleks SSSR v 1920–1950-e gody: Tempy ekonomicheskogo rosta, struktura, organizatsiia proizvodstva i upravlenie* (Moscow: ROSSPEN, 1996), 329.

5. Arnold Wolfers, "The Atomic Bomb in Soviet-American Relations," in Bernard Brodie, ed., *The Absolute Weapon: Atomic Power and World Order* (New York: Harcourt, 1946), 113.

6. Eugene P. Wigner, *The Recollections of Eugene P. Wigner, as Told to Andrew Scranton* (New York: Plenum, 1992), 251.

7. Weart, *Scientists in Power*, 146; Gowing, *Britain and Atomic Energy*, 202–203.

8. E. Kol'man, *Noveishie otkrytiia sovremennoi atomnoi fiziki v svete dialekticheskogo materializma* (Moscow: OGIZ-Gospolitizdat, 1943), 24–25.

See also Arnold Kramish, *Atomic Energy in the Soviet Union* (Palo Alto: Stanford University Press, 1959), 56–57.

9. G. N. Flerov and K. A. Petrzhak, "Spontaneous Fission of Uranium," *Journal of Physics* 3, nos. 4–5 (1940): 275–80.

10. In Iu. N. Smirnov, "G. N. Flerov i stanovlenie sovetskogo atomnogo proekta," *VIET*, no. 2 (1996): 114. For further discussion, see E. A. Negin et al., *Sovetskii atomnyi proekt: Konets atomnoi monopolii. Kak eto bylo . . .* (Nizhnii Novgorod/Arzamas-16: Izd. Nizhnii Novgorod, 1995), 58; I. N. Golovin, *Academician Igor Kurchatov*, trans. George Yankovsky (Moscow: Mir Publishers, 1969), 47–48.

11. Smirnov, "G. N. Flerov i stanovlenie sovetskogo atomnogo proekta," 120.

12. Mark Walker, *German National Socialism and the Quest for Nuclear Power, 1939–1949* (New York: Cambridge University Press, 1989), 156.

13. Langmuir testimony to U.S. Senate Special Committee on Atomic Energy, November 30, 1945, *Atomic Energy: Hearings on S. Res. 179*, 79th Cong., 1st sess., 1945–1946, 114. See also E. U. Condon to Walter Lippmann, August 12, 1955, Condon Papers, Series I, Box 82, Folder: "Lippmann, Walter": "This action of General Groves resulted in quite a lot of unfavorable comment in England, questions were asked in Commons, and, of course, the General had let out the fact of the existence of an atomic bomb project which was itself supposed to be secret at the time . . . Personally I believe a great mistake was made which must have alerted the Russians to the importance of the information they were getting from Los Alamos through [Klaus] Fuchs and [David] Greenglass, their spies who were operating at Los Alamos without detection by General Groves' hordes of security officers." This episode is only rarely referred to by historians, although it was of undoubted contemporary importance. See, for example, Lieberman, *The Scorpion and the Tarantula*, 194.

14. Quebec Agreement, signed by Franklin D. Roosevelt and Winston Churchill, August 19, 1943, Harrison-Bundy Files, Roll 1, Target 3, File 3: "Discussion on Atomic Energy with British and Canada." For helpful discussions of this wartime atomic framework, see Bernstein, "The Quest for Security"; and Sherwin, *A World Destroyed*.

15. Stimson to Truman, September 11, 1945, inserted immediately after Stimson's diary entry of September 12, 1945. For the most careful and thorough account, see Sean L. Malloy, *Atomic Tragedy: Henry L. Stim-*

son and the Decision to Use the Bomb Against Japan (Ithaca: Cornell University Press, 2008).

16. Dean Acheson, *Present at the Creation: My Years in the State Department* (New York: Norton, 1987 [1969]), 123. Truman wrote to his wife Bess on September 22, 1945, that the meeting "lasted two hours and every phase of national and international politics was discussed. It was very helpful." Letter in Robert H. Ferrell, ed., *Dear Bess: The Letters from Harry to Bess Truman, 1910–1959* (New York: Norton, 1983), 523.

17. Entry of September 21, 1945, Forrestal Diaries, Volume III, Sept. 4, 1945–Jan. 5, 1946; see Richard F. Haynes, *The Awesome Power: Harry S. Truman as Commander in Chief* (Baton Rouge: Louisiana State University Press, 1973), 66.

18. Entry of September 18, 1945, Forrestal Diaries, Volume III, Sept. 4, 1945–Jan. 5, 1946.

19. Entry of September 21, 1945, ibid. On Wallace and the Manhattan Project, see J. Samuel Walker, *Henry A. Wallace and American Foreign Policy* (Westport, CT: Greenwood Press, 1976), 122–23.

20. Henry Wallace, diary entry of September 21, 1945, in John Blum, *The Price of Vision*, 483.

21. Felix Belair, Jr., "Plea to Give Soviet Atom Secret Stirs Debate in Cabinet," *NYT*, September 22, 1945, 1, 3; "Truman Says He'll Decide Atomic Policy," *LAT*, September 24, 1945, 1–2.

22. Entry of December 24, 1946, Forrestal Diaries, Volume VI, Oct. 1, 1946–March 31, 1947; Henry L. Stimson and McGeorge Bundy, *On Active Service in Peace and War* (New York: Harper, 1948), 646.

23. For the distribution of positions, see Notes on Cabinet Meeting, September 21, 1945, Connelly Papers, Box 1, Folder: "September 21, 1945."

24. Entry of September 21, 1945, Forrestal Diaries, Volume III, Sept. 4, 1945–Jan. 5, 1946.

25. Acting Secretary of War Robert Patterson to Truman, September 26, 1945, PSF: General File, 1940–1953, Box 96, Folder: "Atomic Bomb," 2.

26. Vannevar Bush to Truman, September 25, 1945, PSF: Subject File 1940–1953, National Security Council—Atomic Files, Box 173, Folder: "Atomic Bomb: Cabinet: James F. Byrnes," 5.

27. John Lewis Gaddis, *The United States and the Origins of the Cold War, 1941–1947* (New York: Columbia University Press, 1972), 273; Martin Weil, *A Pretty Good Club: The Founding Fathers of the U.S. Foreign Service* (New York: Norton, 1978), 220–23.

28. David Robertson, *Sly and Able: A Political Biography of James F. Byrnes* (New York: Norton, 1994); Robert L. Messer, *The End of an Alliance: James F. Byrnes, Roosevelt, Truman, and the Origins of the Cold War* (Chapel Hill: University of North Carolina Press, 1982), 222; Alonzo L. Hamby, *Man of the People: A Life of Harry S. Truman* (New York: Oxford University Press, 1995), 327.

29. Robert L. Beisner, *Dean Acheson: A Life in the Cold War* (New York: Oxford University Press, 2006), 103. Only in Truman's second term did he acquire administrative apparatus proportionate to the job. See Hamby, *Man of the People*, 298–305; Jonathan Daniels, *The Man of Independence* (Philadelphia: Lippincott, 1950), 304.

30. Susan M. Hartmann, *Truman and the 80th Congress* (Columbia: University of Missouri Press, 1971), 4–5.

31. Hamby, *Man of the People*, 384–85.

32. Randall Woods, "Congress and the Roots of Postwar American Foreign Policy," in Arnold A. Offner and Theodore A. Wilson, eds., *Victory in Europe 1945: From World War to Cold War* (Lawrence: University Press of Kansas, 2000), 167–81; Henry W. Berger, "Bipartisanship, Senator Taft, and the Truman Administration," *Political Science Quarterly* 90 (1975): 221–37; Hartmann, *Truman and the 80th Congress*, 13–14; C. David Tompkins, *Senator Arthur H. Vandenberg: The Evolution of a Modern Republican, 1884–1945* (Lansing: Michigan State University Press, 1970), 241; Lynn Rachele Eden, "The Diplomacy of Force: Interests, the State, and the Making of American Military Policy in 1948" (Ph.D. dissertation, University of Michigan, 1985), 168–75; and James T. Patterson, *Mr. Republican: A Biography of Robert A. Taft* (Boston: Houghton Mifflin, 1972), 339–40.

33. In U.S. Department of State, *The International Control of Atomic Energy: Growth of a Policy* (Washington, D.C.: GPO, 1946), 112.

34. See Arnold A. Offner, *Another Such Victory: President Truman and the Cold War, 1945–1953* (Palo Alto: Stanford University Press, 2002), 108; Gregg Herken, *The Winning Weapon: The Atomic Bomb in the Cold War, 1945–1950* (New York: Knopf, 1980), 100.

35. Deborah Welch Larson, *Origins of Containment: A Psychological Explanation* (Princeton: Princeton University Press, 1985), 214; Gaddis Smith, *Dean Acheson* (New York: Cooper Square Publishers, 1972), 40; David Horowitz, *The Free World Colossus: A Critique of American Foreign Policy in the Cold War* (New York: Hill and Wang, 1965), 266.

36. Hazel Gaudet Erskine, "The Polls: Atomic Weapons and Nuclear Energy," *Public Opinion Quarterly* 27 (1963): 164–68.

37. Press and Radio Conference #34, November 20, 1945, PSF: Press Conference File, Press Conference Transcripts, Box 51, Folder: "April–December, 1945 (Nos. 1–40)," 8.

38. Alice Kimball Smith, *A Peril and a Hope: The Scientists' Movement in America: 1945–47* (Chicago: University of Chicago Press, 1965); Donald A. Strickland, *Scientists in Politics: The Atomic Scientists Movement, 1945–1946* (Lafayette, IN: Purdue University Studies, 1968). The FAS began to wither in the late 1940s under FBI scrutiny. By late 1949 their membership had dropped to 1,500 from a onetime high of 3,000. The FBI terminated their investigations on April 21, 1950, concluding that the FAS was no longer important enough to investigate. Jessica Wang, *American Science in an Age of Anxiety: Scientists, Anticommunism, and the Cold War* (Chapel Hill: University of North Carolina Press, 1999), 82.

39. James R. Newman and Byron S. Miller, *The Control of Atomic Energy: A Study of Its Social, Economic, and Political Implications* (New York: McGraw-Hill, 1948); Herbert S. Marks, "Congress and the Atom," *Stanford Law Review* 1 (November 1948): 23–42.

40. Alonzo L. Hamby, *Beyond the New Deal: Harry S. Truman and American Liberalism* (New York: Columbia University Press, 1973), 224; Robert J. Donovan, *Conflict and Crisis: The Presidency of Harry S Truman, 1945–1948* (New York: Norton, 1977), 26.

41. David E. Lilienthal, entry of December 20, 1946, in *The Atomic Energy Years, 1945–1950: The Journals of David E. Lilienthal, Volume 2* (New York: Harper, 1964), 120.

42. Lilienthal, entries of June 24, 1947, and January 14, 1949, ibid., 207, 445.

43. Lilienthal, entry of September 19, 1949, ibid., 568. There are several ways to interpret this conflict. Lilienthal's biographer comments, "Ironically, much of the conflict arose from coincidence of personality. Both men had large egos and a capacity for arrogant bearing." Steven M. Neuse, *David E. Lilienthal: The Journey of an American Liberal* (Knoxville: University of Tennessee Press, 1996), 205.

44. Forrestal to Truman, July 21, 1948, and Lilienthal to Truman, July 21, 1948, in Dennis Merrill, ed., *Documentary History of the Truman Presidency, Volume 21: The Development of an Atomic Weapons Program Following World War II* (Bethesda, MD: University Publications of America, 1998), 221–25; and Carl Spaatz to Lieutenant General Lewis H. Brereton (Chairman of MLC), October 31, 1947, Spaatz Papers, Box 256, File: "Atomic Bombs and Tests." See also Haynes, *The Awe-*

some Power, 142–43; Steven L. Rearden, *History of the Office of the Secretary of Defense, vol. 1: The Formative Years, 1947–1950* (Washington, D.C.: Historical Office, Office of the Secretary of Defense, 1984), 426–27, 432; and Townsend Hoopes and Douglas Brinkley, *Driven Patriot: The Life and Times of James Forrestal* (New York: Knopf, 1992), 378–79. On Truman's nuclear-launch authority, see Steven T. Ross, *American War Plans, 1945–1950* (New York: Garland Publishing, 1988), 13–14; and Offner, *Another Such Victory*, 272.

45. James R. Newman, "Control of Information Relating to Atomic Energy," *Yale Law Journal* 56, no. 5 (May 1947): 769–802.

46. C. R. Attlee, *As It Happened* (New York: Viking, 1954), 162. On the British involvement at Los Alamos, see Ferenc Morton Szasz, *British Scientists and the Manhattan Project: The Los Alamos Years* (New York: St. Martin's Press, 1992).

47. Graham Spinardi, "Aldermaston and British Nuclear Weapons Development: Testing the 'Zuckerman Thesis,' " *Social Studies of Science* 27 (1997): 550–51; Gowing, *Independence and Deterrence*, 1:21.

48. Quoted in Gowing, *Independence and Deterrence*, 1:183. See also the discussion in Kenneth O. Morgan, *Labour in Power, 1945–1951* (New York: Oxford University Press, 1984), 280.

49. Entry of July 8, 1947, Forrestal Diaries, Volumes VII–VIII, April 1, 1947–Oct. 31, 1947.

50. Entry of November 5, 1947, ibid., Volumes IX–X, Nov. 1, 1947–April 30, 1948.

51. Harry S. Truman, *Memoirs*, Volume II: *Years of Trial and Hope* (Garden City, NY: Doubleday, 1956), 298.

52. David Mayers, *George Kennan and the Dilemmas of US Foreign Policy* (New York: Oxford University Press, 1988), 304.

53. Timothy J. Botti, *The Long Wait: The Forging of the Anglo-American Nuclear Alliance, 1945–1958* (New York: Greenwood Press, 1987), 34–35; S.J. Ball, "Military Nuclear Relations Between the United States and Great Britain Under the Terms of the McMahon Act, 1946–1958," *Historical Journal* 38 (1995): 439–54; James L. Gormly, "The Washington Declaration and the 'Poor Relation': Anglo-American Atomic Diplomacy, 1945–46," *Diplomatic History* 8 (1984): 125–43; Nicholas J. Wheeler, "British Nuclear Weapons and Anglo-American Relations 1945–1954," *International Affairs* 62 (1985–1986): 71–86.

54. Acheson-Lilienthal Committee, "Proposals for Discussion," December 21, 1945, Harrison-Bundy Files, Roll 4, Target 9, File 63: "Working Committee (State Department)."

55. Dean Acheson to David Lilienthal, January 16, 1946, Lilienthal Papers, Series 3, Box 112, Folder: "Acheson, Dean 1946."

56. Acheson, *Present at the Creation*, 153.

57. Lilienthal, entry of February 25, 1946, *The Atomic Energy Years*, 23. One of Lilienthal's biographers did not think the idea *that* original, noting some clear parallels between the report and the organizational structure Lilienthal had established at the TVA. See Willson Whitman, *David Lilienthal: Public Servant in a Power Age* (New York: Henry Holt, 1948), 144.

58. Chester I. Barnard et al., *A Report on the International Control of Atomic Energy* (Washington, D.C.: U.S. Department of State, 1946), 52–53.

59. Ibid., 11–13.

60. Acheson testimony, February 10, 1947, before JCAE, Senate Section, *Confirmation of Atomic Energy Commission and General Manager: Hearings*, 80th Cong., 1st sess., 1947, 296. Statements like this belie the extent of Acheson's personal commitment to the proposal. See David S. McLellan, *Dean Acheson: The State Department Years* (New York: Dodd, Mead, 1976), 79.

61. Truman, *Years of Trial and Hope*, 7–8. On Baruch's health, see James Grant, *Bernard Baruch: The Adventures of a Wall Street Legend* (New York: Simon & Schuster, 1983), 304.

62. Baruch to Truman, March 26, 1946, PSF: General File, 1940–1953, Box 96, Folder: "Atomic Energy Commission—United Nations"; James Byrnes to Baruch, April 19, 1946, PSF: General File, 1940–1953, Box 97, Folder: "Baruch, Bernard M."

63. Acheson, *Present at the Creation*, 154.

64. Lilienthal, entry of March 19, 1946, *The Atomic Energy Years*, 30. Despite his disappointment, Lilienthal would publicly back the Baruch Plan in his January 27, 1947, testimony during his confirmation hearings: JCAE, *Confirmation of Atomic Energy Commission and General Manager*, 18.

65. Bernard M. Baruch, *Baruch: The Public Years* (New York: Holt, 1960), 364. James B. Conant shared these views and felt the appointment made sense only to assuage senatorial qualms: Conant, *My Several Lives: Memoirs of a Social Inventor* (New York: Harper, 1970), 493. The real zenith of Baruch's congressional influence, however, was in 1931–1932. See Jordan A. Schwarz, *The Speculator: Bernard M. Baruch in Washington, 1917–1965* (Chapel Hill: University of North Carolina Press, 1981), 4.

66. Baruch, quoted in Lilienthal, entry of December 22, 1946, *The Atomic Energy Years*, 123.

67. Larry G. Gerber, "The Baruch Plan and the Origins of the Cold War," *Diplomatic History* 6 (1982): 69–95; John Lewis Gaddis, *We Now Know: Rethinking Cold War History* (New York: Oxford University Press, 1997), 90; Robert Gilpin, *American Scientists and Nuclear Weapons Policy* (Princeton: Princeton University Press, 1962), 62.

68. Bernard M. Baruch, "United States Atomic Energy Proposals," Statement to the UNAEC, June 14, 1946, Baruch Papers, Unit VII, Vol. 4, 1946–1950, 5–6.

69. On procedure as a Soviet stalling tactic, see the analysis in Joseph L. Nogee, *Soviet Policy Towards International Control of Atomic Energy* (Notre Dame: University of Notre Dame Press, 1961), 282.

70. James S. Allen, *Atomic Imperialism: The State, Monopoly, and the Bomb* (New York: International Publishers, 1952), 7. See also Lloyd C. Gardner, *Architects of Illusion: Men and Ideas in American Foreign Policy* (Chicago: Quadrangle Books, 1970), 175–76; and Joyce Kolko and Gabriel Kolko, *The Limits of Power: The World and United States Foreign Policy, 1945–1954* (New York: Harper, 1972), 105.

71. Andrei Gromyko, *Memoirs*, trans. Harold Shukman (New York: Doubleday, 1989), 140.

72. Molotov, "The Soviet Union and International Cooperation," speech at Plenary Meeting of the General Assembly of the United Nations, October 29, 1946, in V. M. Molotov, *Problems of Foreign Policy: Speeches and Statements, April 1945–November 1948* (Moscow: Foreign Languages Publishing House, 1949), 258. This was a main strand of the official discourse about atomic arms control. See V. M. Khaitsman, *SSSR i problema razoruzheniia, 1945–1959: Istoriia mezhdunarodnykh peregovorov* (Moscow: Nauka, 1970), 50; A. Gromyko and B. N. Ponomarev, eds., *Istoriia vneshnei politiki SSSR*, 5th rev. ed., vol. 2 (Moscow: Nauka, 1986), 87–89.

73. "Staff Memorandum, Subject: Points Raised by Mr. Ickes' Letter of August 22, 1946," August 29, 1946, Baruch Papers, Unit X, Section 1, Box 52, File: "Policy Correspondence, Memoranda, and Notes on Conferences (Post June 14)—General," 4.

74. John M. Hancock, memorandum for the staff, November 21, 1946, Baruch Papers, Unit X, Section 1, Box 56, File: "On the Subject of Bomb Manufacture," 2.

75. In Department of State, *The International Control of Atomic Energy*, 210.

76. "Progress Report of the First Two Months of Negotiations," August 14, 1946, Baruch Papers, Unit X, Section 1, Box 52, File: "Policy Correspondence, Memoranda, and Notes on Conferences—State Department," 20–21.

77. Smith to Byrnes, June 26, 1946, *FRUS* 1946, 6:766. Wallace's position was paraphrased in Émile Benoit-Smullyan, "Control of Atomic Energy by the United Nations," *Antioch Review* 6 (Winter 1946): 488.

78. Molotov, "The Reduction of Armaments and the Draft Decision," speech at meeting of the First Committee of the General Assembly of the United Nations, December 4, 1946, in Molotov, *Problems of Foreign Policy*, 323. Similar logic, interestingly, was invoked by isolationists in the U.S. Congress, insisting on the veto to prevent the UN from dragging America into unnecessary foreign "entanglements." See Justus D. Doenecke, *Not to the Swift: The Old Isolationists in the Cold War Era* (Lewisburg, PA: Bucknell University Press, 1979), 49. On veto deliberations at the San Francisco meeting, and their importance for the Soviet Union, see Stephen C. Schlesinger, *Act of Creation: The Founding of the United Nations: A Story of Superpowers, Secret Agents, Wartime Allies and Enemies, and Their Quest for a Peaceful World* (Cambridge, MA: Westview Press, 2003), 193; and Adam B. Ulam, *The Rivals: America and Russia Since World War II* (New York: Viking, 1971), 107.

79. D. F. Fleming to Bernard M. Baruch, July 2, 1946, Baruch Papers, Unit X, Section 2, Box 62, File: "Atomic Energy—Fleming D. F. 1946," 1.

80. "The Rock of the U.N. Veto," *LAT*, August 27, 1947, A4; Bernard G. Bechhoefer, *Postwar Negotiations for Arms Control* (Washington, D.C.: Brookings Institution, 1961), 57–60.

81. Chester Barnard to David Lilienthal, January 20, 1947, Lilienthal Papers, Series 3, Box 121, Folder: "Barnard, Chester I. 1947."

82. In Bertrand Goldschmidt, "A Forerunner of the Non-Proliferation Treaty? The Soviet 1947 Proposals," in A. Boserup, L. Christensen, and O. Nathan, eds., *The Challenge of Nuclear Armaments: Essays Dedicated to Niels Bohr and His Appeal for an Open World* (Copenhagen: Rhodos International, 1986), 64.

83. Frederick H. Osborn, "Negotiating on Atomic Energy, 1946–1947," in Raymond Dennett and Joseph E. Johnson, eds., *Negotiating with the Russians* (Boston: World Peace Foundation, 1951), 231.

84. Walter Lippmann, "Britain, Russia and the Bomb," *WP*, March 8, 1947, 7.

85. For contemporary arguments that compromise was possible, see "Bomb Control: The Two Plans," *NYT*, June 21, 1946, 22; that it was impossible, see "Mr. Gromyko Vs. Mr. Baruch," *LAT*, June 21, 1946, A4.

86. Bernard M. Baruch to Harry S. Truman, September 17, 1946, Baruch Papers, Unit X, Section 1, Box 52, File: "Policy Correspondence, Memoranda, and Notes on Conferences—President," 16.

87. Walter Lippmann to Chester I. Barnard, June 25, 1946, Lilienthal Papers, Series 3, Box 114, Folder: "Barnard, Chester I. 1946."

88. George T. Mazuzan, *Warren R. Austin at the U.N.: 1946–1953* (Kent, OH: Kent State University Press, 1977).

89. J. Robert Oppenheimer to Robert F. Bacher, August 6, 1947, Oppenheimer Papers, Case File, Box 18, File: "Bacher, Robert F. (correspondence)," 4.

90. Frederick Osborn, entry of February 18, 1948, "United Nations Atomic Energy Commission Diary," Osborn Papers, Box 2. For the evolution of Oppenheimer's views on international control, see J. Robert Oppenheimer, "International Control of Atomic Energy," *Foreign Affairs* 26, no. 2 (January 1948): 239–52; and James G. Hershberg, " 'The Jig Was Up': J. Robert Oppenheimer and the International Control of Atomic Energy, 1947–49," in Cathryn Carson and David A. Hollinger, eds., *Reappraising Oppenheimer: Centennial Studies and Reflections* (Berkeley: Office for History of Science and Technology, University of California, 2005), 149–83.

91. Edward A. Shils, "The Failure of the United Nations Atomic Energy Commission: An Interpretation," *University of Chicago Law Review* 15 (Summer 1948): 872.

92. Lieberman, *The Scorpion and the Tarantula*, 393.

93. Marshall D. Shulman, *Stalin's Foreign Policy Reappraised* (Cambridge, MA: Harvard University Press, 1963), 22; Nogee, *Soviet Policy Towards International Control of Atomic Energy*, 272; Lawrence S. Wittner, *One World or None: A History of the World Nuclear Disarmament Movement Through 1953* (Palo Alto: Stanford University Press, 1993), 308.

94. William O. McCagg, Jr., *Stalin Embattled: 1943–1948* (Detroit: Wayne State University Press, 1978), 26.

95. John Murray Clearwater, "The Evolution of Soviet Military Doctrine in Regards the Atomic Bomb" (Ph.D. dissertation, Dalhousie University, Halifax, Nova Scotia, 1990), 36–37.

96. Russell D. Buhite and Wm. Christopher Hamel, "War for Peace: The Question of an American Preventive War Against the Soviet Union, 1945–1955," *Diplomatic History* 14 (1990): 367–84; Raymond L.

Garthoff, *A Journey Through the Cold War: A Memoir of Containment and Coexistence* (Washington, D.C.: Brookings Institution Press, 2001), 15; William Reitzel, Morton A. Kaplan, and Constance G. Coblenz, *United States Foreign Policy, 1945–1955* (Washington, D.C.: Brookings Institution Press, 1956), 326; Gaddis, *We Now Know*, 89.

97. Robert A. Divine, "The Cold War and the Election of 1948," *Journal of American History* 59 (1972): 90–110; Avi Shlaim, *The United States and the Berlin Blockade, 1948–1949: A Study in Crisis Decision-Making* (Berkeley: University of California Press, 1983); Leffler, *A Preponderance of Power*, 205; Harold F. Gosnell, *Truman's Crises: A Political Biography of Harry S. Truman* (Westport, CT: Greenwood Press, 1980), 439; Vojtech Mastny, "Stalin and the Militarization of the Cold War," *International Security* 9 (Winter 1984–1985): 109–29; Melvyn P. Leffler, *The Specter of Communism: The United States and the Origins of the Cold War, 1917–1953* (New York: Hill and Wang, 1994), 66.

98. Kerr to Bevin, December 3, 1945, *FRUS 1945*, 2:83–84.

TWO: HOW MUCH TIME DO WE HAVE?

1. Erskine, "The Polls," 175.
2. Social Science Research Council, Committee on Social and Economic Aspects of Atomic Energy, *Public Reaction to the Atomic Bomb and World Affairs: A Nation-wide Survey of Attitudes and Information* (Ithaca: Cornell University, 1947), 105.
3. "Report Gives Soviet A-Bomb Excelling U.S.," *CSM*, January 8, 1946, 8. For the presidential refutation, see Press and Radio Conference #41, January 8, 1946, PSF, Press Conference File, Press Conference Transcripts, Box 51, Folder: "January–June, 1946 (Nos. 41–71)," 4; "Atom Is Still a U.S. Secret, Says Truman," *CDT*, January 9, 1946, 10.
4. ORE, Special Study No. 3, August 24, 1946, in Woodrow J. Kuhns, ed., *Assessing the Soviet Threat: The Early Cold War Years* (Washington, D.C.: Center for the Study of Intelligence, CIA, 1997), 79.
5. "Russia Has Death Ray, Scientist Says," *LAT*, March 10, 1949, 1; "Warns Russia May Be Making Bomb by Spring," *CDT*, November 21, 1945, 5; "Rumor of New Red Ray Bomb Unfounded," *WP*, September 20, 1946, 6; Professor Irving Fisher to Bernard M. Baruch, August 30, 1946, Baruch Papers, Unit X, Section 2, Box 61, File: "Atomic Energy Commission (Special Correspondence, A–F)"; "Pole Says Reds Have Mastered Atomic Energy," *LAT*, December 5, 1945, 1; "Physicist Says Soviet Has 'Tons' of A-Bombs," *CSM*, July 22, 1947, 6; "London Professor Says Reds Have Atom Bomb," *WP*, April 3, 1948, 6; "Rus-

sians Have A-Bomb Secret, Says Scientist," *CDT*, March 23, 1949, 21; "Refugee Author Says Russia Has A-Bomb," *WP*, April 8, 1949, 26.

6. For example, John Thompson, "Red Scientists Reported Far Beyond A-Bomb," *CDT*, March 12, 1947, 14, reported from *De Volkskrant*, organ of the Netherlands National Catholic Party; "Soviet A-Bomb Test Reported," *CSM*, November 11, 1947, 12, reported from *L'Intransigeant*; "Paris Paper Reports Russ A-Bomb Tests," *LAT*, July 26, 1949, 1, reported from *Samedi-Soir*. For Britain, "Russia Will Have A-Bombs by June, Union Leaguers Told," *CDT*, November 24, 1948, 7.

7. Chargé in Soviet Union Durbrow to Byrnes, September 13, 1946, *FRUS* 1946, 6:782.

8. "Atomic Bombs," [April 1945], Harrison-Bundy Papers, Roll 1, Target 15, File 15: "History of the Atomic Bomb," 17.

9. Stalin, *Sochineniia*, 3:62.

10. Molotov, "Thirtieth Anniversary of the Great October Socialist Revolution," speech at celebration meeting of the Moscow Soviet, November 6, 1947, in Molotov, *Problems of Foreign Policy*, 488.

11. "Reds 'Possibly' Have A-Bomb—Vishinsky," *LAT*, November 7, 1947, 1; "U.S. Monopoly on Atom Bomb 'Illusion,' Vishinsky Tells UN," *CSM*, October 1, 1948, 6; "Reds' A-Bomb Hint Called 'Dishonest,' " *WP*, October 3, 1948, M3; Zhdanov quoted in Sydney Gruson, "U.S. Monopoly of Bomb Cited," *NYT*, October 23, 1947, 3.

12. Smith, *My Three Years in Moscow*, 327–28. See also Neal Stanford, "U.S. Doubts That Soviet Has A-Bomb 'Know-How,' " *CSM*, November 7, 1947, 9. In a minority view, Igor Gouzenko, the famous defector who will be discussed in the following chapter, felt that perhaps Molotov actually meant that the Soviet Union had proliferated. See Gouzenko, *The Iron Curtain* (New York: Dutton, 1948), 255.

13. Few historians have addressed the existence of this disparity, and their explanations for the diversity have usually been cursory. See Ethan Pollock, "Oshibki, vyzvannye emotsiiami: Predstavlenie amerikantsev o vozmozhnosti sovetskikh atomnykh razrabotok, 1945–1949 gg.," in E. P. Velikhov, ed. *Nauka i obshchestvo: Istoriia sovetskogo atomnogo proekta (40-e—50-e gody)*, vol. 3 (Moscow: IzdAT, 2003), 200–206; and Charles A. Ziegler, "Intelligence Assessments of Soviet Atomic Capability, 1945–1949: Myths, Monopolies and *Maskirovka*," *Intelligence and National Security* 12, no. 4 (October 1997): 1–24.

14. The reasons for the failure of the German uranium project to produce a nuclear device have been heavily disputed in the historical literature, with answers ranging from "dictatorships are unable to exploit scientific

talent" (Samuel A. Goudsmit, *Alsos* [New York: Henry Schuman, 1947]), to "the scientists did not know how" (Paul Lawrence Rose, *Heisenberg and the Nazi Atomic Bomb Project: A Study in German Culture* [Berkeley: University of California Press, 1998]; and Jeremy Bernstein, *Hitler's Uranium Club: The Secret Recordings at Farm Hall* [Woodbury, NY: AIP Press, 1996]), to "the scientists sabotaged the project" (Thomas Powers, *Heisenberg's War: The Secret History of the German Bomb* [New York: Knopf, 1993]; and Robert Jungk, *Brighter than a Thousand Suns: The Story of the Men Who Made the Bomb*, trans. James Cleugh [New York: Grove Press, 1958]), to "they were trying to make a reactor, not a bomb" (Walker, *German National Socialism and the Quest for Nuclear Power*; Mark Walker, *Nazi Science: Myth, Truth, and the German Atomic Bomb* [Cambridge, MA: Perseus Publishing, 1995]; Mark Walker, "German Work on Nuclear Weapons," *Historia Scientiarum* 14, no. 3 [2005]: 1–18), to "they actually *did* make a bomb" (Rainer Karlsch, *Hitlers Bombe: Die geheime Geschichte der deutschen Kernwaffenversuche* [Munich: Deutsche Verlags-Anstalt, 2005]). This is not the place to try to adjudicate this issue; I simply note that it is still difficult to come to an answer for why nations take as long (or as short) as they do to produce nuclear weapons.

15. Samuel A. Goudsmit, "Science and the Atom Bomb," letter to the editor, *NYT*, February 11, 1947, 26.

16. P.M.S. Blackett, *Atomic Weapons and East-West Relations* (Cambridge, England: Cambridge University Press, 1956), 41.

17. Norris Bradbury, "Los Alamos—The First 25 Years," in Lawrence Badash, Joseph O. Hirschfelder, and Herbert P. Broida, eds., *Reminiscences of Los Alamos, 1943–1945* (Dordrecht: D. Reidel, 1980), 167.

18. For Forrestal, see the entry of November 8, 1945, Forrestal Diaries, Volume III, Sept. 4, 1945–Jan. 5, 1946.

19. "Notes of a Meeting in the Office of Secretary of War Concerning Atomic Energy Legislation, 9:30 a.m.–11:00 a.m., September 28, 1945," Harrison-Bundy Files, Roll 5, Target 4, File 68: "Interim Committee—Legislation," 6.

20. Groves testimony, October 9, 1945, U.S. House of Representatives, Committee on Military Affairs, *Atomic Energy: Hearings on H. R. 4280*, 79th Cong., 1st sess., 1945, 18.

21. Groves testimony, November 29, 1945, U.S. Senate, Special Committee on Atomic Energy, *Atomic Energy: Hearings on S. Res. 179*, 79th Cong., 1st sess., 1945–1946, 62. Groves reiterated the shorter end of

this estimate while debriefing one of Bernard Baruch's associates on atomic arms control in 1946. Franklin Lindsay recalled that Groves "considered the four-year estimate entirely too short and stated that he would stick by his original estimate of five to seven years." When pressed further, "he stated that he believed the time required would be a minimum of seven years." Franklin A. Lindsay to Bernard M. Baruch, September 12, 1946, Baruch Papers, Unit X, Section 2, Box 56, File: "On the Subject of: <u>Bomb Manufacture</u>," 2. Presumably, Groves was factoring in the possibility that the Baruch Plan would pass and thus the Americans would share some information and technology with the Soviets.

22. Transcript of telephone call between Leslie R. Groves and G. M. Read, 9:45 am, May 21, 1945, Top Secret Files, Roll 2, Target 6, File 12: "Intelligence and Security."

23. Snyder to Truman, September 25, 1945, PSF, General File, 1940–1953, Box 96, Folder: "Atomic Bomb."

24. Entry of September 24, 1948, Forrestal Diaries, Volumes XI–XII, May 1, 1948–Sept. 30, 1948.

25. John F. Hogerton and Ellsworth Raymond, "When Will Russia Have the Atomic Bomb?" *Look*, March 16, 1948, 32, 34 (I have removed the boldface of the original). The Pulitzer Prize–winning "atomic journalist" William L. Laurence agreed in "How Soon Will Russia Have the A-Bomb?" *Saturday Evening Post*, November 6, 1948, 181.

26. A. Neubauer, "Nemetskie khimiki i sovetskii atomnyi proekt posle 1945 g.: Maks Fol'mer," *VIET*, no. 4 (1991): 22.

27. Groves interview in Joseph J. Ermenc, ed., *Atomic Bomb Scientists: Memoirs, 1939–1945* (Westport, CT: Meckler, 1989), 254.

28. Groves, testimony of April 15, 1954, United States Atomic Energy Commission, *In the Matter of J. Robert Oppenheimer: Transcript of Hearing Before Personnel Security Board and Texts of Principal Documents and Letters* (Cambridge, MA: MIT Press, 1971 [1954]), 175. On the centrality of uranium supply for Groves's assessments, see Ziegler, "Intelligence Assessment of Soviet Atomic Capability"; Herken, *The Winning Weapon*; and Robert S. Norris, *Racing for the Bomb: General Leslie R. Groves, the Manhattan Project's Indispensable Man* (South Royalton, VT: Steerforth Press, 2002), 475.

29. Fred Searls, Jr., to James F. Byrnes, October 24, 1946, Baruch Papers, Unit X, Section 2, Box 64, File: "Searls, Fred, Jr.," 2.

30. Jonathan E. Helmreich, *Gathering Rare Ores: The Diplomacy of Ura-*

nium Acquisition, 1943–1954 (Princeton: Princeton University Press, 1986); Bertrand Goldschmidt, *Atomic Rivals*, trans. Georges M. Temmer (New Brunswick, NJ: Rutgers University Press, 1990), 185.

31. Leslie R. Groves, *Now It Can Be Told: The Story of the Manhattan Project* (New York: Harper, 1962), 33.

32. Groves to Patterson, December 3, 1945, *FRUS* 1945 2:84–85. For the ore figures, see Norris, *Racing for the Bomb*, 327.

33. Herken, *The Winning Weapon*, 101–105.

34. V. Merkulov to Beria, February 28, 1945, *APSSSR* I.ii.236.

35. Paul C. Fine to Joseph Volpe, Jr., October 3, 1947, AEC Records, Records of the Office of the Chairman, Office Files of Robert F. Bacher, Entry 17, Box 1, Folder: "Intelligence."

36. Leslie R. Groves to Nat C. Finney, July 9, 1949, Groves Papers, Entry 2, Box 3, Folder: "F."

37. V. A. Makhnev to L. P. Beria, January 17, 1945, *APSSSR* I.ii.202.

38. D. B. Shimkin, "Uranium Deposits in the USSR," *Science*, n.s., 109, no. 2821 (January 21, 1949): 58–60; V. I. Bulatov, *Rossiia radioaktivnaia* (Novosibirsk: TsERIS, 1996), 9.

39. Ziegler and Jacobson, *Spying Without Spies*, 25–26; Ronald E. Powaski, *March to Armageddon: The United States and the Nuclear Arms Race, 1939 to the Present* (New York: Oxford University Press, 1987), 30.

40. Quoted in "Russ A-Bomb Doubted, With or Without Secret," *LAT*, November 7, 1947, 7.

41. Leslie R. Groves to Nat C. Finney, July 9, 1949, Groves Papers, Entry 2, Box 3, Folder: "F."

42. Franck Report, memorandum on "Political and Social Problems," transmitted by Arthur H. Compton on June 12, 1945, Harrison-Bundy Files, Roll 6, Target 5, File 76: "Interim Committee—Scientific Panel."

43. Staff members of Los Alamos via Robert Wilson to Interim Committee via J. Robert Oppenheimer, September 7, 1945, ibid., 3. Nobel laureate Irving Langmuir consistently argued for a low estimate, at times as low as two years, and was usually cited at the time as the foil to Groves. See Langmuir at Conference on Atomic Energy Control at the University of Chicago, September 20–21, 1945, in Lilienthal, *The Atomic Energy Years*, 643; and Langmuir testimony to Senate Special Committee on Atomic Energy, November 30, 1945, *Atomic Energy*, 111. Further development of his estimate, based on the fact that the Soviet Union could spend money without any concern for its citizenry, can be found in Irving Langmuir, "An Atomic Arms Race and Its Alternatives,"

in Masters and Way, *One World or None*, 48–53; and "Russia Given 3 or 4 Years to Get A-Bomb," *LAT*, March 26, 1946, 1.

44. Szilard testimony to House Committee on Military Affairs, October 18, 1945, *Atomic Energy, H.R. 4280*, 88. See also the two-to-ten-year estimate in "Russia and the Atomic Bomb," *BAS* 1, no. 5 (February 15, 1946): 10–11.

45. Frederick Seitz and Hans Bethe, "How Close Is the Danger?" in Masters and Way, *One World or None*, 45, 47.

46. "Compton Sure Russia Doesn't Have A-Bomb," *LAT*, May 1, 1948, 14.

47. Oppenheimer letter of April 14, 1948, read during Oppenheimer testimony of April 12, 1954, USAEC, *In the Matter of J. Robert Oppenheimer*, 47.

48. Entry of September 21, 1945, Forrestal Diaries, Volume III, Sept. 4, 1945–Jan. 5, 1946.

49. Conant, *My Several Lives*, 488. In retrospect Conant does not seem the most reliable prognosticator; he also predicted that it would take Germany only ten years to get the bomb after the war, an eventuality that obviously never happened. James G. Hershberg, *James B. Conant: Harvard to Hiroshima and the Making of the Nuclear Age* (New York: Knopf, 1993), 214.

50. Ross, *American War Plans*, 6.

51. Lawrence Aronsen, "Seeing Red: U.S. Air Force Assessments of the Soviet Union, 1945–1949," *Intelligence and National Security* 16 (2001): 121.

52. Arthur H. Vandenberg, Jr., *The Private Papers of Senator Vandenberg* (Boston: Houghton Mifflin, 1952), 228. This short estimate was identical to that of the left-leaning Norman Cousins: Cousins and Thomas K. Finletter, "A Beginning for Sanity," *Saturday Review of Literature*, June 15, 1946, 5.

53. Vandenberg to L. G. Carnick, April 18, 1946, in Vandenberg, *Private Papers*, 252–53. For Pearson's similar views, see Drew Pearson, "Russia Bitter Over Atom Secret," *WP*, September 30, 1945, B5.

54. Truman paraphrased in entry of October 22, 1945, in Edward R. Stettinius, Jr., *The Diaries of Edward R. Stettinius, Jr., 1943–1946* (New York: New Viewpoints, 1975), 439. See also Acheson to Truman, September 25, 1945, *FRUS 1945*, 2:48; Byrnes, *All in One Lifetime*, 283.

55. Herman Kahn, *On Thermonuclear War*, 2d ed. (Princeton: Princeton University Press, 1961), 428. See also Karl T. Compton, 5 *Atomic Bombs and the Future* (Birmingham, AL: Rushton Lectures Founda-

tion, 1959 [1948]), 60; John Prados, *The Soviet Estimate: U.S. Intelligence Analysis and Russian Military Strength* (New York: Dial Press, 1982), 18–19; and Herbert F. York, *Arms and the Physicist* (Woodbury, NY: AIP Press, 1995), 6–7.

56. "Shall We Keep Atom Secret?" *LAT*, September 16, 1945, A4; "Wilson Fearful of Soviet Power," *NYT*, September 23, 1945, 18; "Russians Believed Near Atomic Secret," *NYT*, October 15, 1945, 4; "Reds Will Develop Own Atom Bomb, Scientist Says," *WP*, September 27, 1945, 16; "Nazi Atomic Secrets Captured by Soviet?" *CSM*, October 15, 1945, 1; "Claims German Scientists Aid Reds on A-Bomb," *CDT*, October 24, 1945, 2; Waldemar Kaempffert, "Science in Review: Secrecy and Censorship Seen as Fatal to Progress in Atomic Research," *NYT*, October 14, 1945, E9; Kaempffert, "Science—and Ideology—in Soviet Russia," *NYT Sunday Magazine*, September 15, 1946, 3, 58–60; "Scientist Tells of Reds' Race to Get A-Bomb," *CDT*, March 26, 1947, 2; "Educator Asserts Russians Have A-Bomb Know-How," *LAT*, June 19, 1947, 2; Malvina Lindsay, "Shrugging off the Bomb," *WP*, August 2, 1947, 4; "Scientist Predicts Russian A-Bomb by January, 1953," *WP*, April 17, 1948, 9; "Canadian Doubts Russia Has Bomb," *CSM*, September 22, 1948, 10.

57. Prados, *The Soviet Estimate*, 4–5.

58. Hayden B. Peake, "Soviet Espionage and the Office of Strategic Services," in Warren F. Kimball, ed., *America Unbound: World War II and the Making of a Superpower* (New York: St. Martin's Press, 1992), 107–38; Gaddis, "Intelligence, Espionage, and Cold War Origins," 194.

59. "Spaatz Board Report," October 23, 1945, Spaatz Papers, Box 22, File: "Personal, October 1945," 7.

60. Laqueur, *A World of Secrets*, 9–10; Philip S. Meilinger, *Hoyt S. Vandenberg: The Life of a General* (Bloomington: Indiana University Press, 1989), 72; Trevor Barnes, "The Secret Cold War: The C.I.A. and American Foreign Policy in Europe, 1946–1956," *Historical Journal* 24 (1981): 400; Danny D. Jansen and Rhodri Jeffreys-Jones, "The Missouri Gang and the CIA," in Rhodri Jeffreys-Jones and Andrew Lownie, eds., *North American Spies: New Revisionist Essays* (Lawrence: University Press of Kansas, 1991), 123–42.

61. The military intelligence outfits did not even correlate with each other, let alone the CIA, until after the outbreak of the Korean War. Aronsen, "Seeing Red," 105.

62. Omar N. Bradley and Clay Blair, *A General's Life: An Autobiography* (New York: Simon & Schuster, 1983), 514. On "denied territory" and

the attempted infiltration program, see Garthoff, *A Journey Through the Cold War*; Matthew M. Aid, "The National Security Agency and the Cold War," *Intelligence and National Security* 16 (2001): 30–31; Clarence E. Smith, "CIA's Analysis of Soviet Science and Technology," in Gerald K. Haines and Robert E. Leggett, eds., *Watching the Bear: Essays on CIA's Analysis of the Soviet Union* (Washington, D.C.: Center for the Study of Intelligence, CIA, 2001), 106; Oleg Bukharin, "US Atomic Energy Intelligence Against the Soviet Target, 1945–1970," *Intelligence and National Security* 19 (2004): 663.

63. ORE 3/1, October 31, 1946, in Kuhns, *Assessing the Soviet Threat*, 87.

64. Entry of July 8, 1947, Forrestal Diaries, Volumes VII–VIII, April 1, 1947–Oct. 31, 1947.

65. Lilienthal, entry of June 30, 1948, *The Atomic Energy Years*, 376.

66. Lilienthal, entry of March 17, 1949, ibid., 486.

67. Goudsmit to Carroll L. Wilson, March 11, 1948, AEC Records, Records of the Office of the Chairman, Office Files of Robert F. Bacher, Entry 17, Box 1, Folder: "Intelligence." See also Draft Minutes of the GAC Eighth Meeting, February 6–8, 1948, Seaborg Papers, Atomic Energy Commission, Committees, General Advisory Committee, Box 615, Folder 2, 4–5, 13; and Bacher to Hickenlooper, January 29, 1948, AEC Records, Records of the Office of the Chairman, Office Files of Robert F. Bacher, Entry 17, Box 1, Folder: "Intelligence."

68. Paul Maddrell, "British-American Scientific Intelligence Collaboration During the Occupation of Germany," *Intelligence and National Security* 15, no. 2 (2000): 74–94.

69. Abram Bergson, "Russian Defense Expenditures," *Foreign Affairs* 26 (1947–1948): 373.

70. The best of the open-source studies of the Soviet program is Kramish, *Atomic Energy in the Soviet Union*. On Wringer, see David Alan Rosenberg, "The Origins of Overkill: Nuclear Weapons and American Strategy, 1945–1960," *International Security* 7 (1983): 21.

71. CIG, Office of Research and Evaluation, ORE 1, July 23, 1946, in Michael Warner, ed., *The CIA Under Harry Truman* (Washington, D.C.: Center for the Study of Intelligence, CIA, 1994), 67, 76.

72. Intelligence Memorandum No. 59 for Secretary of Defense, September 20, 1948, CIA Records, Box 110, Folder: "26519," 9.

73. Indeed, early public estimates often referred to reactors, and, over time, began to refer more and more to "stockpiles." See, for example, "Russ A-Bomb Outlook Told," *LAT*, January 18, 1946, A1; "Warns of Russian Bombs," *NYT*, June 24, 1946, 18; Hanson W. Baldwin, "Has

Russia the Atomic Bomb?—Probably Not," *NYT*, November 9, 1947, E3; "Russ Bombs Derided," *NYT*, March 29, 1948, 9; and "Soviet Atom Bomb Held 20 Years Off," *NYT*, May 6, 1948, 37, 43.

74. Laurence, "How Soon Will Russia Have the A-Bomb?" 181.

75. David E. Lilienthal, speech at the National Press Club, April 10, 1946, Lilienthal Papers, Series 2, Box 30, Folder: "April 10, 1946, Speech: National Press Club, Washington, D.C.," 5.

76. Oppenheimer, testimony of April 12, 1954, USAEC, *In the Matter of J. Robert Oppenheimer*, 36. For more on the Tolman declassification committee, see Norris, *Racing for the Bomb*, 449.

THREE: LARGER THAN ENORMOZ

1. See, for example, the 1984 autobiographical comments by Iakov Zel'dovich in J. P. Ostriker, ed., *Selected Works of Yakov Borisovich Zeldovich*, vol. 2: *Particles, Nuclei, and the Universe* (Princeton: Princeton University Press, 1993), 637. See also Ulrich Albrecht, "The Development of the First Atomic Bomb in the USSR," in Everett Mendelsohn, Merritt Roe Smith, and Peter Weingart, eds., *Science, Technology and the Military* (Dordrecht: Kluwer, 1988), 352.

2. Norris, *Racing for the Bomb*, 276.

3. Memorandum to Byrnes, August 20, 1948, *FRUS* 1948, 1:390.

4. Groves memorandum included in Patterson to Byrnes, December 11, 1945, *FRUS* 1945, 2:97.

5. R. B. Landry to Truman, April 6, 1949, WHCF: Confidential File, Box 4, Folder: "Atomic bomb and energy, 1948–1949," 1–2.

6. Robert M. Hutchins, "Peace or War with Russia?" *BAS* 1, no. 6 (March 1, 1946): 1. Matthias Correa reported to Secretary of the Navy Forrestal, echoing this view, that "Commodor[e Lewis] Strauss, for example, gives it as his view that sufficient information has already been made public about the atomic bomb to enable the Russians to solve the so-called secret of the bomb in a relatively short period and that in consequence this country would gain by making the best trade possible in obtaining a mutual exchange of information." Matthias F. Correa to James V. Forrestal, September 27, 1945, Forrestal Papers, Box 28, Folder: "Atomic Energy Comm. 1-23-46," 2.

7. McGeorge Bundy, *Danger and Survival: Choices About the Bomb in the First Fifty Years* (New York: Random House, 1988), 135. Henry DeWolf Smyth, *Atomic Energy for Military Purposes: The Official Report on the Development of the Atomic Bomb Under the Auspices of the United States Government, 1940–1945* (Palto Alto: Stanford University Press,

1989 [1945]). The most comprehensive account of the writing and impact of the Smyth Report is Rebecca Press Schwartz, "The Making of the History of the Atomic Bomb: Henry DeWolf Smyth and the Historiography of the Manhattan Project" (Ph.D. dissertation, Princeton University, 2008). I owe much of my analysis here to Schwartz's insights.

8. Groves, foreword to Smyth, *Atomic Energy for Military Purposes*, xiii. For the security rules of what was permissible to include, see Leslie Groves to Henry DeWolf Smyth, June 15, 1945, Smyth Papers, Series I, Box 17, Folder: "Groves, Leslie R. #2."

9. Henry DeWolf Smyth, "The 'Smyth Report,'" *Princeton University Library Chronicle* 37 (1975–1976): 180.

10. H. D. Smyth, "Memorandum on the History of the Preparation of my Report on Atomic Energy for Military Purposes," draft of January 10, 1947, Smyth Papers, Series I, Box 8, Folder: "Conant, James B. #2."

11. Smyth, *Atomic Energy for Military Purposes*, 226. For more on Operation Candor, see Chapter 6 below.

12. Smyth, *Atomic Energy for Military Purposes*, 166–67. Ellipses added.

13. Stimson, diary entries of August 1 and 9, 1945. On Groves's central role in pushing for the Smyth Report, see Smith, *A Peril and a Hope*, 83.

14. Gowing, *Independence and Deterrence*, 2:119; Goldschmidt, *Atomic Rivals*, 270.

15. Szilard testimony, October 18, 1945, U.S. House of Representatives, Committee on Military Affairs, *Atomic Energy: Hearings on H. R. 4280*, 79th Cong., 1st sess., 1945, 80, 87. Many contemporaries (although not many scientists) echoed this view: Bernard Brodie, "War in the Atomic Age," in Brodie, ed., *The Absolute Weapon*, 65; William A. Reuben, *The Atom Spy Hoax* (New York: Action Books, 1955), 3.

16. Bernard M. Baruch to Harry S. Truman, September 17, 1946, Baruch Papers, Unit X, Section 1, Box 52, File: "Policy Correspondence, Memoranda, and Notes on Conferences—President," 3.

17. Henry Wallace to Truman, September 24, 1945, PSF: Subject File 1940–1953, National Security Council—Atomic Files, Box 173, Folder: "Atomic Bomb: Cabinet: Henry A. Wallace," 1.

18. Lilienthal testimony, January 28, 1947, U.S. Congress, Joint Committee on Atomic Energy, Senate Section, *Confirmation of Atomic Energy Commission and General Manager: Hearings*, 80th Cong., 1st sess., 1947, 32.

19. "The Atom Bomb and Security," *LAT*, February 6, 1947, A4. See also

Goudsmit, "Science and the Atom Bomb"; and Bertrand Goldschmidt, *The Atomic Complex: A Worldwide Political History of Nuclear Energy*, rev. ed. (La Grange Park, IL: American Nuclear Society, 1980), 69.

20. Groves testimony to House Committee on Military Affairs, October 9, 1945, *Atomic Energy*, 13.

21. Vannevar Bush, *Pieces of the Action* (New York: Morrow, 1970), 294. See also his statement in Minutes of Combined Policy Committee Meeting, July 4, 1945, Harrison-Bundy Files, Roll 3, Target 1, File 37: "(Minutes of) Meeting, July 4, 1945, Combined Policy Committee," 5.

22. David E. Lilienthal, "Atomic Energy and the Engineer," speech before the American Society of Mechanical Engineers, December 2, 1947, Lilienthal Papers, Series 2, Box 34, Folder: "December 2, 1947: Speech: American Society of Mechanical Engineers. 'Atomic Energy and the Engineer,'" 17.

23. Seitz and Bethe, "How Close Is the Danger?" 47.

24. Bohr statement in Iu. N. Smirnov, " 'Dopros' Nil'sa Bora: Svidetel'stvo iz arkhiva," *VIET*, no. 4 (1994): 119, 114.

25. Ia. P. Terletskii, "Operatsiia 'Dopros Nil'sa Bora,' " *VIET*, no. 2 (1994): 41.

26. Minutes of the twelfth meeting of the Special Committee of the Sovnarkom SSSR, January 29, 1946, APSSSR II.i.63. See also Holloway, *Stalin and the Bomb*, 173.

27. Henry DeWolf Smyth, *Atomnaia energiia dlia voennykh tselei*, ed. G. N. Ivanov (Moscow: Transzheldorizdat, 1946), 234, 235.

28. Henry DeWolf Smyth, *Atomenergie und ihre Verwertung im Kriege*, trans. Friedrich Dessauer (Basel: Ernst Reinhardt Verlag, 1947); *L'Énergie atomique et son utilisation militaire*, trans. Maurice E. Nahmias (Paris: Éditions de la Revue d'Optique Théorique et Instrumentale, 1946); *Atomová energie pro vojenské úcely*, trans. Vilém Santholzer (Prague: Masarykova Akademie Práce, 1946).

29. Andreas Heinemann-Grüder, *Die Sowjetische Atombombe* (Münster: Verlag Westfälisches Dampfboot, 1992), 85.

30. James Chadwick to Field Marshal Sir Henry Maitland Wilson, August 4, 1945, Top Secret Files, Roll 2, Target 6, File 12: "Intelligence and Security."

31. Andrei Sakharov, *Memoirs*, trans. Richard Lourie (New York: Knopf, 1990), 92. See also P. A. Zhuravlev, *Moi atomnyi vek: O vremeni, ob atomshchikakh i o sebe* (Moscow: Khronos-press, 2003), 8.

32. V. F. Kalinin, "Ot pervykh reaktorov do atominforma," *VIET*, no. 2

(1996): 127. Or, as another pair of scientists put it, "This book clarified a great deal for those of us who were professionally very close to the subject matter." Veniamin Tsukerman and Zinaida Azarkh, *Arzamas-16: Soviet Scientists in the Nuclear Age: A Memoir*, trans. Timothy Sergay (Nottingham: Bramcote Press, 1999 [1994]), 47.

33. A. P. Aleksandrov, "Gody s Kurchatovym," *Nauka i zhizn'*, no. 2 (1983): 23.

34. N. M. Sinev, *Memuary. Vospominaniia* (Moscow: IzdAT, 2000), 59.

35. Heinz Barwich and Elfi Barwich, *Das rote Atom* (Munich: Scherz Verlag, 1967), 75.

36. Minutes of the fourteenth meeting of the Special Committee of the Sovnarkom SSSR, February 19, 1946, APSSSR II.i.69. See also Pavel V. Oleynikov, "German Scientists in the Soviet Atomic Project," *Nonproliferation Review* (Summer 2000): 24.

37. V. S. Gubarev, *Belyi arkhipelag Stalina: Dokumental'noe povestvovanie o sozdanii iadernoi bomby, osnovannoe na rassekrechennykh materialakh "Atomnogo proekta SSSR"* (Moscow: Molodaia gvardiia, 2004), 25, 104; Barwich and Barwich, *Das rote Atom*, 83, 88–89.

38. Bernard M. Baruch to J. Edgar Hoover, February 11, 1950, Baruch Papers, Unit X, Section 2, Box 61, File: "Atomic Energy Commission (Special Correspondence, G–L)."

39. Hans Thirring, *Die Geschichte der Atombombe* (Vienna: Neues Österreich, 1946), 129–30. Some Americans had come to the same conclusion. See the analysis in Kaiser, "The Atomic Secret in Red Hands?"

40. U.S. Congress, Joint Committee on Atomic Energy, *Soviet Atomic Espionage* (Washington, D.C.: GPO, 1951).

41. In their memoirs, Soviet spymasters predictably emphasize the amount of material excluded from the Smyth Report: Feklisov, *Za okeanom i na ostrove*, 150. For a sampling of the post–cold war "exposé" literature on the Soviet atomic espionage network, see Pavel Sudoplatov and Anatoli Sudoplatov, *Special Tasks: The Memoirs of an Unwanted Witness—A Soviet Spymaster* (Boston: Little, Brown, 1994); Allen Weinstein and Alexander Vassiliev, *The Haunted Wood: Soviet Espionage in America—the Stalin Era* (New York: Random House, 1999); Harvey Klehr, John Earl Haynes, and Fridrikh Igorevich Firsov, *The Secret World of American Communism* (New Haven: Yale University Press, 1995); and Jerrold Schecter and Leona Schecter, *Sacred Secrets: How Soviet Intelligence Operations Changed American History* (Washington, D.C.: Brassey's, 2002). For a critique of these histories, see Barton J. Bernstein, "The

Puzzles of Interpreting J. Robert Oppenheimer, His Politics, and the Issues of His Possible Communist Party Membership," in Carson and Hollinger, *Reappraising Oppenheimer*, 77–112.

42. Feklisov, *Za okeanom i na ostrove*, 60.

43. Military Policy Committee to Henry A. Wallace, Henry L. Stimson, and George C. Marshall, August 21, 1943, Harrison-Bundy Files, Roll 1, Target 6, File 6: "Military Policy Committee Papers—Minutes," 19.

44. Vladimir V. Pozniakov, "Commoners, Commissars, and Spies: Soviet Policies and Society, 1945," in Offner and Wilson, *Victory in Europe 1945*, 193; David J. Dallin, *Soviet Espionage* (New Haven: Yale University Press, 1955), 248, 288; Gregg Herken, *Brotherhood of the Bomb: The Tangled Lives and Loyalties of Robert Oppenheimer, Ernest Lawrence, and Edward Teller* (New York: Henry Holt, 2002), 88.

45. Each assignment in the Soviet espionage plan carried its own set of cryptonyms for places and agents. For example, in Enormoz, Washington was Carthage, New York was Tyre, and San Francisco was Babylon. See Herken, *Brotherhood of the Bomb*, 87.

46. Plan of Enormoz by 1st administration of NKGB, no earlier than February 1, no later than February 28, 1944, *APSSSR* I.ii.31.

47. A. A. Adams to chief of GRU on American developments, March 7, 1944, *APSSSR* I.ii.44. On encouraging spies to accept cash payments, whether or not their primary motivation was financial, see Dallin, *Soviet Espionage*, 20–21.

48. Christopher Andrew and Vasili Mitrokhin, *The Sword and the Shield: The Mitrokhin Archive and the Secret History of the KGB* (New York: Basic Books 1999), 131. See also V. Merkulov to M. G. Pervukhin, May 15, 1944, *APSSSR* I.ii.68.

49. Dallin, *Soviet Espionage*, 432–34.

50. See the trenchant critique in David Holloway, "Charges of Espionage," *Science* 264 (May 27, 1994): 1346–47.

51. Sudoplatov and Sudoplatov, *Special Tasks*, 184; Joseph Albright and Marcia Kunstel, *Bombshell: The Secret Story of America's Unknown Atomic Spy Conspiracy* (New York: Times Books, 1997), 155.

52. Holloway, *Stalin and the Bomb*, 82–83; Weinstein and Vassiliev, *The Haunted Wood*, 172.

53. Yuri Modin with Jean-Charles Deniau and Aguieszka Ziarek, *My Five Cambridge Friends*, trans. Anthony Roberts (London: Headline, 1994), 117.

54. Robert Cecil, *A Divided Life: A Personal Portrait of the Spy Donald Maclean* (New York: Morrow, 1989), 78; Modin, *My Five Cambridge*

Friends, 119; Christopher Andrew and Oleg Gordievsky, *KGB: The Inside Story of Its Foreign Operations from Lenin to Gorbachev* (New York: Harper, 1990), 311; and Helmreich, *Gathering Rare Ores*, 253. On Maclean's nonnuclear spying during the Berlin crisis, see Sheila Kerr, "The Secret Hotline to Moscow: Donald Maclean and the Berlin Crisis of 1948," in Ann Deighton, ed., *Britain and the First Cold War* (New York: St. Martin's Press, 1990), 71–87.

55. Canada, Royal Commission, *The Report of the Royal Commission Appointed under Order in Council P.C. 411 of February 5, 1946 to Investigate the Facts Relating to and the Circumstances Surrounding the Communication, by Public Officials and Other Persons in Positions of Trust, of Secret and Confidential Information to Agents of a Foreign Power, June 27, 1946, Honourable Mr. Justice Robert Taschereau, Honourable Mr. Justice R. L. Kellock, Commissioners* (Ottawa: Edmond Cloutier, 1946), 11–12.

56. This is not to discount the significant nonatomic espionage—and even direct and open cooperation and exchange—related to military technology during the war. See Donald Avery, "Allied Scientific Co-operation and Soviet Espionage in Canada, 1941–45," *Intelligence and National Security* 8 (July 1993): 100–28.

57. Canada, Royal Commission, *Documents Relating to the Proceedings of the Royal Commission Established by Order in Council P.C. 411 of February 5th, 1946* (Ottawa: Edmond Cloutier, 1946), 11. On the development of Soviet-Canadian relations, see Robert Bothwell and J. L. Granatstein, eds., *The Gouzenko Transcripts: The Evidence Presented to the Kellock-Taschereau Royal Commission of 1946* (Ottawa: Deneau Publishers, 1982), 6.

58. Gouzenko testimony in Bothwell and Granatstein, *Gouzenko Transcripts*, 48; Amy Knight, *How the Cold War Began: The Igor Gouzenko Affair and the Hunt for Soviet Spies* (New York: Carroll & Graf, 2005), 32–33.

59. Gouzenko testimony in Bothwell and Granatstein, *Gouzenko Transcripts*, 66; John Earl Haynes and Harvey Klehr, *Early Cold War Spies: The Espionage Trials That Shaped American Politics* (New York: Cambridge University Press, 2006), 50–52; Alan Moorehead, *The Traitors* (New York: Harper, 1963 [1952]), 10; Canada, Royal Commission, *Report of the Royal Commission*, 449–50.

60. Canada, Royal Commission, *Report of the Royal Commission*, 617.

61. "Russia Admits Receipt of Atom Bomb Secrets; Assails Canada's Attitude," *LAT*, February 21, 1946, 1, 5.

62. Quoted in "Canadian Atom Bomb Leak Not Alarming, Say Scientists," *CDT*, February 17, 1946, 12.

63. Cockcroft testimony in Bothwell and Granatstein, *Gouzenko Transcripts*, 239.

64. Moorehead, *The Traitors*, 57. See also V. Kulishov, "Konets atomnomu sekretu," in *Professiia: Razvedchik* (Moscow: Izd. Polit. lit., 1992): 105–86; and Michael S. Goodman, "Santa Klaus? Klaus Fuchs and the Nuclear Weapons Programmes of Britain, the Soviet Union and America," *Prospero*, no. 1 (Spring 2004): 47–69. My thanks to John Krige for the latter reference.

65. Norman Moss, *Klaus Fuchs: The Man Who Stole the Atom Bomb* (New York: St. Martin's Press, 1987), 6.

66. Rudolf E. Peierls, *Bird of Passage: Recollections of a Physicist* (Princeton: Princeton University Press, 1985), 163; Otto Frisch, *What Little I Remember* (New York: Cambridge University Press, 1991 [1979]), 201.

67. Moss, *Klaus Fuchs*, 38.

68. Joseph O. Hirschfelder, "The Scientific and Technological Miracle at Los Alamos," in Badash, Hirschfelder, and Broida, *Reminiscences of Los Alamos, 1943–1945*, 86.

69. Bradbury, "Los Alamos," 167.

70. Feklisov, *Za okeanom i na ostrove*, 149, 154.

71. Cecil, *A Divided Life*, 81.

72. Robert Louis Benson and Michael Warner, eds., *Venona: Soviet Espionage and the American Response, 1939–1957* (Washington, D.C.: NSA, CIA, 1996); Nigel West, *Venona: The Greatest Secret of the Cold War* (London: HarperCollins, 1999); Robert J. Lamphere and Thom Shachtman, *The FBI-KGB War: A Special Agent's Story* (New York: Random House, 1986), 79.

73. Robert Chadwell Williams, *Klaus Fuchs: Atom Spy* (Cambridge, MA: Harvard University Press, 1987), 6; John Ranelagh, *The Agency: The Rise and Decline of the CIA* (New York: Simon & Schuster, 1986), 149; Aid, "The National Security Agency and the Cold War," 35.

74. Andrew and Mitrokhin, *The Sword and the Shield*, 131–32; West, *Venona*, 146; Albright and Kunstel, *Bombshell*, 139.

75. Quoted in Weinstein and Vassiliev, *The Haunted Wood*, 208.

76. Albright and Kunstel, *Bombshell*; Haynes and Klehr, *Venona*, 314–17.

77. Williams, *Klaus Fuchs*, 3.

78. Fuchs's confession to William Skardon, January 27, 1950, ibid., 185.

79. Caroline Kennedy-Pipe, *Stalin's Cold War: Soviet Strategies in Europe, 1943 to 1956* (New York: Manchester University Press, 1995), 55; Wil-

fred Loth, "Stalin's Plans for Post-War Germany," in Francesca Gori and Silvio Pons, eds., *The Soviet Union and Europe in the Cold War, 1943–53* (New York: St. Martin's Press, 1996), 23–36; Bruce Kuklick, *American Policy and the Division of Germany: The Clash with Russia over Reparations* (Ithaca: Cornell University Press, 1972), 167. On Soviet scientists' demands for reparations, see the academicians I. P. Bardin and A. E. Fersman to V. L. Komarov and N. G. Bruevich, January 25, 1944, *APSSSR*, I.ii.25. On American looting, see Lloyd C. Gardner, "America and the German 'Problem,' 1945–1949," in Barton J. Bernstein, ed., *Politics and Policies of the Truman Administration* (Chicago: Quadrangle Books, 1970), 120–21.

80. Memorandum of conversation between Averell Harriman and Joseph Stalin, August 8, 1945, Harriman Papers, Public Service Special File, World War II, Moscow Files, Box 181, File: "Chron. File, Aug. 5–9, 1945," 2.

81. Oleynikov, "German Scientists in the Soviet Atomic Project," 4–5; Heinemann-Grüder, *Die Sowjetische Atombombe*, 63.

82. Holloway, *Stalin and the Bomb*, 63.

83. F. I. Vol'fson, N. S. Zontov, and G. R. Shushaniia, *Petr Iakovlevich Antropov, 1905–1979* (Moscow: Nauka, 1985), 34; L. V. Komlev, G. S. Sinitsyna, and M. N. Koval'skaia, "V. G. Khlopin i uranovaia problema," in A. M. Petros'iants, G. S. Sinitsyna, and D. N. Trifonov, eds., *Akademik V. G. Khlopin: Ocherki, vospominaniia sovremennikov* (Leningrad: Nauka, 1987), 42; Iu. N. Elfimov, *Marshal industrii: Biograficheskii ocherk o A. P. Zaveniagine* (Cheliabinsk: Iuzhno-ural'skoe knizhnoe izd., 1982).

84. V. G. Zeliak, *Piat' metallov Dal'stroia: Istoriia gornodobyvaiushchei promyshlennosti severo-vostoka Rossii v 30-50-kh gg. XX v.* (Magadan: Kordis, 2004), 209–10. My thanks to Jeffrey S. Hardy for bringing this reference to my attention.

85. E. P. Slavskii, "Poka atomnaia bomba ne vzorvalas'," *Krasnaia zvezda* (January 6, 1993).

86. Holloway, *Stalin and the Bomb*, 101; Steven J. Zaloga, *Target America: The Soviet Union and the Strategic Arms Race, 1945–1964* (Novato, CA: Presidio Press, 1993), 19. When this news broke, it sparked a right-wing crusade about traitors in the United States "giving" the Soviet Union the bomb. See the accusations in George Racey Jordan, *From Major Jordan's Diaries* (New York: Harcourt, 1952), 95.

87. Groves to Stimson, June 23, 1945, Harrison-Bundy Files, Roll 3, Target 1, File 37: "(Minutes of) Meeting, July 4, 1945, Combined Policy Committee."

88. Iulii B. Khariton, "Vystuplenie v Sarove 27 fevralia 1994 goda," in Khariton, *Put' dlinoiu v vek* (Moscow: Editorial URSS, 1999), 208–10; Holloway, *Stalin and the Bomb*, 111. See also A. P. Zaveniagin and V. A. Makhnev to Beria, June 18, 1945, *APSSSR* I.ii.324.

89. Steinhardt to Byrnes, paraphrase of secret telegram, November 19, 1945, Harrison-Bundy Files, Roll 2, Target 3, File 20: "Russia"; F. Ianoukh, "Chekhoslovatskii uran i sovetskaia A-bomba," in Velikhov, *Nauka i obshchestvo*, 3:292–300; Jiri Kasparek, "Soviet Russia and Czechoslovakia's Uranium," *Russian Review* 11 (1952): 97–105.

90. Norman M. Naimark, *The Russians in Germany: A History of the Soviet Zone of Occupation, 1945–1949* (Cambridge, MA: Belknap, 1995), 238–248; Nikolai Grishin, "The Saxony Uranium Mining Operation ('Vismut')," in Robert Slusser, ed., *Soviet Economic Policy in Postwar Germany: A Collection of Papers by Former Soviet Officials*, (New York: Research Program on the U.S.S.R., 1953), 127–55; Rainer Karlsch, "Der Aufbau der Uranindustrien in der SBZ/DDR und ČSR als Folge der sowjetischen 'Uranlücke,' " *Zeitschrift für Geschichtswissenschaft* 1 (1996): 5–24; Paul Maddrell, *Spying on Science: Western Intelligence in Divided Germany, 1945–1961* (New York: Oxford University Press, 2006), 150; Gubarev, *Belyi arkhipelag Stalina*, 252–53; Dmitrij N. Filippovych and Vladimir V. Zacharov, "Deutsches Uran für die sowjetische Atombombe: Zur frühen Geschichte der Sächsischen Bergverwaltung und der Sowjetischen Staatlichen Aktiengesellschaft 'Wismut,' " *Der Anschnitt* 50, nos. 2–3 (1998): 82–94; and minutes of the fourth meeting of the Special Committee of the Sovnarkom SSSR, September 14, 1945, *APSSSR* II.i.25.

91. "Soviets Flying Saxony A-Bomb Ore to Russia," *LAT*, July 21, 1947, 1; Peter Kihss, "30 Nations Are Pitting Their Scientific Might in Atomic Race," *WP*, August 3, 1947, B12; "Soviet 'Robbing' Czech Uranium Pits, Stefan Says," *WP*, August 8, 1948, M2; and Groves, testimony of April 15, 1954, USAEC, *In the Matter of J. Robert Oppenheimer*, 176.

92. Lucienne Félix, *La Science au Goulag: Au Temps des Charachkas* (Paris: Christian Bourgois, 1981); Werner Keller, *Are the Russians Ten Feet Tall?* trans. Constantine FitzGibbon (London: Thames & Hudson, 1961); Jack Raymond, "German Scientists Held Aiding Soviet," *NYT*, September 24, 1949, 3; "German Brains Get Credit for Soviet A-Bomb," *CDT*, September 26, 1949, 15; Walter Trohan, "Denies Security for U.S. Rests in Atom Bombs," *CDT*, September 21, 1945, 5; Drew Middleton, "Russian Progress on Atom Doubted," *NYT*, January 16, 1946, 3.

93. Albrecht, "Development of the First Atomic Bomb," 366. Some Russian participants lamented this after the collapse of the Soviet Union and argued forcefully for recognizing German efforts: P. Boltianskaia, "Kto delal bombu," *Literaturnaia gazeta*, no. 14 (April 10, 1991): 5.

94. For an insightful analysis of these rocket specialists, see Asif A. Siddiqi, "Russians in Germany: Founding the Post-war Missile Programme," *Europe-Asia Studies* 56 (2004): 1131–56.

95. Heisenberg, Farm Hall transcript of August 6, 1945, in Bernstein, *Hitler's Uranium Club*, 150. See also George A. Modelski, *Atomic Energy in the Communist Bloc* (Melbourne: Melbourne University Press, 1959), 36.

96. S. A. Goudsmit to Robert F. Bacher, October 30, 1947, AEC Records, Records of the Office of the Chairman, Office Files of Robert F. Bacher, Entry 17, Box 1, Folder: "Intelligence." On the price tag for Heisenberg, see "Soviet Said to 'Buy' German Atom Men," *NYT*, February 24, 1947, 1, 7; and Heinemann-Grüder, *Die Sowjetische Atombombe*, 68.

97. Christoph Mick, *Forschen für Stalin: Deutsche Fachleute in der sowjetischen Rüstungsindustrie, 1945–1958* (Munich: R. Oldenbourg, 2000), 15, 91; Maddrell, *Spying on Science*, 30–31; Neubauer, "Nemetskie khimiki i sovetskii atomnyi proekt posle 1945 g."

98. Mick, *Forschen für Stalin*, 150.

99. Heinemann-Grüder, *Die Sowjetische Atombombe*, 66; Heinemann-Grüder, " 'Keinerlei Untergang': German Armaments Engineers During the Second World War and in the Service of the Victorious Powers," in Monika Renneberg and Mark Walker, eds., *Science, Technology and National Socialism* (New York: Cambridge University Press, 1994), 44. Nonetheless, many years later von Ardenne, in his self-serving memoir, claimed the offer had come to him "without my having solicited it." Manfred von Ardenne, *Sechzig Jahre für Forschung und Fortschritt: Autobiographie* (Berlin: Verlag der Nation, 1987), 180.

100. Barwich and Barwich, *Das rote Atom*, 21.

101. Paul Harteck, interview in Ermenc, *Atomic Bomb Scientists*, 113. For more on Hertz, see Josef Kuczera, *Gustav Hertz* (Leipzig: B. G. Teubner, 1985); and Barwich and Barwich, *Das rote Atom*, 16–17.

102. Thirring, *Die Geschichte der Atombombe*, 96n.

103. Gustav Hertz, "Quantensprünge und Isotopentrennung," in G. Lange and J. Moerke, *Wissenschaft im Interview: Gespräche mit Akademiemitgliedern über ihre Leben und Werk* (Leipzig: Urania-Verlag, 1979), 63.

104. Max Steenbeck, *Impulse und Wirkungen: Schritte auf meinem Lebensweg* (Berlin: Verlag der Nation, 1977), 214.

105. On the exception of Riehl, see Riehl and Seitz, *Stalin's Captive*, 68; and Oleynikov, "German Scientists in the Soviet Atomic Project," 7.

106. Rough draft of a collection on the history of the use of atomic energy in the USSR, September 19, 1952, to no later than June 26, 1953, *APSSSR* II.v.830. An interesting analysis of the Smyth Report against this Soviet internal history can be found in Vl. P. Vizgin, " 'Berievskaia istoriia' i 'Otchet Smita': Sravnitel'nyi analiz atomnykh proektov SSSR i SShA," *VIET*, no. 2 (2008): 26–64. See also A. M. Petrosyants, *Problems of Nuclear Science and Technology: The Soviet Union as a World Nuclear Power*, 4th ed., trans. W. E. Jones (New York: Pergamon Press, 1981 [1979]), 12; Iurii Smirnov in Iu. B. Khariton and Iu. N. Smirnov, *Mify i real'nost' sovetskogo atomnogo proekta* (Arzamas-16: VNIIEF, 1994), 29; Golovin, *Academician Igor Kurchatov*, 67; and Smirnov, "G. N. Flerov i stanovlenie sovetskogo atomnogo proekta," 101.

107. Maddrell, *Spying on Science*; John Gimbel, *Science, Technology, and Reparations: Exploitation and Plunder in Postwar Germany* (Palo Alto: Stanford University Press, 1990); Alan Beyerchen, "German Scientists and Research Institutions in Allied Occupation Policy," *History of Education Quarterly* 22, no. 3 (1982): 289–99; Tom Bower, *The Paperclip Conspiracy: The Hunt for Nazi Scientists* (Boston: Little, Brown, 1987); Clarence G. Lasby, *Project Paperclip: German Scientists and the Cold War* (New York: Atheneum, 1971); Linda Hunt, *Secret Agenda: The United States Government, Nazi Scientists, and Project Paperclip, 1945 to 1990* (New York: St. Martin's Press, 1991); Burghard Ciesla, "Das 'Project Paperclip'—deutsche Naturwissenschaftler und Techniker in den USA (1946 bis 1952)," in Jürgen Kocka, ed., *Historische DDR-Forschung: Aufsätze und Studien* (Berlin: Akademie Verlag, 1993), 287–301; and Franz Kurowski, *Alliierte Jagd auf deutsche Wissenschaftler: Das Unternehmen Paperclip* (Munich: Kristall bei Langen Müller, 1982).

FOUR: FIRST LIGHTNING

1. Lillian Hoddeson, Paul W. Henriksen, Roger A. Meade, and Catherine Westfall, *Critical Assembly: A Technical History of Los Alamos During the Oppenheimer Years, 1943–1945* (New York: Cambridge University Press, 1993), 360–61; Leona Marshall Libby, *The Uranium People* (New York: Crane Russak, 1979), 219; David Hawkins, Edith C. Truslow, and Ralph Carlisle Smith, *Project Y: The Los Alamos Story* (Los Angeles: Tomash Publishers, 1983), 236–37.

2. Leslie R. Groves, "Some Recollections of July 16, 1945," in Richard S.

Lewis and Jane Wilson, eds., *Alamogordo Plus Twenty-Five Years: The Impact of Atomic Energy on Science, Technology, and World Politics* (New York: Viking, 1970), 52; Groves, *Now It Can Be Told*, 288–89; George B. Kistiakowsky, "Reminiscences of Wartime Los Alamos," in Badash, Hirschfelder, and Broida, *Reminiscences of Los Alamos*, 56; Hoddeson et al., *Critical Assembly*, 174.

3. Hoddeson et al., *Critical Assembly*, 311.

4. J. B. Conant, "Notes on the 'Trinity' Test," July 16, 1945, Bush-Conant Files, Folder 28: "Bush, V. [1943–1945]."

5. Appendix A in Hawkins, Truslow, and Smith, *Project Y*, 363.

6. Quoted in "Russian A-Bomb Near, Red Scientist Predicts," *LAT*, August 13, 1946, 1.

7. Quoted in Elfimov, *Marshal industrii*, 187. In a similar vein, consider Turchin's assessment: "The scientists-weaponeers understood that the criterion of truth in any theory is experiment. Only tests on a polygon can give a final answer to the question of whether the expected was realized and to create a weapon based on the use of a chain fission reaction, and also the synthesis of light nuclei of matter." I. F. Turchin, *Sorok let na ispytaniiakh iadernogo oruzhiia* (Sarov: RFIaTs-VNIIEF, 1999), 13.

8. Baldwin, "Has Russia the Atomic Bomb?"

9. For such comprehensive accounts in English, the reader can do no better than turn to Holloway's seminal *Stalin and the Bomb*. For details about the transformation of the initial bomb project into a nuclear industry, see Cochran, Norris, and Bukharin, *Making the Russian Bomb*.

10. Beria's biographer assigns Igor Kurchatov credit for pressuring Stalin to appoint Beria instead of Molotov to direct the project. Amy Knight, *Beria: Stalin's First Lieutenant* (Princeton: Princeton University Press, 1993), 134.

11. S. I. Vavilov, *Sovetskaia nauka na novom etape* (Moscow: Izd. AN SSSR, 1946), 78.

12. Iu. N. Krivonosov, "Okolo atomnogo proekta (Po materialam arkhivov TsK KPSS)," in Vizgin, *Istoriia sovetskogo atomnogo proekta*, 396; Anton Antonov-Ovseenko, *Beriia* (Moscow: AST, 1999), 386, 393; Iu. S. Zamiatin, "Vospominaniia ob uchastii v atomnom proekte," *VIET*, no. 2 (1996): 142.

13. Khariton and Smirnov, "The Khariton Version," 26; Slavskii, "Poka atomnaia bomba ne vzorvalas'," 7.

14. Steenbeck, *Impulse und Wirkungen*, 197.

15. On the history of the Uranium Commission, headed by the noted geochemist Vladimir Vernadskii, see Kendall E. Bailes, "Soviet Science in the Stalin Period: The Case of V. I. Vernadskii and His Scientific School, 1928–1945," *Slavic Review* 45 (1986): 20–37; Komlev, Sinitsyna, and Koval'skaia, "V. G. Khlopin i uranovaia problema," 37–52; and D. N. Trifonov, "K istorii komissii po probleme urana," *VIET*, no. 2 (1996): 93–99.

16. David Holloway, "Entering the Nuclear Arms Race: The Soviet Decision to Build the Atomic Bomb, 1939–1945," *Social Studies of Science* 11 (1981): 160, 167. On employment at the laboratory, see the list of employees as of January 18, 1944, APSSSR I.ii.22–23.

17. Holloway, *Stalin and the Bomb*, 94.

18. I. N. Golovin and Iu. N. Smirnov, "Eto nachinalos' v Zamoskovorech'e," in *Nauka i uchenye Rossii v gody Velikoi Otechestvennoi voiny 1941–1945: Ocherki, vospominanii, dokumenty* (Moscow: Nauka, 1996), 203–12.

19. Gubarev, *Belyi arkhipelag Stalina*, 64.

20. Isai I. Gurevich in Boris Volodin, "Povest' ob Igore Vasil'eviche Kurchatove," in *Puti v neznaemoe: Pisateli rasskazyvaiut o nauke*, vol. 16 (Moscow: Sovetskii pisatel', 1982), 73. Not all were so adoring. On the exact same page, G. N. Flerov criticized Kurchatov's poor knowledge of engineering specifics.

21. M. G. Pervukhin, "Vydaiushchiisia uchenyi i talantlivyi organizator," in A. P. Aleksandrov, ed., *Vospominaniia ob Igore Vasil'eviche Kurchatove* (Moscow: Nauka, 1988), 179. We do not have the text of these lectures, but presumably they covered ground similar to that addressed by Robert Serber in his orientation lectures to those at Los Alamos, in Robert Serber, *The Los Alamos Primer: The First Lectures on How to Build an Atomic Bomb*, ed. Richard Rhodes (Berkeley: University of California Press, 1992).

22. Terletskii, "Operatsiia 'Dopros Nil'sa Bora,'" 41.

23. David Holloway, "Physics, the State, and Civil Society in the Soviet Union," *Historical Studies in the Physical and Biological Sciences* 30 (1999): 174.

24. Historians have generally avoided the topic. For some rare exceptions, see Gennady Gorelik with Antonina W. Bouis, *The World of Andrei Sakharov: A Russian Physicist's Path to Freedom* (New York: Oxford University Press, 2005), 75; and Gerhard Barkleit, *Manfred von Ardenne: Selbstverwirklichung im Jahrhundert der Diktaturen* (Berlin: Duncker & Humboldt, 2006), 128.

25. Robert R. Wilson, "The Conscience of a Physicist," in Lewis and Wilson, *Alamogordo Plus Twenty-Five Years*, 72–73. For the climate of the end of the war, the pace of which left little time for careful moral introspection, see Gordin, *Five Days in August*, chaps. 4–5.

26. Charles Thorpe, "Against Time: Scheduling, Momentum, and Moral Order at Wartime Los Alamos," *Journal of Historical Sociology* 17 (2004): 31–55.

27. Quoted in A. I. Ioirysh, *Iadernyi dzhinn* (Moscow: IzdAT, 1994), 291.

28. V. S. Emel'ianov, *O nauke i tsivilizatsii: Vospominaniia, mysli i razmyshleniia uchenogo* (Moscow: Mysl', 1986), 8.

29. Zhuravlev, *Moi atomnyi vek*, 65.

30. Holloway, *Stalin and the Bomb*, 205–206; V. S. Gubarev, *Cheliabinsk-70* (Moscow: IzdAT, 1993), 10.

31. For just a few examples, see L. V. Al'tshuler, A. A. Brish, and Iu. N. Smirnov, "Na puti k pervomu sovetskomu atomnomu ispytaniiu," in Vizgin, *Istoriia sovetskogo atomnogo proekta*, 11; Vladimir Iosifovich Merkin, "Pervyi promyshlennyi atomnyi reaktor Sovetskogo soiuza: Sozdanie i pusk," in N. S. Babaev, ed., *Iadernoi nauke i tekhnike Rossii—50 let: Sbornik dokladov iubileinoi nauchno-prakticheskoi konferentsii, posviashchennoi 50-letiiu sozdaniia atomnoi otrasli, 29–30 avgusta 1995 g.* (Moscow: Moskovskaia tip. No. 2, 1996), 98; V. V. Igonin, *Atom v SSSR: Razvitie sovetskoi iadernoi fiziki* (Saratov: Izd. Saratovskogo universiteta, 1975), 10; Oleg Moroz, "Tak my delali bombu," *Literaturnaia gazeta*, no. 23 (June 6, 1990): 13; N. A. Dollezhal', *U istokov rukotvornogo mira: Zapiski konstruktora* (Moscow: Znanie, 1989), 128–29. In these critiques, the moral authority of British physicist P.M.S. Blackett was frequently cited. See, for example, I.F. Zhezherun, *Stroitel'stvo i pusk pervogo v Sovetskom Soiuze atomnogo reaktora* (Moscow: Atomizdat, 1978), 3.

32. V. B. Adamskii, "Stanovlenie grazhdanina," in B. L. Al'tshuler et al., eds., *On mezhdu nami zhil . . .: Vospominaniia o Sakharove* (Moscow: Praktika, 1996), 37.

33. L. V. Al'tshuler, "Riadom s Sakharovym," ibid., 114.

34. This account of Sakharov's motivations is according to I. L. Rozental', "Proshchaite, Andrei Dmitrievich!" ibid., 543.

35. Sakharov, *Memoirs*, 96–97.

36. Michael Frayn, *Copenhagen* (New York: Anchor, 2000). The argument that the German physicists deliberately sabotaged the Nazi project in order to prevent Hitler from gaining the bomb was articulated fully in Jungk, *Brighter than a Thousand Suns*, and resurrected in Powers,

Heisenberg's War, which served as one of the main sources for Frayn. For detailed attacks on this apologetic position, see Goudsmit, *Alsos*; Rose, *Heisenberg and the Nazi Atomic Bomb Project*; and Bernstein, *Hitler's Uranium Club*. For judicious siftings of the alternative positions, see Matthias Dörries, ed., *Michael Frayn's* Copenhagen *in Debate: Historical Essays and Documents on the 1941 Meeting Between Niels Bohr and Werner Heisenberg* (Berkeley: Office for History of Science and Technology, University of California, 2005); Walker, *German National Socialism* and *Nazi Science*.

37. Max Steenbeck, "On stal moim drugom," in B. B. Kadomtsev, ed., *Vospominaniia ob akademike L. A. Artsimoviche*, 2d ed. (Moscow: Nauka, 1988), 28; and Steenbeck, *Impulse und Wirkungen*, 175–77, 190.

38. Walker, *German National Socialism*, 17.

39. Riehl and Seitz, *Stalin's Captive*, 91.

40. Von Ardenne, *Sechzig Jahre für Forschung und Fortschritt*, 194, 205. On his work for the Third Reich, see Rose, *Heisenberg and the Nazi Atomic Bomb Project*, 136.

41. Boris Gorobets, *Krug Landau* (Moscow: Letnii sad, 2006), 169.

42. Landau, quoted in Sakharov, *Memoirs*, 125, and in Gorelik, *The World of Andrei Sakharov*, 191.

43. V. L. Ginzburg, *O nauke, o sebe i o drugikh* (Moscow: Nauka-Fizmatlit, 1997), 210.

44. Rozental', "Proshchaite, Andrei Dmitrievich!" 543.

45. Yuli Khariton and Yuri Smirnov, "The Khariton Version," *BAS* 49, no. 4 (May 1993): 29.

46. Holloway, *Stalin and the Bomb*, 213. The mechanics of the meeting are complicated to tease out. The interested reader can turn to Ethan Pollock, *Stalin and the Soviet Science Wars* (Princeton: Princeton University Press, 2006), chap. 4; Alexei B. Kojevnikov, *Stalin's Great Science: The Times and Adventures of Soviet Physicists* (London: Imperial College Press, 2004); Holloway, "Physics, the State, and Civil Society in the Soviet Union," 182; S. A. Sonin, "Soveshchanie, kotoroe ne sostoialos'," *Priroda*, nos. 3–5 (895) (March–May 1990); Kalinin, "Ot pervykh reaktorov do atominforma," 125–40; M. D. Akhundov, "Spasla li atomnaia bomba sovetskuiu fiziku?" *Priroda*, no. 1 (1991): 90–97; and G. A. Gorelik, "Fizika universitetskaia i akademicheskaia," *VIET*, no. 2 (1991): 31–46.

47. See Lillian Hoddeson, "Mission Change in the Large Laboratory: The Los Alamos Implosion Program, 1943–1945," in Peter L. Galison and

Bruce Hevly, eds., *Big Science: The Growth of Large-Scale Research* (Palo Alto: Stanford University Press, 1992), 265–89.

48. Fuchs's confession to Michael Perrin, January 30, 1950, in Williams, *Klaus Fuchs, Atom Spy*, 190–91.

49. Kurchatov to Beria, March 13, 1945, *APSSSR* I.ii.243; and Kurchatov memorandum evaluating intelligence material, March 16, 1945, ibid., 246. See also Iu. B. Khariton, "Schastliveishie gody moei zhizni," in S. S. Gershtein and R. A. Siuniaev, eds., *Znakomyi neznakomyi Zel'dovich: V vospominaniiakh druzei, kolleg, uchenikov* (Moscow: Nauka, 1993), 103.

50. Kapitza to Stalin, November 25, 1945, *APSSSR* II.i.613–18.

51. Khariton in Khariton and Smirnov, *Mify i real'nost' sovetskogo atomnogo proekta*, 8.

52. Kojevnikov, *Stalin's Great Science*, 140.

53. Haynes and Klehr, *Venona*, 322.

54. Nikita S. Khrushchev, *Khrushchev Remembers: The Glasnost Tapes*, trans. and ed. Jerrold L. Schecter and Vyacheslav V. Luchkov (Boston: Little, Brown, 1990), 195.

55. According to a leading atomic espionage agent, "From the very beginning [Beria] suspected disinformation in these reports, considering that through this means the opponent tried to lure us into enormous expenditures of resources and effort on work that had no potential." A. A. Iatskov, "Atom i razvedka," *VIET*, no. 3 (1992): 105.

56. Khariton in Khariton and Smirnov, *Mify i real'nost' sovetskogo atomnogo proekta*, 8. For more statements along these lines, see V. N. Novoselov and V. S. Tolstikov, *Taina "sorokovki"* (Ekaterinburg: Ural'skii rabochii, 1995), 27; and Simonov, *Voenno-promyshlennyi kompleks SSSR v 1920–1950-e gody*, 214.

57. Kurchatov to Pervukhin, March 7, 1943, in Iatskov, "Atom i razvedka," 116.

58. On this problem of incompleteness, see V. Zhuchikhin, *Pervaia atomnaia: Zapiski inzhenera-issledovatelia* (Moscow: IzdAT, 1993), 6, 12; Khariton, "Schastliveishie gody moei zhizni," 104; V. A. Tsukerman, "Eto bylo pokhozhe na koldovstvo," in Gerstein and Siuniaev, eds., *Znakomyi neznakomyi Zal'dovich*, 109; and Negin et al., *Sovetskii atomnyi proekt*, 67.

59. Groves, *Now It Can Be Told*, 140. For more detail on compartmentalization and Groves, see Norris, *Racing for the Bomb*, 254–56; Sherwin, *A World Destroyed*, 60; and Charles Thorpe, *Oppenheimer: The Tragic Intellect* (Chicago: University of Chicago Press, 2006), 99. It appears

that compartmentalization actually preceded the Groves regime, having been instituted in the American Uranium Committee by the physicist Gregory Breit. See Stanley Goldberg, "Groves and the Scientists: Compartmentalization and the Building of the Bomb," *Physics Today* (August 1995): 41.

60. On layers of ignorance among Soviet physicists, see Kojevnikov, *Stalin's Great Science*, 150–51; Vladimir Chikov, "Kak sovetskaia razvedka 'rasshchepila' amerikanskii atom," *Novoe Vremia*, nos. 16–17 (2390) (April 23 and 30, 1991); Arkadii Kruglov, *The History of the Soviet Atomic Industry*, trans. Andrei Lokhov (New York: Taylor & Francis, 2002), 112, 119; and Sagdeev, "Russian Scientists Save American Secrets," 33.

61. Khariton and Smirnov, "The Khariton Version," 20; David Holloway, "How the Bomb Saved Soviet Physics," *BAS* 50 (November 1994): 47.

62. Tsukerman and Azarkh, *Arzamas-16*, 71–72.

63. In V. S. Gubarev, *Arzamas-16* (Moscow: IzdAT, 1992), 22. On the systemic problems of "copying" in the nuclear context, see MacKenzie and Spinardi, "Tacit Knowledge, Nuclear Weapons Design, and the Uninvention of Nuclear Weapons," 66.

64. See, for example, his authorization for Khariton: Kurchatov to G. G. Ovakimian (1st Department of NKGB), April 30, 1945, in *APSSSR* I.ii.278. Similar letters exist for the other leading scientists in the Soviet project.

65. Iulii B. Khariton, "Pis'mo v redaktsiiu gazety 'Gorodskoi kur'er' (g. Sarov)," in Khariton, *Put' dlinoiu v vek*, 193. Or consider the statement of Anatolii P. Aleksandrov, eventually president of the Academy of Sciences of the USSR and a leading atomic reactor designer: "We had a strict division of labor and areas of information—I did not concern myself with weapons, and only rarely was I brought in on separate questions." Aleksandrov, "Gody s Kurchatovym," 23.

66. In Khariton and Smirnov, *Mify i real'nost' sovetskogo atomnogo proekta*, 13.

67. Postanovlenie GOKO No. 9877ss/op, "O spetsial'nom komitete pri GOKO," August 20, 1945, *APSSSR* II.i.11.

68. Novoselov and Tolstikov, *Taina "sorokovki,"* 32; Negin et al., *Sovetskii atomnyi proekt*, 64–65.

69. Holloway, *Stalin and the Bomb*, 136.

70. L. V. Al'tshuler, "Nachalo fiziki ekstremal'nykh sostoianii," in Gerstein and Siuniaev, *Znakomyi neznakomyi Zel'dovich*, 116.

71. Vitalii Semenovich Tolstikov, "K istorii realizatsii otechestvennogo atomnogo proekta," *Klio*, no. 1 (2002): 107–14.

72. Holloway, *Stalin and the Bomb*, 99.

73. Ibid., 189–90; Cochran, Norris, and Bukharin, *Making the Russian Bomb*, 8.

74. Khariton quoted in Gubarev, *Arzamas-16*, 22.

75. Thomas Reed and Arnold Kramish, "Trinity at Dubna," *Physics Today* (November 1996): 32; Thomas B. Cochran and Robert S. Norris, "A First Look at the Soviet Bomb Complex," *BAS* 47 (May 1991): 27; V. Novikov, B. Segerstahl, V. Merkin, and V. Popov, "The Construction Period in Mayak 1946–1949," in Velikhov, *Nauka i obshchestvo*, 3: 170–80; Merkin, "Pervyi promyshlennyi atomnyi reaktor Sovetskogo soiuza"; and Zhezherun, *Stroitel'stvo i pusk pervogo v Sovetskom Soiuze atomnogo reaktora*.

76. L. P. Goleusova, " 'Arzamas-16': Kak vse nachinalos' . . . ," *VIET*, no. 4 (1994): 89–97; Tsukerman and Azarkh, *Arzamas-16*; Al'tshuler, "Na puti k pervomu sovetskomu atomnomu ispytaniiu," 22–25, 30; and Zhuravlev, *Moi atomnyi vek*, 109–10.

77. David Holloway, "Parallel Lives? Oppenheimer and Khariton," in Carson and Hollinger, *Reappraising Oppenheimer*, 115–28. For the Beria story, see Sergo Beriia, *Moi otets—Lavrentii Beriia* (Moscow: Sovremennik, 1994), 275.

78. V. I. Gol'danskii, "Fragmenty minuvshego," in A. E. Shilov, ed., *Vospominaniia ob akademike Nikolae Nikolaeviche Semenove* (Moscow: Nauka, 1993), 50.

79. Steenbeck, *Impulse und Wirkungen*, 216.

80. Minutes of fourth meeting of the Special Committee of the Sovnarkom SSSR, September 28, 1945, *APSSSR* II.i.21.

81. Mick, *Forschen für Stalin*, 152. These were only the major projects. For details on the minor projects, see Barkleit, *Manfred von Ardenne*, 98; and Oleynikov, "German Scientists in the Soviet Atomic Project," 13.

82. Mick, *Forschen für Stalin*, 192–93; Ulrich Albrecht, Andreas Heinemann-Grüder, and Arend Wellmann, *Die Spezialisten: Deutsche Naturwissenschaftler und Techniker in der Sowjetunion nach 1945* (Berlin: Dietz Verlag, 1992), 79; and Albrecht, "The Development of the First Atomic Bomb in the USSR," 375. On the ethnic mix of the workers, see Steenbeck, *Impulse und Wirkungen*, 209; and Barwich and Barwich, *Das rote Atom*, 28.

83. Khariton and Smirnov, "The Khariton Version," 20.

84. Zhuchikhin, *Pervaia atomnaia*, 97–98.

85. Decree of Council of Ministers of the USSR No. 1286-525ss, June 21, 1946, *APSSSR* II.i.435.

86. Negin et al., *Sovetskii atomnyi proekt*, 107.

87. Khariton in Gubarev, *Arzamas-16*, 12; Novoselov and Tolstikov, *Taina "sorokovki,"* 167. It is not true that Stalin was actually shown a pluto-nium sphere, either at this incident or at any other time. Khariton and Smirnov, "The Khariton Version," 28. David Holloway has pointed out that Khariton met Stalin only once, in 1947, and that it was likely that this meeting was misdated in Khariton's memory. Holloway, personal communication, June 4, 2008.

88. Negin et al., *Sovetskii atomnyi proekt*, 164–68; and Georgi Kaurow, "Die Atomtestgebiete—der Vorhof zur Hölle," in Siegfried Fischer and Otfried Nassauer, eds., *Satansfaust: Das nukleare Erbe der Sowjetunion* (Berlin: Aufbau-Verlag, 1992), 51–66. The Limonia code name was peculiar to scientists at Nikolai Semenov's laboratory, as reported in Gol'danskii, "Fragmenty minuvshego," 55. On the orders to begin con-struction, see minutes of the twenty-eighth meeting of the Special Com-mittee of the Sovnarkom SSSR, November 11, 1946, *APSSSR* II.i.140.

89. It has been claimed that initial plans for an airdrop test were aban-doned on finding that there was no plane sufficiently sturdy to carry the device. Zaloga, *Target America*, 59. Considering the reluctance to deviate from the model of the Manhattan Project, the more parsimo-nious explanation for the tower was the analogy with the Americans.

90. A. I. Veretennikov, *Riadom s atomnoi bomboi (Zapiski fizika-eksperi-mentatora)* (Moscow: IzdAT, 1995), 20. See also Zhuchikhin, *Pervaia atomnaia*, 72–73; Cochran, Norris, and Bukharin, *Making the Russian Bomb*, 12; Gubarev, *Belyi arkhipelag Stalina*, 355; and Tsukerman and Azarkh, *Arzamas-16*, 76.

91. Zhuchikhin, *Pervaia atomnaia*, 68–70; Turchin, *Sorok let na ispytani-iakh iadernogo oruzhiia*, 14–15.

92. M. A. El'iashevich, "Podgotovka i provedenie opticheskikh nabliudenii pervogo sovetskogo iadernogo vzryva," *VIET*, no. 2 (1996): 160. Others were more verbose, although perhaps less felicitous. See, for example, the rather poor poem to commemorate the "unknown settlement" of the polygon: B. A. Kryzhov, "U neizvestnogo poselka," reproduced in A. I. Veretennikov, *Fol'klor na sluzhbe atomu: Sbornik-stikhov i pesen* (Moscow: IzdAT, 1996), 86.

93. Peter Bacon Hales, *Atomic Spaces: Living on the Manhattan Project* (Urbana: University of Illinois Press, 1997), 301–31.

94. G. A. Goncharov, "Termoiadernyi proekt SSSR: Predystoriia i desiat' let puti k vodorodnoi bombe," in Vizgin, *Istoriia sovetskogo atomnogo proekta*, 78. See the proposed schedule in minutes of the sixty-third meeting of the Special Committee of the Sovnarkom SSSR, June 5, 1948, *APSSSR* II.i.283. The original schedule of 1946 can be found in L. P. Beria to I. V. Stalin, no later than June 21, 1946, *APSSSR* II.i.433. For the final order for the test, which made it clear that no information about it should be leaked either before or after the fact, see minutes of the eightieth meeting of the Special Committee of the Sovnarkom SSSR, July 16, 1949, *APSSSR* II.i.380–81.

95. Stalin, "Ob ispytanii atomnoi bomby," August 26, 1949, appendix to minutes of the eighty-fifth meeting of the Special Committee of the Sovnarkom SSSR, *APSSSR* II.i.389.

96. El'iashevich, "Podgotovka i provedenie opticheskikh nabliudenii pervogo sovetskogo iadernogo vzryva," 161–62.

97. Holloway, *Stalin and the Bomb*, 221.

98. Zhuchikhin, *Pervaia atomnaia*, 93–94; Holloway, *Stalin and the Bomb*, 215–16.

99. Tsukerman and Azarkh, *Arzamas-16*, 77.

100. Zhuchikhin, *Pervaia atomnaia*, 95.

101. In Ioirysh, *Iadernyi dzhinn*, 287. See also Burnazian, "O radiatsionnoi bezopasnosti," 309–10.

102. In Ioirysh, *Iadernyi dzhinn*, 286.

103. El'iashevich, "Podgotovka i provedenie opticheskikh nabliudenii pervogo sovetskogo iadernogo vzryva," 162–63; M. G. Pervukhin, "Pervye gody atomnogo proekta," *Khimiia i zhizn'*, no. 5 (1985): 66; V. I. Vlasov in Gubarev, *Arzamas-16*, 15–16.

104. Quoted in Ioirysh, *Iadernyi dzhinn*, 285.

105. Knight, *Beria*, 139.

106. L. P. Beria and I. V. Kurchatov to Stalin, August 30, 1949, *APSSSR* II.i.639–43, quotation on 639.

107. Beria's final report to Stalin, September 28, 1949, *APSSSR* II.i.654.

108. Kruglov, *History of the Soviet Atomic Industry*, 123–24; Negin et al., *Sovetskii atomnyi proekt*, 178.

109. Holloway, *Stalin and the Bomb*, 218.

110. Decree of Council of Ministers of the USSSR No. 5070-1944ss/op, October 29, 1949, *APSSSR* II.i.530–62.

111. A. P. Alexandrov, "The Heroic Deed," *BAS* 23 (December 1967): 13. On Aleksandrov's declarations of lack of involvement in weapons production, which were also clearly a method of dealing with the morality

question, see I. I. Larin, *Akademik atomnykh del* (Moscow: IzdAT, 1998), 31.

112. Dollezhal', *U istokov rukotvornogo mira*, 152.

FIVE: MAKING VERMONT

1. William T. Golden to Lewis Strauss, November 25, 1947, Strauss AEC papers, Box 68, Folder: "Monitoring Soviet Tests."

2. Lewis Strauss to John E. Gingrich, September 10, 1947, ibid.

3. Lawrence Aronsen, "Seeing Red," 120.

4. Admiral William D. Leahy to Harry S. Truman, August 21, 1946, in Warner, *The CIA under Harry Truman*, 79–80.

5. Richard Pfau, *No Sacrifice Too Great: The Life of Lewis L. Strauss* (Charlottesville: University Press of Virginia, 1984), 95–97, 126; Jeffrey T. Richelson, *American Espionage and the Soviet Target* (New York: Morrow, 1987), 116–17; and Noel Francis Parrish, "Behind the Sheltering Bomb: Military Indecision from Alamogordo to Korea" (Ph.D. dissertation, Rice University, 1968), 297. Ralph Lapp offered a different account, giving primary credit to Vannevar Bush and his Joint Research and Development Board: Ralph E. Lapp, *Atoms and People* (New York: Harper, 1956), 141.

6. Edward Teller with Judith L. Shoolery, *Memoirs: A Twentieth-Century Journey in Science and Politics* (Cambridge, MA: Perseus Publishing, 2001), 279.

7. Lewis L. Strauss to AEC Commissioners, April 11, 1947, Strauss AEC Papers, Box 68, Folder: "Monitoring Soviet Tests."

8. A geophysicist, having learned that Strauss was interested in long-range detection, offered him his services for testing a seismic apparatus: Frank Rieber to Lewis Strauss, November 12, 1947, Strauss AEC Papers, Box 113, Folder: "Tests and Testing." I have been unable to find any record of Strauss's response.

9. Benjamin P. Greene, *Eisenhower, Science Advice, and the Nuclear Test-Ban Debate, 1945–1963* (Palo Alto: Stanford University Press, 2007), 28–29.

10. William T. Golden to Lewis L. Strauss, May 22, 1947, Strauss AEC Papers, Box 68, Folder: "Monitoring Soviet Tests."

11. J. Robert Oppenheimer to David E. Lilienthal, October 10, 1947, Seaborg Papers, Atomic Energy Commission, Committees, General Advisory Committee, Box 614, Folder 6, 6.

12. G. L. Weil and S. G. English, memorandum to file, July 26, 1948, AEC

Records, Office of the Secretary, Entry 67a, Box 8, Folder: "Companies & Corporations."

13. Lewis L. Strauss, *Men and Decisions* (Garden City, NY: Doubleday, 1962), 203.

14. Entry of July 22, 1948, James V. Forrestal, Diaries, Volumes XI–XII, May 1, 1948–Sept. 30, 1948.

15. Strauss to AEC Commissioners and the Director of the Division of Military Application, August 9, 1948, Strauss AEC Papers, Box 68, Folder: "Monitoring Soviet Tests."

16. Lewis L. Strauss, "History of the Long-Range Detection Program," July 21, 1948, Strauss AEC Papers, Box 113, Folder: "Tests and Testing," 1.

17. Ibid., 4; Pfau, *No Sacrifice Too Great*, 96.

18. Strauss to James Forrestal, January 3, 1949, Strauss AEC Papers, Box 68, Folder: "Monitoring Soviet Tests."

19. Demetrios Caraley, *The Politics of Military Unification: A Study of Conflict and the Policy Process* (New York: Columbia University Press, 1966); and Perry M. Smith, *The Air Force Plans for Peace, 1943–1945* (Baltimore: Johns Hopkins Press, 1970).

20. Quoted in Doyle L. Northrup and Donald H. Rock, "The Detection of Joe 1," *Studies in Intelligence* (Fall 1966): 26.

21. Eisenhower, memorandum to JCS, November 5, 1947, letter 1846, in Alfred D. Chandler, Jr., ed., *The Papers of Dwight David Eisenhower*, 21 vols. (Baltimore: Johns Hopkins Press, 1970–2001), 9:2047.

22. Aronsen, "Seeing Red," 107.

23. Ziegler and Jacobson, *Spying Without Spies*, 21.

24. Ibid., 95.

25. Richelson, *Spying on the Bomb*, 73–74.

26. Ziegler and Jacobson, *Spying Without Spies*, 82; John F. Fuller, *Thor's Legions: Weather Support to the U.S. Air Force and Army, 1937–1987* (Boston: American Meteorological Society, 1990), 246–49; Charles C. Bates and John F. Fuller, *America's Weather Warriors, 1814–1985* (College Station: Texas A&M University Press, 1986), 136–37, 166–67.

27. Luis W. Alvarez, *Alvarez: Adventures of a Physicist* (New York: Basic Books, 1987), 120–21; Richelson, *Spying on the Bomb*, 40–50; Ziegler and Jacobson, *Spying Without Spies*, 5–6.

28. T. I. Harriman memo to Commanding Generals FUSAG, FUSA, TUSA, and USSTAF, May 3, 1944, Top Secret Files, Roll 1, Target 8, Subfile 7D: "Operation PEPPERMINT."

29. Ziegler and Jacobson, *Spying Without Spies*, 8. See the summary in Goudsmit, *Alsos*; and Leo J. Mahoney, "A History of the War Department Scientific Intelligence Mission (Alsos), 1943–45" (Ph.D. dissertation, Kent State University, 1981).

30. Ziegler and Jacobson, *Spying Without Spies*, 14.

31. Ibid., 38; Hoddeson et al., *Critical Assembly*, 353. On the fallout studies at Trinity, see Hirschfelder, "The Scientific and Technological Miracle at Los Alamos," 75–76.

32. Ziegler and Jacobson, *Spying Without Spies*, 38–39. On the potential for future atomic bombings of Japan and the tentative state of the Manhattan Project during the final week of the war, see Gordin, *Five Days in August*, chap. 5.

33. J. H. Webb, "The Fogging of Photographic Film by Radioactive Contaminants in Cardboard Packaging Materials," *Physical Review* 76 (1949): 375. See also Richard L. Miller, *Under the Cloud: The Decades of Nuclear Testing* (New York: Free Press, 1986), 58.

34. A. W. Coven, "Evidence of Increased Radioactivity of the Atmosphere After the Atomic Bomb Test in New Mexico," *Physical Review* 68 (1945): 279.

35. B. Gutenberg, "Interpretation of Records Obtained from the New Mexico Atomic Bomb Test, July 16, 1945," *Bulletin of the Seismological Society of America* 36 (1946): 327–30.

36. W. A. Shurcliff, *Bombs at Bikini: The Official Report of Operation Crossroads* (New York: Wm. H. Wise, 1947), iii. For the history of the Bikini tests, see Lloyd J. Graybar, "The 1946 Atomic Bomb Tests: Atomic Diplomacy or Bureaucratic Infighting?" *Journal of American History* 72 (1986): 888–907; and Jonathan M. Weisgall, *Operation Crossroads: The Atomic Tests at Bikini Atoll* (Annapolis, MD: Naval Institute Press, 1994).

37. Bradbury, "Los Alamos," 162.

38. Richelson, *Spying on the Bomb*, 79.

39. Ziegler and Jacobson, *Spying Without Spies*, 48, 54.

40. G. Herzog, "Gamma-Ray Anomaly Following the Atomic Bomb Test of July 1, 1946," *Physical Review* 70 (1946): 227–28; and Dorothy E. Weekes and D. F. Weekes, "Effort to Observe Anomalous Gamma-Rays Connected with Atomic Bomb Test of July 1, 1946," *Physical Review* 70 (1946): 565.

41. B. Gutenberg and C. F. Richter, "Seismic Waves from Atomic Bomb Tests," *Transactions of the American Geophysical Union* 27, no. 6 (December 1946): 776.

42. R. E. Fearson, A. Wendell Engle, Jean Thayer, Gilbert Swift, and Irving Johnson, "Results of Atmosphere Analyses Done at Tulsa, Oklahoma, During the Period Neighboring the Time of the Second Bikini Atomic Bomb Test," *Physical Review* 70 (1946): 564.

43. Victor F. Hess and Paul Luger, S.J., "The Ionization of the Atmosphere in the New York Area Before and After the Bikini Atom Bomb Test," *Physical Review* 70 (1946): 565.

44. "Long-Range Detection of Atomic Explosions," *Intelligence Review*, no. 37 (October 24, 1946): 56.

45. Ziegler and Jacobson, *Spying Without Spies*, 45.

46. "Long-Range Detection of Atomic Explosions," 59.

47. Edward Teller to Norris Bradbury, September 3, 1948, Nuclear Testing Archive, accession #NV0125268. I thank Alex Wellerstein for bringing this document to my attention.

48. William T. Golden to Robert F. Bacher, March 19, 1948, AEC Records, Records of the Commissioners, Office Files of Robert F. Bacher, Entry 17, Box 4, Folder: "Remote Detection."

49. Aerial surveys and photoreconnaissance had been ruled out as ineffective as long ago as the UNAEC negotiations in 1946. Committee 2 of the UNAEC, "Notes on the Twelfth Information Conversation [November 25, 1946]," transcript of December 3, 1946, Baruch Papers, Unit X, Section 1, Box 53, File: "Proceedings—Sub-Committee No. 2 of AEC Informal Meetings," 7.

50. After Sandstone, the AEC began developing test sites within the continental United States. In the late 1950s, because of the prohibitive expense of overseas testing, the proving grounds were moved to Nevada, where they remain today, albeit unused during the current testing moratorium. Miller, *Under the Cloud*, 80.

51. Richard G. Hewlett and Francis Duncan, *Atomic Shield: A History of the United States Atomic Energy Commission, Volume II: 1947/1952* (Washington, D.C.: U.S. Atomic Energy Commission, 1972), 161–65; and Rearden, *History of the Office of the Secretary of Defense*, 440–41.

52. Statement of Lt. Gen. John E. Hull, May 18, 1948, AEC Records, Records of the Office of the Chairman, Office Files of David E. Lilienthal, Entry 1, Box 5, Folder: "Eniwetok," 2.

53. Lilienthal, entry of October 10, 1947, *The Atomic Energy Years*, 245.

54. Lilienthal, entry of April 8, 1948, ibid., 311.

55. Herken, *The Winning Weapon*, 252.

56. Strauss, *Men and Decisions*, 204. See also Lapp, *Atoms and People*, 141–42.

57. Ziegler and Jacobson, *Spying Without Spies*, 131. For more on Mogul, see Curtis Peebles, *The Moby Dick Project: Reconnaissance Balloons over Russia* (Washington, D.C.: Smithsonian Institution Press, 1991); and Norris, *Racing for the Bomb*, 477.

58. Paraphrased in William T. Golden to Lewis L. Strauss, August 12, 1948, Strauss AEC Papers, Box 113, Folder: "Tests and Testing." Johnson, however, had had it with the military, feeling he was not listened to, and quit after Sandstone, being immediately replaced by his deputy, Dr. George Shortley.

59. Richelson, *Spying on the Bomb*, 83–85.

60. Richelson, *American Espionage and the Soviet Target*, 117.

61. Charles A. Ziegler, "Waiting for Joe-1: Decisions Leading to the Detection of Russia's First Atomic Bomb Test," *Social Studies of Science* 18 (1988): 213; Ziegler and Jacobson, *Spying Without Spies*, 113. On countermeasures, see Enrico Fermi's worries about masking nuclear tests reported in Draft Minutes of the GAC sixth meeting, October 3–5, 1947, Seaborg Papers, Atomic Energy Commission, Committees, General Advisory Committee, Box 615, Folder 1, 19, and Draft Minutes of the GAC seventh meeting, November 21–23, 1947, Seaborg Papers, Box 615, Folder 2, 2–3, 37.

62. Lilienthal, entry of July 8, 1948, *The Atomic Energy Years*, 384.

63. Ziegler and Jacobson, *Spying Without Spies*, 110.

64. "Business in Isotopes," *Fortune*, December 1947, 121–25, 150–56, 160–64; Ziegler and Jacobson, *Spying Without Spies*, 125; Angela N. H. Creager, "The Industrialization of Radioisotopes by the U.S. Atomic Energy Commission," in Karl Grandin, Nina Wormbs, and Sven Widmalm, eds., *The Science-Industry Nexus: History, Policy, Implications* (Sagamore Beach, MA: Science History Publications, 2004).

65. Richelson, *Spying on the Bomb*, 86.

66. Kenneth W. Condit, *The Joint Chiefs of Staff and National Policy, Vol. II: 1947–1949* (Washington, D.C.: Office of Joint History, Office of the Chairman of the Joint Chiefs of Staff, 1996), 281.

67. William T. Golden to Lewis L. Strauss, August 12, 1948, Strauss AEC Papers, Box 113, Folder: "Tests and Testing"; Northrup and Rock, "The Detection of Joe 1," 27; Harry R. Borowski, *A Hollow Threat: Strategic Air Power and Containment Before Korea* (Westport, CT: Greenwood Press, 1982), 188. General Roscoe Charles Wilson of USAF commented in 1954 at J. Robert Oppenheimer's security-clearance hearings that he thought there needed to be further research: "It is hard for me to talk about these things. We are not naming names. They were

three [systems]. They were of relative degrees of development or lack of development. The one that appeared to be most immediately promising, the one that perhaps we had the most information on was the one that Dr. Oppenheimer supported to the greater degree." Testimony of April 28, 1954, USAEC, *In the Matter of J. Robert Oppenheimer*, 692. From archival sources, it appears that Oppenheimer pushed for seismic methods. On James Bryant Conant's similar attitude, see Herken, *Brotherhood of the Bomb*, 199.

68. Lawrence R. Aronsen, "American National Security and the Defense of the Northern Frontier, 1945–1951," *Canadian Review of American Studies* 14, no. 4 (1983): 270.

69. Strauss comments in "Minutes of an Executive Meeting of the Joint Committee on Atomic Energy," February 4, 1949, 10:00 p.m., Hickenlooper Papers, JCAE Series, Box 6, Folder: "Committee Minutes, 1948–49," 19.

70. "Detector Reported Perfected to Warn of Any A-Bomb Test," *CDT*, December 18, 1948, 1; "Reveals Russia's 'Atom Bomb' Was a Monster Meteor," *CDT*, December 31, 1948, 9.

71. Ziegler and Jacobson, *Spying Without Spies*, 200.

72. Borowski, *A Hollow Threat*, 81–83.

73. Northrup and Rock, "The Detection of Joe 1," 29.

74. Herbert Friedman, Luther B. Lockhart, and Irving H. Blifford, "Detecting the Soviet Bomb: Joe-1 in a Rain Barrel," *Physics Today* (November 1996): 38–41; Ziegler and Jacobson, *Spying Without Spies*, 190–93; and L. B. Lockhart, Jr., R. A. Baus, P. King, and I. H. Blifford, Jr., "Atmospheric Radioactivity Studies at the U.S. Naval Research Laboratory," *Journal of Chemical Education* 36 (June 1959): 291–95.

75. This narrative has been told many times. I draw my version from the following sources: Richelson, *American Espionage and the Soviet Target*, 117–18; Richelson, *Spying on the Bomb*, 88–89; Northrup and Rock, "The Detection of Joe 1," 23; and Ziegler, "Waiting for Joe-1," 218–19. For more details on the crew and flight paths of the sample missions, see Fuller, *Thor's Legions*, 246–47.

76. Hewlett and Duncan, *Atomic Shield*, 363–64.

77. Moss, *Klaus Fuchs*, 130–31.

78. W. Penney, "An Interim Report of British Work on Joe," September 22, 1949, PSF: Subject File, 1940–1953, National Security Council—Atomic Files, Box 173, Folder: "Atomic Bomb: Reports."

79. M. K. Fleming, Jr. (director of NRL), to AFOAT-1, "Collection and Identification of Fission Products of Foreign Origin," [undated but

received September 22, 1949], ibid.; see also Friedman et al., "Detecting the Soviet Bomb," 40.

80. L. R. Zumwalt, A. J. Stevens, and F. C. Henriques, Jr., "Special Filter Paper Analyses and Preliminary Information Derived Therefrom," September 18, 1949, PSF: Subject File 1940–1953, National Security Council—Atomic Files, Box 173, Folder: "Atomic Bomb: Reports."

81. "U.S. Weather Bureau Report on Alert Number 112 of the Atomic Detection System," September 29, 1949, PSF: Subject File, 1940–1953, National Security Council—Atomic Files, Box 173, Folder, "Atomic Bomb: Reports." See also Lester Machta, "Finding the Site of the First Soviet Nuclear Test in 1949," *Bulletin of the American Meteorological Society* 73, no. 11 (1992): 1798–99.

82. Richelson, *Spying on the Bomb*, 91.

83. Machta, "Finding the Site of the First Soviet Nuclear Test in 1949," 1800–1801.

84. Robert F. Bacher, interview by Mary Terrall, Pasadena, CA, June–August 1981, February 1983, Oral History Project, California Institute of Technology Archives, Pasadena, 115, http://resolver.caltech.edu/CaltechOH:OH_Bacher_R.

85. Ibid., 115–16.

86. Al Christman, *Target Hiroshima: Deak Parsons and the Creation of the Atomic Bomb* (Annapolis, MD: Naval Institute Press, 1998), 241–42; Zachary, *Endless Frontier*, 349. On Parsons's role in the dropping of the atomic bombs, see Gordin, *Five Days in August*, 74–79.

87. Vannevar Bush, testimony of May 4, 1954, USAEC, *In the Matter of J. Robert Oppenheimer*, 910.

88. Kai Bird and Martin J. Sherwin, *American Prometheus: The Triumph and Tragedy of J. Robert Oppenheimer* (New York: Vintage Books, 2005), 416.

89. Herken, *Brotherhood of the Bomb*, 200.

90. Vannevar Bush to David Lilienthal, September 26, 1949, Lilienthal Papers, Series 3, Box 142, Folder: "Bush, Vannevar 1949"; George H. Quester, *Nuclear Diplomacy: The First Twenty-Five Years* (New York: Dunellen, 1970), 35.

91. Quoted in Joseph Alsop and Stewart Alsop, "How Red A-Blast Was Detected," *WP*, December 31, 1950, B5.

92. Bacher interview, 116.

93. Vannevar Bush, testimony of May 4, 1954, in USAEC, *In the Matter of J. Robert Oppenheimer*, 911.

SIX: DRAMATIZING THE SITUATION

1. Shulman, *Stalin's Foreign Policy Reappraised*, 29–30; William Taubman, *Stalin's American Policy: From Entente to Détente to Cold War* (New York: Norton, 1982), 208; and Forrest C. Pogue, *George C. Marshall: Statesman, 1945–1959* (New York: Viking, 1987), 418.

2. Eben Ayers, diary entry of August 31, 1949, in Robert H. Ferrell, ed., *Truman in the White House: The Diary of Eben A. Ayers* (Columbia: University of Missouri Press, 1991), 326.

3. Credit for the name "Joe" for Soviet tests, a universally accepted Western designation that continued throughout the following decades (Joe-4, Joe-23, etc.), has been claimed by different people. Arnold Kramish asserted that he had coined the name: Reed and Kramish, "Trinity at Dubna," 32. It has also been assigned to Anthony Turkevich: Machta, "Finding the Site of the First Soviet Nuclear Test in 1949," 1805n. Both accounts agree that the naming took place in mid-September 1949.

4. Gaddis, *We Now Know*, 99.

5. These are only the first three of Kennan's several points: Kennan, "Political Implications of Detonation of Atomic Bomb by the U.S.S.R.," report of the PPS to Gordon Arneson, August 16, 1949, *FRUS 1949*, 1:515.

6. Keith D. McFarland and David L. Roll, *Louis Johnson and the Arming of America: The Roosevelt and Truman Years* (Bloomington: Indiana University Press, 2005).

7. Ibid., 155; David McCullough, *Truman* (New York: Simon & Schuster, 1992), 741.

8. Eden, "The Diplomacy of Force," 70–73; and Warner R. Schilling, "The Politics of National Defense: Fiscal 1950," in Warner R. Schilling, Paul Y. Hammond, and Glenn H. Snyder, *Strategy, Politics, and Defense Budgets* (New York: Columbia University Press, 1962), 1–266.

9. Hamby, *Man of the People*, 499.

10. Steven L. Rearden, *The Evolution of American Strategic Doctrine: Paul H. Nitze and the Soviet Challenge* (Boulder, CO: Westview Press, 1984), 16.

11. Ross, *American War Plans*, 103. For more on Truman's budget, see Michael J. Hogan, *A Cross of Iron: Harry S. Truman and the Origins of the National Security State, 1945–1954* (New York: Cambridge University Press, 1998), 98.

12. McFarland and Roll, *Louis Johnson and the Arming of America*, 180–81.

13. Donovan, *Conflict and Crisis*, 200; Paolo E. Coletta, *The United States Navy and Defense Unification, 1947–1953* (Newark: University of Delaware Press, 1981), 134. Omar Bradley, for his part, found "the most dishonest and disturbing aspect" of the navy's arguments to be their dismissal of the power of nuclear weapons. See Bradley and Blair, *A General's Life*, 509.

14. Keith D. McFarland, "The 1949 Revolt of the Admirals," *Parameters* 11, no. 2 (1981): 53–63.

15. Bradley and Blair, *A General's Life*, 514.

16. Quester, *Nuclear Diplomacy*, 59.

17. Elsey's notes on his copy of the September 23, 1949, press release, Elsey Papers, Box 88, Folder: "National Defense—Atomic energy—announcement of Russian Atomic Bomb, September 23, 1949."

18. Elsey, longhand notes on interview with Sidney Souers about the Soviet test, ibid., 4.

19. Elsey, longhand "Notes on Interview with the President," ibid., 1.

20. Elsey, notes on interview with Souers, 1.

21. Press and Radio Conference #191, July 28, 1949, PSF, Press Conference File, Box 52, Folder: "January–December, 1949 (Nos. 163–209)," 9.

22. ORE, intelligence memorandum 225, "Estimate of Status of Atomic Warfare in the USSR," September 20, 1949, in Warner, *The CIA Under Harry Truman*, 319.

23. Truman, *Years of Trial and Hope*, 306–307. Bacher recalls that Truman "wanted and got a report written by Van Bush and the rest of us, and signed by all of us individually." Bacher interview, 116.

24. Elsey, notes on interview with Souers, 5.

25. Dean Acheson, entry of September 22, 1949, Appointment Book, March–December 1949, Acheson Papers, Box 46, Folder: "March–December, 1949."

26. Elsey, notes on interview with Souers, 6.

27. Carlton Savage memo, September 29, 1949, *FRUS* 1949, 1:536.

28. Septimus H. Paul, *Nuclear Rivals: Anglo-American Atomic Relations, 1941–1952* (Columbus: Ohio State University Press, 2000), 158.

29. "The Thunderclap," *Time*, October 3, 1949, 7.

30. Neuse, *David E. Lilienthal*, 213.

31. Laconically noted in Gordon Dean's diary entry of September 20, 1949, in Roger M. Anders, ed., *Forging the Atomic Shield: Excerpts*

from the Office Diary of Gordon E. Dean (Chapel Hill: University of North Carolina Press, 1987), 37. This happens to be the first entry in Dean's office diary.

32. Lilienthal, entry of September 21, 1949, *The Atomic Energy Years*, 569–72. Details of Lilienthal's schedule are from David Lilienthal, Office Diary, 1949, AEC Records, Records of the Office of the Chairman, Office Files of David E. Lilienthal, Entry 15, Box 1.

33. Hoyt Vandenberg's desk diary, entry of September 21, 1949, telephone call of 11 a.m. from General David Schlatter, Vandenberg Papers, Box 2.

34. C.C.S. Newton, "The Sterling Crisis of 1947 and the British Response to the Marshall Plan," *Economic History Review*, n.s., 37 (1984): 391–408.

35. Acheson, *Present at the Creation*, 212.

36. Nicholas Mayhew, *Sterling: The History of a Currency* (New York: John Wiley, 2000), 237–39; Samuel I. Katz, "Sterling's Recurring Postwar Payments Crises," *Journal of Political Economy* 63 (1955): 216–26; Philip W. Bell, *The Sterling Area in the Postwar World: Internal Mechanism and Cohesion, 1946–1952* (Oxford: Clarendon Press, 1956).

37. Wilson D. Miscamble, *George F. Kennan and the Making of American Foreign Policy, 1947–1950* (Princeton: Princeton University Press, 1992), 286. Kennan was worried that devaluation boded ill for the future of the British financial system and feared an upcoming collapse: George F. Kennan, "Transcript of Presentation Held in Room 1276, 'Q' Building," October 14, 1949, Kennan Papers, Box 17, Folder 29.

38. Elsey, "Notes on Interview with the President," 2.

39. Elsey, longhand "First Draft, based on interviews with the President," September 24, 1949, Elsey Papers, Box 88, Folder: "National Defense—Atomic energy—announcement of Russian Atomic Bomb, September 23, 1949," 5–6.

40. Eisenhower to Arthur H. Vandenberg, September 19, 1949, in Chandler, *The Papers of Dwight David Eisenhower*, 10:751.

41. Acheson, *Present at the Creation*, 312.

42. On the Hiroshima announcement, see Gordin, *Five Days in August*, 85–86.

43. Truman, *Years of Trial and Hope*, 307.

44. Brien McMahon to Bourke Hickenlooper, September 23, 1949, Hickenlooper Papers, JCAE Series, Box 35, Folder: "McMahon, Brien Sept.–Dec. 1949."

45. Elsey, notes on interview with Souers, 2–3.

46. Matthew Connelly, Notes on Cabinet Meeting, September 23, 1949, Connelly Papers, Box 2, Folder: "September 1949."

47. Alben W. Barkley, *That Reminds Me* (Garden City, NY: Doubleday, 1954), 267.

48. David Lilienthal to J. Robert Oppenheimer, September 23, 1949, Lilienthal Papers, Series 3, Box 147, Folder: "Oppenheimer, J. Robert 1949."

49. Harry S. Truman, public statement of September 23, 1949, PSF, Subject File, 1940–1953, Box 59, Folder: "September, 1949."

50. Press and Radio Conference #200, October 6, 1949, PSF, Press Conference File, Box 52, Folder: "January–December, 1949 (Nos. 163–209)," 4.

51. David E. Lilienthal, Remarks at the Annual Freedom House Award Dinner, October 13, 1949, Clifford Papers, Box 1, Folder: "Atomic Energy—Lilienthal, David E. [1946–49]," 5. These views were fairly widely shared, as in "Russia and the Bomb," *NYT*, September 24, 1949, 12.

52. Walter Lippmann, "End of the Atomic Monopoly," *WP*, September 27, 1949, 13. The rest of the press fairly quickly deduced the rationales for openness on this issue. See, for example, Arthur Krock, "Truman Chose Timing of Bomb Announcement," *NYT*, October 2, 1949, E3.

53. In McGeorge Bundy, "Early Thoughts on Controlling the Nuclear Arms Race: A Report to the Secretary of State, January 1953," *International Security* 7 (1982): 18–20. On the fate of candor in the Eisenhower years, see Ira Chernus, "Operation Candor: Fear, Faith, and Flexibility," *Diplomatic History* 29 (2005): 779–809.

54. Among those who guessed radiological monitoring, see "Science and the Citizen," *Scientific American* 181 (November 1949): 26–27; N. S. Haseltine, "U.S. Learned of Atom Blast Through 'Mechanical Means,'" *WP*, September 24, 1949, 1–2; "The Russian Bomb," *WP*, September 24, 1949, 6; and William L. Laurence, "Soviet Achievement Ahead of Predictions by 3 Years," *NYT*, September 24, 1949, 2. For speculations on photographic plates or remote Geiger counters, see James R. Shepley and Clay Blair, Jr., *The Hydrogen Bomb: The Men, the Menace, the Mechanism* (New York: David McKay, 1954), 3; and Robert Conway, "Stalin Witnessed Testing of A-Bomb," *LAT*, September 24, 1949, 1, 5. For seismic guesses, see Joseph C. Harsch, "Atom Explosion in Russia: Britain and U.S. Weigh Impact of Dual Report," *CSM*, September 23,

1949, 1. For those who insisted on human intelligence as the method of detection, see Robert Conway, "2 Bombs Duds; Stalin Present as 3d Goes Off," *CDT*, September 24, 1949, 1; and Arthur Veysey, "Reveal Czech Bared Blast of Soviet A-Bomb," *CDT*, September 25, 1949, 8.

55. K. D. Nichols, *The Road to Trinity* (New York: Morrow, 1987), 272.

56. "U.S. Detects Atomic Blast in Russia," *Life* 27, no. 14 (October 3, 1949): 18.

57. Dean Acheson, Press Conference at United Nations, September 23, 1949, 2:00 p.m., Acheson Papers, Box 72, Folder: "July–December 1949," 4.

58. "The Soviet Bombs: Mr. Truman's Doubts," *BAS* 9, no. 2 (March 1953): 43. See also the discussion in Ulam, *Expansion and Coexistence*, 497; and Robert J. Donovan, *Tumultuous Years: The Presidency of Harry S Truman, 1949–1953* (New York: Norton, 1982), 102.

59. Erskine, "The Polls," 176.

60. Johnson quoted in "A Little Something," *Time*, October 3, 1949, 55.

61. Statement of September 26, 1945 in "General Groves' Statement," *BAS* 5, no. 10 (October 1949): 267.

62. Quoted in "What They Say: Some Comment on Red A-Bomb," *CDT*, September 24, 1949, 2.

63. Quoted in Walter Trohan, "U.S. Stirred by Disclosure of Atomic Blast in Russia," *CDT*, September 24, 1949, 4.

64. Omar Bradley with Beverly Smith, "This Way Lies Peace," *Saturday Evening Post*, October 15, 1949, 170.

65. George F. Kennan, "Is War with Russia Inevitable? Five Solid Arguments for Peace," *Reader's Digest* 56 (March 1950): 1–9; Walter L. Hixson, *George F. Kennan: Cold War Iconoclast* (New York: Columbia University Press, 1989), 90.

66. Dean Acheson, Press Conference at United Nations, September 23, 1949, 2:00 p.m., Acheson Papers, Box 72, Folder: "July–December 1949," 2. See also Charles G. Ross, "Press and Radio Conference, September 24, 1949," Ross Papers, Box 11, Folder: "Press and Radio Conferences . . . Aug. 16–Sept. 28, 1949," 2–3.

67. Curtis E. LeMay, diary entry for September 23, 1949, LeMay Papers, Box B103.

68. Glenn T. Seaborg, *Journal of Glenn T. Seaborg, 1946–1958*, PUB-676, vol. 3: January 1, 1949–December 31, 1949 (Lawrence Berkeley Laboratory, University of California, prepared for the Department of Energy, July 1990), Seaborg Papers, Box 17, 256, entry for September 23, 1949.

69. Minutes of the Sixteenth Meeting of the GAC, September 22–23, 1949, Seaborg Papers, Historical File, Box 186, Folder 5, 20. For more, see Richard T. Sylves, *The Nuclear Oracles: A Political History of the General Advisory Committee of the Atomic Energy Commission, 1947–1977* (Ames: Iowa State University Press, 1987), 142–43.

70. Carlton Savage, executive secretary of PPS, September 29, 1949, *FRUS* 1949 1:536.

71. Undated document, but certainly late September 1949, PSF: Subject File, 1940–1953, National Security Council—Atomic File, Box 175, Folder: "Atomic Energy: Russia."

72. Mr. Arena, telegram to Truman, September 23, 1949, OF 692a, Box 1529, Folder: "Reaction to President's announcement, 9/23/49 that Russia has the Atomic Bomb, 'A–M.'"

73. Harsch, "Atom Explosion in Russia," 1.

74. "Swift Work by Russians Surprise to Scientists," *LAT*, September 24, 1949, 4.

75. Winston Churchill, "Devaluation of the Pound," September 28, 1949, in Winston S. Churchill, *Winston S. Churchill: His Complete Speeches, 1897–1963*, ed. Robert Rhodes James (New York: Chelsea House, 1974), 7:7845.

76. William S. Parsons to Oppenheimer, October 19, 1949, Oppenheimer Papers, Case File, Box 56, File: "Parsons, W. S.," 2. See also "Russian Bomb Blast Report: No World Policy Change Seen," *CSM*, September 24, 1949, 7.

77. "Foreign Reactions to Announcement of Atomic Explosion," [late September or early October 1949], PSF: Subject File, 1940–1953, National Security Council—Atomic File, Box 175, Folder: "Atomic Energy: Russia"; Arthur Schlesinger, Jr., "First Reactions to Russ Bomb Was Smug One," *WP*, October 2, 1949, B2.

78. "German Expert Sees Peace in Soviets' Atomic Bomb," *CDT*, September 24, 1949, 3.

79. Wittner, *One World or None*, 46. On U.S. nuclear censorship in Japan, see Monica Braw, *The Atomic Bomb Suppressed: American Censorship in Occupied Japan* (Armonk, NY: M. E. Sharpe, 1991).

80. Vojtech Mastny, *The Cold War and Soviet Insecurity: The Stalin Years* (New York: Oxford University Press, 1996), 77; Holloway, *Stalin and the Bomb*, 266–67.

81. Vladislav M. Zubok, "Stalin and the Nuclear Age," in John Lewis Gaddis et al., eds., *Cold War Statesmen Confront the Bomb: Nuclear Diplomacy since 1945* (New York: Oxford University Press, 1999), 55.

82. Bernard Newman, *Soviet Atomic Spies* (London: Robert Hale, 1952), 8–9.

83. William Curti Wohlforth, *The Elusive Balance: Power and Perceptions During the Cold War* (Ithaca: Cornell University Press, 1993), 110.

84. Riehl and Seitz, *Stalin's Captive*, 102.

85. Sudoplatov and Sudoplatov, *Special Tasks*, 211. See also Mastny, *The Cold War and Soviet Insecurity*, 77.

86. Kirk to Acheson, telegram of October 6, 1949, PSF: Subject File, 1940–1953, Box 164, Folder: "Russia: Moscow."

87. TASS statement of September 25, 1949, in S. G. Evans, *Russia and the Atomic Bomb* (London: British-Soviet Society, 1949), 2. For the original Russian, see *APSSSR* II.i.645.

88. See, for example, Igonin, *Atom v SSSR*, 59; Zhezherun, *Stroitel'stvo i pusk pervogo v Sovetskom Soiuze atomnogo reaktora*, 9; and Golovin, *Academician Igor Kurchatov*, 87.

89. Nikolai V. Sivachev and Nikolai N. Yakovlev, *Russia and the United States*, trans. Olga Adler Titelbaum (Chicago: University of Chicago Press, 1979), 228; El'iashevich, "Podgotovka i provedenie opticheskikh nabliudenii pervogo sovetskogo iadernogo vzryva," 163; and Gromyko and Ponomarev, *Istoriia vneshnei politiki SSSR*, 92.

90. "A Spur to Peace Seen in Moscow," *NYT*, September 26, 1949, 6.

91. Mastny, *The Cold War and Soviet Insecurity*, 64; Holloway, *Stalin and the Bomb*, 273.

92. A. M. Aleksandrov-Agentov, *Ot Kollontai do Gorbacheva: Vospominaniia diplomata, sovetnika A. A. Gromyko, pomoshchnika L. I. Brezhneva, Iu. V. Andropova, K. U. Chernenko i M. S. Gorbacheva* (Moscow: Mezhdunarodnye otnosheniia, 1994), 53.

93. Quoted in Eugene Rabinowitch, ed., *Minutes to Midnight: The International Control of Atomic Energy* (Chicago: Bulletin of the Atomic Scientists, 1950), 100. On the UN context for Vyshinskii's speech, see Nogee, *Soviet Policy Towards International Control of Atomic Energy*, 153. See also "Vishinsky Shuns Truman Report on Red A-Bomb," *LAT*, September 24, 1949, 1, 5.

94. Nataliia I. Egorova, "Stalin's Foreign Policy and the Cominform, 1947–53," in Gori and Pons, *The Soviet Union and Europe in the Cold War*, 200.

95. George W. Perkins to Dean Acheson, November 7, 1949, *FRUS* 1949, 5:39.

96. M. Rubinshtein, "Proval atomnoi diplomatii amerikanskikh imperialistov," *Bol'shevik*, no. 6 (March 1950): 46.

97. Kirk to Acheson, October 5, 1949, *FRUS* 1949, 5:664.

98. Vandenberg to his wife, September 23, 1949, Vandenberg, *Private Papers*, 518.

99. "Well, What Have the Russians Got?" *LAT*, September 24, 1949, A4.

SEVEN: THE YEAR OF JOE

1. Lewis Strauss to William L. Borden, December 10, 1952, Strauss AEC Papers, Box 29, Folder: "Fuchs, Klaus," 2; Strauss, *Men and Decisions*, 205; Kramish, *Atomic Energy in the Soviet Union*, 122–23.

2. Intelligence Memorandum No. 269, February 2, 1950, CIA Records, Box 111, Folder: "26514," 1.

3. Quoted in Lincoln Barnett, "J. Robert Oppenheimer," *Life*, October 10, 1949, 121.

4. CIA Weekly Briefing, September 30, 1949, CIA Records, Box 110, Folder: "7303," 5–6.

5. Bernard M. Baruch, statement released to newspapers, October 4, 1949, Baruch Papers, Unit VII, vol. 4, 1946–1950, 5. This is Baruch's first statement on nuclear matters after Joe-1, released in response to requests from media outlets.

6. David E. Lilienthal, entry of October 29, 1949, in *The Atomic Energy Years*, 580.

7. J. Robert Oppenheimer to David E. Lilienthal, September 26, 1949, Oppenheimer Papers, Case File, Box 46, File: "Lilienthal, David E.— FROM JROppenheimer"; and J. Robert Oppenheimer, "Atomic Weapons and American Policy," *BAS* 9, no. 6 (July 1953): 202–205. For the development of the policy of candor, see Chernus, "Operation Candor," 779–809.

8. Reuben, *The Atom Spy Hoax*, 151–52.

9. Assistant Secretary of State for European Affairs Perkins to Deputy Assistant Secretary of State for UN Affairs (Sandifer), September 23, 1949, *FRUS* 1949, 1:170–71.

10. Hartley Rowe to J. Robert Oppenheimer, December 3, 1949, Seaborg Papers, Atomic Energy Commission, Committees, General Advisory Committee, Box 614, Folder 8.

11. Dean, memorandum to Lilienthal, Pike, Strauss, Smyth, Wilson, and Volpe, September 23, 1949, AEC Records, Records of the Office of the Chairman, Office Files of David E. Lilienthal, Entry 1, Box 5, Folder: "Gordon Dean," 1.

12. Leffler, *A Preponderance of Power*, 373–74; Nichols, *The Road to Trin-*

ity, 268; Gaddis, *We Now Know*, 100; Samuel F. Wells, Jr., "The Origins of Massive Retaliation," *Political Science Quarterly* 96 (1981): 48.

13. Eugene P. Wigner, "Where Are We Going in Reactor Development?" *Journal of Metallurgy and Ceramics* 5 (June 1950): 401–402.

14. William W. Waymack to Robert Bacher, October 13, 1949, Lilienthal Papers, Series 3, Box 148a, Folder: "Waymack, William W. 1949." Lilienthal would later emphatically agree: David E. Lilienthal, *Change, Hope, and the Bomb* (Princeton: Princeton University Press, 1963), 116.

15. Edward Teller, *The Legacy of Hiroshima* (Garden City, NY: Doubleday, 1962), 214–15.

16. Chester I. Barnard, "Arms Race v. Control," *Scientific American* 181 (November 1949): 11. Such thoughts were echoed by Edward Cruetz of Carnegie Tech and Arthur Snell, director of physics at Oak Ridge, quoted in "What They Say: Some Comment on Red A-Bomb," *CDT*, September 24, 1949; 2; and Gordon Dean in "Plan," memorandum of September 30, 1949, in Anders, *Forging the Atomic Shield*, 40. See also Nogee, *Soviet Policy Towards International Control of Atomic Energy*, 151.

17. ORE 32-50, "The Effects of the Soviet Possession of Atomic Bombs on the Security of the United States," June 9, 1950, Enclosure A, in Warner, *The CIA Under Harry Truman*, 332. Brien McMahon expected a renewed "peace offensive": McMahon to Truman, September 28, 1949, PSF: General File, 1940–1953, Box 96, Folder: "Atomic Bomb."

18. David F. Cavers, "An Interim Plan for International Control of Atomic Energy," *BAS* 6, no. 1 (January 1950): 13–16.

19. Bernard M. Baruch, "International Control of Atomic Energy," *Air Affairs* 3, no. 2 (1950): 316. See also Frederick H. Osborn, "The United Nations Faces the New Situation," *BAS* 5, no. 10 (October 1949): 267.

20. Robert W. Frase and James R. Newman, "Who Prevents Atomic Agreement?" *New Republic* 122, no. 15 (April 10, 1950): 8.

21. Norris Bradbury, testimony of April 20, 1954, USAEC, *In the Matter of J. Robert Oppenheimer*, 486.

22. Condit, *The Joint Chiefs of Staff*, 2:281.

23. Kuhns, *Assessing the Soviet Threat*, 27; Lawrence Freedman, *U.S. Intelligence and the Soviet Strategic Threat*, 2d ed. (Princeton: Princeton University Press, 1986 [1977]), 31; and Barnes, "The Secret Cold War," *Historical Journal* 25 (1982): 653–54.

24. Maddrell, *Spying on Science*, 113, 219–10; André Steiner, "The Return of German 'Specialists' from the Soviet Union to the German Democratic Republic: Integration and Impact," in Matthias Judt and Burghard Ciesla, eds., *Technology Transfer out of Germany After 1945* (Amsterdam: Harwood Academic, 1996), 119–30; Henry S. Lowenhaupt, "On the Soviet Nuclear Scent," *Studies in Intelligence* 11, no. 4 (Fall 1967): 13–29; and Bukharin, "US Atomic Energy Intelligence Against the Soviet Target, 1945–1970," 662. On "cooling off," see Steenbeck, *Impulse und Wirkungen*, 308.

25. Stuart Symington to Louis Johnson (November 1949), PSF: Subject File, 1940–1953, National Security Council—Atomic File, Box 175, Folder: "Atomic Energy: Russia."

26. Jack H. Nunn, *The Soviet First Strike Threat: The U.S. Perspective* (New York: Praeger, 1982), 81; Richard K. Betts, *Nuclear Blackmail and Nuclear Balance* (Washington, D.C.: Brookings Institution, 1987), 147.

27. Intelligence Memorandum No. 269, February 2, 1950, CIA Records, Box 111, Folder: "26514," 6.

28. Leffler, *A Preponderance of Power*, 332, 440. See also Prados, *The Soviet Estimate*, 21–23.

29. ORE 32–50, "The Effects of the Soviet Possession of Atomic Bombs on the Security of the United States," June 9, 1950, Enclosure A, in Warner, *The CIA Under Harry Truman*, 413n1.

30. Thomas K. Finletter, *Power and Policy: U.S. Foreign Policy and Military Power in the Hydrogen Age* (New York: Harcourt, 1954), 6.

31. Beria to Stalin, March 26, 1951, APSSSR II.v.665; Holloway, *Stalin and the Bomb*, 322. For figures on the actual size of the Soviet stockpile, see Robert S. Norris and William M. Arkin, "Estimated U.S. and Soviet/Russian Nuclear Stockpiles, 1945–94," *BAS* 50, no. 6 (November/December 1994): 58–59; and Pavel Podvig, ed., *Russian Strategic Nuclear Forces* (Cambridge, MA: MIT Press, 2001), 2.

32. William D. Jackson, "The Soviets and Strategic Arms: Toward an Evaluation of the Record," *Political Science Quarterly* 94 (1979): 245.

33. Gordon Dean, *Report on the Atom: What You Should Know About the Atomic Energy Program of the United States* (New York: Knopf, 1953), 307.

34. Richelson, *American Espionage and the Soviet Target*, 118–20; Richelson, *Spying on the Bomb*, 95.

35. David Lilienthal to Admiral Sidney Souers, November 4, 1949, PSF:

Subject File, 1940–1953, National Security Council—Atomic File, Box 173, Folder: "Atomic Bomb: Attack."

36. Andrew D. Grossman, "Atomic Fantasies and Make-Believe War: The American State, Social Control, and Civil Defense Planning, 1946–1952," *Political Power and Social Theory* 9 (1995): 91–120.

37. Ross, *American War Plans*, 61; Joseph, "Commitments and Capabilities," 238; Samuel R. Williamson, Jr., and Steven L. Rearden, *The Origins of U.S. Nuclear Strategy, 1945–1953* (New York: St. Martin's Press, 1993), 101, 189; Robert Jervis, *The Meaning of the Nuclear Revolution: Statecraft and the Prospect of Armageddon* (Ithaca: Cornell University Press, 1989), 47.

38. W. Stuart Symington to Louis Johnson, November 18, 1949, in Merrill, *Documentary History of the Truman Presidency*, 21:338.

39. Ross, *American War Plans*, 139; Borowski, *A Hollow Threat*, 4–5.

40. Rosenberg, "The Origins of Overkill," 3–71.

41. Kahn, *On Thermonuclear War*, ix. On Brodie, see Fred Kaplan, *The Wizards of Armageddon* (Palo Alto: Stanford University Press, 1991 [1983]), 26.

42. Early designs for a thermonuclear bomb (1942 to roughly 1951) assumed that the tremendous heat released by the fission bomb would serve as the trigger for the fusion reaction. The essence of the Teller-Ulam design—the eventual American solution to the trigger problem—was the recognition that radiation pressure, not heat, could be used to ignite the thermonuclear fuel. I thank David Kaiser for underscoring this point.

43. Stanislaw M. Ulam, *Adventures of a Mathematician* (New York: Scribner's, 1976), 209.

44. Oppenheimer, testimony of April 12, 1954, USAEC, *In the Matter of J. Robert Oppenheimer*, 18. All of the primary and secondary literature on the hydrogen bomb points to this linkage: Priscilla J. McMillan, *The Ruin of J. Robert Oppenheimer and the Birth of the Modern Arms Race* (New York: Viking, 2005); Richard Rhodes, *Dark Sun: The Making of the Hydrogen Bomb* (New York: Simon & Schuster, 1995); Barton J. Bernstein, "Truman and the H-bomb," *BAS* 40, no. 3 (March 1984): 12–18; Warner R. Schilling, "The H-Bomb Decision: How to Decide Without Actually Choosing," *Political Science Quarterly* 76 (1961): 24–46; Gordon Arneson, "The H-Bomb Decision," *Foreign Service Journal* (May 1969): 27–29; Truman, *Years of Trial and Hope*, 308; Strauss, *Men and Decisions*, 207; Herbert F. York, *The Advisors: Oppenheimer,*

Teller, and the Superbomb (Palo Alto: Stanford University Press, 1989 [1976]); Shepley and Blair, *The Hydrogen Bomb*; Norman Moss, *Men Who Play God: The Story of the H-Bomb and How the World Came to Live with It* (New York: Harper, 1968); and Alvarez, *Alvarez*, 169.

45. Teller, *Memoirs*, 279. Teller had offered the same phrasing in his testimony of April 28, 1954, USAEC, *In the Matter of J. Robert Oppenheimer*, 714.

46. Oppenheimer, testimony of April 13, 1954, USAEC, *In the Matter of J. Robert Oppenheimer*, 80. See also J. Robert Oppenheimer to George F. Kennan, November 17, 1949, Rabi Papers, Miscellany, Box 89, Folder 5.

47. See the helpful discussion in Peter L. Galison and Barton J. Bernstein, "In Any Light: Scientists and the Decision to Build the Superbomb, 1942–1954," *Historical Studies in the Physical Sciences* 19 (1989): 267–347; and Barton J. Bernstein, "Crossing the Rubicon: A Missed Opportunity to Stop the H-Bomb?" *International Security* 14 (1989): 132–60.

48. Donovan, *Tumultuous Years*, 153; "So It Was Plutonium?" *Time* (December 5, 1949), 50; "New A-Bomb Has 6 Times Power of 1st," *WP*, November 18, 1949, 1.

49. Brien McMahon to Truman, November 21, 1949, Rabi Papers, Columbia University Office File, Box 16, Folder 3, 6.

50. Lilienthal, entry of November 6, 1949, *The Atomic Energy Years*, 591.

51. John Lewis Gaddis, *The Long Peace: Inquiries into the History of the Cold War* (New York: Oxford University Press, 1987), 113. It took substantially longer for the military to incorporate hydrogen bombs into their actual war strategy. See the discussion in David Alan Rosenberg, "American Atomic Strategy and the Hydrogen Bomb Decision," *Journal of American History* 66 (1979): 62–87.

52. Quoted in Rhodes, *Dark Sun*, 407.

53. Audrey Kurth Cronin, "East-West Negotiations over Austria in 1949: Turning Point in the Cold War," *Journal of Contemporary History* 24 (1989): 125; Shulman, *Stalin's Foreign Policy Reappraised*, 125.

54. "Report by the Joint Intelligence Committee to the Joint Chiefs of Staff on Implications of Soviet Possession of Atomic Weapons," February 9, 1950, JCS Records, Geographical Files, Box 88, File: "CCS 4781.6 USSR *(11-8-49) S.1," 2, 5. See the discussion in Ian Clark and Nicholas J. Wheeler, *The British Origins of Nuclear Strategy, 1945–1955* (New York: Oxford University Press, 1989), 11.

55. Charles Bohlen to George F. Kennan, October 6, 1949, Kennan Papers, Box 28, Folder 10, 4.

56. Quoted in Beisner, *Dean Acheson*, 159. See also Lawrence S. Kaplan, *A Community of Interests: NATO and the Military Assistance Program, 1948–1951* (Washington, D.C.: Office of the Secretary of Defense, Historical Office, 1980), 47; Shulman, *Stalin's Foreign Policy Reappraised*, 104; and McLellan, *Dean Acheson*, 167.

57. Trachtenberg, *A Constructed Peace*, 96; Bert Cochran, *Harry Truman and the Crisis Presidency* (New York: Funk & Wagnalls, 1973), 288.

58. Truman to Brien McMahon, October 11, 1949, PSF: General File, 1940–1953, Box 96, Folder: "Atomic Bomb."

59. John Prados, *Keepers of the Keys: A History of the National Security Council from Truman to Bush* (New York: Morrow, 1991), 27–31; Sara L. Sale, *The Shaping of Containment: Harry S. Truman, the National Security Council, and the Cold War* (Saint James, NY: Brandywine Press, 1998); Hamby, *Man of the People*, 311; Anna Kasten Nelson, "President Truman and the Evolution of the National Security Council," *Journal of American History* 72 (1985): 360–78; Alfred D. Sanders, "Truman and the National Security Council: 1945–1947," *Journal of American History* 59 (1972): 369–88; and Thomas H. Etzold, "American Organization for National Security," in Etzold and John Lewis Gaddis, eds., *Containment: Documents on American Policy and Strategy, 1945–1950* (New York: Columbia University Press, 1978), 19.

60. Samuel F. Wells, Jr., "Sounding the Tocsin: NSC 68 and the Soviet Threat," *International Security* 4 (1979): 116–58; Paul Y. Hammond, "NSC-68: Prologue to Rearmament," in Schilling, Hammond, and Snyder, *Strategy, Politics, and Defense Budgets*, 285; Marc Trachtenberg, "A 'Wasting Asset': American Strategy and the Shifting Nuclear Balance, 1949–1954," *International Security* 13 (1988–1989): 5–49; and Brian Easlea, *Fathering the Unthinkable: Masculinity, Scientists, and the Nuclear Arms Race* (London: Pluto Press, 1983), 8.

61. Strobe Talbott, *The Master of the Game: Paul Nitze and the Nuclear Peace* (New York: Knopf, 1988), 50; David Callahan, *Dangerous Capabilities: Paul Nitze and the Cold War* (New York: Harper, 1990), 60.

62. George F. Kennan, *Memoirs, 1925–1950* (New York: Pantheon, 1967), 426, 465–66. See also Gaddis, *Strategies of Containment*, 90; Miscamble, *George F. Kennan*, 292; Phillip A. Karber and Jerald A. Combs, "The United States, NATO, and the Soviet Threat to Western Europe: Military Estimates and Policy Options, 1945–1963," *Diplomatic History* 22 (1998): 400–429; Jerald A. Combs, "The Compromise That Never Was: George Kennan, Paul Nitze, and the Issue of Conventional Deterrence in Europe, 1949–1952," *Diplomatic History* 15 (1991):

361–86; and Mayers, *George Kennan and the Dilemmas of US Foreign Policy*, 303.

63. Nitze in John Lewis Gaddis and Paul Nitze, "NSC 68 and the Soviet Threat Reconsidered," *International Security* 4 (1980): 172–73.

64. Paul H. Nitze, "The Grand Strategy of NSC-68," in S. Nelson Drew, ed., *NSC-68: Forging the Strategy of Containment* (Washington, D.C.: National Defense University, 1996 [1994]), 9–10.

65. Mastny, "Stalin and the Militarization of the Cold War," 125–26; Raymond L. Garthoff, *Assessing the Adversary: Estimates by the Eisenhower Administration of Soviet Intentions and Capabilities* (Washington, D.C.: Brookings Institution, 1991), 48–49.

66. Marc Trachtenberg, *History and Strategy* (Princeton: Princeton University Press, 1991), chap. 4; Kaplan, *A Community of Interests*, 35.

67. Botti, *The Long Wait*, 47.

68. Gowing, *Independence and Deterrence*, 1:318; H. Montgomery Hyde, *The Atom Bomb Spies* (New York: Atheneum, 1980), 174; and Francis Duncan, "Atomic Energy and Anglo-American Relations, 1946–1954," *Orbis* 12 (1969): 1199.

69. Seaborg, *Journal*, vol. 3: January 1, 1949–December 31, 1949, Seaborg Papers, Box 17, entry for September 22, 1949, 253. On Truman's initiative, see Truman, *Memoirs*, 2:303; Donovan, *Tumultuous Years*, 100; and Paul, *Nuclear Rivals*, 157.

70. Gowing, *Independence and Deterrence*, 2:123–24.

71. Brian Cathcart, *Test of Greatness: Britain's Struggle for the Atom Bomb* (London: John Murray, 1994), 112.

72. Robert Lamphere to Meredith Gardner, September 26, 1949, in Benson and Warner, *Venona*, 14; Moss, *Klaus Fuchs*, 130; Haynes and Klehr, *Early Cold War Spies*, 153.

73. Chikov, *Razvedchiki-Nelegaly*, 320.

74. McMillan, *The Ruin of J. Robert Oppenheimer*, 2; Lamphere and Shachtman, *The FBI-KGB War*, 136; Leffler, *A Preponderance of Power*, 313; and Athan Theoharis, "The Rhetoric of Politics: Foreign Policy, Internal Security, and Domestic Politics in the Truman Era, 1945–1950," in Bernstein, *Politics and Policies of the Truman Administration*, 196–241. None of this is to deny that American anticommunism was well established by 1947, with Truman's elaborate loyalty-security program, and certainly by early 1949—after the Chambers demarche to Nixon's committee—with the loyalty-oath requirements instituted for AEC graduate fellowships. This history is recounted in Wang, *American Science in an Age of Anxiety*, 252; and Ellen Schrecker,

Many Are the Crimes: McCarthyism in America (Boston: Little, Brown, 1998).

75. John Simpson, *The Independent Nuclear State: The United States, Britain, and the Military Atom*, 2d ed. (New York: St. Martin's Press, 1986 [1983]), xvii; Francis Williams, ed., *Twilight of Empire: Memoirs of Prime Minister Clement Attlee* (New York: A. S. Barnes, 1962 [1960]), 118.

76. Botti, *The Long Wait*, 2. See also Acheson, *Present at the Creation*, 321; Simpson, *The Independent Nuclear State*, 56; Gaddis, "Intelligence, Espionage, and Cold War Origins," 207; Smith, *Dean Acheson*, 148–49; Oliver Pilat, *The Atom Spies* (New York: Putnam, 1952), 182; Simone Turchetti, "Atomic Secrets and Governmental Lies: Nuclear Science, Politics and Security in the Pontecorvo Case," *British Journal for the History of Science* 36 (2003): 389–415; and Wayne Reynolds, "Rethinking the Joint Project: Australia's Bid for Nuclear Weapons, 1945–1960," *Historical Journal* 41 (1998): 864–65. On Pontecorvo, see Goldschmidt, *Atomic Rivals*, 348–49.

77. Kaiser, "The Atomic Secret in Red Hands?" 38; Ranelagh, *The Agency*, 144.

78. Roger M. Anders, "The Rosenberg Case Revisited: The Greenglass Testimony and the Protection of Atomic Secrets," *American Historical Review* 83 (1978): 388–400.

79. Eugene Rabinowitch, "Atomic Weapons and the Korean War," *BAS* 6, no. 7 (July 1950): 194. See also Leffler, *A Preponderance of Power*, 510.

80. Gordon H. Chang, *Friends and Enemies: The United States, China, and the Soviet Union, 1948–1972* (Palo Alto: Stanford University Press, 1990), 21.

81. Sandifer, memorandum of conversation with Dean Rusk, September 23, 1949, *FRUS* 1949, 1:172.

82. Zubok and Pleshakov, *Inside the Kremlin's Cold War*, 150; Ulam, *The Rivals*, 96; Steven J. Zaloga, *The Kremlin's Nuclear Sword: The Rise and Fall of Russia's Strategic Nuclear Forces, 1945–2000* (Washington, D.C.: Smithsonian Institution Press, 2002), 10; Zubok, "Stalin and the Nuclear Age," 57; and Haynes and Klehr, *Venona*, 11.

83. Sergei N. Goncharov, John W. Lewis, and Xue Litai, *Uncertain Partners: Stalin, Mao, and the Korean War* (Palo Alto: Stanford University Press, 1993), 336n174.

84. Ian Clark, *Limited Nuclear War: Political Theory and War Conventions* (Princeton: Princeton University Press, 1982), 149; Joseph, "Commitments and Capabilities," 261–62.

85. Rosemary J. Foot, "Nuclear Coercion and the Ending of the Korean Conflict," *International Security* 13, no. 3 (Winter 1988–1989): 92–112; Sean L. Malloy, "A 'Paper Tiger'? Nuclear Weapons, Atomic Diplomacy, and the Korean War," *New England Journal of History* 60, nos. 1–3 (Fall 2003–Spring 2004): 227–52; and Roger Dingman, "Atomic Diplomacy During the Korean War," *International Security* 13 (Winter 1988–1989): 50–91.

86. Gaddis, *Strategies of Containment*, 113; Wells, "Sounding the Tocsin," 139; Joseph, "Commitments and Capabilities," 5.

87. Bruce Parrott, *Politics and Technology in the Soviet Union* (Cambridge, MA: MIT Press, 1983), 96–97; Wolfe, *Soviet Power and Europe*, 26.

EPILOGUE: TRACES AND TAILINGS

1. James B. Conant to J. Robert Oppenheimer, January 15, 1952, Oppenheimer Papers, Case File, Box 27, File: "Conant, James B. (correspondence)," 2.

2. Natural Resources Defense Council, "Table of Global Nuclear Weapons Stockpiles, 1945–2002," www.nrdc.org/nuclear/nudb/datab19 .asp.

3. Lilienthal, *Change, Hope, and the Bomb*, 14.

4. Holloway, *Stalin and the Bomb*, 329.

5. H. W. Brands, "The Age of Vulnerability: Eisenhower and the National Insecurity State," *American Historical Review* 94 (1989): 963–89.

6. Henry A. Kissinger, *Nuclear Weapons and Foreign Policy* (New York: Council on Foreign Relations, 1957), 13.

7. Betts, *Nuclear Blackmail and Nuclear Balance*, 22 (United States) and 132 (Soviet Union); Raymond L. Garthoff, *Deterrence and the Revolution in Soviet Military Doctrine* (Washington, D.C.: Brookings Institution, 1990). On the limited utility of the atomic monopoly, see Gaddis, *The Long Peace*, chap. 5. On arguments for the existence of a nuclear taboo, see Nina Tannenwald, "The Nuclear Taboo: The United States and the Normative Basis of Nuclear Non-Use," *International Organization* 53 (1999): 433–68.

8. V. P. Vizgin, "Fenomen 'kul'ta atoma' v SSSR (1950–1960-e gg.)," in Vizgin, *Istoriia sovetskogo atomnogo proekta*, 413–88; Josephson, *Red Atom*; and Josephson, "Atomic-Powered Communism: Nuclear Culture in the Postwar USSR," *Slavic Review* 55 (1996): 297–324.

9. Raymond L. Garthoff, *Soviet Military Policy: A Historical Analysis* (New York: Praeger, 1966); Garthoff, *The Soviet Image of Future War* (Washington, D.C.: Public Affairs Press, 1959), 9; Spencer R. Weart, *Nuclear*

Fear: A History of Images (Cambridge, MA: Harvard University Press, 1988), 136.

10. Larin, *Akademik atomnykh del*, 36.

11. Josephson, *Red Atom*, 246; Podvig, *Russian Strategic Nuclear Forces*, 439.

12. V. I. Bulatov, *200 iadernykh poligonov SSSR: Geografiia radiatsionnykh katastrof i zagriaznenii* (Novosibirsk: TsERIS, 1993), 13–14; Robert S. Norris and William M. Arkin, "Known Nuclear Tests Worldwide, 1945–1995," *BAS* 52 (May/June 1996): 61–63. For annual breakdowns, see Nikolai N. Egorov, Vladimir M. Novikov, Frank L. Parker, and Victor K. Popov, eds., *The Radiation Legacy of the Soviet Nuclear Complex: An Analytical Overview* (London: Earthscan Publications, 2000), 184.

13. Richelson, *Spying on the Bomb*, 96; Holloway, *Stalin and the Bomb*, 219.

14. Frank C. Lakin to AEC, October 1, 1951, Smyth Papers, Series III, Box 4, Folder: "AIC—Russian Atomic Explosions."

15. Olav Riste, *The Norwegian Intelligence Service, 1945–1970* (Portland, OR: Frank Cass, 1999), 192–93; T. A. Heppenheimer, "How to Detect an Atomic Bomb," *Invention & Technology* (Spring 2006): 51.

16. Henry DeWolf Smyth to Mr. Salisbury, October 3, 1951, Smyth Papers, Series III, Box 4, Folder: "AIC—Russian Atomic Explosions."

17. George M. Elsey, memo for file, October 5, 1951, Elsey Papers, Box 113, Folder: "Atomic Bomb, Russian."

18. Stalin, "Otvet korrespondentom 'Pravdy,'" October 6, 1951, in *Sochineniia* 3:183. See also Taubman, *Stalin's American Policy*, 209.

19. Lewis L. Strauss, press release, August 20, 1953, Smyth Papers, Series III, Box 4, Folder: "AIC—Russian Atomic Explosions." On AEC policy, see Kramish, *Atomic Energy in the Soviet Union*, 123–24; and Strauss, *Men and Decisions*, 251.

20. Robert Armory, Jr., to Executive Secretary of NSC, October 19, 1953, NSC Records, Entry 3, "P" Papers, Box 1, File: "P45."

21. Roy B. Snapp to Executive Secretary of NSC, October 28, 1953, NSC Records, Entry 3, "P" Papers, Box 1, File: "P45"; Lewis Strauss, memorandum for file, August 19, 1953, Strauss AEC Papers, Box 68, Folder: "Monitoring Soviet Tests."

22. Lewis Strauss to Eisenhower (draft), October 25, 1954, Strauss AEC Papers, Box 106, Folder: "Soviet Tests."

23. A. P. Vasil'ev, "Sistema dal'nego obnaruzheniia iadernykh vzryvov i sovetskii atomnyi proekt," in Vizgin, *Istoriia sovetskogo atomnogo*

proekta, 237–78; Yuli Khariton, Viktor Adamskii, and Yuri Smirnov, "The Way It Was," *BAS* 52, no. 6 (November–December 1996): 54; Richelson, *Sword and Shield*, 110–11.

24. Daniel Hirsch and William G. Mathews, "The H-Bomb: Who Really Gave Away the Secret?" *BAS* (January/February 1990): 22–30.

25. Arnold, *Britain and the H-Bomb*, 223; Lars-Erik De Geer, "The Radioactive Signature of the Hydrogen Bomb," *Science & Global Security* 2 (1991): 351–63.

26. Holloway, *Stalin and the Bomb*, 312.

27. Lapp, *Atoms and People*, 140.

28. Robin Ranger, *Arms and Politics, 1958–1978: Arms Control in a Changing Political Context* (Toronto: Macmillan of Canada, 1979).

29. Herbert M. Clark, "The Occurrence of an Unusually High-Level Radioactive Rainout in the Area of Troy, N.Y.," *Science*, n.s., 119, no. 3097 (May 7, 1954): 619–22. See also David W. Dorn, "Mike Results—Implications for Spontaneous Fission," *Physical Review* 126 (April 15, 1962): 693–97; and Norman J. Holter and Wilford R. Glasscock, "Tracing Nuclear Explosions," *Nucleonics* (August 1952): 10–13.

30. Barton C. Hacker, *Elements of Controversy: The Atomic Energy Commission and Radiation Safety in Nuclear Weapons Testing, 1947–1974* (Berkeley: University of California Press, 1994); Ernest J. Sternglass, *Secret Fallout: Low-Level Radiation from Hiroshima to Three Mile Island* (New York: McGraw-Hill, 1981 [1972]).

31. The interested reader should turn to United Nations Department for Disarmament Affairs, *The United Nations and Disarmament: 1945–1985* (New York: United Nations, 1985), 59–60; and Greene, *Eisenhower, Science Advice, and the Nuclear Test-Ban Debate*.

32. Special National Intelligence Estimate, "Feasibility and Likelihood of Soviet Evasion of a Nuclear Test Moratorium," SNIE 11-7-57, December 10, 1957, in Scott A. Koch, ed., *Selected Estimates on the Soviet Union, 1950–1959* (Washington, D.C.: History Staff, Center for the Study of Intelligence, CIA, 1993), 264.

33. Samuel Glasstone, ed., *The Effects of Nuclear Weapons*, rev. ed. (Washington, D.C.: USAEC, 1962), Appendix C. For a simplified discussion, see Jay Orear, "Detection of Nuclear Weapons Testing," *BAS* 14, no. 3 (March 1958): 98–101. See also Richelson, *Spying on the Bomb*, 112; Ziegler and Jacobson, *Spying Without Spies*, 217; P. K. Kuroda and J. Nix, "Strontium-90 Fallout from the 1961 Soviet Nuclear Detonation," *Science*, n.s., 137, no. 3534 (September 21, 1962): 991–92; and

Bukharin, "US Atomic Energy Intelligence Against the Soviet Target, 1945–1970," 666–72.

34. V. V. Shustov, *Sovetskii soiuz i problema prekrashcheniia ispytaniia iadernogo oruzhiia* (Moscow: Atomizdat, 1977), 68–73.

35. Frank Costigliola, *France and the United States: The Cold Alliance Since World War II* (New York: Twayne Publishers, 1992), 103.

36. Bundy, *Danger and Survival*, 149; Mitchell Reiss, *Bridled Ambition: Why Countries Constrain Their Nuclear Capabilities* (Washington, D.C.: Woodrow Wilson Center Press, 1995).

37. Chang, *Friends and Enemies*, 141; William R. Harris, "Chinese Nuclear Doctrine: The Decade Prior to Weapons Development (1945–1955)," *China Quarterly* 21 (Jan.–Mar. 1965): 87–95; William Burr and Jeffrey T. Richelson, "Whether to 'Strangle the Baby in the Cradle': The United States and the Chinese Nuclear Program, 1960–64," *International Security* 25 (Winter 2000–2001): 54–99; Shu Gang Zhang, "Between 'Paper' and 'Real Tigers': Mao's View of Nuclear Weapons," in Gaddis, *Cold War Statesmen Confront the Bomb*, 194–215; Mark A. Ryan, *Chinese Attitudes Toward Nuclear Weapons: China and the United States During the Korean War* (Armonk, NY: M. E. Sharpe, 1989).

38. Gloria Duffy, *Soviet Nuclear Energy: Domestic and International Policies* (Santa Monica, CA: Rand, 1979), 2–3; Michael S. Minor, "China's Nuclear Development Program," *Asian Survey* 16 (1976): 571–79.

39. Lewis and Litai, *China Builds the Bomb*.

40. Bertrand Goldschmidt, "A Historical Survey of Nonproliferation Policies," *International Security* 2 (1977): 72–73.

41. Barbara Rose Johnson, ed., *Half-Lives and Half-Truths: Confronting the Radioactive Legacies of the Cold War* (Santa Fe: School for Advanced Research Press, 2007).

42. Cochran and Norris, "A First Look at the Soviet Bomb Complex," 25–31.

43. John M. Whiteley, "The Compelling Realities of Mayak," in Russell J. Dalton, Paula Garb, Nicholas P. Lovrich, John C. Pierce, and John M. Whiteley, *Critical Masses: Citizens, Nuclear Weapons Production, and Environmental Destruction in the United States and Russia* (Cambridge, MA: MIT Press, 1999), 59–96; Vladislav Larin, *Kombinat "Maiak"— problema na veka*, 2d ed. (Moscow: KMK, 2001); Medvedev, *Nuclear Disaster in the Urals*; Bulatov, *200 iadernykh poligonov SSSR*; Egorov et al., *The Radiation Legacy of the Soviet Nuclear Complex*; Oleg

Bukharin, "The Future of Russia's Plutonium Cities," *International Security* 21 (1997): 126–58; Don J. Bradley, Clyde W. Frank, and Yevgeny Mikerin, "Nuclear Contamination from Weapons Complexes in the Former Soviet Union and the United States," *Physics Today* (April 1996): 40–45; Arjun Makhijani, Howard Hu, and Katherine Yih, eds., *Nuclear Wastelands: A Global Guide to Nuclear Weapons Production and Its Health and Environmental Effects* (Cambridge, MA: MIT Press, 1995); D. J. Peterson, *Troubled Lands: The Legacy of Soviet Environmental Destruction* (Boulder, CO: Westview Press, 1993), 144–50.

44. Peterson, *Troubled Lands*, 202–205.

SELECTED SOURCES

ARCHIVAL (UNITED STATES)

American Philosophical Society, Manuscripts Division, Philadelphia
    Edward U. Condon Papers (B:C752)
    Henry DeWolf Smyth Papers (MS Coll. 15)
    Stanislaw M. Ulam Papers (MS Coll. 54)
California Institute of Technology Archives, Pasadena
    Robert F. Bacher, Interview by Mary Terrall, June–August 1981, February
        1983, Oral History Project
Harry S. Truman Presidential Museum and Library, Independence, Missouri
    Dean G. Acheson Papers, Political and Government Files, 1933–1971
    R. Gordon Arneson Papers
    Clark M. Clifford Papers
    Matthew J. Connelly Papers
    George McKee Elsey Papers
    Paul H. Nitze, Oral History Interview by Richard D. McKinzie, June 11
        and 17, 1975
    Frederick H. Osborn Papers
    OF—Official File
    PSF—President's Secretary's Files
    Samuel I. Rosenman Papers
    Charles G. Ross Papers
    John W. Snyder Papers
    Sidney W. Souers Papers
    Harry H. Vaughan Papers
    WHCF—White House Confidential File

Herbert Hoover Presidential Library, West Branch, Iowa
  Bourke B. Hickenlooper Papers
  Lewis L. Strauss Papers, Atomic Energy Commission (AEC) Series
Library of Congress, Manuscripts Division, Washington, D.C.
  Henry H. Arnold Papers
  Vannevar Bush Papers
  W. Averell Harriman Papers
  Curtis E. LeMay Papers
  Brien McMahon Papers
  J. Robert Oppenheimer Papers
  Isidor Isaac Rabi Papers
  Glenn Theodore Seaborg Papers
  Carl A. Spaatz Papers
  Hoyt S. Vandenberg Papers
National Archives and Records Administration, College Park, Maryland
  Atomic Energy Commission Records (RG 326)
  Bush-Conant Files Relating to the Development of the Atomic Bomb,
    1940–1945, Records of the Office of Scientific Research and Develop-
    ment (RG 227)
  Central Intelligence Agency Records (RG 263)
  Defense Threat Reduction Agency Papers (RG 374)
  Leslie R. Groves Papers (RG 200)
  Harrison-Bundy Files Relating to the Development of the Atomic Bomb,
    Records of the Office of the Chief of Engineers (RG 77), Microfilm
    Publication M1109
  National Security Council Records (RG 273)
  State-Army-Navy–Air Force Coordinating Committee Records (RG 334)
    (Interservice Agencies)
  Top Secret Files—Correspondence ("Top Secret") of the Manhattan
    Engineer District, 1942–1946, Records of the Office of the Chief of
    Engineers, Record of the Office of the Commanding General, Man-
    hattan Project (RG 77), Microfilm Publication M1109
  United States Joint Chiefs of Staff Records (RG 218)
Nuclear Testing Archive, Las Vegas
Seeley G. Mudd Manuscript Library, Princeton University
  Bernard M. Baruch Papers (MC 006)
  James Vincent Forrestal Papers (MC 051)
  James Vincent Forrestal Diaries (MC 052)
  George F. Kennan Papers (MC 076)

David Lawrence Papers (MC 084)

David E. Lilienthal Papers (MC 148)

Yale University Library, New Haven, Connecticut

Henry Lewis Stimson Diaries, Microform edition, Manuscripts and Archives

PUBLISHED ARCHIVAL DOCUMENT COLLECTIONS (UNITED STATES AND SOVIET UNION)

APSSSR—Riabev, L. D., ed., *Atomnyi proekt SSSR: Dokumenty i materialy.* Moscow: Nauka/Fizmatlit, 1998–. [Cited as *APSSSR* volume.part.page.]

Benson, Robert Louis, and Michael Warner, eds. *Venona: Soviet Espionage and the American Response, 1939–1957.* Washington, D.C.: National Security Agency and Central Intelligence Agency, 1996.

FRUS—United States Department of State, *Foreign Relations of the United States.* Washington, D.C.: GPO, 1932–. [Cited as *FRUS* year, volume: page.]

Gubarev, V. S. *Belyi arkhipelag Stalina: Dokumental'noe povestvovanie o sozdanii iadernoi bomby, osnovannoe na rassekrechennykh materialakh "Atomnogo proekta SSSR."* Moscow: Molodaia gvardiia, 2004.

Koch, Scott A., ed. *Selected Estimates on the Soviet Union, 1950–1959.* Washington, D.C.: History Staff, Center for the Study of Intelligence, CIA, 1993.

Kuhns, Woodrow J., ed. *Assessing the Soviet Threat: The Early Cold War Years.* Washington, D.C.: Center for the Study of Intelligence, CIA, 1997.

Merrill, Dennis, ed. *Documentary History of the Truman Presidency. Volume 21: The Development of an Atomic Weapons Program Following World War II.* Bethesda: University Publications of America, 1998.

Negin, E. A., et al. *Sovetskii atomnyi proekt: Konets atomnoi monopolii. Kak eto bylo . . .* Nizhnii Novgorod/Arzamas-16: Izd. Nizhnii Novgorod, 1995.

Vizgin, V. P., ed. *Istoriia sovetskogo atomnogo proekta: Dokumenty, vospominaniia, issledovaniia,* vyp. 2. St. Petersburg: Izd. Russkogo khristianskogo gumanitarnogo instituta, 2002.

JOURNALS (AND ABBREVIATIONS)

Bulletin of the Atomic Scientists (BAS)

Chicago Daily Tribune (CDT)

Christian Science Monitor (CSM)

Los Angeles Times (LAT)

New York Times (NYT)

Voprosy Istorii Estestvoznaniia i Tekhniki (VIET)

Washington Post (WP)

ACKNOWLEDGMENTS

The atomic bomb is perhaps no longer, as it was during the cold war, the ubiquitous subject of politics and culture, yet it still proves remarkably persistent in periodically forcing itself upon the world's attention. No matter how distracted we become, something nuclear emerges to grab the headlines—a North Korean nuclear test, weapons inspectors in Iraq, revelations about a new Soviet atomic spy at Los Alamos during World War II. In the last several years, while researching this book in an attempt to excavate the early days of this nuclear omnipresence, I have drawn on many strands of excellent scholarship in a broad variety of fields: American political and military history, Soviet history, diplomatic history, the history of the physical sciences, nuclear strategy, intelligence studies, postwar European history, and studies of science policy. These debts are poorly discharged in the scholarly apparatus to this volume, and I want to acknowledge them up front.

That said, I have the pleasure of being more explicit and comprehensive in expressing my heartfelt gratitude to the numerous people whose support, insights, suggestions, and criticisms have made this book possible. My deepest appreciation goes to Lorraine Daston, who generously sheltered me for a year in her group at the Max Planck Institute for the History of Science in Berlin. Raine not only granted me space and freedom to write the manuscript but also shared her astute observations on multiple aspects of the project (as well as kindly reading the entire manuscript). This project would not have emerged in the form it has without her support. Similarly, I thank the History Department at Princeton University for allowing me the time to take advantage of her offer for a friendly home in Germany.

Several archives and libraries allowed me access to the materials that have made this exploration possible. I thank the staff at the Seeley G. Mudd Manuscript Library at Princeton, the American Philosophical Society Library, the National Archives and Records Administration at College Park, Maryland, the Manuscripts Division at the Library of Congress, and especially everyone at the Harry S. Truman Presidential Museum and Library who assisted me greatly during a bitterly cold visit in January 2007. Matthew Schaefer at the Herbert Hoover Presidential Library and the staffs at the Yale University Library and the Caltech Archives generously allowed me to use their materials remotely by sending them to Princeton, for which I am very grateful. A special thanks goes to the Article Express office at the Princeton University Library, who stoically put up with my egregious impositions on their services to obtain materials both near and far relating to the history of nuclear weapons. Their heroic efforts have not gone unappreciated.

Many colleagues and friends have read all or part of the manuscript and offered sometimes bracing criticisms that have tremendously improved the final product. My thanks to Daniel Andersson, Charlotte Bigg, Angela Creager, Loren Graham, Ludmila Hyman, David Kaiser, Philip Kitcher, Ursula Klein, John Krige, Daryn Lehoux, Zia Mian, Erika Milam, Gregg Mitman, Tania Munz, Catherine Nisbett, Gwen Ottinger, Skúli Sigurdsson, Matthew Stanley, Annette Vogt, Robin Wasserman, and Alex Wellerstein. Alex also generously shared with me some materials he had located in his own research on nuclear history, especially a very interesting document from the Nuclear Testing Archive in Las Vegas, Nevada. Finally, my deep gratitude to David Holloway, the preeminent Western historian of the Soviet nuclear project, for his helpful comments and guidance on chapters 3 and 4 of this book. His work has been a touchstone throughout.

Don Lamn was indispensible in encouraging this project, providing valuable comments on all stages from the early gestational thoughts to the final product, and for finding it a home at Farrar, Straus and Giroux. I especially want to thank my editor, Eric Chinski, for his enthusiasm and careful labor over these pages as they began to cohere into a book. It would have been a much poorer effort without him.

Finally, I dedicate this book to Loren Graham, one of the founders of the history of Russian science in the West, whom I was fortunate enough to have had as a teacher in my freshman year in college, and as a friend ever since. This entire book stemmed, in part, from a heated intellectual argument we had over dinner one evening, and many of the ideas in it have likewise emerged from other (calmer) discussions with him. For that, and for so many other things, my sincere thanks.

INDEX

Page numbers in *italics* refer to illustrations.